# Subjects and Sovereigns

# Subjects and Sovereigns

## The Grand Controversy over Legal Sovereignty in Stuart England

CORINNE COMSTOCK WESTON

Professor of History, Herbert H. Lehman College
The City University of New York

JANELLE RENFROW GREENBERG

Assistant Professor, Department of History
University of Pittsburgh

CAMBRIDGE UNIVERSITY PRESS

Cambridge
London   New York   New Rochelle
Melbourne   Sydney

Published by the Press Syndicate of the University of Cambridge
The Pitt Building, Trumpington Street, Cambridge CB2 1RP
32 East 57th Street, New York, NY 10022, USA
296 Beaconsfield Parade, Middle Park, Melbourne 3206, Australia

First published 1981

Printed in Great Britain by The Anchor Press Ltd
and bound by Wm Brendon & Son Ltd
both of Tiptree, Essex

*British Library Cataloguing in Publication Data*
Weston, Corinne Comstock
Subjects and sovereigns.
1. Monarchy, British
2. Political science – England – History – 17 century
I. Title II. Greenberg, Janelle Renfrow
321.6'0942   JC385   80–40588
ISBN 0 521 23272 4

# Contents

THIS BOOK IS DEDICATED TO

Arthur Weston
Martin Greenberg
Janelle Copeland Renfrow

# Preface

A number of people and institutions have facilitated the completion of this study, and we would like to express our appreciation to them. Acknowledgement should be made of two grants to Corinne Comstock Weston from The City University of New York Faculty Research Award Program (1970–71, 1971–72) and grants to Janelle Renfrow Greenberg from the American Bar Foundation (1967) and the Horace H. Rackham School of Graduate Studies, University of Michigan (1965). These made it possible to use the pamphlet collection in the North Library of the British Museum, now the British Library, and the McAlpin Collection in the Union Theological Seminary Library in New York City, to whose gracious and competent staffs thanks are due. To one person in particular we are grateful for the help he so generously gave. Very special thanks must go to Professor Ivan Roots for his scholarly examination of the study while still in typescript and the steady encouragement that aided immeasurably in its publication. The quality of the study was also improved by critical comments from Dr Mark N. Brown and Professor Francis Oakley and as the result of conversations with Dr Ian Roy and Dr M. J. Mendle. Finally, we have received advice and information from Dr Joel Fishman, Professor W. Speed Hill, Professor Peter Karsten, Professor Hugh Kearney, Professor Lois Schwoerer, and Professor Fred Whelan.

Much attention has been given to pamphlet literature in a discussion of what we see as the two leading political ideologies of Stuart England. Sometimes tracts have been deemed important because their authors wrote at the behest of such powerful and representative figures as James, duke of York, or the prominent whig leader, Arthur Capel, earl of Essex, who was one of the earl of Shaftesbury's closest associates. Others merited analysis because they seem to have been widely read, as evidenced by frequent citation in contemporary writings or testimony to that effect in such writings and by their appearance in multiple editions. Still another kind of tract was considered worthy of note. Penned by a hack writer or published anonymously, it would seldom enjoy national acclaim; but the number of such tracts is too great to be ignored, their existence indicating a market for this kind of political literature. A sampling of political tracts written to justify or condemn the English civil war and the Glorious Revolution reveals that a majority of them reflect the two major antithetical political ideologies that are central to this study.

A few other items require mention. The dating in this study is new style where the year is given, but the day and the month remain as in the contemporary usage. The spelling in contemporary quotations has been modernized but not the titles of books and pamphlets.

When reference is made in the following pages to the king's dispensing power, that term may encompass as well the suspending power. The two powers are facets of the same royal prerogative; and the distinction between them, drawn for example in the Bill of Rights (1689), seems to have emerged only in the late seventeenth century as contemporary attention centered on the law-making power and its relationship to ideas of legal and political sovereignty.

Corinne Comstock Weston
*Herbert H. Lehman College and
The Graduate Center, The City
University of New York*

Janelle Renfrow Greenberg
*University of Pittsburgh*

# I

# The shift in political thought

Two political ideologies shaped the political thought of Stuart England at mid-century : a political theory of order or an order theory of kingship and what is termed in this study a community-centered view of government. Both were utterly compatible with the outward forms of the traditional governmental structure with its emphasis on a king and two houses of parliament. Neither was completely new since elements of both ideologies were earlier present, but their full articulation and dominant characteristics are properly dated from the extended quarrel between Charles I and the long parliament in the months preceding and following the outbreak of civil war. The exchange of political ideas at this time provided the main inspiration for the pamphleteers whose reflections and speculations on government flooded the England of the 1640s. It is a major theme of this study that the rival ideologies emerging from this amalgam provided thereafter the intellectual framework of seventeenth-century political contro-versy and, further, that the success of one of them, the community-centered view of government, brought about the radicalization of Stuart political thought.

Each ideology had a distinctive cluster of ideas centering on issues crucial to the political thought of every age. How was a person's allegiance enjoined? Why was he obliged to obey one government rather than another? What ideas, in other words, justified and legitimated the exercise of political authority? Seventeenth-century royalists settled such issues in terms of the political theory of order, a subject on which the modern historian W. H. Greenleaf has shed much light.[1] As he pointed out, political theories of divine right and patriarchalism were frequently voiced in early modern England where the belief in a divinely ordered world was ubiquitous, their advocates arguing that since God, the author of the universe, had ordained kings to rule as his vicars on earth, the English king was the human source of law and political authority generally. As such he exercised a reserve of power, a royal discretionary authority analogous to God's miracle-working power and the father's discretionary authority within the family. No legitimate ground existed for disobeying the kingly will. In elaborating this style of thought theorists of order relied on arguments of correspondence and analogy to prove, as Charles I put it, that subjects and sovereigns were 'clean different things'. The king was like God : both were the supreme governors of their respective universes. Or else he resembled the sun, the *primum mobile* of the heavens. Analogies were frequently invoked to illustrate the relationship between king and subject. The king was the head, the subject the member; the king the physician, the subject the patient; the king the master of the ship, the subject the deck hand, and so on. The king was, then, the supreme governor of the realm, the keeper of the kingdom, so to speak, to whom allegiance and obedience were properly due and as God's vicegerent his position was one of lofty eminence. He had no equal, no one shared his political authority, and as the human source of political power and authority he was the center of the body politic and political society, his position unrivalled by that of any other person, agency, or aggregate of powers within the kingdom. This meant that the rights of all political bodies including those of parliament flowed directly from him – a conclusion the more significant because a derived authority seemed to contemporaries in every way inferior to an original authority.

Not unexpectedly, the pattern of power in parliamentarian political thought was very different. The theory of order was rejected unequivocally in favor of the community-centered view that certainly political authority flowed from God to the king but only with community consent. Since the community (or people) determined the nature of the governmental system within which royal power was exercised and even chose the ruler or rulers, the community was the human source of political authority. Government in general was from God, the particular form or species from the community – here was the highly successful formula by which the parliamentarians and their intellectual successors legitimated the government of their choice and conception.[2] The implications were subversive of the order theory of kingship. To differ from the royalists on so important a matter as the human source of political power and authority was also to reject a hierarchical relationship between the king and the two houses of parliament and to open the way for a substitute political belief, one intrinsically levelling in nature that could only weaken the king in relationship to the two houses. Here the parliamentarian theorists made a distinctively original contribution to Stuart political thought, the effect of which was to remove the king from the lofty political position envisaged in the theory of order and to place him firmly alongside the two houses on the same political plane. Whether he was now described as dethroned or as flanked by companions who shared his great power, the conception of a political parity among king, lords, and commons was new.

That conception arose when the parliamentarian theorists invented the thoroughly novel principle of a co-ordination in the legislative power – a principle which became the linchpin of the community-centered view of government. Dependent on the assumption that the community was the human source of political power, the revolutionary principle was gleaned from Charles I's vastly influential Answer to the Nineteen Propositions of June, 1642. Under its terms the king was no more than a single member of three co-ordinate estates of parliament, the others being the house of lords and the house of commons. Such a principle must affect the kingship, leading to encroachments by the two houses on royal power. Alarmed at the prospect, conservative theorists denounced co-ordination vehemently as conducive to confusion and even to civil war.[3] Equally to the point was a comment of Dr Peter Heylyn, the conservative theologian and devoted assistant to Archbishop Laud. His civil-war tract supporting the kingship was written 'to preserve the dignity of the supreme power [the king] . . . and fix his person in his own proper orb, the *primum mobile* of government, brought down of late to be but one of the three estates, and move in the same planetary sphere with the other two'.[4]

The divergent ideologies illuminate the major controversy of the Stuart century in the realm of politics and ideology. At its center was the single question : 'Who makes law?' It loomed during the civil war when Englishmen concluded that law-making constituted the distinctive and pre-eminent mark of political sovereignty. For the first time the legislative power began to be treated consistently as subject only to the will of the legislator or legislators and as uncontrollable by any other person or agency in the state. That power was now said to be the final political authority, from which no appeal was possible. In an unprecedented and unparalleled fashion certain leading royalists agreed with the parliamentarians that law-making and political sovereignty went together. They agreed also that law-making took place only in parliament. No claim was advanced, for example, that the king was a law-maker who exercised the legislative function outside of parliament, in complete independence of the two houses. But disagreement did exist as to who made law within parliament, a matter of the highest practical importance because law-making was associated with political sovereignty. The remaining issue was this: did the king make law singly in parliament, acting with the advice and consent of the two houses but without actually sharing the legislative power with them, or was a law the shared product of three equal estates – king, lords, and commons – each member of the trinity meriting the description of legislator? That is, was law made by the king in parliament or by king, lords, and commons in parliament?

Imbued with the theory of order, the royalists placed that power, undivided and unshared, in the king alone. He was the sole law-maker because he was the human source of political authority while parliament's power and authority were at best derivative. Granted that the king performed certain functions in parliament, indeed that if law were made at all, it was made there with the two houses' assistance. Still he was properly the sole legislator because he acted of his own volition whenever law was being made. And other reasons could be mustered to support this view of law-making. The king's assent converted parliamentary measures into law, and parliament's very existence was dependent on his will. His writs of summons assembled the two houses, and only he might end their sitting. As one royalist declared, 'The king is *caput, principium,* and *finis parliamenti,* as confesseth Sir Edward Coke.'[5] A king who was the exclusive law-maker in parliament must in ordinary times occupy the heights in relationship to the two houses; and the prerogatives intertwined with law-making such as summoning, dissolving, and proroguing parliament, vetoing parliamentary measures, and dispensing with statutes must rest secure and uncontested in a general esteem, to be exercised at his discretion. Moreover, the problem of allegiance if raised would be settled in his favor. Finally, the royalist who viewed law-making as the supreme power in the state was likely to assign legal sovereignty to the king; and under these circumstances it was the king in parliament who was sovereign.

The more radical community-centered ideology afforded a sharp contrast when its advocates placed law-making in king, lords, and commons in parliament. Since they too placed a high value on the law-making power, their theory of legal sovereignty was actually the modern theory of parliamentary sovereignty. From the seventeenth-century standpoint, its distinctive characteristic was the stress placed on a shared law-making power; and it will appear repeatedly during this study that to apply the adjective 'shared' to the legislative power was to impart a distinctive tone to a political tract or argument. According to the community-centered ideology, parliament as the representative of the community was the primary law-giver; and the law made there was the shared product of king, lords, and commons legislating as three co-ordinate estates. Not all parliamentarians were equally generous, however; and some of them thought in terms of a supremacy in the two houses. This appeared when they opposed a royal veto in law-making. The new reasoning was clearly conducive to denying this important power to the king since as only one of three co-ordinate estates he might be termed subordinate to the two houses together. After all, the political authority of the three estates was said to flow from the same human source, the community; and one estate was numerically less than two. Surely, this situation demanded that the king assent to measures said by the two houses to be of common right and justice and for the public good. Presumably such considerations underlay the warning from John Selden in his famous *Table Talk* : 'The king is not one of the three estates, as some would have it. Take heed of that for then if two agree, the third is involved.'[6]

Here was a more radical version of co-ordination, but whatever its form the principle was full of danger to the kingship. Besides menacing the king's veto in law-making, it jeopardized the dispensing power, earlier exercised on a broad scale with relative impunity. Any idea of a discretionary authority in the king above the law must become anachronistic should the idea gain ground that he was no more than a single member of three co-ordinate estates who shared equally in law-making. Why should one legislator set aside the work of three? Or, to put the matter differently, the law enacted by three co-ordinate estates was the measure of royal power. As one prominent parliamentarian theorist asserted roundly, no almanac was needed to reckon that one was less than three.[7] Questions might also be raised about the king's discretion in summoning, proroguing, and dissolving parliament and the problem of allegiance in a civil war or revolution be settled against him and in favor of the two houses. The latter was no small consideration in a century as troubled as the seventeenth, and it goes far to explain the great appeal of this ideology after 1642. Even a staunch royalist would grant that resistance to the king was legal if the two houses were indeed co-ordinate with him in law-making.

It was the community-centered view of government that prevailed in the course of the seventeenth century although the political theory of order had stout advocates as late as the Glorious Revolution. The shift in thought was momentous for the political system and the development of the English state. It meant among other things that just as the theory of parliamentary sovereignty became ascendant, a sudden twist was imparted by which that sovereignty was seen as shared. Whereas earlier the view taken of the king as law-maker pointed to a parliamentary sovereignty vested in the king in parliament, it was the parliamentarian version that proved successful. Public understanding of the lines of political authority altered irrevocably when the community-centered ideology became popular during the civil war, and the process of intellectual erosion continued unabated after 1660 despite the best efforts of apologists for the Stuart monarchy. Unmistakably, this ideology, with its emphasis on a co-ordination in law-making, the highest power, occupied a central place in the political thought of Charles II's reign, its tenets accepted in whig and tory camp alike. There also appeared in whig writing a coherent and articulated common-law argument for early parliaments that added a new dimension to Stuart political thought. It strengthened the already widespread conviction that the community but not the king constituted the human source of law and political authority, promoting the political idea indispensable to the co-ordination principle that the two houses were in fact independent of the king.

The transformation in national outlook had virtually run its course by 1689, being so far advanced by that time as to make possible the conclusion that the Glorious Revolution marked in ideological terms the completion of an intellectual process at work since 1642. The principle of a co-ordination in law-making held the most conspicuous place in the triumphing parliamentarian ideology. Providing the ideological axis that joined the civil war to the Glorious Revolution, this principle more than any other in Stuart political thought fostered the growth and spread of the modern theory of a parliamentary sovereignty in king, lords, and commons and by radicalizing Stuart political thought effectually destroyed the substance of the kingship.[8] The history of the acceptance of such a theory by the seventeenth-century political nation affords not only a substantial explanation for the Glorious Revolution but also an important means of assessing the significance of that remarkable event.

# 2

# The keeper of the kingdom

Of the two political ideologies, it was the royalist that was more
firmly rooted in English experience and tradition of the late
sixteenth and early seventeenth centuries. It grew out of the theory
of order that distinguished late Tudor and early Stuart political
thought, nourished and sustained in turn by a network of legal
and constitutional ideas concerning kingship. Prominent among
the Tudor and early Stuart Englishmen who wrote in terms of
the order theory was the eminent common lawyer, Sir Edward
Coke, whose judicial and parliamentary careers spanned Elizabeth I's and James I's reigns and included the first years of
Charles I. Taking a high view of the royal position – unexpectedly
so for an authority whom the parliamentarians revered as the
oracle of the law – Coke wrote that 'the kingdom of England is
an absolute monarchy', of which 'the king is the only supreme
governor', having been empowered 'immediately of almighty
God'. He was, according to the ancient laws of the realm, the
kingly head of the body politic, and as such he possessed 'plenary
and entire power, prerogative, and jurisdiction'. The purpose of
this power was 'to render justice and right to every part and
member of this body . . .; otherwise he should not be a head of
the whole body'.[1] The language sounds like hyperbole but was by
no means unusual in discussions of the kingship. To another
lawyer, Henry Finch, the king was the head of the commonwealth
immediately under God. 'Carrying God's stamp and mark among
men, and being . . . a God upon earth, as God is a king in heaven',
it followed that the English king had 'a shadow of the excellencies
that are in God'.[2] Other Tudor lawyers wrote similarly. For
Edmund Plowden, 'king is a name of continuance, which shall
always endure as the head and governor of the people'.[3] And to

James Morrice, a serjeant at Middle Temple, the king was 'supreme head and governor' of the body politic of the kingdom, 'adorned with princely rights and dignities'.[4]

Writing in this vein was Sir Thomas Elyot, who served as clerk to the justices of assize for the western circuit, chief clerk to the council, and ambassador to Emperor Charles V. Best remembered for his *Boke Named Governor* (1531), Elyot reasoned that because one God, one perpetual order, and one providence governed all things in heaven and on earth, the best and surest governance was a king ruling for his people's welfare. This manner of governance had the sanction of time; it was the best approved, the longest continued, and the most ancient.[5] In another passage the king was referred to as the 'principal bee', an analogy common in a period when bees were described as abhoring anarchy, 'God having showed in them unto men an express pattern of a perfect monarchy, the most natural and absolute form of government'.[6]

To dismiss such descriptions as mere rhetoric, as if to imply that the words ought not to be taken seriously, is to obscure the fact that these statements held meaning for Tudor and early Stuart Englishmen, the choice of language expressing the assumptions of the prevailing theory of kingship and political society. A corollary of the premise that the most natural form of government was monarchy, in which the king ruled as God's vicar, was an idea extremely important to the seventeenth-century mind, namely, that the king was the human source of political authority. This was assumed by so representative a figure as Sir Thomas Smith, whose highly influential *Discourse on the Commonwealth of England* was written sometime after 1562 and published posthumously in 1583. Smith had enjoyed a varied political career as ambassador to France, privy councillor, and secretary of state; and the circulation of his little treatise was commensurate with his eminence. By 1640 it had passed through eleven editions and was much quoted thereafter, especially as publicists, preoccupied with the distribution of political power in the English state, gave prominence to his remarks on parliament's high power. But his description of royal power was equally valuable. The king was the life, the head, the authority of all things done in England, though he might sometimes distribute his authority and power to lesser agencies within the state. Law-making provided the conspicuous example : while the king legislated in parliament, still he was the fountain of that institution's power.[7] Although his view of the human source of political authority was more complicated than this, William Lambarde, the Tudor antiquary, considered the king to be God's earthly vicar,[8] and Edmund Forset found that 'all superiority and command in the state' branched from 'the supreme principality', that is, the king, with regard to whom God had announced : 'By me . . . kings do reign.'[9] There is little need to multiply examples beyond noting that as late as the *Ship Money Case* (1637) Sir John Finch, lord chief justice of common pleas, referred to the king as the immediate source of political authority. Kings had existed before parliaments and were the human sources of their power.[10]

The king was, then, a very special person; and the law took note of his specialness. Because he was no mere man, he was treated differently from others. 'All honour, dignity, prerogative and pre-eminence' pertained to him, the prerogative extending not only to the king's person but also to his possessions, goods and chattels.[11] His uniqueness was evident from his privileges. He was free, for example, from being sued; an aggrieved subject could only petition. Nor were the king's goods and chattels subject in any way to either toll or tribute. Further, it was impossible to term him a joint tenant, for who was his equal? As for fictions such as common recoveries, he was legally immune from them. The king's privileges could be stated more positively. He might sue in the court of record of his own choice and might choose the procedures there. There was no requirement that he accept the method of pleading which his opponent chose. And then there was the principle known as *nullum tempus occurrit regi* : time did not run against him; his rights were generally imprescriptible.

This uniqueness was further evidenced in discussions of the primary function of the kingship. According to theorists of order, the king, as supreme governor of the realm, was charged with the *merum imperium*, the power of the sword and the right to command. Or, as some lawyers asserted, he was possessed of *gubernaculum*, meaning that he was charged with the business and welfare of the kingdom. To carry out his high responsibilities the king possessed certain royal prerogatives, which included making war and peace, coining money, appointing ministers and councillors, summoning and dissolving parliament, and mitigating the rigor of the law and facilitating justice by means of the dispensing power and its corollary, the pardoning power. These prerogatives were said to be inseparable from the king. Indeed, even an act of parliament, to which the king had given his consent, could not take them from him. As Coke forcefully stated, 'no act can bind the king from any prerogative which is sole and inseparable to his person, but that he may dispense with it by a *non obstante* [the operative words in a clause of dispensation]'. Such prerogatives were the essence of the kingship; they were what it meant to be king and to sever them from him would be to deprive him of the kingship itself.[12]

These royal prerogatives were attached to the king's political office as distinct from his natural person, a distinction derived from the medieval doctrine of the king's two bodies or capacities, which became prevalent in Tudor England largely as a result of Plowden's law reports. The king was in one sense a natural person, subject to the infirmities and disabilities afflicting a private person. He might succumb to illness and death. But in addition the king possessed a public capacity, a political office which never died. Legal comment assigned to this body 'the office, government and majesty royal'. The political office was said to consist 'of policy and government' and to be constituted 'for the direction of the people, and the management of the public weal'. In his public capacity the king was said to have 'sole government'.[13] The two bodies were usually deemed inseparable, but in political terms the political body was superior. The prerogatives attached to the king's office were described as both absolute and inseparable from him. According to Morrice, whose viewpoint was typical, 'the king, in . . . cases concerning his royal government hath a preeminence above the law'.[14]

But there was always more said than this about the royal prerogative, and even more striking is the marked tendency to treat it as essentially dual in character. If the king possessed an absolute prerogative, he also had an ordinary prerogative. Included within the latter were rights such as purveyance, *primer seisin*, and, in the opinion of some lawyers, the *nullum tempus* privilege.[15] The distinction between the absolute and ordinary prerogatives clearly underlines the discretionary nature of the former. The absolute prerogative was *legibus solutus*: it was above or outside positive law. The ordinary prerogative, on the other hand, was regulated and bound by the rules of law. The dual nature of the royal authority was consistently acknowledged by Tudor and early Stuart theorists. Smith, for one, noted that the royal prerogative consisted of both an absolute power and a royal power regulated by laws.[16] Equally to the point were the remarks of Sir Francis Bacon, who served under Queen Elizabeth and James I as solicitor general, attorney general, privy councillor, and lord chancellor. Writing toward the end of the sixteenth century, Bacon distinguished between the king's absolute and ordinary prerogatives, the former – 'a free jurisdiction' or 'sovereign power' – enabled the king to dispense with the law: *pro bono publico* he could 'temper, change, and control' the common law and mitigate and even suspend parliamentary statutes. A discretionary authority was necessary because the law could not provide for all occasions; and the king possessed, accordingly, a reserve of power upon which the dispensing power drew. Yet there was no suggestion here of an extraparliamentary power of law-making in the king. The latter with the three estates – that is, lords spiritual, lords temporal, and commons – made statute law in parliament.[17]

Nor was the king always above the law. Royal grants were limited by law and regularly argued in the law courts; and the king had no power, for example, to forbid the youngest son to inherit wherever the custom of borough English was applicable. He could not alter the nature of pleading or grant that a man should be judge in his own cause. In matters such as these the royal authority was restricted by ordinary rules of law.[18] Typically it was the ordinary prerogative that was involved in conducting the government. The absolute prerogative was unsuitable for everyday use and should be held in reserve for unusual occasions. Bacon made an apt comparison: its exercise was comparable to God's miracle-working power. Just as God consented to rule the universe according to the law of nature, so kings 'ought as rarely to put in use their supreme prerogative, as God does his power of working miracles'.[19] The comparison between the miracle-working power of God and the royal absolute prerogative illustrates graphically the discretionary dimension of the latter. Sir John Davies – James I's attorney general for Ireland, later appointed chief justice of common pleas – put it well when he wrote of the king that by restricting 'his absolute power' and limiting 'himself to the ordinary rules of the law, in common and ordinary cases', he 'doth imitate the divine majesty which in the government of the world doth suffer things for the most part to pass according to the order and course of nature, yet many times doth shew his extraordinary power in working miracles above nature'.[20]

James I himself drew the distinction between the absolute and ordinary prerogatives. His remarks on the absolute nature of the kingship are well known. 'The state of monarchy', he wrote, 'is the supremest thing upon earth'. Because kings reigned as God's lieutenants on earth, the absolute prerogative was unbounded by law and indisputable. Indeed, just as it was 'atheism and blasphemy to dispute what God can do', so was it 'presumption and high contempt in a subject to dispute what a king can do'. But a king, as head of the commonwealth, had obligations to his subjects. One was to interpret and mitigate 'doubtsome or rigorous' laws. According to James the royal authority might mitigate and even suspend 'general laws, made publicly in parliament' upon 'causes only known to him'. Yet certain other royal prerogatives were less high in nature. The powers which he termed his 'private right' were bounded by law. Where such rights were concerned, the courts should treat him as a private person.[21]

These pronouncements were more representative of contemporary opinion than one might think. The same distinction was expressed in Lambarde's writings, and there also comes to mind in this connection the comment on the dual nature of the royal authority in *Bate's Case* (1606), where the judges, sitting in the exchequer chamber, upheld the king's right to levy extraparliamentary impositions. Explaining the need for an absolute discretionary authority Lambarde wrote that 'in the government of all commonweals, sundry things do fall out both in peace and war that do require an extraordinary help'. The king exercised of necessity, therefore, an 'absolute power and irregular authority'. The reason for this 'absolute and regal' power was that the king was sworn to see justice done to his subjects when no 'ordinary law' provided for it.[22] And at the time of *Bate's Case* Chief Baron Thomas Fleming explained that the government of the realm was intrusted to the king, whom God had empowered for the purpose of governing. The royal power was not, however, of uniform quality, and Fleming drew a careful distinction between what he called the ordinary and the absolute power of the king. In his words,

The king's power is double, ordinary and absolute, and they [sic] have several laws and ends. That of the ordinary is for the profit of particular subjects, for the execution of civil justice, the determining of *meum*; and this is exercised by equity and justice in ordinary courts, and by the civilians is nominated *jus privatum* and with us, common law : and these laws cannot be changed, without parliament.

On the other hand,

The absolute power of the king is not that which is converted or executed to private use, to the benefit of any particular person, but is only that which is applied to the general benefit of the people and is *salus populi*; as the people is the body, and the king the head; and this power is [not] guided by the rules, which direct only at the common law, and is most properly named policy and government; and as the constitution of this body varieth with the time, so varieth this absolute law, according to the wisdom of the king, for the common good.

All royal actions aimed at attaining this common good were *ipso facto* lawful. In other words, the question of impositions was 'material matter of state, and ought to be ruled by the rules of policy; and if it be so', the chief baron concluded, 'the king hath done well to execute his extraordinary power'.[23]

Such descriptions of the royal authority strongly suggest that representative and articulate Englishmen in the sixteenth and early seventeenth centuries assigned to their king a dual position by which he was both above and below the law. His prerogatives were both absolute and ordinary, the first unlimited by ordinary rules of law, the second bound by positive law. That such views were prevalent appears from the comment made on the eve of the civil war by a leading member of the opposition. Speaking in the short parliament of 1640, John Pym would grant that the king had a transcendent power in many cases whereby he might by proclamation prevent and guard against sudden accidents.[24]

The two spheres of authority delineated here were by no means of equal rank and quality. The absolute prerogative, just because it pertained to the king's public role, was superior to the ordinary prerogative – a fact of cardinal importance. Since the rationale of a royal discretionary authority was that the king as supreme governor must have a reserve of power with which to govern, he might on occasion disregard positive law. The primary weapon in such situations was the dispensing power by which statute law was set aside whenever this course was, in his judgment, dictated by equity or the public welfare. It should be stated that this power, if used to suspend a statute for the benefit of a large number of individuals, can be termed the suspending power. Until the late seventeenth century, however, Englishmen did not as a rule distinguish between the two; and properly in law there is but a single prerogative – the dispensing power. The discretionary authority expressed in the dispensing power made the king superior to parliament; that is, the king out of parliament could at times legally overrule the decisions taken by the king in parliament. In a word, adherence to the theory of order entailed the view that the king was sovereign governor of the realm, equipped as such with the authority required for acting outside or above positive law whenever the action seemed to him essential to the kingdom's welfare.

This account of the kingship, and especially of the royal prerogative, departs sharply from that advanced by modern scholars such as Charles H. McIlwain. According to McIlwain, the distinction between *gubernaculum* and *jurisdictio*, terms used by the thirteenth-century medieval lawyer, Henry Bracton, was central to medieval and early modern constitutionalism. By *gubernaculum* McIlwain concludes Bracton had meant the government of the kingdom, while *jurisdictio* was intended to encompass the rights of subjects, these being outside the legitimate bounds of the royal administration. Where *gubernaculum* was concerned, McIlwain seems at first to state that the royal authority was absolute, the king above the law, but an important qualification was then added. *Gubernaculum* was limited whenever *jurisdictio* was involved because subjects had an interest that had to be respected in the areas of justice and jurisdiction. In this way two spheres were created within the state, one of the king's rights and powers, the other of his subjects', each of equal weight and authority. A kind of balance was the result, a dualism in the state. If the king could not legally abridge his subjects' rights, neither could they infringe the royal interest. In support of this proposition McIlwain points to the occasional invocations, especially in the sixteenth and seventeenth centuries, of Seneca's maxim, *Ad Reges potestas omnium pertinet, ad singulos proprietas* – 'to kings belongs government, to subjects property'. McIlwain interprets *potestas* as the equivalent of *gubernaculum*, while *proprietas* is seen as being analogous to Bracton's *jurisdictio*. It was the tension between the two equal spheres in the early seventeenth century that was largely responsible for the breakdown of the constitution and the coming of civil war.[25]

This interpretation of Bracton's thought has not held up, but McIlwain's account of sixteenth and seventeenth-century constitutionalism continues to influence historians of Tudor and Stuart England, some of whom have accepted his distinction between two equal spheres of interest.[26] But not all. The groundwork was laid for a different view when Sir William Holdsworth, writing well before McIlwain's distinction was made public, stressed the king's high authority where matters of state were concerned; and working from Holdsworth's conclusions, Francis Oakley carries the argument further in a noteworthy article on the absolute and ordinary powers of the king. Oakley argues convincingly that appeals to this distinction in Tudor and early Stuart England usually 'postulated the existence, not of two parallel or co-ordinate powers each confined by law to its own proper sphere, but rather of two powers, one of which was in essence superior to the other, and which in time of necessity or for reason of state could transcend the other and encroach upon its domain'.[27] So if the king was charged with the welfare of the kingdom and if he might act in certain circumstances above the law, his rights were clearly superior to and not equal with those of his subjects. In other words, the effect of the royal discretionary authority was to exalt the king's rights and assign his subjects' to an inferior status. This was so even if the legal exercise of the dispensing power was confined to exceptional and temporary occasions. The subjects' sphere of interest was not parallel with the king's or equal to it. The royal interest was *salus populi*, and the welfare of the kingdom superseded that of private persons.

It would seem, then, that the key to understanding early seventeenth-century political thought does not lie in viewing the relationship between the king and subject in terms of two parallel and equal spheres of authority in a state of tension, with the destruction of this delicate balance leading to the civil war. Rather it is to be found in perceiving the prevalence and pervasiveness of the theory of order, with its theological overtones, which placed the king in a position of undoubted superiority in the years before 1642, this superiority manifested, in particular, in his exercise of a dispensing power in the name of equity or the public welfare. The king as God's vicar had a discretionary authority like God's miracle-working power, an analogy that carried conviction in the intellectual climate of the early seventeenth century.

Moving in the direction set by Holdsworth and Oakley, one might offer an interpretation very different from McIlwain's in discussing the ideological pattern before 1642 and afterwards. It would run thus. The order theory of kingship was the prevailing theory when civil war came, but once upset in the storm and stress of the 1640s, the old predominance was destroyed and never regained. In an astonishingly brief period of time, its tenets were first challenged and then superseded by the new and revolutionary community-centered ideology with its stress on a legal sovereignty in king, lords, and commons, a sovereignty hostile by its very nature to the dispensing power and its traditional exercise. This line of thought obviously departs from McIlwain's interpretation in its key points. Going further and discussing the post-1642 years in ideological terms, one would be tempted to make the following generalizations. After the rise of the more radical ideology, the political nation undertook to wrest from the king the discretionary authority that had been the hallmark of *gubernaculum* and make that authority its own. Progress was made in this direction before the Glorious Revolution, but it was that event which proved ultimately decisive. Expressed in ideological terms, the sweeping transfer of political authority which took place in the course of the seventeenth century owed much to the co-ordination principle and the community-centered ideology generally. The final result at the Revolution was an official acceptance by the court of the theory of parliamentary sovereignty in king, lords, and commons, the three co-ordinate estates so much cherished by parliamentarian writers. At the very heart of this theory was the clear recognition that the essence of sovereignty, that is, the highest power in the state, was the right to make laws.

## II

But these developments lay in the future. Prior to the advent of the parliamentarian ideology most Englishmen failed to face squarely what was to become the cardinal issue of the seventeenth century. It was this: who makes law – the king alone though legislating in parliament (that is, the king in parliament), or king, lords, and commons as three equal and co-ordinate estates (king, lords, and commons in parliament)? Before 1642 this question defied an unequivocal and unambiguous answer because few Tudor and early Stuart Englishmen either isolated the law-making power for an independent consideration or perceived in that power the key to sovereignty in the state. If Englishmen were to comment precisely on the law-making power, they must needs be in the habit of assigning law-making a position of primacy in their political system. They did this only after learning to equate the legislative power with the control and exercise of supreme political authority or sovereignty. Until then, the more usual practice was to define sovereignty or the supreme power in terms of various governmental functions. Writers like Smith and Raleigh usually made mention of 'marks' or attributes of sovereignty, which included the pardoning power, the dispensing power, the right to coin money, summoning and dissolving parliament, and the right to legislate. That is, law-making was only one of several marks of sovereignty which were identified with the totality of the royal prerogative.

On those occasions when the law-making power was singled out for special consideration, the commentator was likely to assign it to the king alone even if the power was admittedly exercised in parliament. Thus Morrice stated that 'the king . . . solely and alone is rightly said by his prerogative to be the maker and ordainer of laws and statutes in and by his court of parliament'.[28] The *Homily of Obedience* of 1547 referred to 'the high power and authority of kings, with their making of laws',[29] and Raleigh writing in the early seventeenth century listed the making or

annulling of laws among the royal rights.[30] Also to the point was
Lambarde's conclusion regarding law-making. The king, he stated,
is, 'as the head, to give life (that is to say) to yield the highest and
last assent'.[31] These were by no means the antiquary's only
remarks on this important subject, but for the moment it should
be noted that the Elizabethan divine, Richard Hooker, spoke
similarly. Though scholars have usually focused on his high claims
for parliament and community, Hooker was specific as to the
identification of the proper legislator. He wrote :

> Touching the supremacy of power which our kings have in this
> case of making laws, it resteth principally in the strength of a nega-
> tive voice; which not to give them, were to deny that without which
> they were but kings by mere title and not in exercise of dominion.
> Be it in states of regimen popular, aristocratical, or regal, principality
> resteth in that person, or those persons, unto whom is given the right
> of excluding any kind of law whatsoever it be before establishment.
> This doth belong unto kings, as kings; pagan emperors even Nero
> himself had not less, but much more than this in the laws of his own
> empire.[32]

Thus even Hooker had admitted that the king in a sense made
law.

The political language of early Stuart Englishmen ran on
similar lines. To the comments on law-making found in Raleigh
should be added those of Sir James Whitelocke, later justice of
king's bench, and Oliver St John, the prominent parliamentarian
of the civil-war years who had served as counsel for Hampden in
the famous *Ship Money Case* of 1637. Speaking in the house of
commons in 1610, Whitelocke – in a passage usually interpreted
as limiting royal power and exalting that of parliament – actually
pointed to the king as the law-maker in parliament when he stated
that 'in acts of parliament, be they laws, grounds, or whatsoever
else, the act and power is the king's, but with the assent of the
lords, and commons, which maketh it the most sovereign and
supreme power above all and controllable by none'.[33] Since this
was what Whitelocke meant in describing the power of the king
in parliament as greater than that of the king out of parliament,
it is little wonder that his remarks were useful to civil-war royalists
who undertook to demonstrate that Charles I was the single law-
maker in parliament.[34] Five years before the civil war Oliver St

John agreed. The king was the *pars agens* or active part of parliament whereas the two houses were but *consentientes* or consenting members.[35]

Nowhere was the point made more controversially than by Dr John Cowell, Cambridge professor of civil law and vicar general to the bishop of London. After *The Interpreter* (1607) became the center of heated controversy, James I prudently recalled it and renounced Cowell's views. Yet S. B. Chrimes, a respected authority on constitutional history, discerns much good law in the civilian's pronouncements.[36] Cowell's description of the king as the human source of political authority was reminiscent of theorists of order, and he was in good company on the question of who made law. Placing that power in the king alone, Cowell insisted that the English king was absolute because 'all learned politicians do range the power of making laws *inter insignia summa et absolutae potestatis* [among the highest insignia of absolute power]'. Even if the king permitted parliament, the representative of the community, to participate in the law-making process, it was he who made law, parliament's power being merely derivative. Only by custom of the kingdom did he make law with the consent of the three estates (the lords spiritual, the lords temporal, and the commons), and he could quash or dispense with whatever they prepared.[37] Whether or not Cowell has been maligned, his writings excited an antipathy that may be traced to other passages in *The Interpreter* where the king was described as above the laws without the accompanying recognition that he likewise possessed ordinary powers restricted by law. Perhaps the very precision with which the civilian's views were expressed helps explain the attention that they elicited from contemporaries. Yet he merely drew conclusions implicit in the order theory of kingship, which assigned the law-making power to the king in parliament.

To do so was a step towards placing legal sovereignty in the crown, but it was no more than that. Modern authorities on the whole have agreed that the ideological climate of these years was inimical to theories of legal sovereignty, whether these were favorable to the king or to king, lords, and commons. Few Englishmen discussed political problems in these terms, and the notion of an unrestricted legislative power was foreign to them. Much more

inclined to think in terms of fundamental law and limited authority, some of them might even describe parliament primarily as
a court and only secondarily as a legislature, a tendency in turn
related to a belief in a ruling fundamental law, which parliament
was said to interpret. It was a tendency which might have been
counteracted had parliament been actively legislating in these
years, but it was not.[38] Its meetings were irregular and the business
of the kingdom was accomplished primarily by means of royal
ordinances and letters patent. Indeed, the parliaments of 1614 and
1621 passed no laws at all. Before theories of legal sovereignty
could become common coin, much would have to change. Parliament must meet regularly and contemporaries treat it primarily
as a legislature, a condition and a transition in political thought
that came only with the civil war. But before the civil war little
or no conception of sovereignty existed in the modern sense of
that word. Whitelocke's comments to the effect that the parliamentary power was uncontrollable fell on stony ground, and other
pronouncements such as those made during the earl of Strafford's
trial reveal that Englishmen as late as 1641 continued to define
their political problems within the traditional theory of order
while basing their political arguments on fundamental law.[39] The
changed outlook, when it emerged, may have been partly due to
the great wave of statute-making in the first year of the long
parliament that was aimed at dismantling the machinery of
prerogative government associated with Charles I's personal rule.
Even so, a modern authority has written that there was 'less talk
than might be expected about the nature of the legislative power,
perhaps because men were too busy legislating to talk much about
the great power that they were exercising'.[40]

Yet the overwhelming obstacle to a theory of legal sovereignty
in king, lords, and commons and, to a lesser degree, to such a
power in the king in parliament, is to be found not in the acceptance of fundamental law, which parliament interpreted as a high
court, but rather in the prevalence of the order theory of kingship.
Its tenets fostered a different pattern of political power in the
political mind. After all, how was it possible to assert an unlimited
legislative power in king, lords, and commons or to describe this
trinity of law-makers as omnipotent in the legal sense when the
royal dispensing power might free a subject from the obligation

to obey a particular statute or statutes? The point bears repetition. A theory of legal sovereignty vested in king, lords, and commons was incompatible with the idea of a powerful dispensing power in the king by which statutes were rendered inoperative. That is, so long as the king's discretionary authority remained uncontested, there could be no accepted theory of a legal sovereignty in king, lords, and commons, not as such theories are known today.

## III

Unmistakably, the dispensing power went hand in hand with an acceptance of the order theory of kingship. That prerogative was the pre-eminent mark of the royal discretionary authority, and the *raison d'être* of that authority was the conviction that the king as sovereign governor was possessed of a reserve of power with which to govern his kingdom and secure the public welfare. He was the sole judge of the occasions when considerations of equity or *salus populi* required setting aside statute law for the benefit of a particular person or class of persons. In a word, to adhere to the order theory of kingship was to acknowledge the validity of the royal dispensing power. Conversely, to deny that theory and to espouse the rival community-centered view of government – the intellectual process so noticeable after 1642 – was to deny the dispensing power as traditionally conceived. The ideological change set in motion by the English civil war, namely the growing acceptance of the community-centered ideology, rendered the dispensing power obsolete. It followed that its use in the late seventeenth century on lines such as those found earlier in the century must make that power the storm center of an acute political and constitutional conflict.

But earlier, in what might appropriately be termed the golden age of that power, English monarchs applied the dispensing power with little controversy to important areas of national life: to justice, the administration of government, the regulation of trade and industry, and even to ecclesiastical matters.[41] How normal the usage actually was is perhaps best conveyed by an examination of its workings and its prevalence in the period when the theory of order governed political assumptions. One of its most valuable exercises was in the area of justice, where its operation was subject to a variety of restrictions and limitations. It should be noted first of all that the dispensing power was closely related to the pardoning power, the latter being viewed as a special manifestation of the dispensing power because it involved dispensing with a particular punishment. Their interdependence was illustrated in another fashion, when the dispensing power was utilized to defeat medieval statutes that had been framed for the purpose of circumventing the king's right of pardon.[42] The usual means was to prohibit the pardoning of felonies except in express terms and to enjoin the recipient of the pardon to find sureties for good behavior. The royal right was affirmed on several occasions. It was readily acknowledged, for example, that the king might dispense with the medieval statutes restricting the pardoning power by including a *non obstante* clause in the charter of pardon.[43] Commenting upon the *Sheriff's Case* (1487) in the early seventeenth century, the respected Welsh judge, David Jenkins, explained the necessity for such an exercise of the dispensing power. 'The king', he wrote, 'by his royalty is trusted with the government, pardons, and public business : particular cases may happen which deserve remission, upon consideration of circumstances'.[44]

Clearly the pardoning power had limits. For one thing, the king might not dispense with the penalties so long as a private person had a right of vengeance, a limitation that might conceivably leave the king without an effective power of pardon if an aggrieved party wished to appeal the convicted person. That is, if A murdered B's father, B might appeal A despite a royal pardon of the offense. As Coke noted, the appeal was at the suit of the party, 'to have revenge by death'.[45] Several sixteenth and seventeenth-century cases illustrate the principle involved. In the *Queen v. Saunders and Archer* it was suggested in an aside that a convicted murderer, who had received a pardon, was nevertheless vulnerable to action on the part of the victim's wife. She might still appeal him.[46] The justification for restricting the royal prerogative rested on this ground : the aggrieved party, in this instance the victim's widow, was entitled to have the revenge of death, and her interest could not be discharged. The queen's pardon was good, however, if the plaintiff abandoned the case of his own volition or at the court's order because of insufficient

evidence. The suit then belonged to the monarch to prosecute.[47]
On the other hand, the plaintiff's desire to cease prosecution was
insufficient to bar the queen's proceedings if she did not wish to
grant a pardon.

Another rule governing the exercise of the pardoning power
concerned convictions upon a popular action. Specifically, if an
informer brought an action upon a statute which divided the
penalty between him and the king, the latter could not defeat the
informer's interest in the judgment. If the king wished to pardon
the entire penalty he had to issue the pardon before the action
commenced; otherwise, the informer was considered to have an
interest in the outcome.[48]

One other restriction on the royal pardoning power ought to
be mentioned. The king had only a limited power to pardon a
common nuisance such as an enclosure or a bridge or a road in
disrepair. Nuisances harmed the subject and such offenses belonged properly to the people and not to the king. If, for example,
the king were to pardon a breach of the statutes prohibiting
enclosures, the pardon would excuse only the recipient's past
behavior. It would not extend to the continuance of the enclosure. If the offense persisted after the pardon, the offender was
liable to an action on the statute, the continuation being treated
as a new offense.[49] That the king could not pardon a nuisance
unconditionally was illustrated in *Nichol's Case* (1576), a complicated proceeding that involved conflicting leases on a piece of
land. One judge explained that a subject who was obliged to
repair a bridge and failed to do so could not be discharged by a
royal pardon 'because others, *viz.* all subjects of the realm, have an
interest in it'.[50]

The dispensing power might also expedite the administration
of government, as in the *Sheriff's Case*. In this frequently cited
case it was stated that the king could dispense with the statutes
prohibiting a man from holding the office of sheriff for more than
one year. The decision was of the greater interest because it was
also held that parliament could not prevent the exercise of the
dispensing power by labeling a statute nondispensable.[51] The
dispensing power was also affirmed in 1564 when it was decided
'that the queen by her prerogative may make a sheriff . . . notwithstanding any statute to the contrary'.[52] Jenkins commented

upon another Elizabethan case in which the judges of an unnamed court declared valid the appointment of a commission to hold trials of piracy contrary to the statute 28 Hen. 8, c. 15, the reason being that such things as 'concern the government of the public' the king might do, statutes to the contrary notwithstanding.[53]

Yet there were limitations on this use of the dispensing power. The king could not dispense with all acts of parliament regulating office holders. Specifically, he was bound by statutes dealing with actions which were termed *mala in se* and not merely *mala prohibita*. According to Lord Chancellor Ellesmere and Coke (then chief justice of king's bench), the king had no power to dispense with statutes prohibiting simoniacal grants, simony being *malum in se*. But the dispensing power was applicable whenever the actions involved were *mala prohibita*.[54]

The dispensing power was freely applied to so important an area of national life as trade and industry. Monarchs often dispensed with the navigation acts and statutes circumscribing the business activities of aliens. Henry VII, Henry VIII, and Elizabeth, for example, all dispensed with the statutes which required that denizens pay double customs.[55] Henry VII also on occasion defeated the navigation acts of 1485 and 1488 so as to enable Spanish merchants to bring wine and woad into England. The practice continued under Henry VIII, who granted hundreds of licenses dispensing with the navigation acts, and Queen Elizabeth, who permitted French subjects to import wines in their own ships despite the navigation laws. The queen also dispensed with the statute 23 Eliz. c. 7, which confined to English vessels the shipping of fish caught in home waters.[56]

A high royal prerogative was also observable whenever the crown exercised control over the flow of bullion from the kingdom in defiance of the statute book or regulated the armaments industry. Grants of *non obstante* defeated medieval statutes prohibiting the export of gold. Henry VIII on one occasion licensed one Augustine Pinelle, a merchant of Genoa, to export 25,000 ducats of gold; and Queen Elizabeth made use of the same power to permit the export of £600 in gold for the resettling of Munster. James I also dispensed with acts prohibiting the export of bullion.[57] The royal discretionary authority also extended to the armaments industry. Early Tudor statutes notwithstanding, royal licenses

B

containing clauses of *non obstante* frequently permitted the expor-
tation of metals essential to making instruments of war. Thus
Henry VIII licensed William Clyftoune, a merchant tailor of
London, to buy and export 120,000 pounds of bell metal, the
prohibitory statutes notwithstanding. And Sir Philip Hobby, a
gentleman of the privy chamber, received a similar grant. Both
Queen Elizabeth and James I dispensed with the statutes regulating the export of war materials.[58]

Moreover, statutes in this period were on occasion suspended,
not merely dispensed with for a particular person's benefit. This
was a broad exercise of the dispensing power, the implication
clear that if the king could suspend one statute, the same discretionary power might be applied to numerous statutes. As later
Stuart Englishmen asked cogently: Why could not a king who
suspended one act of parliament, suspend forty? The usual method
of announcing such a suspension was by royal proclamation. An
example may be taken from Queen Elizabeth's reign. Notwithstanding a prohibitory statute (7 Edw. 6, c. 6), the queen licensed
merchant adventurers to carry sums of money out of the realm.
Such proclamations were likewise issued by the first two Stuarts,
and the royal right of dispensing with or entirely suspending
statutes appears to have gone unquestioned in the late sixteenth
and early seventeenth centuries.[59]

One of the most valuable uses of the dispensing power was to
facilitate the conveyance of land. In order to permit lay and
ecclesiastical corporations to hold or acquire estates and leases
the king often dispensed with the medieval statutes of *mortmain*
and *quia emptores*. Thus in the case of *Grendon v. Bishop of
Lincoln* (1577) the justices in common pleas ruled that the queen
might ignore statutes circumscribing her right to bestow lands
upon corporations.[60] The dispensing power further facilitated the
conveyance of estates and leases by allowing the monarch to
ignore the rules regulating royal grants. These restrictions rose
out of the requirement that the king's grant be expressed in
certain and precise language because it was a matter of public
record. Serious defects in the content or wording often served to
void it since mistakes raised the possibility of the king's having
been misinformed or deceived. Thus a grant from the king to A
and 'his heirs male' instead of the 'heirs male of his body' was

void, because the king's intention was to convey a fee tail. If 'body' had been mentioned, the grant would have been good and would have conveyed a fee tail. On the other hand, if a subject made an identical grant, a fee simple would have passed, because private grants, unlike royal grants, were taken more beneficially for the grantee and against the grantor. But in the king's case, when more passed by the grant than was intended, he was presumed to be deceived and the grant was therefore void.[61]

Several rules aimed at preventing such deception. One enjoined that existing leases on a unit of land be cited in any new grant concerning it. For example, if the king leased Blackacre to A for a term of years, and then conveyed the reversion of Blackacre to B, B's letters patent ought to recite A's lease. Otherwise, the grant was void because the king was deceived in the sense of lacking full knowledge of his estate. The reasoning behind this rule enjoining the recital of leases was that the king had the charge and care of the kingdom and could not therefore attend to his private business. The subject's duty, in this case B's, was to inform the king as to the condition of his estate, for the existing lease was a matter of record of which the subject ought to take notice. If this obligation went unfulfilled, the king was said to be deceived in his grant, and it might be declared void.[62]

This restriction was sometimes defeated by clauses of *non obstante*. In 1575, for example, the justices in the court of common pleas decided a case in which the queen, who was seised in fee of a certain manor, leased part of it for a term of years. Later, without making recital of this lease, Elizabeth granted the same manor to another in fee farm. The letters patent included the words *'ex certa scientia et mero motu nostris'*, indicating that the grant had been made of her own certain knowledge and 'mere motion' and not at the suit of the party. Since it was a rule of law that leases ought to be recited in such a grant, the queen included the words *'non obstante* non-recital and bad recital'. In the opinion of the justices, the clause of dispensation served to make the grant good.[63]

Finally, ecclesiastical matters might necessitate the exercise of the royal dispensing power. The monarch sometimes granted dissenting groups the right to worship by suspending statutes that enjoined religious conformity. Both Edward VI and Elizabeth, for example, dispensed with the act of uniformity, thereby permitting Walloon congregations to worship freely,[64] and the lot of Protestant dissenters was eased early in the seventeenth century when James I dispensed with the statutes prohibiting aliens from exercising certain trades. The Walloons were also given relief when informers brought actions against them, the king commanding that 'all informations already preferred against them be discharged, and the names of such informers or other persons as shall presume to molest them . . . be presented to this [council] board'.[65] The command was followed by a proclamation in 1616 directing the justices to see to it that French and Flemish aliens were unmolested and promising protection from informers. James in addition renewed the Elizabethan licenses to Huguenot congregations in Southampton and Rye.[66]

The royal mercy went beyond Protestant dissenters. It is of interest, in view of the later Stuart controversy centering on the dispensing power, that Tudor and early Stuart monarchs often relaxed the rigor of the law for the benefit of their Roman Catholic subjects. Many of them were freed from the penalties of the ecclesiastical laws. Thus Queen Elizabeth followed a policy that was tantamount to a partial suspension of the recusancy laws when in 1586 she dispensed with the statute of the same year granting her two-thirds of their lands and for a fee protected them from the danger of the law, the daily vexation of informers, and other circumstances and inconveniences. Similar practices are found in James I's reign. At times the king dispensed with the oath of supremacy so as to enable Roman Catholics to hold governmental office. Such a dispensation was granted to the earl of Clanricarde, who, when indicted in 1627 as a Roman Catholic, pleaded letters patent from James. Charles I ordered the justices to honor his father's dispensation and to refrain from molesting the earl. A more general toleration occurred as a result of the marriage contract between Prince Charles and Princess Henrietta Maria, in accordance with which all law officers were commanded to cease religious prosecutions against Roman Catholics.[67]

The same policy was in evidence when Charles I granted a dispensation in 1639 to a Frenchman, one Peter la Dore, by which he was allowed to become a denizen without taking the oath of supremacy.[68] Such dispensations were neither isolated nor unique.

Charles issued more than seventy licenses to Roman Catholics, some of which protected the recipient from the actions of informers. He also frequently employed Roman Catholics in his service by dispensing with the requisite oaths. Commenting on the royal clemency, Sir Edward Hyde, later earl of Clarendon, remarked that 'the papists had for many years enjoyed a great calm, being on the matter absolved for the severest parts of the law, and dispensed with the greatest'.[69]

The dispensing power was, then, a valuable instrument of legal flexibility in the Tudor and early Stuart periods of English history. But more than this: since the exercise of the dispensing power permitted the king to override the highest legal enactment in the land, the royal prerogative also had far-reaching constitutional and even ideological implications. To be sure, the dispensing power was encased within certain forms and boundaries; and there were always certain statutes immune from its application. But it should be stressed that the fact that the king might dispense at all with statutes entailed automatically the assumption that he was above or outside positive law, under certain circumstances and for certain purposes.[70] This is an important fact, but it is not all that may be said about this distinctive royal power. Contemporaries usually viewed the exercise of the royal discretionary authority as virtually unlimited in time of emergency. The king might suspend law entirely in wartime. Or in case of fire he might ignore all statutes protecting the subject's freehold by entering land without the owner's permission and tearing down burning buildings. What matters even more, perhaps, is that he was the sole judge of the emergency. While he might choose to consult with his council or with parliament or with both, he could just as easily act alone if the occasion warranted.[71] Such, indeed, was the essence of the kingship; such was what it meant to be king before 1642.

## IV

The monarch's great power, rising out of the royal discretionary authority, was plainly revealed on several occasions when Tudor and early Stuart parliaments undertook reform. The uproar about monopolies late in Queen Elizabeth's reign provides the example *par excellence* of the dilemma posed under such circumstances. This is what happened. The house of commons, seeking to recall the more obnoxious licenses, debated in 1601 the proper way of approaching the queen. Was it advisable to proceed by way of a bill curtailing the creation of monopolies? Or should that house petition Elizabeth for a redress of grievances? Speeches were made on behalf of the royal prerogative by both Sir Robert Cecil and Bacon, but perhaps the greatest interest attaches to those emanating from more ordinary members when they reminded their colleagues that the queen possessed the power to dispense with any statute restricting the royal authority. The final decision to proceed by way of petition may well have reflected their reasoning. Thus the moderate Sir George More of Loseley explained the situation in this graphic language: 'We know the power of her majesty cannot be restrained by any act, why therefore should we thus talk? Admit we should make this statute with a *non obstante*, yet the queen may grant a patent with a *non obstante*, to cross this *non obstante*'.[72] These words brought out the futility, in More's view, of any attempt to circumscribe the queen's powers with regard to the harmful monopolies. Even if a statute included a clause of *non obstante* aimed at precluding a dispensation (that is, notwithstanding a royal license of dispensation), the dispensing power was not thereby restrained; the queen might ignore the prohibition by including in her patent of monopoly a clause dispensing with the prohibiting statute. More had even voiced the conviction that an act of parliament could not restrain the royal prerogative.

William Spicer, member for Warwick, spoke in the same vein. The house ought to proceed by petition: it was 'to no purpose to offer to tie her [the queen's] hands by act of parliament, when she may loosen herself at her pleasure'. And Francis Moore, a Berkshire lawyer and member for Reading, took a similar line as he stressed the futility of proceeding by statute against monopolies. 'To what purpose is it to do anything by act of parliament', he asked, 'when the queen will undo the same by her prerogative?'[73] Apparently the houses of parliament accepted this reasoning since a majority petitioned Elizabeth for a redress of grievances resulting from the monopolies. The decision seems the more noteworthy in view of certain aspects of the situation. The queen had promised in the preceding parliament (1597–98) to deal with the abuse of monopolies, but the pledge had gone unfulfilled in part because of the Essex rebellion. As Sir John Neale drily remarks, the episode was not conducive to administrative efficiency; but his comments nevertheless implied that a better performance might rightfully have been expected from the queen's government. The tone of the parliament meeting in 1601 was disappointed and angry, and its final decision under these circumstances seems almost surprisingly moderate, suggesting that the hold of the order theory of kingship was exceedingly powerful.[74]

The viewpoint regarding the dispensing power, noted above, was also enunciated in James I's parliaments. On one occasion, when purveyance was at issue in the parliamentary session of 1606, Sir Richard Spencer noted the uselessness of contracting with the king for the abolition of purveyance. If the king broke the agreement, the only recourse was to petition. Proceeding by bill, he continued, was equally futile, for 'if a law pass on that behalf no man can forbid the king to dispense with it'. With regard to the same issue, Lord Chancellor Ellesmere reportedly reminded the lower house in April, 1606, that the king could dispense with any bill abolishing purveyance. Further, no statutory restriction, even one with a clause prohibiting the use of the dispensing power, could prevent the exercise of this prerogative. Citing the *Sheriff's Case* in proof of this contention, Ellesmere was quoted as stating

that by this bill the king is tied so, as with a *non obstante* he shall be able to do nothing, which . . . is void, for the statute of [23 Hen. 6, c. 7] is, that no man shall be sheriff longer than one year, no not with a *non obstante* and yet the king with a *non obstante* of that *non obstante* may continue sheriffs longer than one year.[75]

Clearly, in the lord chancellor's opinion, the royal authority could not legally be restricted by statute, at least where purveyance was involved.

Still other examples may be cited. Not long afterward, the problem of placing meaningful statutory limitations on royal power came to the forefront. In May, 1606, at a time when the house of commons had under consideration an act to prohibit the retailing of beer and ale by their brewers, the decision was finally taken to abandon the measure on the ground that a courtier might procure a patent of dispensation.[76] And in June, 1607, the house of commons took up a bill aimed at 'abolishing hostile laws', in an apparent attempt to extend protection to Englishmen who were accused of committing felonies in Scotland. The bill's supporters wanted the accused brought to trial in northern England before the ordinary justices of assize, as if the offenses had been committed there. A provision in the bill specifically prohibited remanding the prisoners to Scotland. Despite its presence one member of the house of commons, Henry Yelverton, expressed concern lest the king dispense with the act and empower a commission to do just that. The only way to prevent such a turn of events, in his opinion, was to impose penalties on those sending persons back to Scotland contrary to the act.[77]

## V

In summary, an active dispensing power meant a very real and concrete authority in the king over statute law.[78] This use of the royal discretionary authority seemed both necessary and legitimate to contemporaries, to whom that power was an essential feature of the order theory of kingship. Central to that theory was the potent political idea that the king was the sovereign governor of the realm, who as keeper of the kingdom was equipped with the requisite authority to act outside or above statutory law whenever he considered the exercise of a royal discretionary authority essential to equity or the kingdom's welfare. Very probably, this widespread and general acceptance of the order theory of kingship accounts for the absence of recorded attacks on the dispensing power during the sixteenth and early seventeenth centuries when its validity seems not to have been denied. Admittedly, there were occasions when the exercise of the dispensing power aroused anger, as in the creation of monopolies[79] and the relaxation of the ecclesiastical penal laws; but even the complainants seem not to have questioned the dispensing power itself. Nor was that prerogative at issue during the controversies of the civil-war years. It received less attention than one might anticipate in royalist political literature, and it passed unmentioned in the tracts written on the side of the two houses. But the calm ended with the restored monarchy in 1660, the situation taking a startlingly new turn when the

dispensing power became literally overnight the object of controversy in the strongly royalist cavalier parliament. On more than
one occasion its members acted as if Charles II had no legal right
to set aside penal laws in ecclesiastical matters. Although that
king exercised the dispensing power in other areas of government
without exciting a similar storm, many politically articulate
Englishmen plainly believed now that the exercise of this power
was contingent on the approval of the two houses. In a word,
much of sixteenth and early seventeenth-century law concerning
the dispensing power was now abandoned – summarily, unequivocally, indeed, almost casually.

The explanation for this curious turn of events is not far to
seek. It lies in a radical alteration in the ideological climate of
Stuart England, an alteration that was tantamount to an intellectual revolution. Beginning in the civil-war years an antithetical
political ideology, the community-centered view of government,
first rivalled and in the end replaced the early modern view of
kingship and royal authority. There was no place in the new way
of reasoning for the royal dispensing power since the advocates of
the community-centered ideology, sensitive to the importance of
the law-making power, placed legal sovereignty in king, lords,
and commons, the trinity of co-ordinate estates so much cherished
and admired by parliamentarian theorists. Once the political
nation as a whole embraced this ideology, the right to dispense
with the law was increasingly coupled with the right to make law.
Because law was made by the three co-ordinate estates, it followed
as the night the day that they were the ones who legally dispensed
with it – certainly not he who was but a third of the legislature.
Here was a legal and constitutional argument, based on ideology,
to which no counterpart existed in Tudor and early Stuart England; and this meant that when Charles II ascended the throne,
the dispensing power as known to his royal predecessors was
anachronistic, clearly suited to another age and another theory of
kingship.

That theory had flourished in an age when little interest was
manifested in the law-making power. The usual practice was to
include law-making among the marks of sovereignty appertaining
to the king and not to isolate it for separate consideration, and
even a theorist who placed that power in the king in parliament

was unlikely to give it a sustained consideration. This situation changed with the civil war when the question of who made law in parliament became primary. When this happened, theories of political and legal sovereignty pushed their way to the forefront of political consciousness and controversy, and there they remained during the rest of the century.

# 3

## The new age of political definition

### I

Ironically, the elegant and fastidious Charles I, whose aloofness from his subjects contributed to the coming of civil war, introduced the new age of political definition. He did so when he inadvertently provided the parliamentarians with the main elements of their ideology: the tenet that the community was the human source of political authority in the state and the radicalizing principle of a co-ordination in the law-making power. Revolutionary in its implications for the pattern of power in government, the co-ordination principle became overnight the center of an intensive debate over matters of power and authority. That such a debate existed is undoubted. 'In all the controversies that have arisen', a contemporary wrote, 'there is nothing (to my observation) that hath been so universally, really, and continuedly insisted on as this matter of power.'[1] Not that the king had foreseen the results; he had not. Yet the co-ordination principle sprang, nevertheless, from his language in 1642, the year when an unprecedented series of declarations and counter-declarations flowed from Charles I and the long parliament.

### II

That principle was rooted in the Answer to the Nineteen Propositions (June 18, 1642), which Charles issued on the eve of the civil war. The king was responding to the Nineteen Propositions (June 2), in which the two houses had put forward demands for naming the king's counsellors, ministers, and judges, controlling the militia, and reforming the church with parliamentary participation. Despite their sweeping character there was one notable omission: the Nineteen Propositions made no mention of law-making as such even though the two houses in the preceding March had legislated without the king in the militia ordinance. In its wake had come a declaration of May 26, which invoked the coronation oath to deny the king a veto in law-making; and this revolutionary position would be repeated and elaborated, six months later, in the very important declaration of November 2, 1642. Not that the parliamentarians claimed the right to legislate without the king: they would freely grant that his assent was needed to make a bill a law. What they now asserted, however, was that this assent must be automatically forthcoming. He was obliged by his coronation oath to give assent to bills that the two houses approved. It is the more surprising, then, that the Nineteen Propositions made no mention of this matter. But the subject of law-making had been raised, and Charles I's response was in the Answer to the Nineteen Propositions, penned for him by Sir John Colepeper, the chancellor of the exchequer, and Lucius Viscount Falkland, secretary of state, and approved for publication by Sir Edward Hyde. With the claim that the two houses' demands must subvert the government, the king rejected them; but historically more significant than this action was the decision to include in the Answer a description of the government itself.[2]

Almost from its inception, the description was treated as authoritative. England had a mixed government, in which the king's power and his subjects' liberties were nicely poised. Further concessions from the king might destroy the balance and admit tyranny, and Charles I now offered what may appropriately be termed a classical theory of the constitution. Classifying the three main forms of government as absolute or pure monarchy, aristocracy, and democracy, he found that the government, with its three estates of king, lords, and commons, combined the pure forms of government so as to retain their conveniences while eliminating their inconveniences. This admirable mixture, the result of the experience and wisdom of his subjects' ancestors, was in evidence whenever laws were made. In an extremely influential statement stressing an equal partnership among the three estates in law-making and stoutly defending his veto, Charles declared: 'In this kingdom the laws are jointly made by a king, by a house of peers, and by a house of commons chosen by the people, *all having free votes* [italics added] and particular privileges.'[3]

Besides having a share in law-making, each estate had distinctive powers of its own. Government (*gubernaculum*) was the king's
preserve. He made treaties of war and peace, created peers, chose
officers and councillors for state and judges for law, named
commanders of forts and castles, gave commissions for raising
men to fight wars abroad and prevent insurrections at home,
exercised the power of pardon, etc. Although the dispensing power
was closely related to the power of pardon and frequently
appeared in such lists, no mention was made of it here. To prevent
the abuse of these powers or the exploitation of the king's authority
in matters of public necessity for the gain of favorites, the house
of commons was empowered to raise money and impeach. But
it was barred from one important area : it had no share in government or in selecting those who governed. As for the house of lords,
its role was mediatory : it served as an excellent screen and bank
between the prince and people by means of a judicial power that
protected each branch of the government from encroachment.
Since the two houses' power was more than enough to prevent
and restrain tyranny, and acceptance of their demands must
unbalance this admirable government, Charles refused them,
repeating the dictum ascribed to the barons at Merton in 1236,
*Nolumus Leges Angliae mutari*.[4]

The Answer was speedily made known to the country at large.
The king issued a warrant to the speaker of the house of lords to
provide for its being read in both houses, and the royal declaration
reached them on June 21.[5] He also ordered that the Nineteen
Propositions and his Answer be read and made public in the
churches and chapels of England and Wales by the several parsons,
vicars, and curates; and this was done.[6] Published with his seal in
at least seven editions, the declaration reached an ever-widening
audience. Thus the Answer was considered for a week in the
house of commons, and a distinguished committee was named to
reply to what was termed 'the preamble of his majesty's Answer to
the Nineteen Propositions'. The membership included Bulstrode
Whitelocke, its chairman, and such leading parliamentarians as
Sir Thomas Barrington, John Crewe, Nathaniel Fiennes, John
Hampden, Denzil Holles, William Pierrepoint, John Pym, John
Selden, and Sir Henry Vane the Younger.[7] The roster of those
familiar with the Answer was equally distinguished in the late

seventeenth century since Charles' declaration was known to the leaders of the Glorious Revolution who wrote the Bill of Rights and prepared a new coronation oath for King William and Queen Mary.[8]

From the first the Answer to the Nineteen Propositions fastened attention to law-making. A ripening concern over the royal veto, to which the two houses' declaration of May 26 had expressed unfeigned hostility, led to placing the statement on law-making close by the felicitous account of the mixture and balance in the political system. After praising the equilibrium among the three estates as a means of retaining the conveniences of the simple forms of government without their inconveniences, Charles illustrated the theme by pointing to the legislative power, a term used in the Answer. His statement that king, lords, and commons made law jointly, all having free votes, had a magical effect, the words echoing throughout the century with consequences unforeseen by their authors and with far-reaching implications for political thought and its vocabulary. Charles I had imparted, literally overnight, a central importance to the law-making aspect of parliament; and an active controversy centering on legal sovereignty now began that stretched over half a century to the Glorious Revolution. Other passages in the Answer reinforced the public image of parliament as pre-eminently a law-making body. Perhaps haunted by ordinance-making, the king was firm that all laws must be made in parliament, of which the crown was the historic center. 'What concerns more the public, and is more (indeed) proper for the high court of parliament,' came the rhetorical question, 'than the making of laws?' Laws not only ought to be transacted there; they could be transacted nowhere else.[9] If theories of legal sovereignty were at a premium before 1642 because of the failure to distinguish with sufficient precision between the judicial and legislative aspects of parliament, this obstacle was removed very early in the civil war.

A theory of parliamentary sovereignty was by no means inherently damaging to the king's power. Certainly not, if he was described as the exclusive law-maker within parliament, that is, if he was said to make law as king in parliament. But, unmistakably, the Answer provided for a very different law-maker. That power was shared: king, lords, and commons made law jointly in parliament. The impact of this description can hardly be overstated. It could now be said on the word of a king, and such a king – a king, poised on the threshold of a great civil war with the two houses of parliament, whose tragic death at its end made him a royal martyr to his subjects – that law-making was a shared power, residing in the three estates of king, lords, and commons. Nothing was left to the imagination on this critical point. The Answer to the Nineteen Propositions referred unequivocally to the king's 'share in the legislative power'.[10] These authoritative public pronouncements, ultimately so injurious to the king's power, provide mute testimony that his advisers did not identify the legislative power with the sovereign and controlling authority in the kingdom. Hyde, Falkland, and Colepeper were thinking in terms other than those of legal sovereignty.

A major reason for this conclusion is that the authority now surrendered was so staggering from the viewpoint of legal sovereignty. Even if the king had embarked upon a policy of concession, as some contemporaries believed, he would hardly have gone this far. How much more likely that Charles I fell victim to a swiftly changing opinion about the value of law-making. It looks as if Falkland and Colepeper, concerned to protect the king's veto in law-making, had adopted without deliberation or self-consciousness certain phrases and expressions, such as 'share in the legislative power', that had been bandied about in the first years of the long parliament when the great reform statutes were enacted to end extraparliamentary taxation and the prerogative courts. In this unusual period there must have been a ferment of ideas applied to law-making; and words, seen in retrospect as significant, were tossed about carelessly. But sporadic use in parliament is one thing, the appearance of such language in a public statement, issued in the king's name and given wide publicity under the royal seal, is quite another. Further, these ideas were expressed before 1642 within a variety of contexts, with a subsequent weakened impact. The situation must be otherwise when such ideas and phrases formed the staple of an articulated political argument, made public by the king's authority, in which law-making had a conspicuous place. The king's advisers failed to anticipate how the Answer might be interpreted, and their lack of foresight explains why he advanced an ideological argument so advan-

tageous to his political enemies. An authorized public pronouncement that king, lords, and commons shared law-making jointly,
at this juncture, was literally destined to become a statement of a
shared legal sovereignty; and this was, in fact, the outcome.[11]

Moreover, the law-making power was equally divided. That
contemporaries quickly grasped the point became evident when
an anonymous writer asserted: 'The three estates are co-essential
[that is, of the same substance or nature], coequal, co-ordinate,
and co-workers in the political power.'[12] This description of the
position of king, lords and commons was much more radical than
appears at first sight, its novelty lying in the power relationship
now seen as characterizing these three elements. Working from
the pattern of power that Charles I's Answer to the Nineteen
Propositions appeared to sanction, the parliamentarians urged that
a king who was but a single member of three co-ordinate and
coequal estates in law-making could no longer be described in
truth as the supreme governor of the realm, ruling his kingdom as
God ruled the universe. Quite the contrary. The king was only
one of three, and it was in the trinity of king, lords, and commons
that sovereign power resided. Thus it was that the parliamentarians
used Charles I's own words to dethrone the king and subvert the
hitherto received view of the king as keeper of the kingdom. Thus
it was, too, that the parliamentarian ideology radicalized Stuart
political thought.

To describe this aspect of parliamentarian ideology as radical
may appear at first glance to contradict G. R. Elton's influential
writings on the modern parliament. Although his scholarly interest
centers on Henry VIII's reign, his generalizations have been
extrapolated at times to apply to the period from roughly 1530
to 1642. In brief, Elton suggests that a marked change occurred
in parliament during the English reformation, a change reflected
in the growing omnicompetence of statute and in the emergence
of a full doctrine of sovereignty, based on law-making, in which
the highest power was vested in king, lords, and commons. Implicit in the 'mixed sovereign' was an equality among the three
law-making partners.[13] If this conclusion is accepted without
qualification, whether or not it is expanded to encompass late
Tudor and early Stuart England, one must question the description of the parliamentarian ideology in the 1640s as 'radical'.

Would it not be preferable, working from Elton's writings, to state that the parliamentarians in advocating a sovereignty vested in king, lords, and commons were only returning to the normal Tudor pattern, as this was established during the English reformation? This pattern, such an argument might run, had been set aside by innovating Stuart kings, determined to expand their power at the expense of parliament; and in this situation it was the parliamentarians who stood for traditional constitutionalism while the royalists were advocates of the radical cause.

Such an interpretation has been rejected in this study, on the ground that the political ideas of Tudor Englishmen were not in fact prototypes of the parliamentarian ideology of the 1640s. A key reason for this judgment is the pervasiveness in Tudor England of the order theory of kingship, with its emphasis on the king as the supreme governor of the realm, possessed with a discretionary authority to dispense with statutes when necessity or justice required him to do so. This theory is a major barrier to accepting a shared legal sovereignty in which supreme power resides in king, lords, and commons as equal partners. Moreover, the modern notion of parliamentary sovereignty, with its insistence on the high authority of statute, was automatically precluded by a power of dispensation vested solely in the king. There is one other consideration that ought to be mentioned. It appears that Englishmen in the sixteenth century, in so far as they gave thought at all to law-making, tended to place that power exclusively in the king although it was admittedly exercised in parliament with the two houses' consent. Any convincing demonstration that pre-1642 Englishmen placed the law-making power in king, lords, and commons requires firm evidence that they widely accepted the co-ordination principle in law-making so much discussed during the civil war and afterwards. As the remainder of this study will show, the co-ordination principle in the seventeenth century was explicitly stated, knowingly applied to law-making by a majority of the political nation, and vigorously attacked and defended over a very substantial period of time. Nothing in Elton's writings indicates the constant presence of such a principle in the years with which he deals or its broad acceptance by the political nation. Under these circumstances his work is best described as supplementary to this study but not as hostile to its premises.

Despite surface similarities the parliamentarians were not returning to the precepts of the Tudor age. On the contrary, theirs was
a radical position, on the whole indigenous to their own day; and
this position in the course of time radicalized Stuart political
thought.

From 1642 until the end of the century political argument over
legal sovereignty typically took the form of a debate over the
membership of the three estates. Royalists contended that despite
Charles I's words in the Answer to the Nineteen Propositions, the
three estates who made law in parliament were, properly speaking,
the lords spiritual, the lords temporal, and the commons, with
the king at their head. Indeed, excluding the king from this
definition became a shorthand way of denoting the royalist view
of kingship. Invoking the tenets of the order theory, supporters
of the court frequently quoted Coke in the effort to offset Charles
I's definition of the three estates and his description of the power
relationship among them. In contrast, parliamentarians habitually
insisted that the king was one of the three estates, along with the
lords and commons, an argument essential to the co-ordination
principle at the heart of the community-centered view of government.

Interestingly, both definitions of estates were current in 1642,
and each had deep roots in medieval and early modern law and
politics. Yet prior to the civil war the membership of the three
estates was not a matter of active political concern or dispute;
and both definitions appear to have been used if not indiscrimin-
ately then usually without reference to constitutional considerations or patterns of political power. Thus the Elizabethan John
Hooker deemed the king to be one of the three estates but at the
same time placed him at the head of parliament and the kingdom.[14] In 1642, with the inauguration of a new age of political
definition, the situation underwent dramatic change. Following
the publication of Charles I's Answer to the Nineteen Propositions, the rival definitions of estates surged to the front and center
of the stage of political debate. Their advocates accepted either
the concept of kingship in the political theory of order or else that
in the community-centered view of government – depending on
the definition of estates adopted. The royalist definition of the
three estates, which excluded the king, was linked firmly and

irrevocably to the position of the king as keeper of the kingdom, while the parliamentarian definition, which included the king, became the unmistakable hallmark of the ideology in which the king was no more than a single member of three co-ordinate and coequal estates. Because of the pattern of power among king, lords, and commons – authoritatively sanctioned by Charles I himself – parliamentarians could now write confidently of these three estates as sharing equally in law-making, this at a time when that power was about to be treated as the most important by far in the political system.

The king's party was early aware that a cardinal mistake was being committed but took the decision to push ahead all the same. Charles I's definition was soon everywhere. Like a brush fire exploding in a bone-dry field, it spread rapidly, finding its way into political literature written by royalist and parliamentarian alike in the first years of the civil war. But royalist writing by the end of 1643 was increasingly cautious, and in the following year Charles I's government seems to have attempted an explicit repudiation. To this subject it will be necessary to return, but it is to be noted here that the popularity of the king's definition of estates, along with his description of their relative power, made this matter central to Stuart political thought. By the eighteenth century, if not earlier, Charles I's definition permeated parliamentary oratory, even settling into the schoolbooks, from whence it was removed only by the scorn of late Victorian historians. One of them, S. R. Gardiner, writing in his *History of the Great Civil War*, noted that this 'error . . . was being widely adopted since the breach with the king', a point also made in the 1640s. According to Heylyn, the king was everywhere conceded to be but one estate; and another royalist wrote, at the end of the civil war, that the king was 'confessedly one estate'.[15]

Above all, this particular definition of estates is important because it gave rise to the principle of a co-ordination in law-making that ran a prosperous course in the seventeenth century. Indeed, had Charles I simply labeled himself one of the three estates and refrained from drawing conclusions about the power relationship among the three, it is unlikely that the king's opponents could have turned his words against him with such devastating effect. As it was, the combination of his description of the three estates with his insistence on an equality among them in law-making proved fatal, enabling as it did the parliamentarians to fashion the co-ordination principle. This principle early became the hallmark of anti-court writing, and no political idea in Stuart England inspired more fear and dread among the advocates of a high prerogative. This was due to the fact that the co-ordination principle, from the very first, was the taproot of the seventeenth-century theory of a parliamentary or legal sovereignty in king, lords, and commons. The line of reasoning that was followed may be seen from the axioms listed by a contemporary in 1643. These were :

1. All persons are subject to the king.
2. The king is subject to the laws.
3. The laws are subject to the powers that make them.
4. The powers that make laws are political.
5. This political power is in three estates [king, lords, and commons].
6. These three estates are co-ordinate.
7. Co-ordination is in parliament.
8. The parliament is above all persons.
9. All persons are bound to obey it.
10. All obedience is active or passive.
11. No man may resist in any thing.
12. They that resist shall receive damnation.[16]

Obviously, there are important ingredients here of the modern doctrine of parliamentary sovereignty. The trinity of king, lords, and commons in parliament made the laws that bound both the king and his subjects but was itself above those laws, which were 'subject to the powers that make them'. At the same time the co-ordination principle, though this was not spelled out, by assuming a parity among king, lords, and commons in law-making, permitted the two houses in practice to assert a superiority to the king in governing the kingdom. It was dangerously easy to describe them as the chief legislators.

Heylyn made this point graphically in his *Stumbling-block of Disobedience* (1658), written at Oxford as early as 1644. Denying that the king could properly be termed one of three estates, he warned of the pitfalls for the kingship in the co-ordination principle. By its very nature it opened the way for a superiority in the two houses in the all-important area of law-making, no matter what was being said about an equality among king, lords, and commons. He wrote:

If the king be granted once to be no more than one of the three estates, how can it choose but follow from so sad a principle, that he is of no more power and consideration in the time of parliament than the house of peers, which sometimes hath consisted of three lords, no more; or than the house of commons only, which hath many times consisted of no more than 80 or an hundred gentlemen : but of far less consideration to all intents and purposes in the law whatever, than both the houses joined together. What else can follow hereupon but that the king must be co-ordinate with his two houses of parliament, and if co-ordinate, then to be over-ruled by their joint concurrence, bound to conform unto their acts, and confirm their ordinances : or upon case of inconformity and non-compliance to see them put in execution against his liking and consents, to his foul reproach.

Moreover, the view that the king was an estate of parliament had brought him 'into an equal rank with the other two [estates] in reference to the business and affairs of parliament'. The whole matter could be dismissed as ridiculous if the co-ordination principle were not so dangerous. Clearly, it was that, for the popularity of that principle, in Heylyn's opinion, provided the prime explanation for the beginning and continuance of the civil war.[17]

The principle did have a far-reaching impact, raising, for one thing, the whole question of allegiance. Whereas earlier it had gone freely to the king as the supreme governor, the matter was clearly more complicated if there existed more than one claimant to the highest power in the kingdom. It was now possible to think in terms of three sovereigns – the king, the house of lords, and the house of commons. Or of two, the king and the two houses. If the two houses shared sovereignty with the king or if king, lords, and commons were equally sovereign, as the co-ordination principle permitted men to assert, the long parliament might use force legally against the king. The competing claims, and the importance of the issue, led royalists to denounce what they termed a *regnum in regno*, the source of the difficulty lying, it was said, in 'that groundless invention which denies subordination, and introduces an unheard of co-ordination, such as creates *regnum in regno*, and rents this country into distinct kingdoms'.[18] Thereafter, it was not uncommon to explain the outbreak of the civil war in terms of the new beliefs, as Heylyn had; and supporters of the two houses, seeking after the restoration to vindicate their civil-war conduct, did so in terms of Charles I's definition of estates.[19]

The co-ordination principle entered political controversy with another equally subversive idea, namely, that the community was the human source of political power and authority. The reference in the Answer to the origins of government was short and pointed. The experience and wisdom of their ancestors, Charles I informed his subjects, had molded the mixed and balanced government under which they lived. It was this statement that impressed contemporaries, though its tenor was contradicted elsewhere in the Answer when Charles referred to his regal authority, which God had intrusted to him for the good of his people.[20] The matter was already past remedy when the mistake was recognized. Yet the slip of the pen on so vital a point rendered imperative the attempt at correction made at Nottingham on August 12, 1642, ten days before the raising of the king's standard signalled the formal opening of the civil war. He was upholding, Charles I declared, 'the whole frame and constitution of this kingdom so admirably founded and continued by the blessing of God and the wisdom of *our ancestors* [italics added]'.[21] Despite the attempted public correction this error in so fundamental a principle haunted the Stuarts until the end of their dynasty.[22] Like the admission about shared law-making and the concomitant principle of a co-ordination in law-making, Charles I's apparent recognition that the community was the human source of government could only erode his authority and enhance that of the two houses.

These statements on the constitution had appeared at an opportune time for the two houses. They had not as yet formulated an ideology to make their encroachment on the king's authority legitimate to the political nation; and until this was done, they stood tarred with treasonous rebellion against their lawful sovereign. Logic dictated that they seize legal sovereignty with the claim of binding him by virtue of their predominance in law-making and that they also capitalize on Charles' apparent admission that the community was the human source of political authority. But they took these steps only after the development of a political vocabulary, on the lines that have been described, which permitted their reaching this goal by a circuitous route. Still the two houses had been moving towards an assertion of their sovereignty by the spring of 1642, and the pace quickened noticeably after Charles I left London to take up residence at York. The situation was this. After accepting the bill to exclude the bishops from the house of lords, Charles left his capital early in February and journeyed northward in a leisurely manner, reaching York on March 19. While he was en route the long parliament aggressively attacked his role in law-making. Converting the militia bill into an ordinance, the two houses moved towards denying the king a veto in legislation, a position reached, it will be remembered, in their declaration of May 26. The next step, logically, would be to claim legal sovereignty over the king, but this step the two houses refrained from taking at this time.

Yet the need remained for a public justification; and their case was presented in another declaration of late May, this one on the 27th of that month. At this time they turned to the concept of the king's two bodies, which was now used in a manner fruitful for the parliamentary cause. As noted earlier, the distinction between the political and natural capacities had a long history. The new action by the long parliament was first separating the king's two capacities and then claiming to control one of them, namely his political capacity. The two houses asserted the right and power to bind the king in his political capacity despite opposition from his natural person, alleging, so Heylyn wrote, 'that the king was present with the houses of parliament, in his political capacity, though in his personal at York'. The distinction permitted the further conclusion that the two houses could fight legally against the king in his personal capacity though not in his political. They might, in Heylyn's words, 'destroy Charles Stuart, without hurting the king'.[23] This argument, carried to its ultimate conclusion, would justify the two houses' encroachment upon the king, permitting them to invest themselves with the full power and rights of the king and the crown. To put the matter in its simplest terms, they were annexing *gubernaculum*, the government of the kingdom.

To justify so revolutionary a stroke the two houses relied on the dual capacities of parliament as a court of judicature and a great council, with no mention, however, of the legislative power. The omission makes it exceedingly difficult to assign a theory of legal or parliamentary sovereignty to the two houses as late as May 27, 1642, less than a month before the Answer to the Nineteen Propositions was made public. The appearance of such a theory now depended on restoring the legislative power to the list of parliament's capacities. This was an indispensable step which, once taken, would clear the way for an appreciation of the legislative power as the primary function of parliament. Had the two houses claimed to bind the king in his political capacity by virtue of the legislative power, it could be stated flatly that their members, guided by a theory of parliamentary sovereignty, had consciously claimed supreme power for the two houses because of their predominance in law-making.

The failure to do so puzzled J. W. Gough, a modern authority on the constitutional history of Stuart England who has carefully examined the position taken by the two houses on May 27 in the light of the modern theory of parliamentary sovereignty. His comment delimits the distance travelled by the two houses towards parliamentary sovereignty before they stopped short of it. Noting that the long parliament was claiming to interpret fundamental law as a high court, he wrote :

If parliament could act as a high court apart from the king, and even against his personal wishes, why should it not similarly act in its legislative capacity? The logical implication of such an argument would be the doctrine of parliamentary sovereignty, but this was a conclusion that the houses did not explicitly draw, for they did not clearly distinguish between the judicial and the legislative sides of their functions. It is doubtful if they fully realized what their claim amounted to, yet they evidently felt that their actions were not adequately covered by the idea that they were interpreting the law as a high court, for they inserted the significant admission that the high court of parliament was 'not only a court of judicature . . . ; but it is likewise a council, to provide for the necessities, prevent the imminent dangers, and preserve the public peace and safety of the kingdom, and to declare the king's pleasure in those things as are requisite thereunto'.

This came close to a claim of sovereignty basically incompatible with any claim of acting in conformity with fundamental law, and Gough thought it 'not easy to explain why the houses so insistently denied that they really meant what was logically implied by their demands'. Possibly prevarication was present, though he rather thought not. Instead, he suggested that the two houses were short-sighted, entering new territory while still unwilling to abandon the time-honored principles that had hitherto guided them. Their supporters among the pamphleteers were less hesitant; they soon 'made it plain that nothing less than legislative sovereignty was the real conclusion, if not the deliberate objective, of the policy of parliament'.[24]

What, then, was the ideological bridge by which the two houses and their supporters finally passed to a position of stressing their supreme power as the dominant members of the legislature, the real citadel of sovereignty? This was the problem posed by Gough, only to be brushed aside at the last moment. It is the more pertinent since he believes 'that it was through the very fact that parliament was the highest court in the realm that it achieved legislative supremacy'.[25] How, then, were Englishmen led to the needed transition in political thought so as to state, indeed to recognize, that parliament was to be viewed pre-eminently as a legislative body? On this point Heylyn supplied vital clues. He had noticed two things: (1) that the claim of co-ordination, which had grown out of Charles I's definition of estates, was being applied to law-making; and (2) that this definition had brought 'the king into an equal rank with the other two estates in reference to the business and affairs of parliament'. The immediate source of these ideas, as Heylyn recognized, was the Answer to the Nineteen Propositions,[26] where Charles I had pointed specifically to the joint participation of the three estates in law-making, each having free votes, as the prime characteristic of English mixed government and had singled out law-making as the proper function of the high court of parliament. The king had asked in a memorable passage: 'What concerns more the public, and is more (indeed) proper for the high court of parliament, than the making of laws; which not only ought there to be transacted but can be transacted no where else?' It was the Answer, then, that provided the long parliament with the element missing from the declaration of May 27.

More precisely, the idea of three co-ordinate estates engaged

jointly in law-making, so conspicuous in the Answer to the Nineteen Propositions, provided the needed ideological element. It
transformed the claim of the two houses from one of binding king
and kingdom as a court of judicature and a great council to one
of making the same claim, but this time by virtue of three functions
in parliament, namely, interpreting the law, counselling the king,
and making laws. The difference is fundamental to the theory of
a parliamentary sovereignty in king, lords, and commons. Once
the two houses began to stress their role in law-making as two
estates, the needed condition for a theory of this type had finally
been supplied; and thereafter the theory of a parliamentary
sovereignty in king, lords, and commons spread rapidly, its domi-
nance clear before the civil war was over. That this theory of
parliamentary sovereignty was gaining ascendancy in this period
has on the whole been overlooked by modern historians, whose
interest has usually centered on the democratic ideology of the
Levellers. But if modern scholars have found the Presbyterian
pamphleteers who elaborated the new theory less interesting than
contemporary democrats, this was not the case with the leading
men of the kingdom. They were fascinated by the pattern of
power rising out of Charles I's definition of estates; and the
assumption was soon widespread that his description of the
government, modified in its essence by parliamentarian pamphleteers, was not only valid for England in the 1640s but was also
an accurate account of that system throughout English history.
It was as if Englishmen had always lived under such a government. Thus Richard Baxter, the beneficiary of the lively discussion
of political power and authority during the civil war, found no
difficulty in employing the following language in the 1650s. His
words seemed perfectly normal and traditional to countless contemporaries, despite their being anything but that, when he wrote:
'The legislative power (that is, the sovereignty) is jointly in king,
lords, and commons as three estates'.[27]

Baxter's comment is the final product of an intellectual process
by which the long parliament's position, as expressed in the
declaration of May 27, was assimilated with Charles I's Answer
to the Nineteen Propositions. It was under way not long after the
king's declaration was made public. War began in August, and
on October 23 the two houses attempted once more to clarify

their legal and constitutional position. Progress had clearly been made. Parliament had to be considered, it was now said, in three respects: 'first, as it is a council, to advise; secondly, as it is a court, to judge; thirdly, as it is the body representative of the whole kingdom, to make, repeal or alter laws'. The third capacity, missing from the declaration of May 27, had reappeared; and another declaration of the two houses, that of November 2, 1642, carried the argument still further. They were responding to Charles I's insistence that they constituted only a temporary body, having nothing to do with discharging the king's trust, summoned only to counsel him, not to command and control him, indeed only to counsel in some things and not in all. Their lengthy response contained a few significant sentences reflecting his concept of estates. Is parliament not a court? – they asked. It was granted that the two houses were a council. Then came once more the third theme, already partly enunciated in October. 'And are we not also two estates', asked the two houses, 'and two estates comprising the persons of all the peers, and the representative body of all the commons of England? And shall the collective body of all the kingdom have nothing to do to look into the discharge of that trust?'[28]

By the end of 1642, then, the position was being taken formally and officially once more that parliament had three functions: it was a legislature as well as a high court and a council. In addition, the two houses had adopted the definition of estates in the Answer, one rendered the more plausible with the bishops' disappearance from the house of lords. These political ideas, when coupled with the version of the king's two bodies in the declaration of May 27, made it possible to take from the king his political office and lodge it with the two houses. If parliament controlled *gubernaculum*, in addition to its historic functions, the necessary elements were present for a theory of parliamentary sovereignty in king, lords, and commons and even in the two houses, since two estates were palpably more than one. Such conclusions were distasteful to the royalists, once they became aware of what was in the wind; and they moved, if only gradually, to deal with two main points in the emerging parliamentarian ideology. The king was not one of three estates, they now said; and he did not share the law-making power with the two houses.

From this conflict of opinion over the most fundamental aspects of government arose the constitutional controversy that marked the remainder of the seventeenth century. To be sure, doubt about parliament's main function now disappeared. Whoever read the tracts of the contending sides came to view parliament as pre-eminently a law-making body. As Michael Hudson, one of Charles I's chaplains, asserted categorically in 1647: 'The principal power and work of the parliament is in law-making.' But his next comment was contentious: it was the king who made law in parliament.[29] Although this proposition seems to have reflected the outlook of the royalists around Charles I late in the civil war, it was by no means characteristic of the political nation as a whole. That is, just as the pieces were falling into place for a theory of parliamentary sovereignty, no agreement prevailed as to who made law in parliament. By the time that Hudson was writing, law-making was widely viewed as a shared power, and many would have placed it unequivocally in king, lords, and commons as three co-ordinate estates. In short, the major premises of Stuart political thought had altered fundamentally and radically, the changes clearly perceptible before the civil war had run its course. Indeed, before the end of 1642, a new era was forming in the critical realms of political ideology and definition; and highly conspicuous in the emergent outlook were rival and contending theories of legal or parliamentary sovereignty. This was a startling development, and one of much consequence.

### III

The new era was first perceptible in the parliamentarian camp, where Presbyterian publicists working outside of parliament elaborated the highly contagious community-centered view of government. Their tracts, published from late 1642 to 1644, spread the new political ideas everywhere. The royal venture into the thorny thicket of political definition had given rise to various political ideas and principles from which the dexterous parliamentarians might pluck arguments favorable to the long parliament; and they exploited swiftly and skillfully the king's phraseology, in particular, his definition of estates and remarks on law-making and the human source of political power and authority. When these were combined with the two houses' declarations of May 26 and November 2, and with concepts drawn from continental sources such as Huguenot theories of popular sovereignty,[30] the result was the theory of mixed monarchy that contemporaries associated with two Presbyterian clergymen, Charles Herle and Philip Hunton. Both of them, but especially Herle, laid the foundations for a theory of parliamentary sovereignty in king, lords, and commons that rested four-square on the Answer to the Nineteen Propositions; and aiding and abetting them was the strong-minded William Prynne, whose writings had a more extremist tone.

Differences among them went beyond tone, extending to their versions of co-ordination. Thus Hunton assigned a genuine equality to king, lords, and commons in law-making, as did Herle in his most influential tract, *A Fuller Answer to a Treatise written by Dr. Ferne* (1642).[31] But Prynne was a latecomer to the scene; and there is very little about co-ordination in his enormous *Soveraigne Power of Parliaments and Kingdomes* (1643). Yet his comments had a widespread effect when he treated the two houses as two co-ordinate estates, who had a preponderance of the legislative power, indeed, virtually the whole of it. So little was left to the king that it looked as if the two houses were the law-makers, the king having but a concurring voice. To this position, Herle moved at a later stage of his writings although he gave the subject very little attention by comparison with Prynne. But even in Prynne's pages, to be supreme was not to be sovereign; and the two houses and their supporters did not advance this claim. Both Herle and Prynne accepted a point which the long parliament made in the declaration of November 2 – that the king's assent was requisite for law-making. But if the two houses could not legislate without him, neither could he deny his assent to measures which they sent to him.[32]

Under these circumstances the writings of all three may be treated as promoting the theory of a parliamentary sovereignty in king, lords, and commons. There is no problem regarding Herle and Hunton, but it is more difficult to apply the generalization to Prynne. He would grant a co-ordinate status to the two houses, as two estates, but not to the king. The latter was to have no veto in law-making. But Prynne, as noted above, did not deny that the king's assent was essential for a measure to become law, and in this sense his writings conveyed that there were three co-ordinate estates in law-making. In short, Prynne promulgated a radical version of the co-ordination principle but not one that precluded the idea of three co-ordinate estates as law-makers. The alternative is to describe him as assigning a parliamentary sovereignty to the two houses, and he was very close at times to this position. Yet he did not reach it because he advanced no argument for law-making without the king.[33] This interpretation of Prynne's political thought is the more warranted because these were the key writers who taught a political generation about the co-ordination principle; and the overriding impression left with contemporaries, no matter what was said in contemporary tracts about the two houses being the chief legislators, was that king, lords, and commons made law in parliament.[34]

Herle's authorship of the distinctive co-ordination principle makes him the central figure in the rise and spread of the theory of a shared parliamentary sovereignty in Stuart England. This aspect of his career goes far to explain his contemporary reputation. According to Anthony Wood, he was 'esteemed by the factious party [the leadership of the long parliament?] the prime man of note and power among the clergy'.[35] The description may have been partly due to his having been elected by the two houses in 1646 to be prolocutor of the Westminster Assembly but more likely is traceable to Herle's activity as a publicist for the long parliament. Very probably, his eminence among his peers was derived ultimately from his authorship of the *Fuller Answer*. Published anonymously, it was circulating in London on December 29, 1642, when George Thomason picked it up and named Herle as its author. It went at once through four editions, one of them revised and enlarged, but unlike other leading parliamentarian tracts was apparently not reprinted after 1660.

This entry into the quarrel between Charles I and the long parliament provides a dividing line in the political tracts of 1642–43, which may be sorted into two main categories. The first consists of pre-co-ordination tracts reflecting the inconsistent arguments advanced for the two houses in the search for public vindication and legitimacy; the second, the co-ordination tracts that provided the badly needed consistency and coherence. Keeping the first category in mind, one is tempted to describe the long parliament's position as confused and contradictory and to assign the king the victory in the war of manifestoes. But such a verdict is by no means acceptable if the co-ordination tracts are kept steadily in view.

The words 'co-ordinate', 'co-ordinative', and 'co-ordination' leap from the pages of the instantaneously successful *Fuller Answer*. The government was 'a co-ordinative and mixed monarchy', it was announced forthwith, the co-ordination or mixture present in 'the very supremacy of power itself'. This language was equivalent to asserting a legal sovereignty in king, lords, and commons. As Herle stated, 'Here the monarchy, or highest power is itself compounded of three co-ordinate estates, a king and two houses of parliament', and 'unto this mixed power no subordinate authority may in any case make resistance'. This mixture, which Charles I had himself applauded, meant that the two houses occupied the same plane as the king. They were co-ordinate with him and in no way subordinate. The house of commons was a 'co-ordinative part in the monarchy'; and as for the peers, the very style 'comites and peers' implied a 'co-ordinative society with his majesty in the government'. Only if the co-ordination or mixture were in the highest power of government could the monarchy be described as mixed. Fortunately, no problem existed on this score. The two houses were 'a co-ordinative part in the monarchy or highest principle of power, in as much as they bear a consenting share in the highest office of it'. Significantly, this highest office was 'the making of laws'.[36] Nor should one be misled by the reference to a consenting share in law-making. In writing the *Fuller Answer*, Herle was concerned to establish that each of the two houses had a co-ordinate share in law-making; by the time that he wrote his *Answer to Dr. Ferne's Reply* (1643), the claim was more far-reaching. This share was close to a monopoly on the part of the two houses. Their share, as the two houses had claimed in their declarations of May 26 and November 2, was to contrive, consent, and offer measures, the king's to ratify them. And Herle even assigned to the two houses a co-ordinate share as well in the execution of laws, an area that more conservative exponents of mixed monarchy, such as Hunton, were content to leave to the king. Both legislation and administration were as proper arenas for the two houses as for the king.[37]

The co-ordination of the three estates permitted a revolutionary conclusion. Two estates being greater than one, the houses might on occasion override the king, the justification, 'reason of the state'. The two houses 'must not desert their trust'; and, therefore, though the king's consent was requisite for law-making, they might, nevertheless, pass ordinances of binding force. Such ordinances amounted to 'an occasional supply of this co-ordination of the government (in case of one part's refusal) lest the whole should [fall to?] ruin'. Herle's doctrine of supply implied that the two houses, not the king, possessed the discretionary authority associated with *gubernaculum*, which was intended to secure the kingdom's welfare. Significantly, he made no mention of either the king's discretionary authority or the dispensing power.[38]

The exposition of the ordinance-making power grew more elaborate as Herle developed the ingenious formula of the king's virtual presence at Westminster despite Charles I's departure from London before the civil war. Its effect was to concentrate political power in the two houses while strengthening at the same time their claim to the subject's allegiance. What Herle did was to combine the royal definition of estates with the idea of the king's two bodies so as to claim that Charles I was virtually present with his two houses in a political sense though he was physically at York. Faced with royalist insistence that the two houses at Westminster had no legal existence after Charles left London, Herle found the king present there in his public and political capacity if not in his physical and natural body, the conclusion being the more valid, so he stated, because Charles had bound himself through legislation not to dissolve the long parliament without its consent.

Herle first divided the king's two bodies and then assigned the political body to the keeping of the two houses on the ground that two estates were greater than one. His argument went like this. Granted that no law could be made without the consent of the three estates and that no subordinate authority could offer resistance to the three estates working in unison as a corporation, certain circumstances made it incumbent on the two houses to supply a co-ordination of the government until a law could be made. As he said in a much quoted phrase, '*co-ordinata invicem supplent*, co-ordinates supply each other'. At such a time they might, for example, issue ordinances. A justifiable expedient whenever the kingdom was endangered, it might also be used on the ground that the two houses as two estates form 'a part in the supremacy of power, and in case of the other part's absence and refusal both, virtually the whole'. By fighting for the law and the kingdom the two houses protected the king in his political capacity: indeed, he was, in fact, politically present at Westminster despite the distance of his person from it.[39] The advantages of urging the doctrine of the king's virtual presence with the two houses are apparent. His prerogatives and his claim to allegiance were thereby effectually transferred to the two houses, now fast becoming, in theoretical terms, the only center of political power and authority.

But was it not fundamentally contradictory to assign a share of legal sovereignty to Englishmen in parliament when they were, in their persons, the king's subjects? Herle's solution was ingenious. The case resembled that of a father and son, jointly intrusted by deed of enfeoffment with the use of certain lands. The son was subordinate to his father within the family, but not when he was feoffee in the trust. Under these circumstances he was co-ordinate and joint with his father. By analogy, the king's subjects were co-ordinate and joint with him in parliament, and Herle's description made it unmistakable that co-ordination carried with it a share in the sovereignty.[40]

Finally, the *Fuller Answer* reflected the view that the community was the human source of political authority as Herle invoked the formula that while government in general came from God, the particular form was from the people. This was the proper interpretation of *Romans* 13:1: 'Let every soul be subject unto the higher powers for there is no power but of God, the powers that be, are ordained by God.' To reach this conclusion Herle relied on I *Peter* 2:13, which was often used to counter *Romans* 13:1. The former exhorted: 'Submit yourselves unto every ordinance of man for the Lord's sake.' This meant that government was an ordinance of man, a human ordinance, as contemporaries explained. According to Herle, mixed monarchy had arisen from the consent of both king and people at the beginning

c

of government and was confirmed thereafter by the oaths of both parties in succeeding reigns and by customary practice time out of mind. This ideological foundation yielded results hostile to the king's power. Because his title was not derived immediately from God but mediately from the community, his power was derivative, assigned by the people in the first constitution of government. Parliament's power had originated in the same way; but after the grant was made, it could not be resumed.[41]

Although the formula was by no means new, Herle's comments compel attention. For these reasons. This was an early statement in the civil-war years of a viewpoint that rapidly became a commonplace as the direct result of parliamentarian pamphleteering. Moreover, in the new age of political definition the assertion that government was a human ordinance usually appeared with the co-ordination principle; and both were often authenticated by Charles I's public statements. No such lofty patronage was present before 1642 nor would it have been present afterwards had not a harried king undertaken to define publicly his constitutional position in the face of an unprecedented assault on his power.

Another tract that, along with the *Fuller Answer*, provided the main foundation of the theory of mixed monarchy was Philip Hunton's *Treatise of Monarchie* (1643). Hunton, too, was a Presbyterian clergyman, and he is said to have enjoyed Oliver Cromwell's patronage. Hunton became provost of Cromwell's northern university at Durham and also received the rich living of Sedgefield. The university disappeared at the restoration; and Hunton was ejected from his living in 1662, living thereafter in obscurity. But his *Treatise of Monarchie* had much influence during the remainder of the century. Writing at the end of the period, Wood commented that it 'hath been and is still in great vogue among many persons of commonwealth and levelling principles', and Hunton was reputed to be the most learned of the parliamentarian writers.[42] Granted that he belonged to one party in the dispute wracking the kingdom, his exposition of the governmental system was more conservative than either Herle's or Prynne's, at least at this stage of Prynne's career. Finding the English government to be a mixed monarchy, as Charles I had himself affirmed in the Answer to the Nineteen Propositions,

Hunton described the mixture as in the very root and supremacy of power because the legislative power, the supreme power, resided in three distinct concurrent estates, each independent of the other. Yet his claims for the two houses were relatively discreet and modest. Disagreeing with the insistence of Charles' supporters that the king's power alone gave force to the law, still he stopped short of claiming that the two houses were either co-ordinate with the king or equal to him in areas outside of law-making. The king was the head and fountain of the power that governed and executed established laws, and his was the larger share of the sovereign power in which all three estates shared.[43]

Hunton avoided the term 'co-ordination' in discussing the legislative power but implied, nevertheless, that the three estates of king, lords, and commons were coequal and co-ordinate in making laws. Despite his hesitation about describing the two houses as co-ordinate with the king, even in law-making, he found their position to be by no means subordinate. That theme was constant. All three – king, lords, and commons – shared the supreme power, all of them had a negative voice, and 'the consent and concourse of all' were 'most free, and none depending on the will of the other'. The power of the two houses was 'radically their own'. Pressed by royalist writers, Hunton found it easier to employ in a later tract the term 'co-ordinate' in discussing law-making; and undeniably his supreme power encompassed the idea of a legal sovereignty in king, lords, and commons. Law-making was the highest power in the state, the 'height of power'.[44] Mixed monarchy meant, then, a parliamentary sovereignty in king, lords, and commons; and to substantiate this view of the constitution Hunton relied not only on the authoritative Answer to the Nineteen Propositions but also on the enacting clauses in statutes. In doing so, he was probably responding to Dr Henry Ferne, who had evoked such clauses to support the royalist case. But Hunton himself had much to do with adding this essential ingredient to the debate over the legislative power. It appeared from acts of parliament, he wrote, 'that every of the three estates hath a legislative power in it; every act being enacted by the king's most excellent majesty, and by the authority of the lords and commons assembled in parliament'.[45] Thereafter enacting clauses figured in the controversy over the law-making power, and the constant examination of statutes to settle the issue of who made law had a lasting impact. Englishmen were learning about legal sovereignty; and if they accepted the radical principle of a co-ordination in the legislative power, they were likely to accept as well the theory of a parliamentary sovereignty in king, lords, and commons.

Unlike Herle, Hunton was circumspect and equivocal in discussing the human source of political authority. He was, in fact, one of the very few civil-war polemicists writing on the side of the long parliament to insist on the dual nature of the king's title. Kings were God's ministers with a deputed commission from Him, and it was God and the laws that conferred power and authority on them. Hunton would also grant that tenable arguments existed for the belief that the king was the human source of all power, even that of the houses of parliament. But he found weighty arguments on the other side, too. First of all, the authority of the two houses, simply because it was legislative in nature, could not be derivative. The law-making power was supreme, and a power that caused the supreme effect could not be derivative and subordinate. As for the immediate human source of the houses' authority, it was the community, which empowered both kings and parliaments. This was how it had come about. The people had used a public compact to institute a sovereign to rule over them and in their wisdom and experience had created a mixed sovereign, that is, a king who could make no laws of his own will but was limited by the important circumstance that king, lords, and commons as three estates shared the legislative power.

This emphasis on a dual source of royal authority diminished when Hunton stressed the importance of community sanction. Monarchy had no monopoly on divine providence, he found, as he now employed the formula that became so prevalent in anti-court literature. Whereas government in general was from God, the particular form came from the people. 'For a general binding ordinance', wrote Hunton, 'God hath given no word, either to command or commend one kind [of government] above another.' To the contrary, 'men may according to their relations to the form they live under, to their affections and judgments in diverse respects, prefer this or that form above the rest'. His conclusion was unqualified. Whatever form the community chose, God's hand could be seen at work.[46]

The theory of mixed monarchy, as expounded by Herle and Hunton, made no allowance for a discretionary authority by which the king dispensed with or otherwise acted above the law whenever he thought the public benefit required a relaxation of its rigor. The law in all instances limited the king's power. Concluding that the law was the measure of his power – language reminiscent of Charles I's at Newmarket on March 9, 1642 – Hunton would vest a discretionary authority in the king only if it were exercised in conjunction with the two houses in matters affecting the public safety and welfare. He had no discretionary authority even in wartime since the house of commons had to be consulted when money was raised for the realm's defense. Since laws were also needed at such times, the king must work with the two houses. 'The two houses in virtue of the legislative authority in part residing in them' were 'interested in the preservation of laws and government, as well as the king'. If anything, emergency action resided in the two houses without the king. Should he misemploy the militia during an emergency or even refuse to take action despite danger to the laws and government, the two houses were justified in assuming arms by means of temporary and extraordinary ordinances and then performing the king's trust.[47] Such language was consistent with the political realities of 1642. Not only had the two houses assumed a power of supply in an emergency, but Charles himself had also set aside tacitly, for the time being at least, any claim of a discretionary authority to override the laws. His declarations in 1642 made no such claim.

A more radical twist entered the co-ordination argument with the appearance of Prynne's notorious *Soveraigne Power of Parliaments and Kingdomes*, licensed for printing by the house of commons on January 13, 1643. It made a lasting impression on Stuart political thought. According to Prynne, the second edition, which appeared a few months later, was due to earnest entreaties by members of the long parliament and his own opinion that lately printed pleas on its behalf were insufficient because they lacked precedents and authorities.[48] One of the lately printed pleas was Herle's *Fuller Answer*, which shaped Prynne's own argument at a critical juncture.

Yet, as contemporaries noted, the *Soveraigne Power of Parliaments and Kingdomes* is more sharply radical than the *Fuller
Answer*. The difference was due to the manner in which they were
written. Herle had worked directly from the Answer to the Nineteen Propositions to produce the new co-ordination principle,
which Prynne encountered only after the important second
volume of his *Soveraigne Power of Parliaments and Kingdomes*
was virtually complete. The latter's point of departure was the
position taken by the two houses, notably in their declarations of
May 26, and November 2, in which they attacked the king's veto.
Prynne was especially influenced by the second of these declarations, in which the two houses categorized themselves as two
estates, who together constituted the collective body of all the
kingdom. Building on this foundation they had advanced striking
arguments for their supremacy that relied on the following: (1)
*singulis major, universis minor,* a maxim prominent in late medieval political thought and sixteenth-century Huguenot political
argument, now imported into England; (2) a quotation asserting
the manifest superiority of the two houses to the king, attributed
here to the tract known as *Fleta* but subsequently in political
literature to Henry Bracton's *De Legibus et Consuetudines Angliae*
and to *Fleta* (which owed much to Bracton), the citation running
'Bracton L.2, c.16; Fleta L.1, c. 17'; and (3) the Latin tag *quas
vulgus elegerit,* taken from the coronation oath before Charles I
and translated to take away the king's veto in law-making. The
quotation from Bracton and Fleta, as later developed, justified
the two houses if they used force against the king, but for the
moment the long parliament was content to assert it to be 'no new
doctrine' that 'the king hath *in populo regendo superiores, legem,
per quam factus est rex, & curiam suam videlicet comites &
barones,* etc'. This was translated to read that the king in ruling
the people had masters – the law through which he was made king
and his high court of earls and barons.[49]

It will be seen that Prynne, by adding these arguments to
Herle's co-ordination principle, created a second and more overtly
radical version of co-ordination by which the two houses emerged
unmistakably as the principal law-makers. The arguments of
November 2, used sparingly and moderately in the *Fuller Answer*,
are conspicuous in the *Soveraigne Power of Parliaments and*

*Kingdomes*, where *singulis major, universis minor* and *quas vulgus elegerit*, in particular, are elaborately developed and given much prominence.

According to Prynne, the high court of parliament, and the whole kingdom that it represented, was truly and properly the highest sovereign power, above the king himself. The proof lay in its binding the king, even in cases of the highest concern that encroached furthest upon the prerogative. Both statute and common law were superior to the prerogative, which parliament might change at will. Working through parliament, the kingdom might not only augment but also abridge, abolish, and even resume branches of the king's power and prerogative if there were just cause; that is, if the prerogative appeared onerous or dangerous to the subject and inconsistent with the laws or the people's welfare, safety and liberty. Prynne believed there were ample historical precedents for his thesis that parliamentary sovereignty bound the prerogative. Witness, for example, Magna Carta, the Petition of Right, and medieval statutes limiting the power of pardon. No notice was given to the fact that grants of pardon had usually dispensed with the medieval statutes. Significantly, Prynne placed no such limitations on parliamentary power. He waxed eloquent as he defended the actions of the two houses in levying and collecting taxes during the civil war. Parliament was the absolute sovereign power within the realm, not subject to any laws; it was the sole law-maker, endowed with an absolute sovereignty over the laws themselves, including Magna Carta and other statutes, and capable of repealing, changing and enacting laws whenever public safety and defense required such actions. Despite the last phrase there is no reason to think that the power cited was dependent on a state of emergency.[50]

Moreover, and this was a key point, the two houses were to all intents and purposes the sovereign parliament. One reason was that the king, as only a third estate, was bound by the other estates, whether personally present or not. Prynne was working at this point from the *Fuller Answer* but now went beyond Herle in the use made of *singulis major, universis minor*. The king as a single person, although he was the chief and principal member of parliament and the kingdom, was subordinate to the two houses. The collective body of all the kingdom, they constituted the greatest and most considerable part of parliament. As he said, 'Doubtless the whole, or major part of the parliament (which in law is the whole) is above the king, the chief member of it.' And he explained the relationship :

Thus in all our corporations, the court of aldermen and common council is of greater power than the mayor alone, though the chief officer; the chapter of greater authority than the dean, the dean and chapter than the bishop; the whole bench, than the lord chief justice, the whole council than the president; the whole parliament than either of the houses : and by like reason than the king; especially, since one of the three estates is lesser than the three estates together; who in parliament . . . are not subordinate, but co-ordinate parts of the great common council of the kingdom [the parliament].[51]

Thereafter *singulis major, universis minor* was often combined with the co-ordination principle. Writing in Charles II's reign, Sir Roger L'Éstrange noted the relationship : 'To colour the invention [of co-ordination]', its advocates 'tell us that the king is *singulis major, universis minor*; greater than the diffusive body of the people but inferior to the collective'.[52]

This view of the kingship shaped Prynne's comments on law-making. According to him, the chief power of enacting and making laws resided in the two houses. One reason was that public acts were the laws of the kingdom; and common justice dictated that the two houses, who constituted the collective body of all the kingdom, should be the principal law-makers. It was also the law, and Prynne turned to the phrase *quas vulgus elegerit* to explain this position.

The phrase is a shortened version of a key portion of the coronation oath before Charles I. It was also used in the statute of provisors (25 Edw. 3), to which reference was frequently made. The point is that the king solemnly promised to '*corroborare justas leges & consuetudines quas vulgus elegerit*', and the problem was to ascertain the nature of his promise. Parliamentarians, and later anti-court writers, translated *vulgus* as 'the people' or 'the two houses', and *elegerit* as 'shall choose' or 'should choose' to conclude that the king had promised assent to 'such laws as the people shall choose' or 'should choose'. The claim of a supremacy in law-making for the two houses was thus associated with the future tense of the verb and conveyed that the coronation oath obliged the king to accept all such bills as the two houses sent him in the name and for the good of the whole kingdom. If he vetoed them, he was guilty of perjury for violating his coronation oath.[53]

The aspect of the coronation oath, commonly referred to as *quas vulgus elegerit*, became current, but not before the parliamentarian interpretation met with challenge. One of Charles I's declarations, by translating *elegerit* as 'hath chosen', associated the court position with the past perfect, or, as contemporaries said, the preterperfect tense of the verb.[54] This was no academic exercise for grammarians: the king's translation gave his public promise an altogether different cast. Whereas the parliamentarian made the two houses the principal law-makers, the royalist provided for the king's executing laws already made. Prynne's statement of the differing interpretations was succinct. The king must accept such measures as 'the lords and commons in parliament (not the king himself) shall make choice of'. The disputed expression referred to 'future new laws, to be chosen and made by the people's consent, not to laws formerly enacted'.[55]

A king without a veto on legislation could hardly dispense with a measure after it became law. This conclusion was implicit in Prynne's argument of 1643 and became explicit in a tract published in the last year of his life. By this time, as will be seen, Prynne's political thought was more conservative; but as a firm believer in the co-ordination principle (now on the lines enunciated by Herle), he asserted that no such power existed in the constitution. A king who 'might dispense with acts of parliament and penal laws, made with the greatest deliberation and advice for public good, by king, lords, and commons' could 'subvert and blow up the sovereign power, authority, jurisdiction [and] honour of parliaments'.[56] Prynne might just as well have remarked that the ideas of parliamentary sovereignty and co-ordination barred the way to a discretionary authority in the king that placed him at times above the law. As only one of three equal estates, he was no longer the sovereign head of the kingdom: the two houses were partners in sovereignty. Moreover, if law-making was the supreme act within the state, it was inappropriate for the king to dispense with a law.

The context of Prynne's thought is predictable and requires

only a brief statement. According to his *Soveraigne Power of Parliaments and Kingdomes*, it was the kingdom that created kings, and parliament as representative of the kingdom – the original and supreme human authority – empowered the ruler. Indeed, the kingdom and parliament were the most sovereign and primitive power, from which all other powers were derived. In summary, Prynne had rejected completely the assumptions about kingship that had prevailed in Tudor and early Stuart England. The king was in no sense above the law. He was only below it, and the community was the sole, immediate human source of political authority.[57]

These were the leading co-ordination tracts, from which parliamentarian political literature took its main lines; and it is time now to discuss their influence, which was by any standard very great.

## IV

On this score Richard Baxter's help was invaluable when he pointed to the contemporary tracts that were, in his opinion, most advantageous to the parliamentarian cause. At the top of his list was Henry Parker's *Observations upon some of his Majesties late Answers and Expresses* (1642), a tract in circulation by July 2, that reflected the early influence of the Answer to the Nineteen Propositions. Great as was contemporary interest in it, it belongs to the category of pre-co-ordination literature.[58] But other tracts mentioned by Baxter did reflect the co-ordination principle. Besides the *Observations*, he thought no works of greater advantage to the long parliament than Hunton's *Treatise of Monarchie* and Prynne's book on the sovereign power of parliaments.[59] He also referred his readers to Nathaniel Bacon's *An Historical Discourse of the Uniformity of the Government of England* (1647–51),[60] a discussion seemingly of English history from early times to Queen Elizabeth's reign but, in fact, a thinly disguised enunciation of the community-centered view of government that made Anglo-Saxon England the major source of Stuart political institutions. It contained a view of co-ordination much like Prynne's.

Baxter's judgment can hardly be faulted. These were the key

tracts written on behalf of the long parliament. Moreover, Hunton's, Prynne's, and Bacon's writings continued to shape polemical warfare during the remainder of the century. Hunton's *Treatise of Monarchie* was twice republished at the time of the exclusion crisis, was burned by Oxford University in 1683, and was reprinted, in two editions, at the Glorious Revolution.[61] Prynne's *Soveraigne Power of Parliaments* was likewise a continued object of suspicion and distrust in pro-court circles. The center of acute controversy during the civil war, it was of much interest to the anonymous author of the *Freeholders Grand Inquest* (1648), a tract repeatedly republished in the last years of Charles II's reign. It will be urged in this study that its author was the royalist lawyer and administrator, Sir Robert Holbourne, an attribution, admittedly, that runs contrary to the opinion of modern authorities.[62] The *Soveraigne Power of Parliaments* attained a new notoriety after 1660 when two formidable high tory controversialists, Dr George Hickes and Dr Robert Brady, singled it out for hostile comment;[63] and the government even seized a written copy that someone had made for his personal use, apparently as a preliminary to having the tract reprinted.[64] As for Bacon's tract, it is frequently mentioned in the *Calendar of State Papers* for Charles II's reign. In 1682, a writer informed the government of a recent reprinting by a certain John Starkey, 'who will possibly pretend it is only an old book reprinted and an historical discourse of past times without any application to the present'. Not so. In this writer's opinion, 'it was dedicated to the service of a rebellion'.[65]

Conspicuously missing from the list, however, was the *Fuller Answer*. Its absence is the more surprising because Baxter himself assumed that the co-ordination principle was indigenous to the political system. If effect on contemporaries is the acid test, this was the most influential civil-war tract: its repercussions are discernible in the pamphlets of the period, the comments of leaders in the long parliament and the votes of that body, and even in the political tenets of Charles II's and James II's reigns. The *Fuller Answer* had an immediate impact when it influenced both Hunton and Prynne, who had their own readers, and drew responses from such leading royalist writers as Ferne, Dudley Digges, and Heylyn. Herle was answered at the restoration by Robert Sheringham and on the eve of the Glorious Revolution by Dr Nathaniel

Johnston, writing under active court sponsorship.[66] He continued
to elaborate the new principle as late as 1644.[67] Its attraction for
parliamentarian pamphleteers, as the civil war went on, appears
from William Stafford's *Reason of the War* (1646), which was
viewed as representative of the parliamentarian position. According to Stafford, the government was 'not simply a subordinative
but a co-ordinative and mixt monarchy'. 'The highest supremacy
itself', he explained, was 'compounded of three estates, co-ordinate, king, lords and commons'. At times the two houses, who
shared the supremacy of power, were 'virtually the whole'.[68] To
Judge Jenkins, who denounced the argument, it came close to
placing a legal sovereignty in the two houses.[69]

These ideological elements found an echo within the long parliament. Indeed, it looks as if the leadership there fashioned from
co-ordination its major propaganda weapon against Charles I.
The assumption was widespread in the late seventeenth century,
and the charge frequently made, that the influence of the new
principle provided the root explanation of the rise and spread of
rebellion against royal authority that culminated in the king's
death. In a word, co-ordination had killed the king. Even if this
is to assign too early an origin to that principle, the mistake is
understandable; and the conclusions of contemporaries – especially noticeable in conservative circles – point to its conspicuous
place in political controversy. It is worthwhile, accordingly, to
pursue the links between Herle and the long parliament so as to
learn more about his role in the 1640s. A suitable point of departure has been provided by John Nalson, a highly conservative
pamphleteer and historian, who, in the early 1680s, asserted
categorically that leading men in the long parliament took up the
co-ordination principle at once after the Answer to the Nineteen
Propositions was made public, with consequences fatal to the
king. The definition of estates, wrote Nalson, 'once dropt from
him [Charles I] fell not to the ground, but was immediately taken
up by some of the leading men of the parliament, who made use
of it as a foundation for their usurped co-ordinancy of authority'.[70]
While the value of this statement is not easily decided, it may be
inquired whether Nalson was actually giving a valid description
of parliamentarian ideology in high places or seeking to discredit
the co-ordination principle in his own day by associating its pre-

valence in the 1640s with Charles I's martyrdom. Motives are difficult to disentangle; but probably Nalson's words had a dual purpose: to denigrate the co-ordination principle, certainly, but also to pinpoint the ideological position of the long parliament.

For leading men there did express their political positions in terms reminiscent of Herle. Prominent among them was Nathaniel Fiennes, who spoke for others in declaring that his party did not intend 'a total alteration of the government from a mixed monarchy, duly bounded as this is, into something else' but rather to keep 'the three estates co-ordinate equally to poise and balance each other'.[71] Later commissioner of the great seal under Cromwell, Fiennes was the second son of Lord Saye and Sele, an influential leader in the long parliament. Fiennes' acquaintance with the Answer to the Nineteen Propositions was long-standing since he had been named to the committee of the house of commons to consider its preamble and return an answer. Another representative member of the long parliament, the earl of Manchester, sometime speaker of the house of lords, used the king's definition of estates at the end of the civil war. Denouncing the ordinance for a court to try Charles I, he insisted that it was impossible for the king to be a traitor. As he said, 'the parliament of England, by the fundamental laws of England' consists 'of three estates, 1. king, 2. lords, 3. commons'. Since the king, 'the first and chief estate', summoned and dissolved parliament and confirmed all of its acts, none was possible without him. It was absurd, therefore, to describe the king as a traitor to parliament.[72]

This language supports Nalson's contention that the co-ordination principle was basic to the position taken by the leadership in the long parliament. Further, Fiennes and Manchester were prominent members of John Pym's middle group, which is said to have held the balance of power in the long parliament during the first years of the civil war. Fiennes and Manchester, in employing the language of co-ordination, were probably representative of their party. This is the more likely because of certain signs that the middle group took up Herle and in a sense sponsored him. The evidence, highly circumstantial in nature but well worth noting, comes from the record of what are called fast sermons, which prominent Puritan clergymen preached before the two houses.[73] Herle's name appears on a number of occasions, and the invitations to preach appear to have come from the middle group.

The record of the fast sermons is more meaningful if the membership of that group is kept constantly in mind and the fast sermon viewed as a political instrument. According to J. H. Hexter, who pioneered research on the middle group, its main connectional axis was supplied by two Essex grandees – Robert Rich, second earl of Warwick, and Sir Thomas Barrington, both men of great political influence in Essex. They worked closely with John Pym.

It was in the period when the middle group under his direction controlled the long parliament that a set pattern of fast sermons took shape. Beginning on February 23, 1642, these lasted until April, 1649, coming to an end after the civil war was over and the commonwealth established. The success of the system rested with the Puritan clergymen who preached the fast sermons; and, as might be anticipated, the most prominent among them were associates of Pym and the Essex grandees. Two names in particular come to mind in this connection – Stephen Marshall and Edmund Calamy – both Warwick protégés. Their fiery sermons, highly colored and spiced with Biblical imagery, brought the outbreak of civil war perceptibly closer and maintained morale on the parliamentarian side after war began. Much the same may be said of Herle although his contribution was more clearly political. While he seems not to have attained an intimacy with Pym and Warwick like Marshall's and Calamy's, he made an equally great contribution to the parliamentary cause; and the long parliament plainly valued his services. By the summer of 1643 he had the confidence of the leadership, and his name was linked with Marshall and Calamy as one of the most trusted extraparliamentary allies of the middle group.

The outcome is the more astonishing because Herle was a relatively obscure provincial clergyman at the beginning of the war, without visible links to Pym and the Essex grandees. A new arrival on the London scene, come from Lancashire, he presumably was in the city by the autumn of 1642 when the house of commons voted, on October 26, to invite him to preach at St Margaret's. It was a signal honor for a newcomer. Referring to the fast sermon, preached on November 30, Herle described himself as a stranger without notes and books when it was penned.[74] The explanation was an apology for the lack of quoted matter. That he should have received an invitation to preach a fast sermon before the house of commons at all is remarkable under the circumstances, but some question marks are dispelled when it is noticed that the invitation came from John Moore, also from Lancashire. He was a wealthy Liverpool merchant and real-estate owner with strong political convictions, who eventually became a regicide. Of enough importance in the first years of the long parliament to be named to key committees, he was subsequently a colonel in the parliamentary army and even outfitted a ship at his own expense for the war in Ireland.[75]

Circumstances had changed, however, when Herle next preached before one of the houses, this time before the house of lords on June 15, 1643. He now enjoyed a new-found eminence as a leading publicist for the long parliament and stood forth as the author of the brand-new co-ordination principle. The parliamentarian ideology, known to contemporaries as mixed monarchy, was enunciated for the first time in an extended controversy between him and Dr Henry Ferne, chaplain to Charles I and a major defender of royal policies. Herle had been drawn into the arena after the royalist published in November, 1642, his well-known *The Resolving of Conscience*. This tract, the first printed in the king's defense, provoked a storm of controversy from which Herle emerged with an assured future. Fortunately, Thomason dated the exchange of tracts. *The Resolving of Conscience* was countered almost at once by the *Fuller Answer*, on the streets of London by December 29, 1642; but several months elapsed before the royalist published his *Conscience Satisfied*. Thomason's copy is dated April 18, 1643. Herle's response was his *Answer to Dr. Ferne*, which was in circulation by May 17, 1643; and less than a month later he was invited to preach before the house of lords on a great and solemn occasion.

The chronology of publication links the peers' invitation with the appearance of the tracts that introduced the co-ordination principle to the civil-war generation. In the period of approximately eight months following his arrival in London, Herle had published two consequential tracts, the first, and the more important, containing his formulation of the new principle, the second its elaboration and defense. His argument was bound to find a sympathetic audience among leading men in the long parliament, in particular, among those named in 1642 to reply to the preamble of the Answer to the Nineteen Propositions. On the appropriate committee were, for example, Pym, Barrington, and Hampden. That Herle's writings were welcome to parliamentarian leadership is evident, moreover, from the invitation to preach before the house of lords.

The invitation is the more significant when one notices the occasion for the fast sermon and the names of the other clergymen invited to preach. The occasion was a by-product of the crisis facing Pym with the disclosure of Sir Edmund Waller's plot to turn London over to the royalists. This was the first major test of his war leadership, and Hexter caught the gravity of the situation when he wrote of panic in a London beset by 'terror of visible enemies without the gates and dread of secret enemies within'.[76] Arrangements were hurriedly made for a public thanksgiving for deliverance from the plot, at first to be celebrated by the two houses, the cities of London and Westminster, and the suburbs but subsequently extended to the whole kingdom.[77] Since only the most dependable clergy would have been intrusted with preaching before the two houses at so critical an hour, it is of much interest to learn the identity of the clergymen besides Herle who undertook the delicate mission.

The house of commons turned in haste to the familiar when its members voted on June 9 to invite Marshall to preach before them and also the less well-known but equally faithful – some would have said equally seditious – Obadiah Sedgwick. Like Marshall and Calamy, he was closely associated with the Essex grandees. After his opposition to Laud cost him his London lectureship, Sedgwick received from Warwick the living of Cogge-shall, Essex.[78] Preaching before the house of lords was Calamy, on the morning of June 15, followed in the afternoon by Herle.[79] As one of four who were invited to preach a sermon of thanks-giving before a house of parliament in the wake of the Waller plot, he stood forth as a clerical ally of the middle group in the long parliament, his name associated with Marshall, Calamy, and Sedgwick, all clergymen identified with the ruling middle group. Of the invited preachers the only one who cannot be linked directly with Pym and the Essex grandees on the basis of their pre-war records was Herle, and this fact certainly suggests that his invitation rested on a different ground. Moreover, unlike the others, he seems not to have been known before the civil war as an opponent of Laud, the usual requisite for an invitation to preach at Westminster. It may be assumed, then, that Herle, his tracts hot off the press, was invited to preach in the emergency as the author of the co-ordination principle, his unique and telling contribution to the world of political propaganda. It was, after all, no small feat to have supplied the long parliament with the political ideology required for vindicating to public opinion an unprecedented opposition to Charles I and establishing the intellectual basis that permitted Englishmen to give their allegiance in good conscience to the two houses. In summary, to paraphrase Nalson, the leading men of the long parliament took up the author of the co-ordination principle not long after Charles I dropped his definition of estates on a startled political world; and if they thought it proper to honor Herle publicly and to rely upon him in what they saw as a national emergency, it may be supposed that they likewise made use of the co-ordination principle on the lines of Nalson's generalization. The supposition is the more reasonable in light of the language, cited earlier, of Fiennes and Manchester, both members of the middle group in the long parliament and representative of the political outlook in their respective houses.

The two houses recognized Herle's contribution to the parliamentarian cause in other ways, lending weight to the idea that he had the patronage of the middle group. On June 20, 1643, he was named, with Calamy and Sedgwick, to license books of divinity and about the same time received appointment to the original membership of the Westminster Assembly, which had the task of suggesting a religious settlement for the kingdom.[80] The picture comes even more sharply into focus when the record of the fast sermons is once more consulted. After Pym's death Herle was invited to preach before the house of commons on November 5, 1644 (Guy Fawkes day), a day of remembrance much cherished by Puritans; and this time his patron can be determined. It was Anthony Nicolls, Pym's nephew and right-hand man, who had served in the preceding year as the liaison between the two houses and the parliamentary army.[81] Herle subsequently preached before the house of commons on two other occasions, in 1646 and in 1647, the invitation in both instances coming from Sir Benjamin Rudyerd, who belonged to the middle group.[82] The days of pamphleteering were now over for Herle with a great victory won in the allied spheres of political ideology and propaganda. After his election as prolocutor of the West-minster Assembly his energies turned to elaborating a Presbyterian church system for the kingdom. But his services to the parliamen-tarian cause were signally recognized once more when he was named one of the clergymen who attended the parliamentarian commissioners during the treaty of Newport.[83]

His political ideas were now common currency.[84] The descrip-tion of the power relationship among the three estates which Herle and his fellows had received from Charles I underlay, for example, the vote of the house of commons, on April 28, 1648, when it was resolved by a large majority (165 to 99) that the house would not 'alter the fundamental government of the kingdom by king, lords, and commons'.[85] The language presents difficulty in this sense. It is by no means clear whether 'government' referred to the sovereign law-making power or to the administration of the government; but there is no problem with the reference to king, lords, and commons, which connoted the three co-ordinate estates in parliament.[86] The popularity of the community-centered ideology was also apparent when contemporaries described the government as a mixed monarchy. The term was rooted in the Answer to the Nineteen Propositions where Charles I, after praising the mixture of monarchy, aristocracy, and democracy in the government, pointed to a joint law-making in king, lords, and commons. Mixed monarchy was often said to have confused ideas of allegiance. In a passage remembered as late as the Glorious Revolution, the royalist Dudley Digges declared: 'I am very confident a mistake of this mixed monarchy hath engaged many well-meaning men against the king, to the overthrow of our laws, which the simpler part are persuaded they fight for.'[87]

Numerous contemporary statements attest to the great popu-larity of the new political ideas and their vocabulary.[88] But one of the most revealing, surely, came from the elder Edward Bagshaw, a parliamentarian who abandoned Pym for the king. Making his way to Oxford, Bagshaw sat in the parliament that Charles I summoned in December, 1643. Taken prisoner in the following year, he wrote during his imprisonment his *Rights of the Crown of England* (1660). The timing tells much about political discussions in the royalist capital and the Oxford parliament during the months before he was taken prisoner. Clearly, Herle's doctrines were a source of much uneasiness to the royalist party. Excoriating the parliamentarians for denying that the king was the supreme governor, whose title was directly from God, Bagshaw described the leading objections to this viewpoint. From one of them, 'the most giant-like', all other objections arose 'like hands from the shoulders of Briareus'. This particular objection rested, significantly, on two newly coined distinctions: (1) 'A subordinate power to the king, and a co-ordinate power with the king', and (2) 'An actual power or presence of the king, and a virtual power or presence of the king'. From these distinctions came the insistence that three co-ordinate estates of king, lords, and commons made law and also that two of the three co-ordinate estates – the lords and the commons – might lawfully control the king as a third estate, even to the point of denying him a veto in law-making. This reasoning – to Bagshaw, manifestly absurd, irrational and illegal – was 'greatly countenanced by men of the gown'.[89]

Bagshaw also noted the prominence of *singulis major, universis minor* in parliamentarian ideology. As he said, 'It is confessed to be true, that the king is greater than any one single person in the kingdom.' But it was also being said, he added, that 'he is not greater than all the people of the kingdom put together'. This was 'a new distinction kindled from a new-found-light of *singulis major*, and *universis minor*'.[90] It will be recalled that the maxim was in the two houses' declaration of November 2, 1642, where it was utilized to demonstrate the superiority of the two houses to the king, and that Prynne had taken it up in his *Soveraigne Power of Parliaments and Kingdomes*. No more is needed to explain its popularity.

Not that all parliamentarians were receptive. Clement Walker, for one, was openly hostile.[91] But the maxim, nevertheless, won wide acceptance and became, according to J. H. M. Salmon, 'the basis of English theories of resistance',[92] or perhaps better, in terms of this study, one of the bases of a radical version of co-ordination and hence parliamentary sovereignty. There is an interesting account of its influence during the civil war in Sir William Dugdale's *A Short View of the Late Troubles in England* (1681). Charles I's enemies, he reported, inserted a passage on *singulis major, universis minor* into Richard Hooker's respected and highly influential *Ecclesiastical Polity* when the last three books were published posthumously. According to Dugdale :

They did at length gain those very books into their hands; and . . . most shamefully corrupted them in sundry places, omitting diverse passages . . . unsuitable to their purposes; and instead thereof inserting what they thought might give countenance to their present evil practices : amongst which was this, *in terminis,* that, *though the king were singulis major,* yet *he was universis minor,* and having so done, caused them to be published in print. By which fallacy diverse well-meaning people were miserably captivated and drawn to their party. And at length were not ashamed, in that treaty which they had with his majesty in the Isle of Wight, to vouch the authority of this venerable man, in derogation of his supremacy, and to place the sovereign power in the people [the two houses?] : that great antimonarchist, William late Viscount Saye and Sele, being the person who boldly urged it. Whereunto the good king answered; that 'though those three books were not allowed to be Mr. Hooker's; yet he would admit them so to be, and consent to what his lordship endeavored to prove out of them, in case he would assent to the judgment of Mr. Hooker, declared in the other five books, which were unquestionably his'.[93]

Only two of the last three books were published at the time indicated, appearing in 1648 and again in 1651. But one of them was the critical eighth book, which contained surprisingly strong anti-monarchical sentiments including a citation of *singulis major, universis minor* by name.[94]

Had the text been tampered with? Ever since the late seventeenth century the central problem in Hooker scholarship has been the authenticity of the last three books, and there can be no suggestion that so complicated a problem can be disposed of in a few sentences. It can be said, however, that the twentieth-century editor of the eighth book, believing it compatible with Hooker's whole conception of society and government, thought not and treated Dugdale's charge as without merit. There is much support for this verdict in scholarly circles,[95] and from the stand-point of civil-war political ideology a number of reasons for accepting it. For one thing, Hooker's use of *singulis major, univer-sis minor* does not carry the stamp of civil-war argument and in borrowing from Bracton he does not resort to the quotation from Bracton and Fleta, to which the long parliament had called attention on November 2, 1642. The radicalism of the eighth book is Elizabethan. This does not mean, however, that Dugdale's account should be dismissed out of hand. The description of Lord Saye and Sele's encounter with the king is plausible. Saye and Sele was a parliamentarian commissioner during the treaty of Newport, and contemporaries remarked on the vigor with which he pressed an accommodation. With the eighth book of the *Ecclesiastical Polity* eminently exploitable for parliamentarian purposes, it would have been natural for him to call upon an authority so revered by Charles I. The royalists, reluctant to believe that Hooker of his own initiative would consciously choose language which they saw as so manifestly injurious to the kingship, responded with the charge of tampering. It is fruitless to ask whether the charge was rooted in sincerity or born of desperation. What does seem self-evident is that news of Hooker's name being enlisted in support of the radical version of the co-ordination principle was a damaging blow to the royalist party.

Even if Dugdale's charge was unfounded, his party had reason to be suspicious. Here the history of what happened to Hooker's papers – or at least certain papers – becomes pertinent. Some of them, including, it was said in the seventeenth century, the manu-scripts of the last three books of the *Ecclesiastical Polity*, passed after Hooker's death to the archbishop of Canterbury (George Abbot) and remained at Lambeth until Laud's library came under the control of the long parliament. After December 28, 1640, Laud's library was in Prynne's custody and on June 27, 1644 was voted to Hugh Peter. The latter, who would play a conspic-uous role in the events leading to Charles I's death, has been compared as a political clergyman with Marshall. Whether he tampered with the *Ecclesiastical Polity* is however another matter. Rumor had it that he received the posthumous books with Laud's library, but more evidence is needed on this point than has appeared. There is the further negative fact that, of the Hooker manuscripts known to modern scholars, none of what has come down can be traced with confidence back to Peter although there are presently two manuscripts of the eighth book at Lambeth, one of which could have been for a time in Peter's possession.[96] That parliamentarian figures of this kind and prominence were associated in the public mind with the custody of Hooker's papers could only have fostered doubt in the king's party about the trustworthiness of the eighth book and, specifically, about the portion where the maxim *singulis major, universis minor* appears.

The whole episode is of interest for another reason. Prynne was already publicly associated with the revolutionary expression, but it now becomes possible to add Peter to the growing list of parliamentarians familiar with it though admittedly the link in Peter's case is tenuous. And Dugdale's reference to Lord Saye and Sele certainly suggests a broad acceptance of the maxim in parliamentarian ranks late in the civil war. The point received dramatic illustration when John Bradshaw, lord president of the high court of justice, invoked *singulis major* in a harsh indictment of Charles I, prior to sentencing him to death.[97]

The quotation from Bracton and Fleta, also in the declaration of November 2, was equally bold in asserting the supremacy of the two houses vis-à-vis the king. Its influence was intertwined with that of *singulis major*, and it, too, flourished in the 1640s. It will be recalled that the two houses cited only Fleta, saying: 'If we should say the king hath *in populo regendo superiores, legem, per quam factus est rex, & curiam suam videlicit comites & barones*, etc., it were no new doctrine.'[98] This was by no means a complete rendering of Bracton's statement, but its appearance in the declaration of November 2 was sufficient to inspire fuller statements. By the end of the century the learned Peter Allix was writing :

*In populo regendo rex habet superiores, legem per quam factus est rex, & curiam suam, viz. comites & barones: comites dicuntur quasi socii regis, & qui habet socium habet magistrum; & ideo si rex fuerit sine fraeno, id est sine lege, debent ei fraenum ponere.*

and translating the passage into the unequivocal judgment that the two houses were superior to the king :

In ruling the people, the king has above him the law by which he is made king; and his high court, viz. the earls and barons : earls are so called as being the king's companions, and he who has a companion has a master; and therefore if the king be without bridle, that is, without law, they must bridle him.[99]

If the 'earls' were by no means the equivalent of 'parliament' (the two houses), the point was plain enough. Nor was there any difficulty in making the necessary substitution in the appropriate place.[100] The conclusion was unmistakable. A king who had companions in law-making, as the co-ordination principle presupposed, had masters (*superiores*), their identity easily discerned. Moreover, the king was below the law; and should he violate the law, it was the two houses who must return him to the legal way.

The relationship between this quotation and a more radical version of co-ordination is clear. Herle, for one, quoted the long parliament's language but found it too strong for his taste. His translation was as follows : 'The king hath above him besides God, the law, whereby he is made king, likewise his court of earls and barons, etc.' 'But we need not go so high', he added, 'it will serve our turn if the houses be in this mixture or temper of government, not subordinate or subject'.[101] Others were more extreme as the war went on; and the quotation became notorious when Bradshaw called upon it, along with *singulis major*, during Charles I's trial.[102] One would think this usage would have doomed it to obscurity, but it proved surprisingly durable. Despite an increasing notoriety in Charles II's reign, which will be later noticed, the quotation enjoyed a kind of Indian summer of popularity at the Revolution.

There was also the Latin tag *quas vulgus elegerit*. Its appearance in political literature after 1642 signalled a continuing controversy over the king's veto in law-making. Yet the long parliament was by no means consistent on this point. The house of commons resolved in 1647 that the king must accept bills from the two houses, being bound 'by the duty of his office to give his assent to all such laws as by the lords and commons assembled in parliament, shall be adjudged to be for the good of the kingdom'[103] but in the late spring of 1648 voted, with the house of lords, that government was in king, lords, and commons. The two houses held to this position as late as the treaty of Newport, despite Dugdale's account of Lord Saye and Sele's attitude. The conditions for a settlement, presented at this time to Charles I, by omitting to deal with his veto presupposed its continuance.[104]

Meanwhile *quas vulgus elegerit* continued to be discussed in political literature. Bacon considered it, for example, in his *Historical Discourse*, which would be much reprinted after 1660. And the distinguished lawyer, Bulstrode Whitelocke, setting down his views on government at the restoration, noted that the phrase had received a thorough airing in the declarations of 1642. Not unnaturally, the royalists likewise displayed a sustained interest in the coronation oath as it affected the law-making power. Judge David Jenkins examined *quas vulgus elegerit* in a tract first published in 1647 and reprinted during the exclusion crisis, as did the anonymous royalist who wrote the influential *Freeholders Grand Inquest*. Prynne's comments were invariably at issue. Rejecting his argument step by step, the author of the *Freeholders* questioned whether *vulgus* could be properly applied to the two houses, while insisting that *justas* before *leges & consuetudines quas vulgus elegerit* opened the way for the king to judge whether a measure presented to him for approval was 'just' and so deserving of acceptance. He explicitly denied that *quas vulgus elegerit* could properly be interpreted as 'assenting unto, or granting any new laws'.[105]

Whatever the version of co-ordination employed, the tenets of the community-centered view of government were very much in the air after Charles I's death. A convincing sign of their durability came from Whitelocke – according to David Underdown, the most representative figure among the rumpers.[106] If so, they had turned their back on civil-war extremism as it shaped the theory of parliamentary sovereignty. Whitelocke took a conservative path for a parliamentarian, eschewing any reference to *singulis major, universis minor,* the quotation from Bracton and Fleta, or the parliamentarian version of *quas vulgus elegerit.* Indeed, he asserted categorically the king's right to a veto. This moderate temper may have been due in part to the time at which he wrote. Yet his comments reflect the impact of Herle's co-ordination principle and point to the close relationship between the community-centered view of government and the theory of a legal sovereignty in king, lords, and commons.

An ex-parliamentarian, with experience at first hand in the governmental changes during the civil war and interregnum, Whitelocke now summed up his political reflections. Writing about twenty years after the appearance of the Answer to the Nineteen Propositions, he not only used Charles I's definition of estates but also quoted from the Answer as the authoritative exposition of the powers of the several estates. 'The power of each estate', Whitelocke explained, 'is exactly described by the late king in his declaration, and answer to the 19 propositions, which is worthy [of] the recital.' And he quoted the passages so frequently invoked during the civil war. That this was his route to a parliamentary sovereignty in king, lords, and commons appeared when he added:

It will not, I suppose be expected, that I describe the power of parliament; it is too vast for a particular recital of it. Our books say, 'it may do all things': and doubtless it is the supreme power of this nation; and can bind the persons, estates, and liberties of all the people. It orders sea affairs, and land affairs; foreign and domestic. And, although each estate hath its bounds; by law : yet all the three estates together, the king, lords, and commons, have no bounds; but power to do what they please.[107]

Here was a judgment with which the majority of the political nation could agree.

## V

It has been seen that concepts of government underwent a remarkable metamorphosis during the civil war, with visible effects during the commonwealth and protectorate despite the changed political structure. The claim of a parity among king, lords, and commons in law-making had transformed political argument; and as Bagshaw's comments reveal, the process was far advanced and the formulation of the community-centered view of government complete well before the rise of Leveller democracy with its insistence that the only legitimate government was a house of commons elected on a wide franchise. But it should be noted that the ideology expounded by the parliamentarian writers, unlike that of the Levellers, was compatible with the historic framework of government, a matter of the highest importance. It means that there can be no notion that democratic republicanism was as viable in Stuart England as mixed monarchy. The parliamentarian ideology was the more entrenched because its tenets were formulated when Presbyterianism as a religion enjoyed powerful support. Writers like Herle, Hunton, and Prynne must have had an assured audience.[108]

The parliamentarian ideology, as has been seen, was essentially the theory of a parliamentary sovereignty in king, lords, and commons. Despite its earlier antecedents the theory was on balance new with an attractiveness for the political nation rising out of a political vocabulary that concentrated the highest power, with subtlety and finesse, in king, lords, and commons. A great deal was now being said about Charles I's definition of estates, the co-ordination principle in law-making, the idea of dividing the king's two bodies so as to assign his political office to the keeping of the two houses at Westminster, and about the community as the human source of political authority. The new interpretation of the king's two bodies was usually combined with the statute ensuring that the long parliament could be dissolved only with its consent. Publicists also exploited slogans borrowed from the continent and earlier English theorists such as *singulis major universis minor*, which Prynne put to good use in developing a version of co-ordination more radical than Herle's.

The community-centered view of government raised havoc with the older idea that the king, charged as supreme governor of the realm with *gubernaculum* and responsibility for the kingdom's welfare, might act at times above the law, using a discretionary authority to mitigate its rigor. This view was no longer acceptable. The strikingly different political relationships envisaged in parliamentarian ideology meant that the discretionary authority so necessary for *salus populi* was seen as residing not in the king alone but in the law-making trinity of king, lords, and commons. A king without a discretionary authority was in no sense above the law; he was below it in all respects. Though the dispensing power was seldom directly attacked in parliamentarian writings, it was anachronistic and illogical in terms of the community-centered ideology. This appears from the *Humble Petition and Advice*, under which England was governed from May 25, 1657 until April 22, 1659. Assigning the law-making power to 'three estates' – to Cromwell, expected to take the crown, to the 'other house', intended to be a house of lords, and to the house of commons, it also provided that no laws were to be made, altered, suspended, abrogated or defeated unless by act of parliament.[109]

The king's position had worsened in still other ways. Thus his legislative veto had come under fire. It has been seen that the co-ordination principle actually existed in two versions, depending on whether he was or was not assigned a veto. According to George Lawson, writing during the interregnum, the party that accepted mixed monarchy believed 'the king, peers, and commons to be three co-ordinate powers, yet so that some of them grant three negatives, some only two'.[110] The new theory further damaged royal authority by the assertion that a particular form of government was a human ordinance although political authority, indeed authority in general, came from God. Writing in the early 1660s John Locke pointed to the parliamentarian formula when he noticed a possible third way of constituting civil power – separate from an immediate divine institution or the usual contract – that is, 'one in which all authority is held to come from God but the nomination and appointment of the person bearing that power is thought to be made by the people'.[111] Not only did this formula subvert the order theory of kingship by reversing the flow of authority in the government, it also had the advantage of providing an escape from the traditional sanctions compelling political obedience and allegiance to the king.

The parliamentarian formula might also be used positively to transfer sanctions to the form of government contemplated in the community-centered ideology. The seventeenth-century practice was to rely on the Biblical injunction to 'honor thy father and thy mother', contained in the fifth commandment given by God to Moses, to inculcate in subjects the political obligation to obey those in authority above them. The divine duty of obeying parents extended easily to the political sphere : an Englishman who obeyed his parents (his father as head of the family) similarly gave political obedience to the civil magistrate. Such ideas were instilled orally by means of the catechism, and the church was in this sense an active agent for mass political education. The final result is said to have been an essentially conservative, even authoritarian outlook on the part of rank and file Englishmen. At least this seems to be Gordon Schochet's conclusion in arguing that 'these Englishmen understood and accepted political authority in terms of the patriarchal theory of obligation that is usually associated with the name of Sir Robert Filmer'.[112] Probably this description is valid for the period before 1642, when the order theory of kingship was generally accepted; but there is no reason for assuming that the habit of mind, to which Schochet called attention, placed obstacles in the way of the parliamentarian ideology with its emphasis on the high power of king, lords, and commons as a law-making trinity. It, too, thanks to the formula cited above, had a divine sanction; and the fifth commandment could easily be translated into an injunction to give political obedience to the new set of rulers.

The intellectual resources for legitimating so abrupt and violent a shift in political values were more meager than the confident style of parliamentarian writing suggests. Two kinds of evidence were usually adduced. Resort was had above all else to the Answer to the Nineteen Propositions, which increased in authority with Charles I's execution. After all, the public statement of a martyred king on the nature of the English government was not easily gainsaid. Secondly, the enacting clauses of statutes were frequently cited as in Hunton's *Treatise of Monarchie* or his *Vindication of the Treatise of Monarchy* (1644). As supporting evidence was marshalled by the contending sides, polemical tracts increasingly contained lists of enacting clauses, a practice, surely, that heightened awareness of the idea of parliamentary sovereignty or legal sovereignty generally. From the first the parliamentarians drew aid and comfort from the carelessness with which enacting clauses had been framed in the relatively carefree days before the new age of political definition. They liked, in particular, such language as 'be it enacted by this present parliament' or even 'be it enacted by the king's most excellent majesty [or, by the king our sovereign lord] and the lords and commons in the present parliament and by the authority of the same'. It is no accident that Charles II's government early adopted a set form for enacting clauses favorable to the king. To this subject it is necessary to return, but for the moment it should be noted that a change in wording was the more needed because the practice of limiting the word 'parliament' to the two houses dates from the civil-war years. It really would not do for enacting clauses to convey that the two houses' authority made a measure law.

One germane circumstance was steadily on the side of the parliamentarians. Their insistence on a shared legislative power was advanced when the two houses were very active in law-making. Their initiative produced the great reform statutes of 1641; and whatever the disclaimers, their ordinances were perilously close to law-making. After the king's death the house of commons legislated alone. A reminder of legislative activity during the civil war and interregnum is provided by the three stout volumes of acts and ordinances compiled by Sir Charles Firth and R. S. Rait, and it is also clear that the sights of the usual parliamentary politician must have been lifted by the amount of business conducted in parliament. The precedents and experiences of these years could only have haunted post-restoration England, no matter what court-approved ideology held. As D. D. Raphael has remarked, a political doctrine can sometimes be disproved 'by showing that it rests on factual assumptions which are known to be false from the familiar daily experience of everyone, not just of scientists or of philosophers'.[113] Fact, or what seems to be fact, plays a part in support of judgments; and stubborn fact ran against the theoretical claims of the Stuart kings to the law-making power in parliament at the moment when Englishmen first recognized in law-making the highest power in the state, the one determining ultimately who would rule the kingdom.

These points may be underscored by noting Baxter's discussion of parliamentary power in his *Holy Commonwealth* (1659), written in the last years of the Cromwellian regime and in the shadow of the pending restoration. His ideology merits close attention since a strong respect for authority made rebellion difficult for him; or, to put the matter more positively, he would give his allegiance and obedience to the political authority that had the most powerful claim. This was in his judgment the long parliament, and he offered an interpretation of the political system that compelled obedience to the two houses while legitimating resistance to Charles I. The source of political power and authority was ultimately God, who had left the choice of government to the people under his general rules. The result was a mixed monarchy in England, resting on a contract between the king and people, in which parliament (the two houses) acted as trustee for the people's liberty and shared the sovereignty. The latter point was undoubted. Baxter would not depend on historical records[114] as evidence but rely on two other proofs. The first was drawn from common experience, and Baxter's language reflected unmistakably the parliamentarian ideology of the civil-war years when he roundly declared:

Parliaments do make laws: the king was sworn to govern by those laws, *quas vulgus elegerit*: the laws expressly speak their authors, 'Be it enacted by the authority of parliament' or 'by the king's majesty, and the lords and commons in parliament assembled,' etc. It is not 'upon their petition or proposal' only, but 'by them' or 'by their authority'.

Not unexpectedly, the second proof rested on Charles I's authority. His Answer to the Nineteen Propositions was said to make the conclusion unmistakable that the legislative power (that is, the sovereignty) was jointly in king, lords, and commons as three estates. If parliament actually shared legal sovereignty, the two houses might defend their part of the sovereignty against any invader and, further, might exercise it upon any subject.[115]

Beginning in 1642 political thought had entered a radical phase with far-reaching implications for the kingship. What, then, was the royalist response?

# 4

## That 'Poisonous Tenet' of co-ordination

### I

The wellspring of royalist ideology was the political theory of order, which assigned the king a commanding position in the state. Head of the commonwealth and supreme governor of the realm, he was God's vicegerent, his authority to rule dependent on divine commission. Just as God was the immediate source of royal authority, the king was the human source of law and political authority; and as the fountain of jurisdiction he was said to be above all jurisdictions. He possessed as God's lieutenant irresistible political power. It was to him that a binding oath of allegiance and supremacy was taken; and since political obligation was rooted in religious belief, those who commented on obligation usually quoted *Romans* 13:1: 'The powers that be are ordained of God.' The divine injunction to obedience in the fifth commandment might also be invoked. The patriarchal flavor so powerful in the pre-1642 period was reflected in Richard Mocket's *God and the King* (1615), which taught that a stronger and higher bond of duty united subjects with the king than children with the fathers of private families. Subjects must obey the king as God's vicegerent on earth, the bond between them inviolable and indissoluble. So impressed was James I that he made provision for the book to be studied in all the schools and universities and to be purchased by all householders in England and Scotland, and Charles II arranged for its republication in the first years of the restoration.[1] These sentiments explain why royalists equated disloyalty to the king with disobedience to God. Those who fought against Charles I were guilty of high treason for encompassing the king's death and also of a disloyalty to the king that must endanger their souls.[2]

Political ideas of this kind might well have become a theory of legal sovereignty in the king in parliament if the right set of circumstances had been present; but this was not the case until the civil war, preceded by a great wave of statute-making, had the effect of concentrating men's minds wonderfully. But earlier, before the new age of political definition, few reasoned on these lines. One stumbling block was the practice of including law-making among several marks of sovereignty, along with such prerogatives as the dispensing and pardoning powers, the right of summoning and dissolving parliament, command of the militia, etc. And there was the relatively low priority assigned to law-making, which before 1642 was intertwined with the tendency to treat parliament as a court as much as a legislature.

Law-making attained a primacy in some royalist lists, however, when Charles I's party recognized the threat to the kingship embodied in the parliamentarian challenge to royal authority, this recognition coming in particular after the co-ordination principle was applied to law-making. If its appearance compelled royalists to look closely at law-making and evaluate its importance, not all royalists assessed that power similarly. The more traditionalist clung tenaciously to older habits of political thought while rejecting the co-ordination principle as inapplicable to the existing government. Continuing to treat law-making as only one of several marks of sovereignty, they were clear, nevertheless, that the king alone made law in parliament, a subject to which comparatively little attention had earlier been given. Other royalists were more modern. Influenced by Bodin's *République* (1576) and writing with the co-ordination principle firmly in view, they equated the legislative power with political sovereignty and as a consequence placed the law-making power at the very top of their list of royal powers.

Bodin's view of legal sovereignty much affected royalist thought. Writing during the French religious wars of the late sixteenth century, he set out to refute Huguenot theories of popular sovereignty that extolled the powers of legislative assemblies vis-à-vis rulers and in doing so made a very powerful royal authority the center of his system. He defined sovereignty as the most high, absolute, and perpetual power over the citizens and subjects in a commonwealth and singled out the power of giving laws and commands to all in general and to every one in particular as the first and chief mark of sovereignty. Since the law-maker might also abrogate, declare, and correct laws, it seemed at first sight that the English king was being ruled out. But Bodin thought otherwise. Despite the undoubted role of the two houses in legislation, he assigned legal sovereignty unhesitatingly to him. It was the king who made laws, and the law-making power was incommunicable to his subjects since sovereignty admitted no companion. This was so even if the two houses seemed to possess great liberty. After all, the royal power of summons and dissolution determined the life of parliament, and the role of the two houses was limited even in law-making. Bodin was precise. 'In effect', he found, 'they proceed not [in law-making], but by way of supplications and requests unto the king.' The royal power of veto was complete : the king accepted or rejected whatever measures he pleased without regard for the will of the estates.[3]

The analysis at this point rendered Bodin's view of legal sovereignty singularly apposite for the royalists seeking to counter the claim of co-ordination. He found the king's law-making power to be neither lessened nor shared because it was exercised in parliament. On the contrary. The king was actually aggrandized when his people acknowledged him as their sovereign in this way even though he often granted or passed measures at such a time that he would ordinarily deny. Recognizing that there were other marks of sovereignty besides law-making, Bodin established an important precedent by placing this power in a class by itself. He wrote :

Under this same sovereignty of power for the giving and abrogating of the law are comprised all the other rights and marks of sovereignty : so that . . . a man may say, that there is but this only mark of sovereign power considering that all other the rights thereof are contained in this, viz. to have power to give laws unto all and every one of the subjects, and to receive none from them.[4]

While some modern authorities have hesitated to assign a genuine theory of legal sovereignty to Bodin since he admitted some restraint on royal power, Greenleaf believes such hesitation unwarranted. The point is that Bodin's restrictions meant nothing unless the ruler voluntarily observed them.[5]

This view of legal sovereignty echoed repeatedly through the

D

writings of royalists who may properly be described as modern-minded in discussing the law-making power. Conspicuous among them was Heylyn, who objected to the co-ordination principle as one of 'co-ordinative sovereignty' or 'co-ordinative majesty',[6] the choice of terms revealing his awareness that the central ideological issue was the identity of the person or persons who controlled the highest power in the state. Others were equally perceptive. Injecting large doses of Bodinian theorizing into their polemics, the modern-minded royalists projected a legal sovereignty in the king alone, granted its exercise in parliament, as the appropriate antidote to the parliamentarian insistence on a sovereignty in king, lords, and commons.

Whatever the value assigned to law-making, royalist writers were increasingly unified, as the civil war went on, by an unmistakable dread of the co-ordination principle, 'that poisonous tenet of the co-ordination of the two houses with the kings of England in the power legislative', as one conservative observer later put it.[7] In so far as one of them failed to object to it, he either wrote too early to have grasped fully its significance or else, like Sir Robert Filmer, formulated his argument in isolation from the mainstream of royalist political thought, as this was being expressed in pamphlet literature. So much seems clear, but thereafter the situation is more confused. There are signs, as will be seen, that after the civil war the co-ordination principle penetrated the royalist party itself, appearing, for example, among conservative elements in the post-1660 parliaments. But for the moment it is to be noted that the anti-co-ordination sentiment, so pervasive as to be tantamount to a movement, endured among pro-court writers until the Glorious Revolution and was likewise to be found in the ranks of the practicing politician. Their reasoning may be seen in Dr Nathaniel Johnston's comments stigmatizing the long parliament, in a phrase borrowed from Charles I, as a 'black parliament' who had taught the people to view the authority of the two houses as equal to the king's. The sequel was predictable. 'When success had hardened them', wrote Johnston, 'they were not content with a share, they at first challenged, but laid claim to all; wholly excluding the king and denying him his negative voice; usurping and taking upon them the whole power of making laws.' The lesson was unmistakable:

the 'serpent of co-ordinate power' must not be suffered 'to wriggle in its head, lest the whole body glide easily after'.[8]

## II

After the intellectual foundations were laid for the co-ordination principle, an effective counter-attack demanded the isolation of Charles I's definition of estates and its repudiation. The process took time, and ignorance of the pressing need to correct the king's definition coincided at times with a failure among the royalist writers to place a premium on the legislative power as the pre-eminent expression of sovereignty. Given these handicaps, some of them blundered badly by accepting and even applying the word 'co-ordination' to law-making. The practice, more frequent in earlier royalist writings, could only have facilitated the reception of that principle in the political nation. Already sanctioned, even sanctified, by the Answer to the Nineteen Propositions, it must increase in authority with this kind of royalist interpretation abroad in the land. The cumulative effect was catastrophic for the king. The opportunity to stifle the new political heresy passed away even before the royalist defeats at Naseby and Langport in 1645, the double development leaving the parliamentarians victorious on the field of battle and their ideology without a peer in the search for legitimacy and public support.

Yet an apprehension about the definition of estates in the Answer early haunted the circles around the king, or so Hyde's account suggests. Charles I's principal adviser by the spring of 1642, he usually drafted the declarations that helped create a party for the king. At the time the king was taking advice not only from Hyde but also from Falkland and Colepeper. All three were earlier identified with the opposition in the long parliament, where they favored the triennial act, the legislation to end the courts of star chamber and high commission, the Strafford impeachment, etc. Alienated, however, by a rising anti-clericalism, they entered the king's service; and Hyde became active in composing royal declarations in the months before the war. What he did not write was the Answer to the Nineteen Propositions, which was prepared after he went to York, leaving Falkland and Colepeper behind in London. It was apparently Colepeper who wrote the paragraphs on the government. They had then sent the declaration to the king with the request that it be made public after Hyde had perused it, and the matter rested there until they reached York and learned that the declaration was still in Hyde's possession. According to Hyde himself, he had delayed publication because of dissatisfaction with the definition of estates, which he viewed as a mistake in point of right, derogatory to both the king and the bishops. Whereas Colepeper had designated king, lords, and commons as the three estates, Hyde held the view that they were the lords spiritual, lords temporal, and commons, 'the king being the head and sovereign of the whole'. According to Hyde, Colepeper had actually believed the king to be an estate, having 'taken it up [the definition] upon credit, and without weighing the consequence'.[9]

In easier times this language would have occasioned little excitement since the usage had appeared earlier without injuring the kingship; but in the harsher climate of 1642, as civil war loomed, it met perfectly the needs of the king's opponents.[10] If Colepeper's ignorance opened Pandora's box, Hyde was scarcely more alert in safeguarding Charles I's interests. It is by no means apparent that the latter, either at the time or for some years afterwards, realistically appraised the effect on the kingship of this description of the power relationship among the three estates.[11] Yet he had recognized in it an element out of place in a royal declaration published by authority and left to himself would not have made the Answer public, or so he stated. Disturbed by a sharp reproach from Falkland, whom he esteemed, Hyde impulsively sent the Answer to the royal printers, who had been summoned to York. A story later circulated among the royalists that this definition of estates would not have been made public even then if the king's advisers had been able to recall the post.[12] According to Hyde's account, Falkland, recognizing too late the mistake, attributed the unfortunate language to his own inadvertence and to the misunderstanding of some clergymen and the influence of some lawyers who had misled Colepeper.[13] Hyde also described the king as afterwards 'very sensible' of the decision to print the Answer to the Nineteen Propositions, implying that the consequences were markedly painful to him. The idea is borne out by the court's subsequent action. New editions of the

Answer in 1643 omitted either the passages in which the king was described as one of the three estates or else the entire section devoted to the governmental system. A tract such as *The Royall and the Royalists Plea* (1647) borrowed liberally from the Answer without reprinting any passages politically harmful to the king. Yet a lasting damage had been inflicted. The royal machinery of publicity spread the Answer to the Nineteen Propositions far and wide before the consequences for the kingship were fully perceived.[14]

The repercussions in royalist ranks reached well beyond the small group of advisers immediately concerned with preparing the royal declaration and took a rather different form outside the charmed circle. This can be seen from the writings of Sir Philip Warwick, a politician and historian, who was a royalist in the long parliament at the beginning of the civil war and very close to Charles I at its end. His *Memoires*, written some time between 1667 and 1675, and Hyde's *History of the Rebellion* are considered to be the two great royalist narratives of the civil war; and the marked differences in their political and constitutional ideas may well reflect the changes in outlook of the royalist party as the civil war progressed, Hyde's views being more typical of the earlier royalist writers who were caught off guard by the parliamentarian ideology. Warwick's ideas, on the other hand, probably reflected a growing consensus in the ranks of the king's supporters as the parliamentarian challenge was more realistically appraised. In Warwick's estimation the Answer (which he called the declaration at York) had done great damage, and his hostility towards the doctrine of the three estates was pronounced. The ideas to which this definition had given rise constituted, in his judgment, a subversion of the older way of viewing the English government, a point where he agreed with Hyde. He considered that Falkland, Hyde, and Colepeper (whom he named) had initially framed declarations advantageous to the royal cause since they knew the temper of the house of commons and were supposed to know that of the nation. The effect of the Answer, however, was to wound the regality rather than convince the refractory. 'Such doctrines . . . must be planted', he wrote bitingly, 'as make a subversion of the old frame of government', for the king must be made one of the three estates and government march under the banners of king, lords, and commons. Warwick had no objection to the king's being considered as head of his three estates, but he ought not to have been made one of them.[15]

Another passage attributed the coming of the civil war to an attempt on the part of anti-court elements to transfer the royal prerogatives from the king to the joint control of the king and parliament (the two houses). Warwick implied that the attempt was influenced by the co-ordination principle, which he condemned as contrary to the constitution.[16] What was the nature of that constitution? The royalist would demonstrate elsewhere that the king alone was sovereign, there being 'no power co-ordinate with him'. But leaving nothing to chance, he added that neither house of parliament had any more authority in law-making than giving advice or consent. Many heads were 'as unnatural to a politic, as to a natural body'.[17]

The promised tract, full of references to the co-ordination principle, was the *Discourse of Government* (1694), which was written as early as 1678. It was given to the public, as was the *Memoires*, by the non-juring divine and oriental scholar, Dr Thomas Smith.[18] Numerous passages denounced the co-ordination principle as incompatible with peace and tranquillity at home and abroad. The power to preserve peace, ran one passage, was 'capable of no rivalship or co-ordination'. This was so because the presence of more than one power at the center of the government complicated the problem of allegiance for subjects while confusing foreign countries who wanted to place their relationship with England on an orderly basis. No treaties could be made usefully when uncertainty prevailed as to where sovereignty or singleness of power resided. Indeed, Warwick found the principle incompatible with government as a whole: its presence made orderly procedure impossible. As he said: 'Two of equal powers [presumably the king and the two houses]', if they were of several minds, 'must distract, cannot settle, or make peaceable any government'. 'Co-ordination', he added, 'is like to prove the mother of a civil war.'[19]

Fortunately, the English government was free of the principle. No co-ordination marked, for example, the important sphere of law-making: parliaments were dependent on the king's sovereignty and his person. By the time that the *Discourse* was written,

Englishmen were well-acquainted with the meaning of sovereignty; and Warwick, writing under Hobbes' influence, defined sovereignty as arbitrary and unquestionable by divine ordinance – a neat splicing of Hobbesian sovereignty with the order theory of kingship. Warwick concluded accordingly that the sovereign person (or persons) was 'the single soul of the law' – this was 'to avoid the ill consequences of co-ordination'. The king's was the final determining voice whenever laws were made; and wherever the last appeal was, there was the sovereignty. Warwick's description was uncompromising. The English monarchy was 'absolute in parliament', where the king was in his zenith and entirely sovereign.[20] By 'absolute' Warwick meant that the king alone possessed the law-making power, this being complete, perfect, pure, or unmixed. In short, a monarchy was absolute in a parliament where there was no co-ordination in the legislative power. As Warwick's analysis proceeded, the king's high power in parliament became more evident. Here the purse and sword were joined together; and here the king, acting with the two houses' consent, made whatever laws he deemed necessary for the public welfare. The subordinate role of the two houses received much emphasis. That they were subordinate to the king in the process of law-making might be seen from the writs of summons which spelled out their commission. This was the division of labor : 'His houses pray a law, but he enacts it; for authority must be single, and therefore our laws call him the beginning, head, and end of a parliament.' Such relationships between the king and the two houses excluded, in Warwick's words, 'all pretence to co-ordination'. Nor was it constitutionally correct to write of the three estates of king, lords, and commons making law. The king met in the high court of parliament with 'his three estates of the realm – lords spiritual, temporal, and commons'. The correction was repeated in several places.[21]

The co-ordination principle was, then, a source of deep and abiding concern to Warwick, his writings a generation after its formulation revealing how the virus of anti-co-ordination, once implanted in royalist consciousness, remained active during the remainder of the century. That he should have attested the omnipresence of the principle is of more than ordinary interest because he was by no means the usual royalist but rather one with unusual opportunities for knowing the currents of opinion in the leadership elements of his party. A political figure of secondary rank, in no way a Hyde, a Falkland, or a Colepeper, still he had qualities of mind and personality that won the friendship of men of greater political stature and higher social status and to a degree at least was a spokesman for the leading royalists who clustered around Charles I in the later stages of the civil war.[22]

He was uniquely situated for gathering ideas from various royalists and transmitting his own impressions to others. Thus Warwick was sometime secretary to two lord treasurers (Archbishop Juxon and the earl of Southampton) and to Charles I himself. He also sat in the house of commons of the long parliament and in the Oxford parliament. He was present at Hampton Court, when the king was negotiating with the new model army, and on the isle of Wight during the treaty of Newport. One political friendship of conspicuous importance was with the earl of Southampton and Lord Hertford, who held high position in the civilian administration at Oxford. It is of much interest that the two peers were clearly acquainted with the Answer to the Nineteen Propositions. They were at York when the decision was taken to make it public; and it was they who carried it to Westminster, delivering it to the speaker of the house of lords as the preliminary to its being read in both houses. These circumstances suggest the probability that Warwick either discussed the Answer with Hertford and Southampton or else heard them discuss it with their associates. Warwick's critique of co-ordination was likely rooted in these sources; and Southampton could have been the unnamed peer, a wise and good man, it was said, with much influence among his fellow royalists, whose uneasiness about the Answer is recorded at some length in the *Memoires*.[23]

Very likely, Warwick also heard the Answer denounced in the parliament summoned at Oxford by Charles I on December 22, 1643. Little is known of its proceedings since its records were burned before the fall of the city in 1646. It met in two sessions, from January 22, 1644, to April 16 of that year; and again from November 9, 1644, until March 10, 1645, when it was adjourned to October 10 but met no more. An anti-parliament to hostile contemporaries, it was made up of members of the two houses who left Westminster at the king's summons and of those willing to do so on promise of pardon. Apparently the purpose was to condemn the long parliament for inviting the Scots into England; but before it ended, perhaps during the second session, certain lawyers and other members appear to have decried the definition of estates in the Answer. The description depends on a rather confused account, written near the end of the century, by Fabian Philipps, a high tory historian of advanced years with a reputation, nevertheless, for having a singularly retentive memory. He is credited, for example, with supplying Anthony Wood with information.[24]

The need for a public repudiation had grown pressing as the co-ordination principle increased in authority. By the time of the Oxford parliament, royalist political literature reflected a concern that could only have deepened when Herle, near the end of the first session, published the substance of three sermons on 1 *King* 22 : 22, preached before the house of commons at Westminster, the lord mayor and aldermen of London, and a sympathetic audience at Westminster Abbey respectively. Attached to these sermons was an influential postscript calling attention to a concession from Ferne with regard to co-ordination and law-making. The latter's remarks will be noted, but for the moment Herle's response is of more interest. Finding Ferne's concession insufficient, Herle insisted that the two houses were 'not only requisite to the acting of this power of making laws, but co-ordinate with his majesty in the very power of acting'.[25]

This reaffirmation of the co-ordination principle in a manner ensuring the widest possible publicity explains the spate of anti-co-ordination literature that coincided with the Oxford parliament. Alarm must have spread as the royalists recognized how Ferne's unwariness was complicating an already difficult situation. Thus Heylyn specifically condemned Ferne's remarks about co-ordination and law-making while he denounced Herle's writings as a new means of vesting the two houses with the robes of sovereignty – 'not as superior to the king, but co-ordinate with him'. The dangerous doctrine had been built on the idea that the king was one of the three estates in parliament.[26] About the same time Edward Bagshaw, a member of the Oxford parliament, was writing that the co-ordination principle and the doctrine of the king's virtual presence with his two houses at Westminster – two political ideas identifiable with Herle – provided the twin grounds

for the parliamentarian case against the royal supremacy. Bagshaw's comments provide impressive testimony that the supporters
of the crown had by this time discerned in co-ordination the
leading tenet of the adversary parliamentarian ideology and
concluded that the principle must somehow be countered. Since
comments were likewise being made at Oxford about the grand
impostors at Westminster who claimed to possess 'omnipotent
power',[27] it is feasible that Charles I used the Oxford parliament
as a vehicle for repudiating the new theory of a legal sovereignty
in king, lords, and commons. This conjecture is supported by the
identity of the lawyers who decried the royal definition of estates
in the course of the Oxford parliament, their names suggesting
an officially inspired repudiation. Fabian Philipps named Sir
Orlando Bridgeman, Sir Geoffrey Palmer, and Sir Robert Holbourne,[28] indicating that their role was conspicuous in the proceedings. At the time of the Oxford parliament Bridgeman and
Holbourne held office under the crown, and the fact that Palmer
was one of Charles' commissioners at Uxbridge suggests that he
was close to the king. All were lawyers who could be depended on
by training and experience to enunciate the official royalist position regarding the membership of the estates in parliament; and
for this purpose the Oxford parliament was a natural arena.

The three royalists can be associated with still another repudiation of the royal definition of estates, although the association in
Holbourne's case must be stated more tentatively. His repudiation,
if it was his, is in the anonymous *Freeholders Grand Inquest*, in
circulation by January 31, 1648. Of deeply conservative hue, it
was attributed to Holbourne, on Wood's authority, by G. K.
Fortescue, the editor of the Thomason tracts; but a powerful
opinion today makes Filmer its author. The question of authorship
is consequential not only because the pamphlet exerted much
influence in the course of the century but also because it illuminates royalist political thought in the late stages of the civil war.
Since there are substantial reasons for believing that it was written
by a royalist in civil-war Oxford, in this case Holbourne, it has
been urged elsewhere in this study that he was indeed the author.[29]
If so, it can be stated confidently that all three of them – Bridgeman, Palmer, and Holbourne – subsequently made plain their
distaste for Charles I's definition of estates. The condemnation in

the *Freeholders* was coupled with the candid admission that it was widespread.[30] But the audience for that pamphlet was nothing like that familiar with Bridgeman's position. As lord chief baron, he presided over the regicide trials in 1660, during which the royal definition of estates received public correction while the idea of co-ordination was denounced in explicit language.[31] It needs only to be added that Palmer as attorney general prosecuted the regicides for the crown.

A proper instinct had guided Charles II's government in singling out this particular set of ideas for a public correction. But if the choice of a target cannot be faulted, the timing is another matter. The judges were almost twenty years too late. The parliamentarian ideology was by this time strongly entrenched, as a by-product of the civil war, with consequences for the kingship only too well understood by conservative thinkers. Conceivably, the damage would have been lessened had royalist pamphleteers recognized from the very first that the definition of estates in the *Answer* was a political mistake and moved promptly to make a public correction. But the opportunity to place Charles I's statement in the most advantageous light possible under the circumstances vanished early in the civil war when the leading royalist writers failed to appraise accurately the ideological crisis. Yet they could hardly be expected to be more politically acute than Hyde, whose own slowness is unmistakable.[32] Their errors are traceable to the example set by Ferne, who, like Hyde a gifted amateur, succeeded at times only in making an already bad situation worse. Yet his writings reflected faithfully the order theory of kingship, so cherished by conservative thinkers generally; and adherence to its tenets minimized the concessions he was willing to make to the parliamentarian ideology. Reasoning much like Ferne's is present in numerous civil-war tracts, even in such seeming exceptions as the *Jura Majestatis* (1644) of Griffith Williams (bishop of Ossory), and Charles Dallison's stirring *Royalist's Defence* (1648).

## III

Ferne emerged early as a leading royalist pamphleteer. Before the first year of civil war was over, both his *Resolving of Con-*

*science* and his *Conscience Satisfied* were in print, and his *Reply unto Severall Treatises* followed in November, 1643. Yet his constitutional ideas, drawn from a different era, proved ill-suited for protecting the king's interest in the protracted controversy over law-making. Concerned with denying a general co-ordination, Ferne allowed himself to be trapped into admitting an element of co-ordination in the government, though certainly not of the nature and to the extent envisaged by Herle. The concession went much too far for the well-being of the Stuart kingship if the term were admitted at all in relationship to law-making. It was a bad slip when Ferne wrote of the two houses of parliament as 'in a sort co-ordinate with his majesty *ad aliquid*, to some act or exercising of the supreme power, that is to the making of laws by yielding their consent'. And he added that the right belonged to the two houses by a fundamental constitution.[33] Nowhere is the old-fashioned quality of his political ideas better illustrated. Serene in the conviction that law-making was only one mark among many of the royal sovereignty, he considered that his account left the king with the supremacy of power displayed 'in making new laws, and abrogating old, in calling assemblies to that and other purposes, in treaties with foreign princes, sending embassies, [and] appointing officers of state, judges of courts, and other ministers of justice throughout the kingdom'. The description did not include the dispensing power and the power of pardon though these prerogatives were frequently included in such lists. Except in law-making the two houses had no share in the supreme power because the king alone summoned and dissolved parliament, made treaties, appointed officers of state, etc. Herle, said Ferne, was mistaken in insisting that the two houses 'should be *co-ordinati ad omnia*, simply co-ordinate and equal in those powers and acts of supremacy'. The parliamentarian could claim successfully a co-ordination between the king and the two houses only 'in consenting to the making of laws'. The king was solely supreme so far as the other marks of sovereignty were concerned, and all power of administration was derived from him.[34]

While admitting a mixed nature in the legislative power, Ferne continued to assert that the supreme power was unitary. It was in the king and in the king alone. Nor was Ferne actually prepared to grant the two houses a genuinely co-ordinate share of the law-making power, despite the willingness to employ the term in relationship to this aspect of the supreme authority. Even here much the greater power belonged to the king. Ferne's language was unmistakable. Though the king had bound himself to impose laws only with the consent of his people, he explained, still 'the beams of his supremacy' could be seen 'shining in the power of enacting exercised with their consent'. Moreover, he alone had the power of calling the two houses for the purpose of legislation, and the constitution granting them the power of consenting whenever laws were made had left with him the power of dissolving parliament. Other signs might be cited of the king's predominant role in legislation. The enacting clauses of medieval statutes, for example, began with the words 'the king ordains'.[35]

Thus a co-ordination in the government on the scale envisaged by Herle was out of the question. Ferne's tone grew more cautious, notably in his last pamphlet. Whereas earlier he had used the royal definition of estates uncritically, he now corrected the king's language. 'His majesty did never use that phrase with any intent of diminution to his supremacy or headship for properly the prelates, lords, and commons are the three estates of this kingdom, under his majesty as their head.'[36] The nature of the constitution precluded sharing political authority in the fashion of the parliamentarian theorists. Kings were empowered by God; and while the two houses were sometimes co-ordinate with the king, he was as the head to the body in his relationship with them. To support this point Ferne quoted from Henry VIII's act of appeals (24 Hen. 8, c.12), a statute that the royalists and later conservative thinkers subsequently invoked to assert that the crown was an imperial crown, its very nature precluding any idea of a co-ordination in the supreme authority.[37] According to Ferne, the king had been declared in parliament to be the supreme head of the body politic, he having been instituted and furnished by the goodness and sufferance of God with 'plenary, whole [and] entire power, preeminence, authority, prerogative, and jurisdiction' to render justice and final determination in all causes to all manner of subjects within the realm.[38] Because royal authority proceeded from God, the powers of parliament were derived from the king. That is, he and not the community was the human source of political authority. Indeed, even the legislative power was originally in the king;

and, in truth, it was still, 'only this power is excited by the instance and request of the commons, representing to him the grievances of his people abroad'. The king who initially had complete legislative power had agreed to exercise this power only with the two houses' consent.[39] In so far as a mixture existed in the government, this was the area where it could be discerned; and it was all there was.

This exposition so qualified Ferne's initial concession regarding law-making as to render it innocuous to a modern mind. Even so, at the wrong point in history for a king of England, Ferne had made the wrong sort of concession if the slightest impression was left with readers that the word 'co-ordination' might be legitimately linked with the all-important area of law-making. So far as the court's interest was concerned, Ferne had clung much too long to a concept fast becoming obsolete because of rapid changes on the political and constitutional scene and in the vocabulary of political debate. Assuming that law-making was only one of several marks of sovereignty, the royalist had made his individual contribution to Charles I's difficulties rising out of the Answer to the Nineteen Propositions. Nor was the anachronism confined to Ferne. Present as well in other royalists, it made for disunity in countering the parliamentarian claim of a co-ordination in the legislative power. Among those who reasoned on similar lines were Griffith Williams and Dudley Digges; but Williams, though the same cannot be said of Digges, was cautious in his treatment of the law-making power.[40] By the time that his *Jura Majestatis* was in print, the royalists were making a more realistic assessment of the dangers confronting the royal position in the government. They knew that the co-ordination principle must not be associated with the law-making power. That way lay disaster.

The warning had come from Heylyn, who was much more alert and modern-minded than the traditionalist royalists generally. He was bitter about Ferne's failure to grasp the importance of law-making, writing :

Some who have undertook the confutation of these brainless follies [that is, the parliamentarian claim of a co-ordination in the legislative power and the political ideas flowing from it] have most improvidently granted not only that the two houses of parliament are in a sort co-ordinate with the king *ad aliquid*, to some act or exercising of the supreme power, that is to the making of laws; but that this co-ordination of the three estates (of which the king is yielded everywhere for one) is fundamental, and held by the two houses on no worse a title than a fundamental constitution.

These were concessions so far-reaching as to satisfy any reasonable parliamentarian.[41] Heylyn was quite right. Herle, it will be recalled, had seized upon Ferne's concession to reiterate his own view of the constitutional system, providing a vivid illustration that even the slightest cry or whisper of a co-ordination in law-making must give aid and comfort, even advantage, to the advocates of the rival ideology. The king who shared legal sovereignty with the two houses was no longer the single head of the commonwealth and the supreme governor of the realm, empowered directly by God. Nor was he the political symbol to whom allegiance and obedience were due in a nation rent with civil war and embittered by division.

Another royalist whose political ideas placed him among the traditionalist elements in his party was Charles Dallison, recorder of Lincoln and a moderate royalist. His *Royalist's Defence* (1648) was written in the vein of the order theory of kingship, a fact by no means obvious at first sight. Although the tract has recently been described as the first extended treatment of the doctrine of separation of powers, the positions in it so closely resemble those taken by Ferne and other traditionalists as to make the description doubtful. *The Royalist's Defence* was permeated by the order theory of kingship, and the amount of power allotted by Dallison to the king is incompatible with a separation of powers in the modern sense of that term. It will be seen that the low value attached by the royalist to the legislative power also makes for difficulty in assigning him this view of government.

The contours of Dallison's argument are recognizable, then, as belonging to the royalist genre. After searching the law books, he had concluded, so he stated, that the king was the only supreme governor of the realm, to whom the people of England were obliged to give allegiance. Despite his great power, the king was subject to certain limitations, only, however, those that he himself had voluntarily imposed. Notable among these was his making law only in parliament. To be sure, the king made law with the concurrence of the two houses, but the use of the term 'co-ordin-

ation' to describe their relationship was meaningless. He was after
all the head of the three estates in parliament, that is, the lords
spiritual, the lords temporal, and the commons; and it was he
who was 'the soul, adding life' when laws were made. So much
was royalist orthodoxy, as were Dallison's further remarks about
law-making. That the king had agreed to make law in parliament
constituted no diminution of royal power. After all, the monarchy
remained, and the people were governed by the same law under
the same authority as before, that is, by the king's sole authority.
Moreover, the laws were the king's laws, properly said to be made
by him because the enactment clause in the majority of statutes
read : 'Be it enacted by the king's majesty, with the assent of the
lords spiritual and temporal, and the commons, etc.'[42]

Dallison's discussion of law-making became more precise as
it progressed, his remarks providing not only a reminder of the
manner in which royalists in his day viewed that power but also
serving in some respects as a harbinger of the approach to law-
making taken by those who in the late seventeenth century
supported the king's discretionary use of the dispensing power.
Dismissing peremptorily Prynne's conclusion in the *Soveraigne
Power of Parliaments* that the king had little or no hand in making
laws, the royalist stressed that whoever consented to a statute was
properly termed its maker. In his words,

It is the consent which makes the law. When the bill is engrossed,
and read in the house : The question by the speaker is put to the
members, whether it shall be a law or not, and such as are of opinion
to pass it, are directed to say *I*, and those against it, *No*, and being
passed by both houses, it is presented to the king, whose answer if
he confirm it, is *le roy le veilt* [sic]. So that if any difference be, the
king's words are more prevalent, for before that, it is but a written
piece of parchment, not valid, but by the king's words, instantly it
hath life, and is become a law binding the whole kingdom and
people. And this (as before is said) is the king's law.[43]

The king, even if the concurrence of the two houses was required
in law-making, was in fact the exclusive law-maker.

But law-making was only one aspect of royal authority. Besides
making law the king had the responsibility of administering it,
and at this point he might have recourse to his dispensing power.
That the king had a power over the positive laws of the realm

was manifest from his right 'to pardon the transgressions thereof, and [his] authority to dispense with the law itself'. Because he was the sole fountain of justice, mercy, and honor and the only supreme governor of the realm, these powers were his and his alone. Dallison explained how the dispensing power might be utilized to set aside a parliamentary statute :

If by act of parliament it be made felony, or other crime to transport any commodity beyond the seas, and the king after the fact committed, may pardon the offence, and before it be committed, by his letters patent (without assent of the members) [he] may by a *non obstante* dispense with the law itself, and legally authorize any person notwithstanding that statute, to transport that prohibited commodity, and so in all public, and penal acts not prohibiting *malum in se.*[44]

The reasoning was circular. Since the king made laws, he could dispense with them. 'The law itself [is] called his law', wrote Dallison. 'He hath usually dispensed with acts of parliament, [and] at pleasure pardoned trangressors of the law.'[45]

The power of dispensation was inseparable from the king's natural person : no act of parliament could sever it from him. This could be seen from the *Sheriff's Case*, which had determined that the royal prerogative could defeat even a statute with a clause prohibiting its dispensation. 'The king by his prerogative hath authority to dispense with penal laws, which cannot be taken from him by act of parliament,' Dallison asserted roundly, 'although in express terms it be enacted that all such dispensations with a *non obstante* shall be void.' To dissipate any lingering doubt as to the inviolate nature of the royal prerogative, Dallison was firm that the dispensing power was inseparable from the person of the king 'and not to be abolished by act of parliament, no more than his other prerogatives of as high a nature, viz. those of denouncing war and concluding peace, enhancing or debasing of coin, or the like'. These were flowers, inseparably annexed to the crown, and most proper for a king.[46]

These remarks meant, of course, that the king-out-of-parliament was in a sense legally superior to the king-in-parliament, since the legislative body was limited in its activity by the inseparable nature of the absolute prerogatives, including the dispensing

power. There could be, perforce, no legal sovereignty in parliament. Indeed, to a surprising degree the very concept of legal
sovereignty was remote from Dallison's mode of thought, his view
of the inviolate nature of the royal prerogative and his treatment
of the law-making power precluding theories of legal sovereignty.
The value that he placed on the law-making power was surprisingly low : it was not even treated as a mark of sovereignty, much
less as constituting the highest power in the state. To Dallison, the
sovereign power of government and the authority to make laws
were altogether different in rank, and it was the first that he
primarily esteemed. He was explicit when he wrote :

Neither the making, declaring, or expounding the law, is any part
of sovereignty. But regulating the people, by commanding the laws
to be observed, and executed, pardoning the transgressions thereof,
and the like, are true badges of a supreme governor. All which are
the king's.

Imbued with this traditionalist outlook and convinced that the
king was not one of the three estates, Dallison found it possible
to grant a concurrence in law-making to the two houses of parliament while insisting that sovereignty resided in the king alone.
He seems not to have made any specific reference to co-ordination
or mixed monarchy, but the whole tenor of his tract was hostile
to such ideas. The very notion of a mixed monarchy was an
absurdity. Whoever governed was sovereign, and he who was
sovereign governed. Clearly, Dallison asserted, England was a
monarchy : it was governed by a king and not a parliament. The
only point at issue was who should govern, and this point was
resolved in favor of the king. The constitution of the realm had
given government to the king, and to him alone.[47]

Imbued with this conventional view of the constitution, Dallison
not unexpectedly regarded the king as the human source of political authority. In the first place the kingship had existed long
before parliaments. 'This nation', he wrote, 'hath been monarchical above 1200 years before the institution of the two houses
of parliament.' Because all power in the state flowed from the
king, whatever rights the two houses possessed they had at the
hand of their sovereign. The same was true of the powers of the
judges, who were chosen and authorized by the king. Indeed, 'all

legal proceedings [were] in his name, and by his authority'. He was genuinely the fountain of all authority.[48] Significantly, Dallison said nothing of the community, and there is no indication that he considered the people as constituting in any way a source of the royal title and authority. Such a view of the kingship raises the question whether Dallison's assignment of an executive power to the crown, a legislative power to the king in parliament, and an independent judicial authority to the judges actually constituted a modern doctrine of the separation of powers, the superficial likeness notwithstanding.[49]

In sum, the royalists whom Ferne represented were essentially traditionalist, their ideas on government closely resembling those put forward by order theorists before 1642.[50] In one cardinal respect they were different since they were much more inclined to discuss law-making *per se* rather than leaving the subject vague and inchoate. Assigning what they called a sovereignty or supremacy to the king, they believed that he might on occasion act above the law by means of the dispensing power. He did so for the public good, of which he was sole judge. Further, the traditionalist argument usually combined an insistence that the king alone, empowered directly by God, was supreme governor of the realm with a fervid denial that he could properly be depicted as one of the three estates associated with law-making. They were emphatic that the king was not one of the three estates but rather their head, a distinction vital to the order theory of kingship espoused by the royalists. He alone possessed the law-making power, even if that power was exercised exclusively in parliament. That the king was the sole law-maker could be demonstrated, it was often said, by considering the manner in which bills prepared by the two houses became law: it was the royal assent which converted measures into law and imparted a binding force to them. Despite the firm conviction that the king alone made law in parliament, traditionalist royalists nevertheless considered law-making only one sign of the royal supremacy or sovereignty. Another point ought to be made. Faced with the parliamentarian insistence on a legal sovereignty in king, lords, and commons, they might conceivably have taken up an advanced position not only denying the parliamentarian contention but putting forward as well the counterclaim that legal sovereignty resided in the king in parliament. He was, after all, in their view the exclusive law-maker in parliament. But they did not take this action, perhaps because of the difference between their interpretation of the royal supremacy and the idea of a legal sovereignty in the king. It was too great to traverse in so short a period of time.


## IV

Not all royalists were so traditionalist, and some of them agreed with Filmer's pre-civil-war assertion when he wrote : 'That which giveth the very being to a king is the power to give laws.'[51] He wrote as Bodin's disciple well before the advent of the co-ordination principle in political literature, but this was the note reverberating throughout the writings of royalists more modern-minded than Ferne and his fellows. Just as the latter tended like Hyde to underestimate the role of law-making in the modern state, so did the former foreshadow the position that Warwick was to take when he described the English monarchy as 'absolute in parliament', the king being in his zenith there and entirely sovereign. These royalists responded to the co-ordination principle with a full-blown theory of a political and legal sovereignty in the king alone, and they also developed in its support an appropriate and effective methodology of argument. Prominent in their ranks were Filmer's friend, Heylyn, and, in particular, the highly influential Sir John Spelman, the seminal thinker among them. His theory of a legal sovereignty in the king in parliament became the hallmark of this category of royalists.

Spelman was no ordinary royalist writer. Eldest son of the antiquary, Sir Henry Spelman, and a scholar in his own right as author of a life of King Alfred, he was living in Norfolk when the civil war broke out. Not long afterward he was summoned to Oxford by the king, where he rose rapidly in royal favor. According to the *DNB* article on his life, Spelman attended the king's 'private council' and was on the way to becoming secretary of state when camp fever struck him in July, 1643. The reference to Charles I's 'private council' is puzzling. On first sight it looks like a mention of attendance at the privy council, but there seems to be no surviving evidence that Spelman attended the privy council or was one of its members. Neither his attendance nor membership is mentioned in the register of the privy council for the years 1640 to 1645, and it may be that the body in question was a small group of trusted advisers known later as the cabinet council. Rumors of this type or suggestions to this effect imply a certain consequence in Spelman's position at Oxford; and before he died, he successfully imparted a distinctive flavor to royalist political thought.

His writings have this significance. In the new age of political definition he was foremost among the royalists in delineating a theory of a legal sovereignty in the king in parliament with an undivided power of law-making at its core. Two tracts command attention in this context: the first his *View of a Printed Book* (January 26, 1643), in which he tried to repair the damage to the king's power inflicted by the references to law-making in the Answer to the Nineteen Propositions; the second, his posthumous *Case of our Affaires* published at Oxford by January 20, 1644, about six months after his death. Recognizing the need for a supreme, indisputable power in the government, Spelman would place that great power in the king in parliament under the conditions expressed in his corrected version of the Answer to the Nineteen Propositions. A section on law-making, which he placed solely in the king, was inserted between two sets of materials either paraphrased or quoted from the Answer. But the change went beyond this. Not only was supreme power placed unequivocally in the king, Spelman also seized the opportunity to make explicit the subordinate role of the two houses in law-making. Nothing was left to chance on so vital a point. Charles I's statement that the king, the house of peers, and the house of commons made law jointly was now omitted, and stress was placed on the consenting role of the two houses. The strategically placed insertion read:

The supreme power therefore of making laws whereby to govern and judge the people in time of peace . . . rests in a king only, and immovably . . . and again as the king himself acknowledgeth those laws by which he is to govern may not be made but by the consent of the house of peers, and by the house of commons chosen by the people, all having free votes and particular privileges . . .

Passages from the Answer followed directly, the source acknowledged in the margin.[52]

Spelman's constitutional exposition, especially as developed in the *Case of our Affaires*, delighted his fellow royalists[53] and foreshadowed subsequent high tory discussion of the legislative power that lasted until the Glorious Revolution relegated the idea of a legal sovereignty in the king to the dustbin of lost causes.[54] An initial statement set its tone : England was a kingdom, an empire, a well-regulated monarchy, its head a supreme head, a sovereign, a king whose crown was imperial, the kingdom being his kingdom, the people his people, the parliament his parliament, etc. Accordingly allegiance was sworn to him alone. Spelman knew of no oath of obedience made unto parliament or to any other power, in any case of misgovernment or danger, however extraordinary. That sovereignty was in the king appeared not only from the oath of supremacy but also by constant acknowledgment in the acts of parliament, both ancient and modern, that styled the king 'our sovereign lord the king'. Moreover, Henry VIII's act of appeals, declaring England to be an imperial kingdom, made it manifest that although the members of the body of the kingdom might cooperate with the king in a necessary act of state, no co-ordination could be said to exist. There was no 'co-ordination, nor co-equality of any estate, order, or degree, of the subject with the sovereign'. And the royalist sought consistently, though not always successfully, to employ the term 'the three orders of parliament' in preference to the 'three estates' so prevalent in parliamentarian writings.[55]

If the two houses had a role in the state, it was limited in nature and decidedly subordinate to the king. On the other hand, the latter's power, while very high, was by no means absolute since his power and judgment were so far restrained as that he could make no settled law without the consent of the two houses. But in all other matters not expressly restrained by a law, as in providing for the present safety against danger, levying arms, suppressing tumults, convoking and dissolving parliaments, etc., in all of these points of regality, the power and judgment lay with the king. In sum, he possessed a discretionary authority. To be king was to be supreme judge and law-giver, this by the law of God and nature. While the two powers of declaring and making law greatly restrained absolutism, Spelman was firm that in neither sphere did the king part with a whit of his sovereignty.[56]

Within this context the two houses exercised a restraint on law-making much more limited than the parliamentarians admitted. True, the king could make no law without them, but still they had no share in the sovereignty, to which the legislative power was inseparably attached. Spelman was precise on this vital point: 'The sovereignty (and with it the inseparable legislative power) does solely reside in the king.' The two houses – 'merely instruments of regulation and qualification of the king's legislative absoluteness' – were 'no sharers with him in the sovereignty'. They remained his subjects; and the king was their true and only sovereign, as they themselves had frequently acknowledged. But what if the power and authority of parliament was recognized as the highest, most absolute, and most sovereign in the kingdom? Was there no contradiction between this idea, to which Spelman also subscribed, and the insistence that the highest power was in the king?[57]

Spelman thought not. The supposed difficulty was due to the varying meanings being attached to the word 'parliament', which he discussed with the aim of elucidating his main points while destroying the claims advanced for the two houses by Herle. Of the several senses in which the word was used, only one actually ascribed sovereignty: this was when it denoted 'the three orders of parliament agreeing in their votes'. In this sense alone parliament was the supreme court, the highest judicatory, and the most sovereign power and authority in the kingdom. Unmistakably, this character was derived from the king, certainly not from the two houses. Borrowing from Henry VIII's famous statement in the *Ferrers Case*, Spelman wrote of parliament that it was the most sovereign court because every complete and perfect act of it was 'the act of the personal will, and power of the sovereign himself, *standing in his highest estate royal*, and (through the concurrence of those that are instrumentals of his restraint) more freely and absolutely working there, than in any other time and place he can do'. After the consent of the two houses remitted the restraint, the king made law by his inherent sovereignty. Accordingly, any act emanating from all three orders actually proceeded from the king in parliament. Yet the act genuinely came from the high court of parliament 'because every of the three estates [sic] contribute their power according to the diversity of their office and interest, the two houses by remitting through the consenting the restraint, and the king by using his then unrestrained power'.[58]

The king was subject to parliamentary power only if the word 'parliament' was properly understood. Just as Christ was subject only to himself, so the king as sovereign was subject to no one but himself. The high court of parliament could not speak without him; and in that body the will of the king, as Christ's vicar on earth, was the fountain and source of the law, as appeared plainly and frequently throughout the whole body of the laws when it was stated that *the king willeth, the king commandeth, the king ordaineth, provideth, establisheth, granteth, etc.*[59] Little was said beyond this about the human source of political authority, perhaps because Spelman had already written on the subject in his *View of a Printed Book*. There he had discussed the parliamentarian formula while offering the opinion that God himself was the source of the monarchy, having granted royal power directly to the king. When the monarchy began, there had been no election by the people; and Spelman now offered the patriarchal theory of its origin. He would have the king's style continued *Carolus Dei gratia* rather than *Carolus electione populi*. It appears, he wrote, that 'God in the law of nature [the divine moral law] instituted this form of government, and whether we call it paternal or regal, it refers to that institution, and is from thence derived'.[60] To be sure, elections had at times interrupted the succession because of wars and commotions, but these were only restorations of the monarchy. Spelman agreed with Raleigh, who had stated that 'kings are made by God, and laws divine; and by human laws only declared to be kings'.[61] It followed that the king was 'the fountain of all jurisdiction, and above all other jurisdictions', including both legislative and judicial powers. In fact, the legislative power was his by the divine and moral law. He had it before parliament ever existed, and the two houses derived their limited role in law-making from him.[62]

Although Spelman wrote of a supreme, indisputable power in the king in parliament, he imposed a limitation on the legislative power. No statute could disable the heir to the throne. 'The descent of the crown upon him purges all disabilities whatsoever, and makes him capable of it', he concluded. He made no reference to the dispensing power in his *Case of our Affaires*, perhaps because he perceived no infringement on the king's legal sovereignty if he acted of his own free will to alter his own laws. However this problem was solved, Spelman's view of the royal power in law-making approximated a modern doctrine of sovereignty in the crown; and undoubtedly in responding to the parliamentarian principle of a co-ordination in the legislative power, he had taken refuge in a position reminiscent of Bodin, to whom he acknowledged explicitly his indebtedness.[63]

Since the *Case of our Affaires* was published on the eve of the Oxford parliament, it probably contributed to the repudiation of the royal definition of estates during its proceedings. Not that he attacked the definition directly. For some time he seems not to have recognized the need and he had not come down directly against it despite his caution in this area. Yet the emendation of the Answer to the Nineteen Propositions to safeguard the king's control of law-making and his positive enunciation of a legal sovereignty in the king must have helped isolate Charles I's definition of estates as a source of danger to the kingship and set the stage for the public rejection that has been described.

The idea of a legal sovereignty in the king received a powerful reinforcement from the *Freeholders Grand Inquest* (1648), probably written in 1644. Following out the lines in the *Case of our Affaires* and in Heylyn's *Stumbling-block of Disobedience* the tract was in all probability by Holbourne.[64] It contained:

A presentment of divers statutes, records and other precedents, explaining the writs of summons to parliament : showing :
I. That the commons, by their writ, are only to perform and consent to the ordinances of parliament.
II. That the lords or common council by their writ are only to treat, and give counsel in parliament.
III. That the king himself only ordains and makes laws, and is supreme judge in parliament.[65]

Working from the 'constant ancient declaration of this kingdom' – in this case the writs of elections to the house of commons, the writs of summons to the peers, and what were called the 'titles' and 'bodies' of statutes – the author set out to demonstrate that the legislative power belonged historically to the king alone even if he should choose to exercise that power in parliament. The use of the royal writs permitted the further conclusion that the king was the human source of the law and of the political authority in the two houses.

Influenced by Bodin and Spelman, the author of the *Freeholders* placed legal sovereignty in the king in parliament, where the king alone was said to be the author and maker of laws. He was careful in definition. Parliament was properly styled the supreme court only if this language conveyed that the king was in the house of lords; but if this fact was understood, the supreme court must have the supreme power. That supreme power was always arbitrary: there was no superior power on earth to control it. In all government, the last appeal must be to an arbitrary power or else appeals would be endless. That arbitrary power was the legislative power; and since it was in the king alone, it followed that he was legally sovereign in the modern sense of that word.[66]

There was, accordingly, no co-ordination in the English government. This simple ideological message, the *raison d'être* of the tract, was supported by a wealth of evidence that made the *Freeholders* the most formidable anti-co-ordination tract of the seventeenth century. Not that the co-ordination principle was mentioned by name. But that the author had it in mind appears from his correction of Charles I's definition of estates. Citing Prynne's *Soveraigne Power of Parliaments* as containing the example to be avoided, he called attention to the one page in that enormous work where the co-ordination principle was combined with the maxim *singulis major, universis minor* to place a supremacy in the two houses that verged on a legal sovereignty. Moreover, Prynne in this particular passage had named Herle's *Fuller Answer* as the source of the co-ordination principle and supplied his readers with the appropriate page numbers. There is, then, no need for conjecture as to whether the *Freeholders* is an anti-co-ordination tract. The signposts are all in place for moving from the *Freeholders* by way of the *Soveraigne Power of Parliaments* to the *Fuller Answer*; and limited as the notations in the *Freeholders* and Prynne's work may be, their presence is sufficient in itself to cast a flood of light on the ideological origins of the *Freeholders Grand Inquest*.[67] The conclusion is strengthened by the tract itself, which runs on stark lines. The two houses in no way shared the legislative power; that great power, from which there was no appeal, was not a shared power. How could it be when the two houses were not even equal, one with the other, much less either of them with the king? King, lords, and commons were not 'fellow commissioners', indeed not, no matter how carelessly certain statutes had been framed in Charles I's reign.[68]

This anti-co-ordination position rested in the main on the royal writs used to elect the house of commons as well as the writs of summons to the house of lords. They were germane, it was said, because the powers of the house of commons were properly defined in terms of the trust committed to its members when they were elected by the freeholders, unless the king decided to enlarge the house's functions and jurisdiction. Similarly writs of summons to peers might be utilized to delimit the functions and jurisdiction of the house of lords. In establishing royal writs as an appropriate means of defining the two houses' respective powers, the author may have followed a pronouncement on this subject issued by the Oxford parliament, which had declared writs of summons to be 'the foundation of all power in parliament, being directed to the lords (in express terms) to treat and advise with the king and the rest of the peers of the kingdom of England, and for the commons to do and consent to those things, which by that common council of England should be ordained'.[69] The pronouncement was thoroughly in accord with the denunciation of Charles I's definition of estates which had also been forthcoming from the Oxford parliament, and one wonders whether Holbourne were involved with both.

Be that as it may, the pronouncement regarding the royal writs provided a valuable means of identifying the house of commons as a subordinate member of the trinity of law-makers postulated by the parliamentarian ideology. That house was subordinate from its beginnings to the present day to both the house of lords and the king. Working from the writs of election to the house of commons, the author of the *Freeholders* noted that its members had been empowered only 'to perform, and to consent to those things which then by the favour of God shall there happen to be ordained by the common council' of the kingdom, a choice of language conveying that the elected house had originally formed no part of the common council or parliament. The peers and

prelates had composed the parliament, and it was with them that
the king would 'have conference and treat'. One conclusion flowed
inexorably from the commons' writ. 'By this writ', went the
triumphant and provocative words, 'we do not find that the
commons are called to be any part of the common council of the
kingdom, or of the supreme court of judicature, or *to have any part
of the legislative power* [italics added], or to consult *de arduis
regni negotiis*, of the difficult businesses of the kingdom.'[70] Accordingly, the Stuart house of commons had no historical claim to
equality with the king either in law-making or in the great affairs
of the kingdom, indeed, not even any claim of equality with the
peers, to whom the writ assigned much the more important functions. In short, the house of commons had scarcely a genuine title
to be an estate of parliament, much less one of three co-ordinate
estates in whom supreme power was placed. The subordination
of the house of commons was dramatically illustrated whenever
its members stood bare-headed, with hats in hand, at a conference
with the peers. The parliamentary practice provided the irresistible proof that 'the lords and commons' were not 'fellow commissioners, or fellow counsellors of the kingdom'.[71]

But what about the claim that the house of commons had
always formed part of the common council of the kingdom? Here
the author would insist on two points: (1) the house of lords was
anciently the common council of the kingdom; and (2) the house
of commons was in parliament for the first time in Henry I's reign
although its members were not constantly called or regularly
elected by writ until Henry III's day.[72] This meant that the house
of commons was a relatively late comer to Westminster. Indeed,
the earliest extant writ of summons dated from the year 1265;
and in the ensuing great debate over the antiquity of the house of
commons, to which the *Freeholders Grand Inquest* contributed,
it became customary for tory publicists to refer to the house of
commons as originating in that year, the forty-ninth year of Henry
III's reign, usually cited as '49 H.3.'[73]

If the historical credentials of the house of lords were more
impressive, still these stopped far short of establishing any co-
ordination with the king despite the peers' political and social
superiority to the house of commons. Any examination of the
historic relationships among king, lords, and commons must reveal

that a subordination, but not a co-ordination, was characteristic, whether the relationships between the two houses were examined or those between the king and each house of parliament. These conditions of inequality made any idea of a co-ordination in law-making among them patently absurd. That power was proper to the king alone and to no one else. True, the peers had historic-ally occupied a more elevated position in the governmental system than the house of commons. Their writs, which went to individual peers, provided for their treating and giving counsel to the king and assigned them a 'deliberative or a consultive power to treat, and give counsel in difficult businesses'. They also possessed a judicial or decisive power that received no mention in their writs, but little should be made of this fact. The judicial power was derivative and subservient to the supreme power residing in the king and was grounded solely in his grace and favor.[74] Or, as the author might well have remarked, the king was the human source of political authority while that of other agencies within the state was merely derivative.

Above all, the king was the sole law-giver in parliament. Or, to look at the other side of the coin, no co-ordination principle characterized the law-making process. To be sure, the king in giving laws made use of the peers' advice and the consent as well of the house of commons, but the participation of the two houses in law-making was hardly that of equals, either in earlier periods of English history or in the seventeenth century. It was clear, however, that the evidence for this position was stronger if early English history were the subject of consideration. The royalist wrote: 'The higher we look, the more absolute we find the power of kings in ordaining laws: nor do we meet with at first so much as the assent or advice of the lords mentioned.'[75] So great was the early power of the king in law-making that statutes could hardly be distinguished from proclamations. Statutes were made as easily outside of parliament as within it; and when the latter process took place, the king's privy council played a great role, its mem-bers sitting with the peers in parliament to make laws there. The subordination of the house of lords to the king was also evident when he decided who would be peers and receive writs of summons.[76]

The royalist also relied on statutes to make his major points, this kind of evidence being satisfactory if the investigation was confined to the reigns before Edward VI. The titles and bodies of earlier statutes pointed to the king alone as the author and maker of laws. 'The general words used of later times, that "laws are made by authority of parliament" ', it was stressed, 'are particularly explained in former statutes to mean "that the king ordains, the lords advise, the commons consent".'[77] Another passage was equally relevant. 'It appears that even till the time of K. Edw. 6, who lived but in our fathers' days, it was punctually expressed in every king's laws that the statutes and ordinances were made by the king.'[78] Thereafter, the titles became more general; but in the bodies of statutes enacted from Edward VI to James I, mention was made at times of the 'consent of lords and commons, in these or the like words, "it is enacted by the king, with the assent of the lords and commons" '. All this changed when Charles I's statutes made no reference to the king's ordaining measures to be laws or to the consent of the two houses in law-making, and such highly unusual language crept in as ' "be it enacted by the king, the lords spiritual and temporal, and commons" '. This language sounded 'as if they were all fellow commissioners'.[79]

Notwithstanding such statutes, the *Freeholders Grand Inquest* presented a formidable case for royal power, developed purposefully at the expense of the community-centered view of government. It was to exercise much influence, notably when Prynne became fascinated with royal writs as a means of understanding early parliaments. He read the *Freeholders* at a time of deepening disillusionment with the house of commons when he was casting about for some means of curbing that house. The method turned out to be a massive historical enterprise centering on the early history of the English parliament. Once underway it rapidly acquired a distinctive life and character of its own, which entitles Prynne to a special niche in any gallery of seventeenth-century publicists who waged war on the house of commons. His furious bombardment opened a wide breach in the wall of co-ordination into which the equally energetic Dr Brady stepped late in Charles II's reign. The result was the Brady controversy of the early 1680s. Yet Prynne was no upholder of royal power, indeed not even a conscious enemy to the co-ordination principle in the legislative power. His views at this period of his life are distinctive and unique, despite their undoubted usefulness to the anti-co-ordination movement among the royalists, and will have to be considered apart from them.

The *Freeholders Grand Inquest* became influential in still another way in the early 1680s. Republication came in the years when the discovery of the so-called popish plot spawned the impeachment of Charles II's leading minister, the earl of Danby, and the attempted whig exclusion of the Roman Catholic James, duke of York, from the throne. A series of royalist tracts was now reprinted, among them the *Freeholders Grand Inquest*. The work was reprinted as a conspicuous part of Filmer's collected writings in 1679, 1680, 1684, and 1696, on each occasion except the last giving the title to the collection. The reappearance of the *Freeholders Grand Inquest* in the company of known Filmerian tracts led to the late seventeenth-century assumption that he was its author, and on the morrow of the first republication the tract was attributed to Filmer in a list of his writings prefixed to his *Power of Kings And in Particular of the King of England* (1648), when the latter was republished in 1680. Yet the attribution is highly unlikely. The *Freeholders* was in all probability written by a royalist active in civil-war Oxford, who was *au courant* with the most recent discussions of law-making. This was Holbourne, not Filmer.[80]

## V

The establishment of the commonwealth and protectorate denied royalist political ideas a public outlet until Cromwell's death in September, 1658, made possible the restoration of the monarchy. In the intervening period the community-centered ideology may have penetrated the ranks of the silenced party since clearly this had occurred by 1660. To this point it will be necessary to return, but for the moment it should be noticed that the royalist ideas of the civil-war years continued to be discussed and they flourished once more in the reigns of Charles II and James II. They were aided, strangely enough, by Prynne, whose researches in the 1650s and 1660s proved surprisingly helpful to anti-co-ordination forces. Inspired by the *Freeholders Grand Inquest*, he undertook a study of early parliaments, and his literary output ran parallel with the continuing royalist influence. And Sir John Spelman's *Case of our Affaires* was quoted and praised in two royalist tracts published independently of one another – in Heylyn's *Stumbling-block of Disobedience* (1658) and Thomas Tomkins' *Rebels Plea* (1660). The ideas of the traditionalist royalists also found an audience when Digges' *Unlawfulnesse of Subjects taking up Armes against the Soveraigne* (1644) was reprinted in 1647 and again in 1662.

The interest of the *Rebels Plea* arises as much from the authorship as the political argument. Five years after its appearance, the author became chaplain to Gilbert Sheldon, who was made bishop of London at the restoration and not long afterwards archbishop of Canterbury. Along with Hyde, now earl of Clarendon, Sheldon was an architect of the restoration settlement in church and state. The archbishop much valued Tomkins and resolved never to part with him, keeping him a chaplain in his house for many years; and Tomkins' appointment to the rectorship of Lambeth, which he kept to his dying day, was the fruit of this association.[81] While the *Rebels Plea* was published well before Tomkins became Sheldon's chaplain, it is reasonable to suppose that the archbishop was sympathetic to his chaplain's political views and in any case gratified by Tomkins' critique of Baxter's *Holy Commonwealth*.

Tomkins' title page set the tone of his tract. He would take issue with Baxter's views on 'the original of government', the idea of a 'co-ordinate and legislative power in the two houses', the identity of the 'third estate', etc. The refutation was on familiar lines. English liberties were by no means the direct product of a contract between the prince and people, as Baxter had urged, but rather the prince's grant alone. Indeed, the chronicles revealed that the royal power was at its height in earliest times. Since then, Englishmen had either won their rights and privileges from weak kings by using fraud or force or else received them gratefully as acts of grace from stronger kings. That the people, meaning the two houses, were no such sharers in the sovereignty, as Baxter had contended, appeared from the oath of supremacy which recognized the royal supremacy at the expense of any idea of a co-ordination in the government, and Tomkins was scornful in mocking the theory of mixed monarchy.[82]

Nor did any validity attach to the parliamentarian claim that the two houses shared the legislative power. So much was apparent from the statute books, where enacting clauses delineated the respective roles of the king and the two houses in law-making. More important than this type of evidence was the recognition that the king was sovereign head of the kingdom and the judge of its welfare. Even if the two houses gave their consent to making new law, this action provided no cogent proof 'of the partition of the supreme and legislative power'. The interest and duty of kings to make good laws for the country's welfare led them to inform themselves by summoning assemblies of men from all parts of the realm, but Grotius was good authority for the contention that this activity did not constitute a sharing of the legislative power. 'When the assent of the senate is necessary to any of the king's acts', he had written, 'it is not that they share in the doing, but that they truly inform the king what it is he does.' Though the adherents of mixed monarchy believed that the two houses shared the legislative power, Tomkins had no doubt of the real truth in this matter. English history and law proved the king to be the sovereign head of the kingdom, a fact that made this 'groundless fancy of division of supremacy' an absurd and non-sensical position. Since the oath of supremacy asserted the king to be the sole supreme governor, it was impossible for the two houses to be 'co-parceners'.[83] As for the Answer to the Nineteen Propositions, Charles I's remarks on law-making were pertinent only if king, lords, and commons actually constituted the three estates. By showing the clergy to be the third estate, which was as much as the king had been allowed to be of late, Tomkins was insistent that he had removed the main argument for co-ordination.[84]

The exchange between Baxter and Tomkins reveals that the ideological controversy engendered by the quarrel between Charles I and the long parliament was still at white heat. While events would soon demonstrate the greater attractiveness of the com-munity-centered ideology for the political nation, royal authority also had supporters as Heylyn's and Tomkins' tracts underscored. Other new writings in this genre included Robert Sheringham's *The Kings Supremacy Asserted* (1660), first published in Holland and then in London. Writing in exile, he undertook a lengthy scholarly refutation of Herle's and Hunton's theory of mixed

E

monarchy and charged them with distorting the Answer to the Nineteen Propositions to serve their own purposes. There was also Archbishop Ussher's posthumous *Power Communicated by God to the Prince* (1661). The contents of the two tracts suggest an earlier date of composition than their publication, and Ussher's could have been written before the civil war.

The latter argued in the most sweeping terms for the king's lofty position as supreme governor of the realm. In his person the earthly source of political power and authority, he was a living law, the figure of God among men, in Plutarch's words, 'the master bee' among the bees.[85] Although Ussher wrote little in explicit opposition to the co-ordination principle, his tract is properly described as anti-co-ordination because of the famous preface written by Dr Robert Sanderson, regius professor of divinity at Oxford and newly created bishop of Lincoln. Sanderson's own dislike of the co-ordination principle had been expressed as long ago as 1647, when he wrote a course of lectures for the divinity school at Oxford; and the preface to Ussher's tract reveals that the major purpose of publication was to combat it. Sanderson found sovereignty in the king to be so self-evident from the laws of the land and the oath of supremacy as to be apparent to men of ordinary capacity as well as to the deepest statesmen. By comparison, he had only contempt for the rival idea of mixed monarchy: it was 'an errand bull, a contradiction *in adjecto*', since monarchy was by definition the rule of one. The idea of mixed monarchy and the companion dream 'of such a co-ordination in the government, as was hatched amidst the heat of the late troubles' were no more than senseless and ridiculous fancies.[86] Sanderson was a warm friend of Sheldon's (Tomkins' patron), and both were conspicuous among the royalists with whom Warwick mingled late in the civil war.

All of these royalists shared a powerful distaste for the co-ordination principle as applied to the legislative power. If Ussher was less explicit on this score than the others, still his *Power Communicated by God to the Prince* took as high a view of royal power as that in the *Freeholders Grand Inquest* – the king was 'a kind of an image of the divine majesty upon earth'[87] – and the preface contained Sanderson's warning against co-ordination. The hostility displayed by the later royalists towards that principle seemed to seventeenth-century observers the distinguishing characteristic of their political writings. Bishop Nicolson, writing at the end of the seventeenth century, found no difficulty in composing a few sentences intended to convey the essence of Sheringham's *Kings Supremacy Asserted*, a tract of well over a hundred pages. The royalist had learnedly overthrown the arguments of the restless and anti-monarchical scribblers who at that time 'distracted the age with their impertinent and mad discourses about co-ordination of the three estates, superiority of the king's court over his person, etc.'[88] Most of the royalist tracts, mentioned above, were republished during the exclusion crisis of the early 1680s.[89]

At that time a host of new conservative tracts appeared. Chief among them were John Brydall's *Absurdity of that New devised State-Principle* (1681);[90] George Hickes' *Jovian* (1683), written at Archbishop William Sancroft's behest;[91] William Assheton's *Royal Apology* (1684), published when the author was chaplain to the duke of Ormonde;[92] and *Jus Regium* (1684), penned by Sir George Mackenzie, lord advocate of Scotland. Like Hickes, Mackenzie was of some prominence in his own right. His treatment of rebellious elements in Scotland has led to his being compared as a prosecutor with Lord Chief Justice Jeffreys, and not surprisingly his view of royal power was very high. Although he was writing about Scotland, his remarks drawn from Scottish history, the framework of Mackenzie's constitutional argument resembled that of his conservative counterparts in England and was addressed to the same problems. That *Jus Regium* was of interest to readers in both kingdoms is also suggested by its simultaneous publication in London and Edinburgh.[93]

Conterminous with this activity was the widening impact of Prynne's scholarly researches inspired by the *Freeholders Grand Inquest*. His findings, it will be seen, introduced an important new element into the controversy over co-ordination with consequences for political thought plainly perceptible long after he himself was gone from the scene.

# 5

## The curious case of William Prynne

With the exceptions of Charles I and Charles Herle, the Presbyterian William Prynne more than any other individual imparted a distinctive shape and direction to the seventeenth-century controversy over the co-ordination principle in law-making, which was in turn indispensable to the ascendant theory of a parliamentary sovereignty in king, lords, and commons. He was influenced by the principle in writing the notorious *Soveraigne Power of Parliaments*, and it became prominent once more in his angry response to Leveller propaganda and the constitutional changes at the end of the civil war. He now undertook an historical investigation of early parliaments aimed at demonstrating from the past that the king and the house of lords were legitimate elements in the government of his own day. His chief concern was to support the house of lords: the peers were not sons of the Norman conquest, as the Levellers had contemptuously proclaimed; on the contrary, they had sat in parliament for hundreds of years before the conquest.

Prynne's historical studies of the 1650s and 1660s[1] had a mixed effect on the general acceptance of the co-ordination principle. If its credibility was enhanced on the one hand by his successful elevation of the king and the house of lords in public esteem at a time when their political authority was under steady fire, still he set in motion the opposite intellectual process. That principle received a formidable blow when his scholarship raised doubt that the house of commons had been part of parliament long enough to justify the claim of sharing the law-making power on equal terms with the king and the house of lords. Equally serious, his scholarly findings also put into question the related political idea that the community was the human source of political authority.

These aspects of Prynne's activity, which appear to have been unintended and the results unforeseen, proved of greater consequence in the long run. He was only one member of a large group of seventeenth-century publicists who wrote the language of co-ordination – albeit a very important member; but in the nature of his challenge to the house of commons, at the time when he was writing, Prynne stood alone.

It was not clear for some time that his thought would move in the direction just indicated. His primary concern was to protect the king and the house of lords against the Levellers with their stress on election as the only legitimate basis for political authority in the state.[2] Ideology was reinforced by events when a group of officers in the new model army carried out Pride's purge in December, 1648, leaving about fifty members of the house of commons in charge of the nation's affairs, so long as the army was agreeable. Prynne, himself one of the excluded members, never forgave the rump – the part left sitting after the purge – for acquiescing in the military coup; and his writings thereafter reflected a fierce determination to place in the king and the house of lords, particularly the latter, a final control over elections to the house of commons or exclusion from it. His hostility towards the rump hardened when that body in January, 1649, approved a series of resolutions that proved the prelude to destroying the historic framework of the government. Their content reflected Leveller ideology, stating as it did not only that the people were the human source of all just power but that the house of commons alone exercised this power for them. Whatever that house enacted for law bound all Englishmen, even if the king and the house of lords had not assented. The rump then approved an ordinance establishing a high court of justice to try Charles I; and his refusal to accept its jurisdiction was followed by his execution, the abolition of the office of king and of the house of lords, and the establishment of the commonwealth.

To Prynne, the revolution was due to a public ignorance of the historic composition of parliaments that had permitted Leveller propaganda to undermine the king's and peers' legislative and judicial functions while aggrandizing the house of commons as the only elected branch of government. The result was the despised commonwealth. 'Next to God's wrath for our sins', he wrote, 'the gross ignorance of the ancient constitution of our English parliaments, and fanatic dream of a supreme parliamentary and absolute legislative authority in THE HOUSE OF COMMONS ALONE, (yea, in a mere remnant of it)' had provided 'the principal groundwork of all the late unparallelled [and] insolent . . . proceedings, against the late and present king, the house of peers, and secluded majority of the late commons house'.[3]

The situation cried out for remedy; and turning a fast-flowing pen to his self-imposed mission of educating the nation to its historic past, Prynne was soon busy fashioning from all types of historical records – the royal writs, certainly, to which the *Freeholders Grand Inquest* had called attention, but also charters, chronicles, and the works of earlier historians and scholars – an account of the composition, purpose, rights and privileges, and proceedings of the great councils and parliaments that had been held in England from the time of the earliest settlements to the end of Edward IV's reign. Prynne considered that the king and house of lords had composed the parliaments of early English history, and he wrote as if the broad jurisdiction then enjoyed had persisted through the centuries. So diligently did he labor on behalf of the peers, in particular, that he was associated in contemporary opinion with their house. Sir Robert Atkyns had in mind Prynne's activity when, writing late in the century, he referred to 'some late over-zealous and injudicious writers, who, out of a too fond and forward zeal to depress the house of commons, in the late exorbitant power which they took upon them . . . thought they could never sufficiently exalt the power of the lords, to overbalance that of the commons'.[4] Yet Prynne's adherence to the co-ordination principle was unmistakable, and his account of the English government as it normally existed resembled the mixed and balanced government described in Charles I's Answer to the Nineteen Propositions. Placing legal sovereignty in king, lords, and commons, Prynne wrote in a vein reminiscent of Herle, a position radical enough to be sure but less so than his own when the civil war began; and when he referred to the house of lords as the centerpiece of the constitutional system, his language came from Charles I. That house was 'an excellent screen and bank between the prince and people, to assist each against any encroachments of the other; and by just judgments to preserve that law, which ought to be the rule between every one of the three'.[5] Other statements revealed a willingness to allot an influential role to the king and the house of commons. Though changes were to be made the latter was not to be a cipher. Binding legislation required the joint consent of king, lords, and commons, all three personally present in parliament whenever laws were made. Like many another Englishman, Prynne had come a long way from the position of 1643 when he developed a radical version of co-ordination that was tantamount to placing a supremacy in the two houses. He still clung to the co-ordination principle, but now in a form more like the one enunciated in the *Fuller Answer*. On the other hand, the house of commons, as it had been developing, must undergo contraction. It was not to be all, as the Levellers would have it. It must be returned to the ancient bounds of loyalty and sobriety for the sake of the peace and settlement of three kingdoms, which had reached the brink of utter ruin when the rump invaded the rights of their fellow members, the peers, and the king. Parliaments must be restored to their ancient constitution, as Prynne put it, and to their rights and privileges but without harm to popular liberties and without the encroachments of one house upon the other.[6]

These motives led him to elevate the king and the house of lords in the constitutional system by stressing their historic monopoly of the judicial power. It was a subject of prime concern to him. His *Plea for the Lords* had made two major points: (1) the peers had an undeniable ancient right and privilege to sit and vote in all parliaments without any election by, or commission from, the people; and (2) their house, with the king, had exclusive possession of the judicial power. The house of commons participated in the exercise of the judicial power only if invited or if a bill of attainder was being considered. Otherwise no. This meant that the king and the house of lords could curb the house of commons: together they could settle all legal cases proper to parliament. By itself the house of commons could neither expel its own members nor bring them back. This could be done only if the king and the peers consented. They were the ones to make all decisions relating to elections, parliamentary privilege, and misdemeanors, whether these concerned the speaker, the members of the house of commons, or their menial servants.[7]

The king and the peers were in a position thus to curb the house of commons because the kingship and the house of lords were so much older historically than the house of commons. This was the nub of the matter to Prynne, who pounded the point home relentlessly, his advocacy due, as earlier stated, to a fixed resolve to cut back the powers of the house of commons. That house was not in parliament until 1265 (49 H. 3), too late to share the judicial power even though it had been admitted promptly to the law-making power on equal terms with the king and the house of lords.[8] This seemingly innocuous statement created a stir that can hardly be overstated. Prynne's insistence on the relative novelty of the house of commons, buttressed by the massive data which he accumulated, gave rise to the historical argument so conspicuous in the late seventeenth and early eighteenth centuries,[9] in particular, in the extended exchange between whig and tory pamphleteers known as the Brady controversy.[10] The reason why Prynne's dating had so great a contemporary impact may be seen by examining the difference between his date for the beginnings of the house of commons and the views commonly accepted on this point at the time when he wrote. Of special importance in this regard was the intellectual relationship between his choice of date and certain common-law assumptions that were undisturbed before his historical investigations began.

## II

Two schools of thought about the antiquity of the house of commons were ascendant when Prynne wrote – an Anglo-Saxon school that discerned in the witenagemot the first modern parliament, the other a post-Norman-conquest school of thought that looked to Henry I's great council at Salisbury in 1116. Both assumed a much older house of commons than Prynne; and their views were perfectly consonant with what may be termed the common-law argument for early parliaments. The spokesman for the Anglo-Saxon school was the Tudor antiquary, William Lambarde, whose discussion of early parliaments in his *Archeion* (completed by 1591) exercised a surprising influence on Stuart England. Lambarde's ideas received a powerful reinforcement when Coke took them up and passed them on to later writers, and *Archeion* itself was printed twice in 1635, in time to affect the literary warfare between Charles I and the long parliament that ushered in the civil war. Almost certainly, Lambarde's influence shaped Charles I's Answer to the Nineteen Propositions at a critical juncture in the king's analysis;[11] and Lambarde's argument ran a prosperous course during the remainder of the seventeenth century.[12] Prynne answered him about the time of Charles II's restoration to the throne, and Lambarde was liberally quoted in polemical writings not only at the Glorious Revolution but also as late as the age of Blackstone.[13] Another spokesman for this school was Nathaniel Bacon, whose *Historical Discourse* enjoyed an undoubted vogue in the late seventeenth century despite the court's vigorous opposition.

One way of demonstrating the Anglo-Saxon origins of the house of commons was to translate words like *sapientes* and *wites* in old English records so as to comprehend popular as well as aristocratic elements. The word *barones* was similarly treated as impressive evidence for a post-conquest house. And there were other resources. Lambarde relied on this kind of evidence and also on the *Modus tenendi Parliamentum*, a medieval tract viewed in the years before Prynne wrote as an unquestionable authority for the composition and procedure of parliament in the reign of Edward the Confessor (1042–66). Knights, citizens, and burgesses were said to have been summoned to parliament, and this testimony seemed the more creditable because Coke assumed the authenticity of the *Modus tenendi* for Anglo-Saxon England in his law reports (1600–15) and his *Institutes* (1628–44). The former were reprinted in 1656 and 1659, at a time when Prynne's scholarship was approaching its zenith. It is difficult to visualize a more powerful kind of support than that supplied by Coke. The law reports were intended and received as a means of supplying the student of the common law with law cases, while the *Institutes* became the first English textbook on the modern common law.

Particularly disturbing to Prynne was Coke's reliance on the *Modus tenendi* to establish a house of commons in Anglo-Saxon England and to prove its persistence after the Norman conquest. According to the great lawyer, that house had survived the conquest. The *Modus tenendi* was rehearsed and declared before the conqueror, and William's first parliament was held in accordance with it. That tract had also been useful to Henry II in introducing a parliament into Ireland and to the makers of Magna Carta, who had borrowed from it. This description was more than Prynne could bear. Pointing to numerous anachronisms, he argued for a much later date of composition. Prynne thought it might have been written during the wars of the roses, perhaps to serve the Yorkist cause. But in any case, the tract was ridiculous, an imposture foisted on a credulous public by Coke, who had 'overdoted on it for a most ancient record, beyond all exception, relying upon it as an undoubted oracle'.[14]

The other school of thought, the post-Norman-conquest school, held that the first modern parliament was Henry I's great council at Salisbury in 1116. This view seems to have originated with the Tudor historian, Polydore Vergil; and its seventeenth-century advocates turned to him and also to popular chronicles – Grafton, Stowe, Holinshed, Speed, and Daniel – where the statement 'first parliament, 1116' appeared in marginal headings.[15] The popularity of this dating was enhanced by Archbishop Parker's society of antiquaries, which met in the period from 1572 to 1604 and again in 1614. The society's papers on the antiquity of parliament were published for the first time in 1658 and reprinted in 1679 and in 1685, the publication at the later dates due no doubt to Prynne's scholarship, which was hostile to the antiquaries' findings. Not all of them followed Polydore Vergil, but the writings of Judge John Dodderidge, William Camden, and Joseph Holland were in this vein.[16] Others tracing the first house of commons to the great council at Salisbury included Raleigh, Heylyn, and Holbourne. According to the *Freeholders Grand Inquest*, the commons were not regularly summoned or regularly elected by writs until Henry III's reign, but the beginnings of that house were placed in Henry I's reign.[17]

The two schools of thought were anathema to Prynne. No modern parliament was to be found in Anglo-Saxon England, despite Lambarde's solid reputation as a scholar and Coke's mighty support; and no greater political progress was discernible under Henry I (1100–35) or even Henry II (1154–89), as could be seen from Prynne's own *Plea for the Lords* with its 'large account of most of the great councils held under Kings Henry I and II proving there were no knights, citizens or burgesses sum-

moned to them in their reigns, as they have been of later times'.[18]
This meant no house of commons as late as 1189, the year of the
coronation of Richard I, the successor of Henry II. Here was a
negative fact of much consequence, a very disturbing one, it will
be seen, to those who supported the co-ordination principle in
law-making by an appeal to the English common law. Almost a
hundred years would pass before popular elements were summoned by writs to medieval parliaments, this occurring when
Henry III summoned representatives of the counties and boroughs
to Westminster after Simon de Montfort's defeat at Evesham in
August, 1265. That king, determined to strike off aristocratic
control, found the means by building a counterweight to the
baronial class in parliament; and the practice continued under
Henry III's successors. The role of the house of commons was
for some time quite limited, its rise to a consequential position in
the kingdom's affairs very slow. Possessing neither a speaker nor
indeed even a house of their own, its members participated only
gradually in the great affairs of state. Yet the house of commons
had from the first one very important power : it shared with the
king and the house of lords 'their consultative, legislative and tax-
imposing power'. Binding laws required a joint consent. If the
ring of co-ordination in this comment was unacceptable to the
enemies of that principle, other elements in Prynne's commentary
proved unfailingly helpful to anti-co-ordination writers.[19]

At first sight this seems surprising. It might be anticipated that
an insistence on 49 H. 3 as marking the appearance of the house
of commons in parliament would render Prynne's scholarship suspect in conservative circles where resistance to novelty is usually a
marked feature. This is not what happened. His dating was eagerly
taken up by the high tory writers of Charles II's reign while
prominent whig writers such as Sir Robert Atkyns, William Petyt,
and James Tyrrell displayed a cold hostility.[20] The whig response
is of special interest. Prynne's dating and its historical justification
were hateful to members of that party for this important reason :
it raised havoc with their approach to political problems in which
certain common-law concepts such as legal memory and prescription figured large. Their response was to fashion from current
common-law ideas and attitudes a coherent argument for early
parliaments that was replete with implications for their own

political institutions, and their doing so lent a distinctive flavor to the Brady controversy and the political debates generally of the 1680s.

More than this can be said. The whig argument, though elaborated a generation after Prynne's death, tells much about the line of contemporary political thought which seemed to him to endanger his scholarship and make its acceptance impossible. Common to both the whig argument and the line of thought that he disliked were the common-law concepts of legal memory and prescription. The application of these concepts, which are related, to early parliamentary history, especially in the form that they took in whig writings, produced results that supported the assumption, and indeed depended on it, that the house of commons was very old. It had been present either in the witenagemot or else in the great council at Salisbury. But if Prynne was contending correctly that the house of commons first began in 1265, the common-law argument must collapse. This dating had to be rejected, then; but the objective of the whig writers can be stated with a greater precision than this. They were intent, above all else, on finding a house of commons at Westminster before 1189, the year of Richard I's coronation. In the great quarrel over the antiquity of the house of commons, this was ultimately the date at issue.

How may this be seen? The place to begin is with the meaning of prescription. It has been defined as the establishment of a claim or title by virtue of immemorial use and enjoyment. In this context the word 'immemorial' has a special meaning: the adjective conveyed that the right in question had been used and enjoyed in the period of time before legal memory began. When had legal memory begun? It became customary in whig writings to treat September 3, 1189, the date of Richard I's coronation, as the line dividing the time of legal memory from that before legal memory; and this view, described as the rule of 1189, became virtually unassailable as a legal principle when Judge Mansfield gave it his support in the eighteenth century. The outcome was largely due, one suspects, to the conspicuous role played by the rule of 1189 in the controversy over the antiquity of the house of commons. But more doubt surrounded the matter in the seventeenth century. The lawbooks were not unanimous in defining prescription, and some authorities found one in a claim or title that had been exercised for several ages or even within living memory. Apparently Prynne accepted this point of view. Yet the rule of 1189 was acceptable to Henry Rolle (d. 1656), successively chief justice of king's bench, lord chief justice of the upper bench, and member of the council of state in the civil-war and interregnum years. He formed part of the Selden circle of scholarship. That Rolle was associated with the rule of 1189 certainly suggests that Prynne's contemporaries had taken it up and were discussing it at the time when he was writing. This is the more likely since it also found favor with Lord Chief Justice Matthew Hale, who served the Cromwellian regime and emerged thereafter as one of the great judges of Charles II's reign. He too was close to Selden, and it is thought that many of Hale's views took shape during the interregnum. The rule of 1189 was asserted vigorously in the political arena by whig polemists who insisted that a political right existing before 1189 was immemorial if no sufficient proof of record or writing could be adduced to the contrary. In the language of the law such a political right had 'ever' existed and was said to be without a beginning or at least such a beginning as the law takes notice of. It was described as grounded in customary or unwritten law, spoken of as prescriptive, and viewed as authoritative in a law court. A whig writer believed he had uncovered a prescriptive right, it must be stressed, if this right was present in the company of expressions such as 'time out of mind', 'in all times past', 'of old times', 'in a time beyond memory', 'in a time when minds run not to the contrary', and the like.[21] Since medieval statutes and other medieval records were full of such expressions, the grounds were ample in whig opinion for claiming the prescriptive rights of Englishmen.

Historical findings of this kind could be utilized to date broadly the emergence of particular political rights and the political institutions by which they were exercised. The prescriptive right cherished by the whigs, in insisting on the antiquity of the house of commons, was the right to representation in parliament, which was said to reside either in the English people or else in the boroughs and counties, the two descriptions treated as interchangeable. To whig writers the case seemed conclusive if convincing proof were forthcoming that even one borough had returned members to parliament before Richard I's coronation, and this reasoning explains the inordinate attention lavished on the case of the burgesses of St Albans. The history of that borough was said to provide the requisite evidence for sustaining the whig thesis.[22]

From a prescriptive right of representation in the community flowed the inevitable assumption that a house of commons must also have existed before the time of legal memory, its political power and authority based squarely on the community and its longevity, in the language of the law, just as great as that of the king and the house of lords. No one doubted that they had existed before 1189. Thus the door opened wide to an immemorial house of commons, independent in its origins of the king, that might appropriately be described as one of the three estates in parliament and an equal partner in law-making with the king and the house of lords. To those who reasoned in this way there was a coevality principle in law-making as well as a co-ordination principle. Here ideally was the trinity of law-makers so much cherished by the advocates of co-ordination, and the controversy over the beginnings of the house of commons is for this reason inseparable from the larger constitutional issue of who made law in Stuart parliaments. The intellectual relationship between the antiquity of that house and the co-ordination principle in law-making (and hence a parliamentary sovereignty in king, lords, and commons) is at the heart of the matter and explains why the controversy over early English history was long and furious.

One other point must be made about prescription and the right of representation in the house of commons. Prescription depended upon beginnings before the time of legal memory, as has been seen, and likewise on the absence of written records to the contrary. But it also depended upon customary and uninterrupted usage and enjoyment. The whig writers who assigned an immemorial character to the house of commons must insist not only on its early origins but also on its persistence as an institution after the Norman conquest despite the vicissitudes of the late eleventh century. Here surely lies a major explanation for the well-known whig abhorrence of the Norman conquest. It was vital for whig writers to believe that parliaments had somehow survived that event. The techniques of argument used to deny an actual conquest – in the interest of the whig argument – have been noted by modern writers.[23] To admit a conquest in the usual sense of the word was too easily construed as an admission of an actual break in the constitution and accordingly a major flaw in the legal case from prescription for an immemorial representation and its concomitant, an immemorial house of commons. Prynne, writing of Lambarde and others who associated the right to representation with the common law and referring in this context to the compiler of the *Modus tenendi*, which Coke had so much magnified, gave the main lines of their thought thus : the original title and right of ancient English cities and boroughs to elect and send burgesses and citizens to parliament was 'prescription time out of mind, long before the conquest, it being a privilege they actually and of right enjoyed in Edward the confessor's time, or before, and [had] exercised ever since'.[24] Tyrrell was likewise illuminating. His history contained 'the testimonies of divers learned antiquaries, all of this opinion, that it was the ancient right of the commons of England [to representation] by prescription, both before and since the Norman entrance'.[25]

That the prescriptive right to representation was accorded the highest priority in whig political thought is easily demonstrated. A major part of Tyrrell's multi-volume history of England, written after the Glorious Revolution, was intended to prove that 'the people or commons of England have always claimed this right by prescription, *i.e.* time beyond memory, of being so represented'.[26] The same reasoning pervaded Petyt's *Antient Right of the Commons of England Asserted* (1680), which was probably the most influential anti-court tract made public in the decade before the Glorious Revolution. The very title suggested to the reader versed in the common law the existence of an assured prescriptive right in the English people to representation in parliament.[27] Assertion of this right did not pass unnoticed in the early 1680s. Whig writers like Petyt, who combined the political sins of making the house of commons older than 1189 with an insistence on a co-ordination in the legislative power, aroused the ire of high tory polemists like Dr Brady, who felt that his own scholarship must destroy the arguments of those invoking the common law to mislead the English people about their fundamental rights. If Brady's exposition fell short at this point of discussing the nature of these fundamental rights, he knew full well that none was deemed more fundamental in anti-court circles than the prescriptive right to representation in a sovereign parliament, where king, lords, and commons shared the law-making power.[28]

This line of thought in Prynne's own day, less articulate and less coherent, to be sure, but still a powerful force to be reckoned with, explains a great deal about his attack on the use of the common law to unlock the secrets of early English history. It had been authenticated by Lambarde and the venerated Coke, and to overturn their authority on a point now deemed so crucial as the antiquity of the house of commons required much diligence and pertinacity, qualities as it happened that Prynne possessed in abundance.

## III

Prynne's critique centered on Lambarde, whose *Archeion* fixed the terms of discussion whenever polemists wrote in terms of prescription and the early house of commons. The latter's style of reasoning may be glimpsed from his oft-cited proof for an Anglo-Saxon house of commons, drawn from the decayed condition of certain boroughs in Tudor England. Assuming a greater prosperity in these boroughs when they first returned members to the house of commons, Lambarde turned to Anglo-Saxon England as the place where the appropriate conditions had been present. Thus the presence of decayed boroughs in Tudor England proved a prescriptive right to a representation exercised as long ago as the Anglo-Saxon period. Presumably, then, the community was properly viewed as the human source of the political authority exercised by the house of commons through the centuries, and it possessed the right of representation because of prescription. As Lambarde put it, the 'interest' which the boroughs had in parliament grew 'by an ancient usage before the conquest, whereof they cannot show any beginning'.[29]

Lambarde also turned to prescription to establish an early house of commons when he cited what he termed 'a contrary usage in the self-same thing'. Boroughs 'of ancient demesne' had requested not to be obliged to perform certain functions otherwise expected of them. They were exempted by prescription from sending members to parliament and from paying the wages of the knights representing the counties even though the pertinent statutes were written in general language without stated exemptions. But what about the origins of such rights and privileges? How old were they? Had they existed before the Norman conquest? Domesday Book was said to mention boroughs of this type under the name of *terra regis*. That they received any mention there meant that they had existed either immediately before or after the conquest. It must follow that there was also a house of commons at that time. Where otherwise would less privileged boroughs send their representatives?[30]

If the modern parliament had actually existed before the Norman conquest, had it survived the cataclysmic events of the late eleventh century? Here was a fundamental question since customary and uninterrupted usage was just as essential to prescription as an early beginning of the house of commons. Granted the difficulty of finding convincing proof since *silent leges inter arma*, Lambarde concluded that a full parliament had assembled once more in the reign of Henry I, the conqueror's youngest son. This might be seen from the latter's famous coronation charter, which promised to restore Edward the confessor's laws and acknowledged as well that Henry himself had been crowned by the common council of the barons of the realm. If the word *barones* posed obstacles to finding commoners in the common council, Lambarde was resourceful. Not only had the Germans translated *barones* to signify freemen, but Matthew Paris had also applied the word to London's citizens. These facts permitted the conclusion that the 'barons of the realm' comprehended both the nobility and the commonalty of the realm; and Henry I had put the matter past doubt by coupling with this expression the words 'common council', signifying parliament.[31]

Lambarde's analysis also made it apparent that the right to share in the law-making power, as well as the right to representation, was vested in the community and in no way derived from the crown. 'Here again', as he said, 'prescription is ready to serve the turn.' Using the language of estates in a fashion foreshadowing Charles I, the antiquary ascribed what he called the voices of the two houses of parliament to prescription. The positive proof was forthcoming from a particular medieval statute (5 Rich. 2, s. 2.c.4), where political practices and procedures closely related to parliamentary representation were linked in four separate places with the expression 'of old time' and described as having been 'done anciently'. This one statute might serve to interpret all other statutes whenever it was necessary to consider the origin of the political authority in the two houses. That the voice of each house in parliament by way of prescription amounted to a share in the law-making power was conveyed by Lambarde's discussion of the relationships among king, lords, and commons as expressed in the enacting clauses of statutes. Whatever their language, such clauses came finally to this: 'The king, his nobility, and commons, did ordain and enact the same.'[32]

This pattern of political ideas made Lambarde's writings of great interest in the seventeenth century. An unmistakable sign of his continuing influence was the respect constantly paid in whig circles to the statute from Richard II's reign (5 Rich. 2, s.2. c.4), which he had praised as an interpreter for all other statutes whenever prescription and the political authority of the two houses were under discussion. Once more Tyrrell is helpful, translating the statute from Norman French for his readers and at the same time offering a commentary as to its meaning. The statute read:

that all and singular persons and commonalties which from henceforth shall for time to come have summons of parliament, shall come from henceforth as before to parliaments, in the manner as they be bound to do, and hath been accustomed within the realm of England of old time. And whatever person of the said realm, which from henceforth shall have the said summons (be he archbishop, bishop, abbot, prior, duke, earl, baron, banneret, knight of shire, citizen of city, burgess of burgh, or other singular person or commonalty) do absent himself and come not at the said summons (except he may reasonably and lawfully excuse himself to our sovereign lord the king) he shall be amerced, and otherwise punished, according as of old times hath been used to be done within the said realm in the said case. And if any sheriff of the realm be henceforth negligent in making his returns of the writs of the parliaments, or that he shall leave out of the said returns any cities or boroughs which were bound, and of old times were wont to come to parliament, he shall be punished in the manner as was accustomed to be done in the said case of old time.[33]

Using the expression 'hath been accustomed of old time' as a point of departure, Tyrrell explained how a reader versed in the common law interpreted the statute. This was the explanation:

First, that the knights, citizens, and burgesses, are supposed by this statute to have a like right to have summons to parliaments as hath been accustomed of old time, as well as the lords spiritual and temporal here mentioned.

Secondly, that by these words, have been accustomed of old time . . . we are to understand a general custom of the realm, time out of mind, that is, by prescription: so that if the bishops, abbots, and temporal lords, are here acknowledged to have had a right to sit in parliament by prescription; so have the commons likewise by the same words equally applied to all the orders here mentioned.

Lastly, that if any sheriff shall neglect in making returns of any such cities and boroughs, which were thus bound to come to parliament of old time he shall be punished, as hath been accustomed to be done in all time past.

The last point provided evidence that the common law bound the sheriffs to make returns from ancient boroughs. Prescription left them no discretion. As Tyrrell asked, 'With what colour of justice' could sheriffs be punished unless there was a 'certain rule to know what cities and boroughs were bound to come to parliament of old time?'[34] This was a verbal thrust at Prynne, who had insisted that the sheriffs had in fact great discretion in elections, deciding in many cases which boroughs were to return members to the house of commons and those not to receive writs at all.

Since Lambarde's language about early parliaments anticipated in so many respects the civil-war co-ordination principle, his ideas had the rare merit of increasing in relevance with the passage of time. But even before the Answer to the Nineteen Propositions had made of *Archeion* a natural resource for the enemies to royal power, Coke had taken up some of Lambarde's conclusions and given them a wider audience. The parallels were at times striking as Coke referred to tenants in ancient demesne who were bound to plow and husband the royal demesnes before and after the Norman conquest. They enjoyed certain exemptions from parliamentary duties because of these obligations: they were not to be returned as burgesses, for example, nor pay the wages of knights. Privileges of this variety rested on prescription, on custom and

usage before the time of legal memory; and in Coke's opinion
their existence provided evidence that there were parliaments
with houses of commons both before and after the conquest. He
also wrote of ancient boroughs where representatives had come
to parliament time out of mind – a common-law expression associated with the concept of legal memory.[35]

Yet to Prynne it was not Coke but Lambarde who was the
main protagonist of prescription, and it was his spell that would
have to be broken before a genuine historical understanding of
early parliaments was possible. This was Prynne's outlook even
though he did give much attention to what he saw as Coke's
misuse of *Modus tenendi*. The mainstays of the argument from
prescription were in *Archeion* and the *Modus tenendi*, so Prynne
reasoned, as he set out to establish that prescription could not be
used to establish a house of commons before the conquest. Nor
would he admit a prescriptive right to representation in the sense
advanced by Lambarde since most boroughs were not only
founded after 1265 but also failed to return members to the
house of commons on a regular basis after representation was
introduced.

Prynne's rejection was sweeping : the argument from prescription in Lambarde was fallacious and in no way conclusive. A
proof dependent on decayed boroughs in Tudor England was
without merit, as was that based on the supposed exemptions
from parliamentary obligations attributed to boroughs of ancient
demesne. The decayed boroughs of Lambarde's day were just as
mean and inconsiderable when the Domesday Book was compiled;
and, moreover, no history or record established that any of these
boroughs, whether decayed or not or much enlarged and enriched
since the conquest, had ever sent burgesses to any parliament
either before or after the Norman conquest. This had not been
done until 49 H.3, and all the antiquaries of England could not
prove otherwise. The evidence against Lambarde was in the
sheriffs' electoral returns, revealing that the bulk of the decayed
boroughs had returned members to parliament for the first time
after Edward I's reign (1272–1307) and not before, much less by
prescription before the conquest.[36]

As for the proof from knights' wages, likewise in *Archeion*, this
too was worthless. The oldest writs for this purpose came from

the twenty-eighth and twenty-ninth years of Edward I; and no records, histories or lawbooks placed the beginning of such payments earlier. Nor could it be demonstrated that knights were elected for the counties and sent to parliament by the king's writ before 49 H.3. Hence the prescription to be discharged from contributing to their wages could not be pushed back before 49 H.3, certainly not to William I's reign or to Anglo-Saxon England.[37]

Despite the missing records, it was possible to establish an early house of commons by reading a high degree of antiquity into such expressions as 'of old times', 'time out of mind', and others. The free association of these terms with a pre-conquest house of commons, or with such a house in 1116, placed Prynne's scholarship in a *cul de sac* from which escape was impossible. Seeing in this practice an obstacle to be confronted and removed, he undertook to divorce such expressions from the idea that the house of commons had existed either in Anglo-Saxon England or immediately after the conquest. He seems to have acted without any concern for the impact of this action on the co-ordination principle to which he subscribed. The meaning of such expressions was much less sweeping than Lambarde and his disciples believed since he, Prynne, had learned of many prescriptions and customs in use during Edward III's reign (1327–77) and thereafter which were said 'to be time out of mind'. Yet a close examination revealed a beginning long after the conquest, a fact ascertained by reading under the heading of 'custom and prescription' from Brooke's and Fitzherbert's lawbooks and from Coke's *Institutes*. Whatever had been used for two or three ages only or in a period beyond the memory of living men was reputed a legal custom or prescription under Edward III. To associate such expressions with a house of commons before 1265 was a mistake; and Prynne was caustic in denunciation as he declared:

I am certain that at this day tenants in ancient demesne, can plead, that both they and their ancestors time out of mind of man, were never accustomed to pay excise for any thing, for which excise is now generally demanded; will it therefore follow; ergo, all places else now subject to pay excise, were liable to pay it before the conquest, when as it was first set on foot since 1642?

Lambarde's argument for early parliaments was no more relevant: knights and burgesses were in parliament no earlier than Henry III's reign. None of Lambarde's authorities provided satisfactory evidence that such representatives were present in the pre-conquest parliament; indeed, all the histories and records since the conquest refuted this view.[38]

Prynne's determined campaign to destroy the common-law argument for an early house of commons entered a new phase with his highly influential *Brevia Parliamentaria Rediviva* (1662), the third volume of the series on parliamentary writs known as the *Brief Register of Parliamentary Writs* (1659–64). The contents of *Brevia Parliamentaria Rediviva* reflected new evidence that Prynne had accumulated after being appointed shortly after the restoration to be keeper of the records in the tower of London. He had taken up his duties at once after receiving the royal patent and was soon busily uncovering large bundles of original writs of summons in the white tower, where for centuries they had lain in chaos under decaying and putrefying cobwebs, dust, and filth. Working with his clerk, Prynne sorted out the foul-smelling records while the cavalier parliament was in adjournment (August–September, 1661). So uninviting were the records that some of the older clerks were unwilling to touch them for fear of soiling their hands, spoiling their clothes, or even endangering their eyesight and health. But not the zealous and industrious Prynne, who reported finding in this 'dung heap' many rare pearls and golden records, indeed 97 parcels of original writs issued to sheriffs and others in the period from Edward I to Henry VI, with their respective returns, schedules, and indentures dispersed into broken fragments. These were mended and made available for public use, and Prynne also had access to 130 other parcels of parliamentary records. From the assorted materials he prepared a detailed statement regarding the representation of medieval boroughs designed to eradicate any lingering impression that parliamentary representation was based on the common-law principle of prescription.[39] If Englishmen had no prescriptive right to representation, the house of commons had no prescriptive right to a share in the law-making power. Thanks to Lambarde's influence, the two ideas were intertwined.

Already on record as opposing the idea that a house of commons had existed before 1265 – indeed before 1189 – Prynne now completed his assault on the common-law position by establishing that discontinuity had historically characterized the representation of the boroughs after the house of commons arrived in parliament. He would offer special observations concerning 'the number, true original creation, continuance [and] discontinuance of all ancient cities, boroughs [and] ports of England summoned by the king's writs or sheriff's precepts [orders or warrants issued pursuant to the royal writs] to elect [and] return . . . citizens, burgesses and barons of ports to serve in ancient parliaments or great councils of England' from 1272 to 1483.[40]

His study revealed the following. In about two centuries the total of the cities, boroughs, and ports that had received writs of summons or sheriffs' precepts to return members to the house of commons amounted to 170, and no more. Of this number only 161 actually elected and sent representatives to parliament, and their experience was varied. Thus twenty-two boroughs returned burgesses for a single parliament, and eight boroughs sent them for only two parliaments. The boroughs that seldom elected and sent burgesses to parliament were likely to go for long periods of time without elections. One borough in Devonshire after making its first return in 1299 did not elect again until 1420, a time lapse of well over a century. The conclusion was irresistible. How could one insist on a prescriptive right to representation, given a discontinuance of this duranton![41]

Prynne's next conclusion afforded little comfort either to those who believed that prescription governed parliamentary representation or to those who discerned in royal charters the means by which cities and boroughs were enabled to return members to the house of commons. The new ground now taken up was, however, more favorable to the king's power than to that of the community. To Prynne, the discretionary authority of the sheriff was a vital element in the electoral situation during the period from Edward I's reign in the late thirteenth century to that of Richard II at the end of the fourteenth. Parliamentary representation had rested on a combination of the royal writ of summons to parliament, which provided for the election of representatives to the house of commons, and the arbitrary authority of the sheriff, whose great discretion rose out of a general clause in the royal writ. He was empowered to act by virtue of the royal writ, yes; but since the empowering clause did not designate the cities and boroughs by name within each county, he was left free to send the writ, or the precepts grounded on it, to whatever cities and boroughs he pleased. The general clause was executed according to each sheriff's judgment, as this was swayed by his emotions and prejudices, the solicitations of particular boroughs, or even the views of individuals seeking seats in parliament.[42] His great power in elections could be seen on all sides. Sometimes he provided for representation in a given county on a generous scale, but at other times the number of seats was arbitrarily reduced.

Bucks provided a case in point. There the sheriff had made and unmade, continued and discontinued, and revived the boroughs at will. Over the centuries burgesses were regularly returned from Wycombe, but no such regularity marked the representation of other boroughs in that county. On one occasion Agmondesham, Wendover, and Marlowe had also sent two burgesses apiece to parliament, only to have the representation revert in the following election to Wycombe alone. Beginning in 1310 the sheriff provided only for elections in that borough. According to Prynne, such boroughs as Agmondesham, Wendover, and Marlowe had returned two members apiece in that year but did not repeat the experience until after Edward IV's reign (1461–83), or else much later. They had been 'excluded from electing burgesses by prescription by these negative returns, *Nec sunt plures burgi; non habentur plures burgi; non est alius burgus in Com. Bucks,* or *Balliva mea,* besides Wycombe, continuing from 4 Edw. 2 till of late'. This meant that the governing factor in determining the borough representation in Bucks was the will of the sheriff, who at his pleasure had erected, named, returned, omitted, discontinued, and revived whatever boroughs he wished. If the boroughs had been created either by the king's letters patent or by prescription and custom before the conquest, he could not have acted in this way; and what is more, the boroughs had accepted this treatment in silence, never complaining against the sheriff so far as Prynne could learn.[43]

Almost as instructive were examples from such other counties as Cornwall, Dorset, Somerset, Southampton, Surrey, Sussex, and Wilts. Their history also demonstrated the sheriff's power regarding the representation of medieval boroughs though Prynne made one exception, based on his view, mentioned earlier, that prescription did not rest on the rule of 1189. Thus the sheriff was in no position to act arbitrarily with regard to certain ancient, rich, and large boroughs, who by 'custom and prescription' – presumably a customary usage since 49 H.3 – were able and bound to send burgesses to parliament. This exception in no way invalidated his general conclusion. The sheriffs' returns demonstrated one non-controvertible truth : the true origin of all ancient parliamentary boroughs was not by prescription or custom before the conquest or 49 H.3 or by special charters from England's ancient kings, but by the king's writs and the sheriffs' constant precepts to certain principal cities and boroughs in their counties. Writs or precepts were sent to cities and boroughs to elect citizens and burgesses to parliament if they were capable of defraying their representatives' expenses, as they were bound by law to do. Once more the sheriff's discretionary authority was the operative factor. He was likely to omit the poor and inferior boroughs, sending or not sending precepts to them at his pleasure.[44]

## IV

In conclusion, then, Prynne's scholarship constituted a clear and present danger to the common-law argument regarding the nature of early parliaments, this depending as it did on the beliefs that a prescriptive right to representation in parliament was lodged in the community and that an immemorial law-making house of commons was its logical political expression. The consensus before Prynne wrote was that the beginning of the house of commons was safely within the period before legal memory began, whether one discerned a house of commons in Anglo-Saxon England or believed that house to have been present for the first time in Henry I's great council at Salisbury. Royalists as conservative in political hue and as rigorous in analysis as Heylyn and Holbourne had accepted uncritically the idea that the house of commons was present in Henry I's great council at Salisbury. Whatever else they might write about the house of commons, they had not denied its immemorial character. Indeed, quite the opposite. This was left to Prynne to accomplish, and the comprehensive manner in which he demolished the argument from the common law made him the *enfant terrible* to the supporters of a co-ordination in the legislative power and a source of inspiration to high tory writers. It was a curious outcome for the author of the *Soveraigne Power of Parliaments*. The impact of Prynne's later writings could only have been enhanced by his *Brevia Parliamentaria Rediviva* with its revelations regarding the irregularity of parliamentary representation after 49 H.3.

There was very early a close link between the common-law argument for a house of commons before 1189 – and for the persistence of that house after the beginnings of representation were established – and the principle of a co-ordination in the legislative power. This appears from the use made of Lambarde by late seventeenth-century publicists. To many their fates seemed interdependent. If the common-law argument prevailed, the origins of the house of commons were in the community, fixed there irrevocably by the common-law principle of prescription. It was a highly significant idea to seventeenth-century Englishmen, who were deeply concerned about the human source of political authority. Whoever accepted the common-law position conceived of the house of commons as an estate in parliament, entirely independent of the crown, sharing the law-making power, the highest power in the state, on equal terms with the king and the house of lords. Law-making belonged, then, to three co-ordinate and coeval estates, the two qualities interdependent, one unable to subsist without the other, or so at least it seemed to some. It is not fanciful to discern in this formulation the root of Blackstone's observation that the legislature of the kingdom was intrusted to three distinct powers, entirely independent of each other, though he plainly wanted no part in the quarrel over the antiquity of the house of commons.[45]

On the other hand, Prynne's scholarship, if it prevailed, would have erected a great barrier to the forward sweep of the co-ordination principle in the years after Charles II's restoration. His researches, published in the critical decades of the 1650s and 1660s, served to create an ever-widening impression that no elements of the house of commons were present in parliament prior to Richard I's coronation. They were present only in 1265 (49 H.3), almost a hundred years after the beginning of legal memory if this was said to commence in the year 1189. How was it possible, then, to view that house as an independent member of the law-making trinity? After all, as Atkyns pointed out, 49 H.3 was 'within time of memory . . . in a legal understanding'.[46] Writing at the restoration, Whitelocke drew the conclusion dreaded by supporters of co-ordination. Whenever it was stated that writs of summons to the house of commons were first issued in 49 H.3, this meant that the king's action was 'out of mere [pure] grace'. No 'ancient right, or custom' was involved.[47] This was to say nothing of Prynne's further proposition that irregularity had marked parliamentary representation from the beginning. For a century after popular elements entered parliament medieval sheriffs, almost of their own authority, had determined the cities and boroughs to have representation; and this discretionary authority, resting on a general clause in the royal writs, made it impossible, in his opinion, to accept either a pre-conquest prescription or royal charters as the legal basis of the political authority in the house of commons. The elimination of a prescription based on the rule of 1189 was devastating to the proponents of a co-ordination principle in law-making and its corollary that the community was the human source of the political power and authority in the house of commons.[48]

Prynne's researches, leading to the highly controversial conclusion that the king and the house of lords were immemorial while the house of commons was not, provided a great bridge linking the ideological argument of the civil war with new trends in Charles II's reign. This was the most important effect. To be sure, his scholarship was damaging both to the argument from the common-law and the co-ordination principle, damaging but not fatal even though high tory writers in Charles II's reign followed Prynne through the broad breach disclosed in the wall of co-ordination. For this reason. Well before his enterprise of the 1650s was underway the constant application of the co-ordination principle to law-making had served to create the belief that the principle had always formed part of the constitution. This appears from the curious case of Prynne himself when, secure in the conviction that the co-ordination principle prevailed in law-making, he moved unhesitatingly in the name of scholarship and with the aim of taming the vagrant house of commons to destroy a major pillar of its position, that is, the common-law argument for its ancient role as an integral part of parliament.

In sum, the historical findings so creditable to Prynne and Brady from the standpoint of modern scholarship had come much too late to affect the co-ordination principle. It was in place before the civil war was over; and though this fact was obscured in the upsurge of loyalty to the throne accompanying the return of the Stuart kingship, the changed situation was, nevertheless, very much in evidence after 1660. Restoration of the monarchy meant for the majority of the political nation, not the restoration of a single law-maker in parliament, who legislated by and with the consent of the lords spiritual and temporal and commons, as enacting clauses of statutes were soon to state, but rather the re-establishment of a trinity of law-makers – many would have said the three co-ordinate estates of king, lords, and commons – and hence a shared legal sovereignty. This is a fact of much significance although a lot of water would flow over the dam before the changed ideological situation became fully apparent. The Revolution of 1688 was to sanctify a principle which it had not originated – that the king was but a single if impressive member of a singularly powerful law-making trinity, possessed of no more right to employ at will a dispensing and suspending power than any other member of it and of much less right than the trinity as a whole. As Herle had succinctly stated in 1642, one 'need not buy an almanac . . . to reckon . . . that one is less than three'.[49]

# 6

## The idiom of restoration politics

### I

When Charles II entered London on May 29, 1660, he could contemplate ruling a people who lauded the kingship and exalted royal authority. The powerful current of opinion running for the monarchy submerged any thought of formally imposing conditions on the restored monarch. Yet the co-ordination principle, with all of its restraints on the monarchy, was assuredly well-known at the time and widely received. On the eve of the king's triumphal entrance the convention parliament resolved, on May 1, 1660, that 'according to the ancient and fundamental laws of this kingdom, the government is, and ought to be, by king, lords, and commons'.[1]

This language had originated in the traditionally more conservative house of lords; and its speaker, the earl of Manchester, subsequently recommended its adoption successfully at a conference of the two houses. That he should have done so was consistent with earlier phases of his political career. A leading member of the middle party in the long parliament when its leaders sponsored Herle as author of the indispensable co-ordination principle, he was also on record as having used the language of mixed monarchy to oppose the ordinance for Charles I's trial. At that time, too, he was speaker of the house of lords. The convention parliament's resolution was based on the same view of the constitution.

Yet the famous resolution enjoyed a broader basis of support than this description suggests. It carried the sanction not only of Englishmen like Manchester who had opposed Charles I in the civil war but also that of numerous royalists in the convention parliament. The timing of that parliament is also significant. Members of the families who had played a leading role in the civil war sat beside others who were to have a profound influence in coming generations. If an Eliot sat for a Cornish borough and a Fiennes for Oxfordshire, there were likewise present an Onslow for Guildford, a Howard for Cumberland, a Stanley for Liverpool, etc. Notably absent, however, were the bishops, whose presence might have imparted a different ring to the resolution. As it was, it was long remembered. Treated as the keynote of the political restoration, the resolution was evoked by a leading member of the cavalier house of commons to counter Charles II's declaration of indulgence (1672); and a member of the convention parliament of 1689 recommended it as the appropriate foundation for that body's proceedings. The resolution also provided publicists with an authority for the potent political idea that king, lords, and commons shared the legislative power.[2]

That the wording was no accident appears from the 'act for the preservation of the king' (13 Car. 2, s.1, c.1), which the cavalier parliament passed in 1661. This was the first legislative measure of a regular parliament in Charles II's reign and the only one to define the legal nature and effect of the restoration. The product of a protracted deliberation, the act condemned as illegal the proceedings of the usurping governments and singled out for special condemnation certain opinions prevalent in the revolutionary period, among them the view 'that both houses of parliament or either house of parliament have or hath a legislative power without the king'. 'Any other words to the same effect' were equally offensive. Whoever maintained the contrary position was subject to the penalties of praemunire, that is, the loss of all property and imprisonment for life.[3] The purpose was to protect the king's role in law-making : he could not be legally and constitutionally barred from the legislative process. This was clearly a victory for the king in light of the constitutional situation during the civil war and interregnum. In the earlier period the two houses had issued ordinances of their own authority, and the king's veto had come under sustained attack although the situation had improved for him by the time of the treaty of Newport. After Charles I's death the kingship itself had disappeared, and the house of lords was abolished. Now the monarchy was back, as was the house of lords; and there would be no more ordinance-making. It followed that the king's veto was safe since the act for the king's preservation was silent on this critical point and the restoration of the monarchy was unconditional.

Yet the king's victory was by no means unalloyed. To be sure, he was a participant in the law-making process, with a free vote, but unhappily from the standpoint of the restoration court, he was no more than that. Unmistakably, the cavalier parliament had acted on the basis of the co-ordination principle: the act for the king's preservation assumed that the law-making was shared. That this was the contemporary interpretation may be seen from a critic writing in the early 1680s. Before the act was passed, he wrote, some persons held the opinion 'that both or either houses of parliament, had a legislative power without the king: since which time the like principle hath been revived, that both or either houses of parliament hath a co-ordinate power and share in the government with the king and that this is the ancient consti-tution of the government of this kingdom'.[4] In short, the point so strenuously urged in parliamentarian writings and so much resisted by royalists was now conceded without a struggle and given official sanction in a restoration statute enacted by a parlia-ment elected at the height of royalist fervor and described at times as more royalist than the king and more Anglican than the bishops.

Admittedly, the resolution of May 1 was intended to welcome back the monarchy and the house of lords, while the act for the king's preservation restored the king as an integral part of law-making. Moreover, both the convention parliament and the cavalier parliament, by making no reference to the supremacy of the two houses, seem to have turned away from the civil-war past, suggesting that a process was underway by which the co-ordination principle was shedding its more radical overtones and settling into a form more acceptable to the new political gener-ation. That this was indeed the case appears from the political vocabulary employed during the indulgence crisis of 1672–73, a subject to which it is necessary to return. But for the moment it is to be noted that just as clearly an important shift had occurred in political thought when leading members of the political nation, royalists and parliamentarians alike, could apply the co-ordin-ation principle, central to the parliamentarian ideology, to govern-ment in general and law-making in particular. One historian has recognized how bold and innovative parliamentary language was in the early 1660s, when compared with the pre-1642 mode of political expression. To Betty Kemp, the convention parliament's resolution was no recantation of civil-war doctrine. 'A statement of achievement', she wrote perceptively, 'it replaced the old unity of "king in parliament" by the new trinity of "king, lords and commons," and the replacement was perhaps only unchallenged because it was clothed in a restoration.'[5] The resolution may also have passed unchallenged because it appeared much too early for the court to assess the challenge, much less to mount an effective counter-response. That came later, beginning with the regicide trials. Nor is it altogether clear that the resolution was a statement of achievement if this implies that the two houses had acted with deliberation and self-consciousness in asserting their position. The language of mixed monarchy was now so habitual that the resolution may have seemed both traditional and unexceptional. A process that looks to an historian like a replacement may have appeared to contemporaries a restoration of the government after the breakdown of the interregnum, and this aspect of the situation would be in some ways the most disturbing for the court. Imbued with the idea of an ancient constitution that governed the distribution of political power, which had been delineated and defined by Charles I, the political nation had come to see as its central feature a legal sovereignty in king, lords, and commons. It was an idea whose time had come.[6]

## II

The court early found the desired propaganda platform for repressing the community-centered ideology in the regicide trials that began at the Old Bailey in October, 1660. The law-officers of the crown knew full well the ideological problem facing them. Sir Geoffrey Palmer, Holbourne's colleague in the Oxford parliament, was attorney general, while Heneage Finch (later earl of Nottingham and lord chancellor) was solicitor general. Palmer's position is clear, and Finch's was explicitly stated in the subsequent trial of Sir Henry Vane when he denounced the 'venomous principle of co-ordination' as contrary to the oath of allegiance.[7] The language was forthright; and he subsequently published a record of the regicide trials, in which the royal judges aired the same view of government.[8] In 1660 Holbourne was dead; but Sir Orlando Bridgeman, now lord chief baron and later lord keeper – who, with Palmer and Holbourne, was said to have condemned Charles I's definition of estates at Oxford – presided over the trials and set their tone.

Bridgeman's remarks on the kingship reflected royalist arguments, in particular those found in Sir John Spelman's *Case of our Affaires* and Judge David Jenkins' *Lex Terrae* (1647). The second of these tracts rejected what was known as the opinion of the Spencers (the Hugh Despensers of Edward II's reign), which held that the king's two bodies might be severed and, further, that allegiance was due to him more by reason of his political than his natural body. This view had provided the basis for Herle's doctrine that Charles I was virtually present with the two houses at Westminster, and this doctrine was then used to justify issuing ordinances without the king and even forcibly resisting him.[9] According to Bridgeman, no coercive force was legally justifiable against the king. He had an imperial crown, and England was an empire, as Henry VIII's act of appeals stated. Not that the king governed absolutely: clearly, he ought to rule in accordance with the fundamental laws of the land; but if he failed to do so, there was no human recourse. The contrary opinion, found in the opinion of the Spencers, had been judged horrid treason in two statutes and by Coke in *Calvin's Case*. This meant that the king's position was very high: he was immediately subject to God, from whom his power was derived, and to no other power, and was the only supreme governor within the realm. This fact was recognized in the oath of allegiance and supremacy, which under the law all who entered parliament were to take. Since the king was the only supreme governor, the result was a foregone conclusion. Bridgeman was explicit: 'That excludes co-ordination.'[10] Another argument, reminiscent of Charles I's last words on the scaffold, also ruled out the co-ordination principle. Englishmen had a right under their government to their properties, liberties, and lives but not to a share in the government itself, which belonged exclusively to the king. 'It is not the sharing of government', Bridgeman explained, 'that is for the liberty and benefit of the people; but it is how they may have their lives, liberties, and estates, safely secured under government.'[11] Aware that the rival principle was

F

rooted in Charles I's definition of estates, Bridgeman found in Coke the essential correction. The king was 'not only *caput populi*, the head of the people; but *caput reipublicae*, the head of the commonwealth, the three estates'.[12]

That he and his colleagues associated the co-ordination principle with law-making, as well as with what they called government, became unmistakable when Sir Robert Hyde, lord chief justice of king's bench, told the defendants: 'You and all, must know, that the king is above the two houses. They must propose their laws to him: the laws are made by him, and not by them, by their consenting, but they are his laws.'[13] There was no question of a shared legal sovereignty; and no validity attached to the defense advanced, for example, by Major General Harrison that their acts were committed in the name of parliament, 'which was then the supreme authority'.[14]

The regicide trials were the ideological prelude to the judicial proceedings against Vane in June, 1662, culminating in his execution. To explain the result there was twenty years' enmity to the Stuart kings, though this is by no means the whole explanation, indeed, not even its most important aspect. Imprisoned at the restoration, Vane was excepted from the act of indemnity by the two houses, who, however, petitioned the king to spare his life if he were ever attainted. Charles assented, and his word was put to the test. Proceedings began against Vane after the election of the cavalier parliament, and he demonstrated during his trial a boldness to the point of recklessness for which he would pay with his life.

These are well-known facts; but the parliamentarian's defense, which must have deeply offended the king, has been much less noticed. The assertion of the community-centered ideology, with its emphasis on the co-ordination principle, explains as much about Vane's fate as his political career. Probably even more, since he provides a prime example of Nalson's thesis that the leadership in the long parliament embraced the co-ordination principle on its first appearance and used it against Charles I. Unmistakably, the principle was known to Vane, who associated it with the Answer to the Nineteen Propositions. His familiarity with the royal declaration dated from 1642, when he was appointed to the house of commons' committee that was to reply to its preamble; and his attention was called to it once more when Baxter's *Holy Common-wealth* (written partly as a response to Vane) cited Charles I as the principal authority on the constitution. That assessment was acceptable to Vane in the altered circumstances of 1662. Charles I had exactly stated the nature of the government, Vane announced, his language reflecting the pervasiveness of the community-centered ideology. He now enunciated it in its more radical form, advancing high claims for the two houses. If each was co-ordinate with the king in law-making, together they were superior to him in this sphere and in other important aspects of the government. Charles I had recognized that laws were made by a king, a house of lords, and a house of commons, all having free votes and particular privileges. So far Vane was faithful to the Answer, but at this point the community-centered ideology, as developed by Herle, suddenly intruded. Charles was said to have added: 'These three estates making one incorporate body, are they, in whom the sovereignty and supreme power is placed, as to the making and repealing of laws.' But the power of the two houses was more extensive than this. They had been admitted to a share in administering the government when Charles accepted the measure by which the long parliament could be dissolved only with its own consent. This statute had made the king, in conjunction with the two houses, *maxime rex*. Vane now turned to the thoroughly radical *Political Catechism* (1643) – a civil-war tract based on the Answer to the Nineteen Propositions – from which he borrowed directly. The dictum emerged that the two houses, 'co-ordinate' in power and authority with the king, were to maintain the balance of the constitution. If it was necessary to prevent and restrain tyranny, they were the ones to take action, using physical force if need be.[15]

This meant that no charge of treason could be levelled against the two houses, or their agents, the more so since the two houses shared legal sovereignty with Charles I. They 'had a co-ordinancy in the supreme or legislative power for the making, altering, and repealing laws', and *'par in parem non habet imperium* [an equal has no command over his equals]'. To the contrary. The two houses might hold the king accountable. Vane's language took on civil-war overtones of an extremist nature as he called upon the quotation from Bracton and Fleta and the maxim *singulis major, universis minor* to place an outright supremacy in the two houses. He declared : 'And by authorities out of Bracton, Fleta, and others, it may appear what superiors the king himself hath, (who yet hath no peer in his kingdom – *nisi curiam baronum* [except the court of barons]), God, law, and parliament.'[16] He seemed to be arguing that the king had no peer in the kingdom except parliament (the court of barons) – that is, he was *singulis major* – but that the relationship with parliament was not actually one of equals. The parliament was the king's peer, but more than this, was his superior. Such ideas, it will be recalled, were rooted in the long parliament's declaration of November 2, 1642, and had become notorious after Bradshaw made use of them during Charles I's trial. If this were not enough, Vane also insisted that the community was the human source of political power and authority, and his language was again reminiscent of *singulis major*. The roots of government were 'in the common consent of the realm, the will of the people or whole body of the kingdom represented in parliament'.[17] Thus Vane fully repudiated the order theory of kingship, replacing it with the more radical version of co-ordination. His political heresy was complete.

This boldness led directly to his death, or so it appears from Charles II's letter to Clarendon on June 7, 1662, the day after the defense. The king had been informed, he wrote, that Vane was so insolent as to justify all he had done, 'acknowledging no supreme power in England, but a parliament : and many things to that purpose'. If this was so, he was certainly too dangerous to be allowed to live, if he could honestly be put out of the way. The lord chancellor was to ponder the matter and give Charles II an account on the following day.[18] No records seem to have survived of Clarendon's decision, which is easily surmised. One week later Vane was executed on Tower Hill under dramatic circumstances, trumpets blowing to drown out his words. The significance of the proceedings against him has been variously judged. David Ogg believes that contemporaries must have compared the parliamentarian's idealism with the Stuart perfidy that permitted Charles II to break the promise to spare Vane's life.[19] But probably the public impression was of a rather different order. Englishmen must have realized it really would not do, it was not even safe, to apply the co-ordination principle publicly to the political system, certainly not if associated overtly with the supremacy of the two houses, probably not in any form. There is evidence for this view. An anonymous diarist explained succinctly why Vane was considered a source of danger to the state :

The explanation, which in the course of his defence, he [Vane] gave of the power of the English monarchy, as it stands in the best of law books; and his asserting . . . the co-ordinate, and, in some cases, superior authority of parliament, with the uncourtly position, that all power is derived from the people, were treasons of too high a nature to be uttered with impunity.[20]

The essence of Vane's ideology, so neatly extracted by the diarist, must have been apparent to others including the king himself. It is reasonable to assume that the trial made Charles II familiar with the community-centered ideology, which was so bound up with his father's Answer to the Nineteen Propositions, if indeed he was not earlier aware of it. Whether he wholly grasped the implications for the kingship is another matter, but that he had more than an inkling of the stakes involved is strongly suggested by Vane's fate.

By this time a court campaign was underway to crush the community-centered view of government, resulting in what may properly be termed the ideological side of the restoration. The description is the more warranted because tracts from Heylyn, Tomkins, Sheringham, and Ussher were tumbling from the press, while Prynne's historical labors were undermining the co-ordination principle. His appointment as keeper of the tower records was as replete with ideological symbolism as the later appointments of Brady and Petyt. In these years the great volumes of parliamentary writs were completed, *Brevia Parliamentaria Rediviva* appearing, for example, in 1662.

The court was active on four fronts : in clamping a censorship on the press with the aim of driving out seditious political doctrines; in imposing a fixed form on enacting clauses so as to deny aid and comfort to the advocates of co-ordination; in revising the book of common prayer to make it difficult to describe the king with authority as only one of three estates in parliament; and, finally, in founding the cult of King Charles the martyr, perhaps with the hope of countering and curbing the parliamentarian versions of the Answer to the Nineteen Propositions. Add to these

activities the skillful use of the regicide trials to propagate the
order theory of kingship and the treatment meted out to Vane to
threaten whoever would evoke the community-centered view of
government in political argument, and it may be concluded that
the court was in hot pursuit of the enemy ideology.

Of the first priority in establishing the new order of things was
the censorship of the press, which came in 1662. A year later Sir
Roger L'Éstrange, the most celebrated pro-court pamphleteer of
the reign, received appointment as 'surveyor of imprimery' with
the mission of enforcing the needed regulations. The task was
congenial to him : there is no disputing his zeal for his chosen
cause. His fitness for the appointment received public demonstration with the publication of his *Considerations and Proposals
in order to the Regulation of the Press*, (1663). Not surprisingly
he referred to Vane's trial and execution, proscribing his defense
as unfit for the reading public. L'Éstrange's interest in seditious
literature did not stop here. Centering his attention on the justifi-
cations for forcible resistance to Charles I, which were said to have
led to the king's death, he found their fountain and the source
encapsulated in the single word 'co-ordination'. This was all
L'Éstrange wrote, but it was enough. The pernicious principle was
said to be nourished and sustained by the *Holy Commonwealth*,
and to Baxter was attributed this statement : 'The sovereignty
here among us is in king, lords, and commons.' The future tory
simultaneously noticed the civil-war *Parliament – Physick for a
Sin-sick Nation* (1644) with the even more radical position that
the government was 'a mixt monarchy . . . governed by the major
part of the three estates assembled in parliament'. No list of such
doctrines would be complete without materials from Herle, and
L'Éstrange was not remiss on the point. He cited *Ahab's Fall,
with a Postscript to Dr. Ferne* (1644) but without naming its
author. If he did not know the tract was Herle's, others did. From
*Ahab's Fall* had come the doctrine that the two houses of parliament shared legal sovereignty. 'The houses are not only requisite
to the acting of the power of making laws', Herle was quoted as
stating, 'but co-ordinate with his majesty in the very power of
acting.'[21]

Another means of forwarding the court-supported ideology
while undercutting its rival was found when the enacting clauses

of statutes were frozen into a mold favorable to the ideal that the king was the single law-maker in parliament. Almost overnight, such clauses, hitherto singularly fluid in expression, took on the fixed form that has endured to the present. Probably its authors were Palmer and Finch, the crown's law-officers. In any case, enacting clauses, beginning with the statute 13 Car. 2, s.2.c2, now read :

Be it enacted by the king's most excellent majesty by and with the advice and consent of the lords spiritual and temporal and the commons in this present parliament assembled and by the authority of the same.

Two changes reflected the order theory of kingship. The king was depicted as the single law-maker in parliament, the role of the two houses confined to giving advice and consent; and at the same time he was unambiguously divorced from membership in the three estates. These were the lords spiritual, the lords temporal, and the commons, the return of the bishops to the house of lords earlier in the year making the definition the more plausible.[22]

This effort was reinforced when the book of common prayer was revised. About 600 changes were made in 1662, these originating in the Canterbury convocation over which Bishop Sheldon (soon to be archbishop) presided; and it was William Sancroft, later archbishop of Canterbury but at this time chaplain to Bishop Cosin of Durham, who supervised the printing. If the church of England was the buttress of the restored monarchy, as is so often stated, no better reflection of this working partnership is to be seen than in the annexation to the revised book of common prayer of what are called the state services. Three forms of prayer and service were set forth for November 5, January 30, and May 29, the dates chosen in commemoration of the deliverance from the gunpowder plot of James I's reign, the martyrdom of King Charles, and Charles II's birthday and return to the throne. The last two were new, but not the form of prayer with thanksgiving to be used yearly on November 5. The service of November 5 now underwent revision, however; and the correction was frequently cited in conservative literature to refute the claim of co-ordination.

The new language clarified the reference to 'states' in the earlier form of the service. Whereas the rubric of the gunpowder treason service had formerly referred to 'the happy deliverance of his majesty, the queen, prince and states of parliament, from the most traitorous and bloody intended massacre by gunpowder', it now recited 'the happy deliverance of the king, and the three estates of the realm' from the intended massacre by gunpowder; and the morning prayer made it unmistakable that the three estates were 'the nobility, clergy, and commons'. Any remaining ambiguity was eliminated when another passage in the service referred to 'the three estates of this realm assembled in parliament'. Clearly the king was distinct from the three estates of parliament. As one writer noted at the end of the century, anyone who consulted the book of common prayer would know that the king was not one of the three estates, even if he had never seen a law book. And this writer added that those who cited the rival definition of estates were more interested in reading Calvin than the liturgy of the church of England.[23]

While it is impossible to state certainly who revised the service of November 5, it was probably Dr Robert Sanderson, bishop of Lincoln, whose anti-co-ordination preface to Ussher's *Power Communicated by God to the Prince* enjoyed conservative esteem. Since his name has been linked to the formulation of the prayers for January 30 and May 29, his service to the court may well have extended to the service of November 5. The conjecture is the more reasonable because Sanderson was the outstanding figure in revising the prayer book. That the state services were valued as a means of propagating the official view of the kingship received a dramatic illustration when an order in council from Charles II annexed them as a unit to the prayer book. Since Anglican clergymen, under the act of uniformity (1662), were obliged to assent to everything in the revised prayer book, they in a sense received the mission of propagating the definition of estates that it contained.[24]

Just as important was the provision for an annual sermon to commemorate Charles I's death. In addition to the state service already mentioned, a restoration statute (lasting until 1859) provided that January 30 be kept as an anniversary of humiliation. The cult of Charles the martyr provided an opportunity to elevate the official ideology at the expense of its rival. By meeting the ordeal of his trial and execution with great composure the king had laid the basis for a martyrdom unparalleled in modern England : he was dying, so he said, 'for the laws and liberties of this land and for maintaining the true Protestant religion'. Whatever else was to be forgotten of the events since 1642, those on the wintry day when the king went to his death at Whitehall were not part of them. Remembrance of things past must include the martyrdom of the best of kings, as the tories were accustomed to stating; and Charles I's execution was regarded with a horror exceeding that induced by the gunpowder plot. The cult of the martyred king was used early and late to discredit the community-centered ideology, such tories as Nalson and Hickes insisting that Charles I's death was due to the co-ordination principle and the related political idea that the community was the human source of political power and authority.[25]

## III

The powerful emotion aroused in conservative circles by the claim of co-ordination was also rooted in the politics of the present; and the conflict of rival ideologies typically surged to the forefront of restoration politics whenever the issue of who made law in parliament became prominent. That issue was likely to be present when the dispensing power was utilized to defeat statutes. Not that the dispensing power invariably excited controversy. At times it met with a minimum of fuss, even with approbation; and on a number of occasions it was evident that many members of the political nation – in no way advocates of a high royal power or even of the argument that the king was the sole law-maker in parliament – would grant the need for a power of this type. But its exercise was now deemed proper only when the two houses concurred. As this qualification reveals, attitudes towards the dispensing power differed markedly from those prevailing at the beginning of the century. It must now be exercised according to rules differing significantly from those of the sixteenth and early seventeenth centuries. 'Legality' was no longer to be determined by reference to the traditional restrictions laid down in law courts and in legal treatises, for example, the rules concerning *malum prohibitum* and *malum in se*. It was now a matter of parliamentary consensus; and if this condition were observed, the king retained a sphere within which he might dispense.

Nowhere was the necessity for statutory relaxation more apparent than in carrying out the navigation act of 1660 and its sister statutes, and nowhere was the dispensing power exercised with less controversy. Charles II frequently dispensed with these statutes during periods of national emergency such as the second and third Dutch wars. Thus a proclamation of March 22, 1665, permitted English merchants to make use of foreign ships to protect their goods from the Dutch, the suspension lasting three months.[26] The fire of London in 1666 also necessitated a relaxation of the navigation acts because rebuilding the city required prohibited commodities such as timber and glass. This particular suspension endured a full year.[27] And then there was the royal navy, its needs leading to a suspension of the navigation acts when the duke of York was authorized to import timber.[28] Similar practices were noticeable in peacetime, and a frivolous example will perhaps illustrate the point. Mindful of his personal comfort, Charles authorized the importation of two shiploads of fruit from the Levant and shipments of tea and lobsters for the royal household, the prohibitory statutes notwithstanding.[29]

It may be concluded, then, that the king had no difficulty after 1660 in exercising his power to dispense with legislation in the case of a particular person or group of persons, so long as his objectives were acceptable to the two houses. The qualification matters since dispensing power had at times a very different effect. Whenever the affected statutes were deemed critical, public objections were strongly voiced in influential quarters. Given the anti-Roman Catholic bias of these years, this usually meant statutes restricting the religious and political activities of the Roman Catholics; and Protestant dissenters were likely to fall under the same ban. Any attempt to set aside this kind of statute aroused vigorous resentment, mostly centering on the proposition that parliament was the ultimate judge of the public welfare.

Of particular interest in this connection is the political vocabulary employed in the quarrel over religious toleration that erupted on two notable occasions in Charles II's reign, in the years 1662–63 and again, at greater length and more decisively, in 1672–73. The dispensing power was at issue on both occasions, but the constitutional and ideological implications were clearer in the 1670s because the indulgence of 1672 constituted a much more

far-reaching exercise of that power. To this subject it is necessary
to return, but it is to be noted here that the use of the dispensing
power was by this time, to a surprising degree, a matter of ideology. To a modern scholar the declaration of 1672 might seem an
assertion of the king's ancient prerogative. Not so to the typical
late Stuart Englishman, who was much more likely to view the
dispensing power through an ideological prism that converted it
into the badge of a particular view of law-making. The controversy over the indulgence seemed to him ultimately a collision
between two rival ideologies, divided by very different opinions
as to law-making and, indeed, about the human source of political
authority in the state. A contemporary description might well run
on these lines. A king who was the single law-maker in parliament,
with political power and authority derived immediately from
God, might lawfully, as a matter of course, exercise the dispensing
power to set aside penal laws in religion. But the situation must be
very different if the community was treated as the human source
of political power and authority and the law-making power
assigned to king, lords, and commons. Only the trinity of law-
makers, under these circumstances, could defeat a given statute;
and the declaration of indulgence of 1672 was automatically
illegal and unconstitutional.

As opinions about law-making shaped current political vocabulary, it became customary in some quarters to refer to the
dispensing power as a menace to the law-making power residing
in king, lords, and commons. Leading Englishmen opposed the
application of the prerogative to ecclesiastical matters as opening
the way to setting aside all laws. If the king might dispense with
some laws, it was asked, why not all? And dispensing with statutes
was described as tantamount to their abrogation. The political
vocabulary was strikingly novel. The dispensing power had not
been so described in the sixteenth or early seventeenth centuries.
On the whole little interest had been displayed towards law-
making in the earlier period; and while Englishmen might recognize that the dispensing power had the effect of setting aside a
statute in a particular case, its exercise was not treated as a threat
to law-making as such. That kind of concern, rooted in civil-war
developments, was the logical corollary of the community-centered
ideology; and, specifically, it was due to the increased importance

attached to law-making and the powerful tendency to place that power in king, lords, and commons. The new political vocabulary was in evidence during the indulgence crises of Charles II's reign.

The catalyst that produced the crises was the king's attempt to grant a wide toleration to Roman Catholics and Protestant dissenters in the form of a declaration of indulgence. Two such declarations were issued, and both times a crisis ensued. Yet the declaration of 1662 looks surprisingly mild. The king was careful to convey that the toleration must rest on statute law, the dispensing power to be exercised only with parliamentary concurrence. On the other hand, the much more provocative declaration of 1672 set aside statutes hostile to the king's policy, and as a consequence his power was more deeply affected by the outcome. Another difference should be noted. In the early 1660s the king withdrew in good order, giving way to a storm in the house of commons before the house of lords was engaged. Left behind was a mélange of conflicting statements pointing to Charles II's failure to think through his constitutional position before undertaking the indulgence policy. By comparison the events of 1672–73 were much more dramatic, and the monarchy was left in a weaker position, though this time Charles II had decided in advance just what theory of the constitution he was advocating. Following the advice at crucial points of his lord chancellor, the earl of Shaftesbury, the king insisted on maintaining a high prerogative almost to the end before surrendering under humiliating circumstances to the combined objections of the two houses of parliament.

The real testing of the dispensing power came, therefore, in the indulgence crisis of 1672–73, which began during a recess of the cavalier parliament at a time when England, aligned with France, was entering a war against Holland. The declaration of indulgence, issued on March 14, 1672, suspended the penal laws and permitted Protestant dissenters to worship publicly while Roman Catholics could do so only privately.[30] After the cavalier parliament reassembled on February 4, 1673, the king took a strong line, warning: 'I shall take it very, very ill to receive contradiction in what I have done.' And he added: 'I will deal plainly with you, I am resolved to stick to my declaration.'[31] Events then waited on the house of commons, where it became immediately apparent that the passage of time had not brought acquiesence in its wake. The reading of the declaration was followed by a long and unusual silence.[32] With the growing realization that the declaration was in peril, the court's supporters tried to limit the house's response to a petition to the king, but with no success. The decision was taken, on February 10, by 168 to 116, to insist on a formal vote on the constitutional and ideological issue; and the house of commons then resolved that penal statutes in ecclesiastical matters could be suspended only by act of parliament. The chairman of the committee now named to draft the appropriate address to the king was Henry Powle, a lawyer whose political record made him a representative figure in the opposition to Charles II and James II.[33]

A lawyer-politician in Charles II's parliaments, he would be appointed to the privy council in 1678 when Charles was wooing his political enemies. Out of office in the following year, Powle was named to the Sacheverell committee of the house of commons, which was active in the Danby impeachment. This facet of Powle's career is important since that committee prepared an influential public pronouncement on the government known as the *Narrative and Reasons* (1679), in which the Answer to the Nineteen Propositions was invoked against Charles II. Though the law-making power was not at issue, it is of much interest that the Answer, so closely associated with the theory of a legal sovereignty in king, lords, and commons, should have been called so dramatically to public attention a decade before the Glorious Revolution. Moreover, many members of the Sacheverell committee were subsequently appointed to the committee of the convention house of commons that in 1689 wrote the Bill of Rights. Powle stood aside at the time of the exclusion crisis, apparently unwilling to use the legislative power to determine the line of succession to the throne; but his role became prominent once more at the Revolution. In the months preceding it he was in touch with William Bentinck, later duke of Portland and William of Orange's leading adviser. Powle was speaker of the convention house of commons and master of the rolls in the new regime. He died early in William's and Mary's reign.[34]

Powle's chairmanship of the committee appointed on February 10, 1673, is then of much interest, establishing as it does that an influential figure during the Glorious Revolution was linked as early as this with the idea of a legal sovereignty in king, lords, and commons. The Powle committee's report received the approval of the cavalier house of commons on February 14, but the failure to elicit a favorable response from Charles II led to the appointment of still another Powle committee and, on February 26, a second address, stiffer in tone than the first.[35] The tenor of the debates surrounding these addresses not only revealed the ideological temper of the house of commons but also provided an important corollary to the community-centered ideology, which had taken shape in the years when the dispensing power was outside the arena of polemics and was now, for the first time, examined within the context of the new political ideas. Not surprisingly it was found wanting in legality.

The declaration of indulgence was described during the debates as exceeding the limits of royal power and usurping a jurisdiction that belonged properly to parliament. The declaration, it was said, was tantamount to the repeal of the statutes affected and the power thus invoked lay with those who made law. This argument, presupposing a shared law-making power in parliament, was new after 1660, a fact stressed earlier in this chapter. A few examples will illustrate the manner in which the argument developed. The moderate Sir Thomas Meres claimed to have learned from books and learned persons that a general suspension of penal statutes was contrary to English law.[36] Powle's stand was similar. The indulgence was illegal and fraught with implications for the legislative power: if the king could dispense with all penal laws, he might 'dispense with all laws, with a *non obstante*'. He would grant the possibility of special cases arising where a law could not be implemented, but in others the king could not dispense. A general suspension of law was an abrogation, Powle added; and this power was parliament's. Such an abrogation had indeed taken place: Charles II's declaration had suspended some forty acts of parliament.[37]

Others would entirely deny a dispensing power to the king. From Colonel Giles Strangeways, usually a reliable court supporter, came just such a denial. He would lay down 'some *postulata* of . . . government'. There must be a legislative power in all kingdoms, and it could not exist in England without the consent of the two houses. Granted the problem of obsolete laws, still the proper way to proceed was their repeal by law, meaning apparently by statute and not prerogative. Admittedly kings possessed a 'power to dispense with the punishment, by pardon'. Yet Charles could not 'dispense with a man to be a papist, or nonconformist'.[38] Further emphasizing the legislature's superiority, Strangeways complained that the king's counsellors should have consulted with parliament about the indulgence just as the justices of the peace advised with the judges at Westminster.[39] Sir Thomas Lee agreed. What was the use of parliament but to inform the king that his privy council had misled him?[40] Granted that laws might be useful today but not tomorrow, still the judgment ought to be in parliament, the proper judge in cases of necessity. Nor would it fail to act when the occasion arose. All men would see the need for mitigation if it were sufficiently great and no parliament would question it.[41]

The terms of rejection recall the parliamentarian polemics during the civil war. Strangeway's and Lee's remarks concerning obsolete laws were compatible with the acceptance of a co-ordination in the legislative power. If parliament were the proper instrument for mitigating the law, the two houses were at least equal to the king. This partnership involved, moreover, a function which had been assigned to the king exclusively in the sixteenth and early seventeenth centuries. The co-ordination principle was also implicit in the contention that the king had no power to dispense because the legislative power was in the parliament. That is, the king had no discretionary authority with which to mitigate the rigor of the law because legal sovereignty was vested in king, lords, and commons in parliament and not in the king in parliament.

But other spokesmen took a different tack, among them the future tory leader, Sir Edward Seymour, who became not long afterwards the speaker of the house of commons. He is reported to have remarked later from the chair that laws existed only with the king's permission, but at this earlier stage in the proceedings he merely insisted, though consistently with this position, that the king might dispense with that part of a penal statute belonging to him. In the present case no man's property had been invaded. Did the house intend to bind the king's hands? If an act restrained the king's power, it was void.[42] Secretary Coventry's argument for a royal discretionary power was based on equally good law and history. The present proceedings were dangerous. What would become of them all in emergencies, Coventry asked, if the king were restrained from breaking into houses that were on fire and from invading men's properties in wartime? The house ought not to inquire into the just extent of the royal power. Like the master of a ship who had to be able to throw goods overboard during a storm, the king must have a dispensing power or else be obliged to put the penal laws into execution.[43] Attorney-General Finch likewise spoke for the court. There was no question of the king's dispensing power whenever the forfeiture was his own. Moreover, the problem at hand was not one of repeal, as Charles' opponents seemed to believe. The king had simply suspended particular statutes to secure peace : surely he could dispense with laws for the preservation of the kingdom. It was the king, moreover, who was the judge of necessity.[44]

Statements such as these, eminently acceptable earlier in the century to even the more radical members of parliament, were out of place in the changed atmosphere of the 1670s. Much more congenial was the Powle committee's address that was read on February 14. Repeating the resolution approved four days earlier by the house of commons, the committee insisted on the illegality of the indulgence while calling on Charles to surrender his religious policy to parliamentary control. Penal statutes in ecclesiastical matters could not be legally suspended except by act of parliament. The address was accepted without a division, and provision was made for sending it on to Charles II.[45] But the constitutional crisis was by no means over. It entered a new phase with the king's response on February 24 when, tactful but firm, Charles II clung tenaciously to his position. He had advanced no claim opposed to his subjects' rights, properties, and liberties, nor had any thoughts been entertained of avoiding or precluding parliamentary advice. His design was only to remove the statutory penalties on dissenters, an action, Charles II implied, that would be acceptable to the house after further deliberation. But the gains made by this display of tact were erased by the king's insistence on his power in ecclesiastical matters. The prerogative at issue had never been questioned in preceding reigns.[46]

On February 26, the cavalier house of commons approved a

second address to the king, this one prepared by the second Powle committee; and on the following day it was sent to the king. Carefully defining the issue, this second address contained the unequivocal pronouncement that the legislative power, a shared power, was superior to the dispensing power. As for the point that the dispensing power had never been questioned in earlier reigns, it cried out for correction. The king's predecessors had never claimed or exercised this power and once admitted it might alter the legislative power. The second Powle committee's position was crystal clear: '[This power] if it should be admitted, might tend to the interrupting of the free course of the laws, and altering the legislative power, which hath always been acknowledged to reside in your majesty, and your two houses of parliament'.[47]

So provocative a pronouncement on the legislative power was bound to arouse objections from members whose interpretation ran on more traditional lines. Foremost among them was Attorney-General Finch, who rejected out of hand the proposition that the legislative power was in the king and the two houses. His correction was based on the order theory of kingship. He would grant that the king legislated in parliament; but when all was said and done, he was the one who made law – '*rex solus non si solus* [the king solely is legislator, but not the king alone]'. This could be proved from enacting clauses in the statutes predating Henry IV (1399–1413), that king's reign being a dividing line. Having received the crown as a result of Richard II's deposition, Henry IV was noticeably weaker than his predecessors. Finch thought it apparent from the earlier enacting clauses that the two houses had no share in the royal sovereignty. They were seldom mentioned, and the change in enacting clauses after Henry IV's accession was due to his holding the crown from parliament.[48]

This stand is by no means remarkable. What is striking is the expression of the contrary opinion among members of the government. So typical a conservative as Solicitor-General Francis North, found in the suspension of statutes a tendency 'to alter the legislative power in king, lords, and commons'.[49] Little wonder that conservative writers expressed astonishment at the casual manner in which the men of the long robe accepted a definition of estates that included the king.[50] Agreement with North came from John Swinfen, a member of the second Powle committee. His steady support of toleration made his hostility towards the indulgence the more significant. Swinfen would grant that the nature of the legislature was a matter of much controversy, in his phrase 'a tender point'; and he too discerned in enacting clauses the evidence required for settling the controversy. Unlike Finch, however, he concluded that 'the united authority' in statutes flowed 'from the three estates', that is, from king, lords, and commons. Chiding Finch for placing the legislative power only in the king, Swinfen, who had sat in the convention parliament of 1660, called to mind its vote to restore Charles II when it declared that 'the legislative power resides in king, lords, and commons'.[51]

These remarks mirrored the prevailing sentiment in the house of commons, and the memorable vote was taken on February 26 to accept without change the second Powle committee's report. A vote of 180 to 77 declared the action unanimous.[52] It would be difficult to overstate its significance. A majority of the cavalier house of commons had agreed that Charles II lacked the power to dispense with ecclesiastical penal laws. As one law-maker among three, he only shared the legislative power with the two houses; and as such he was in no position to undo the work to which all three had contributed. Despite the absence of the term 'co-ordination' from the recorded debates, it must surely have been familiar to the speakers. The close relationship between that principle and the constitutional position of the cavalier house of commons was stressed by Shaftesbury, at the time lord chancellor and a leading member of the cabal. In pointing to this intellectual relationship he spoke for Charles II, and their perception of the point at issue must have been shared by the cavalier house of commons even if it preferred a less radical political vocabulary.

As important as Shaftesbury's statement was the occasion for making it. His remarks formed part of Charles II's strenuous if belated attempt to reverse the tide of opinion. The strategy adopted was to appeal to the house of lords, by-passed in the proceedings to this point, to offset the position assumed by the house of commons in the address of February 26. Charles II was following Shaftesbury's advice. The king's own inclination was to seek the money bill from the house of commons needed to outfit a fleet in support of the French, even if the dispensing power was allowed to go by default. Shaftesbury persuaded the king to hold out for both the desired revenue and the high prerogative on which the declaration of indulgence rested. Urging that the house of lords would stand by the king, he noted that referral of the issue to the peers would provide time for supply to be granted before the constitutional question was settled.[53] By accepting this advice Charles II made himself party to an open appeal to the house of lords against the house of commons on the central question of who made law. The king and his brother, the duke of York, were even present when the peers were asked to reverse the verdict that had come from the house of commons.

The constitutional issue had penetrated to the center of restoration politics when first Charles II and then Shaftesbury addressed the house of lords on March 1, 1673. After complaining about the two addresses from the house of commons the king commanded Shaftesbury to acquaint the peers with the transactions to this point, saying: 'I am sensible for what relates to me; and I assure you, my lords, I am not less so for your privileges and the honour of this house.' Shaftesbury then read the two addresses as the preliminary to discussing the king's proceedings in relationship to them.[54] It was soon apparent that no prospect of an accommodation was being entertained. The indulgence was legal and constitutional and to claim otherwise was to invoke the co-ordination principle that had wreaked such havoc in the civil-war years – this was the thrust of the remarks now made. Calling attention to the key sentence in the address of February 26, in which the legislative power was said to reside in the king and the two houses of parliament, Shaftesbury attacked. This wording implied 'a co-ordination of the three estates' of parliament, in which the king was reduced to being merely one of three. 'I am commanded', he continued, 'to open to you what foundation this co-ordination laid for the late war.' It had 'produced the ordinances which were the cause of it'. Here was a theory that the civil war was due essentially to a quarrel over legal sovereignty between Charles I and the long parliament. Given the events of 1642, the analysis has some validity, but its significance is of another kind. To have employed this political vocabulary at all reveals an ever-present awareness in the court of the implications of the co-ordination principle for the kingship. What aspect of the principle made it unacceptable? Shaftesbury was helpful: it assumed that the two houses were equal to the king in law-making and must, therefore, be rejected. Since the king's sanction converted a measure into law, he alone made law; and no claim was possible that the two houses shared the legislative power on equal terms with him. What else could Shaftesbury have meant when he asserted : 'Co-ordination [which he had just condemned] makes the two houses equal with his majesty in the legislature, whereas the sanction of laws is in the king alone'.[55] With this extraordinary statement, Charles II, speaking through his lord chancellor in the house of lords, laid claim to being the only law-maker in parliament – so much is clear from Shaftesbury's language. This claim justified the declaration of indulgence if it could be made good. To strengthen his own position and to isolate the house of commons, Charles II had charged it with championing the co-ordination principle in the address of February 26, apparently assuming that this language would deter the peers from lining up with the house of commons. The bid for the peers' support was bold, and to it the king added, on March 3, a personal appeal : 'I will always be very affectionate to you', he stated to the peers, 'and I expect you shall stand by me, as I will always by you.'[56]

The king gambled; but despite Shaftesbury's assurances, he lost. The house of lords may have been more moved by religious considerations than the house of commons, but the issue to which the peers addressed themselves was constitutional and ideological. Their response on March 4, despite the soft language in which it was couched, was unmistakable. The proper and natural course for settling 'the points now controverted' was to leave them 'to a parliamentary way by bill'. In the peers' opinion, an answer of this kind from the king would be 'good and gracious'.[57] Only a few sentences were involved, but the response meant that no matter how much the peers disliked and abhorred a course that had been labelled as one of 'co-ordination', they preferred it to abandoning the position that the cavalier house of commons had taken up. On the most important constitutional and ideological question of the Stuart century – that of who makes law in parliament – the peers voted that the primary function of their house was to make laws co-ordinately with the king and the house of commons, not to act as a shield to the crown when the house of commons was charged with overstepping the limits of the constitution. The house of lords, equally with the house of commons, had committed itself publicly and formally to the proposition that the legislative power was in king, lords, and commons. It was to contemporaries an obvious conclusion from what had happened. If Charles II was in fact the only law-maker in parliament, as he and Shaftesbury had asserted, there was no need to abandon the declaration of indulgence for a bill. Whoever made law could dispense with it, so went contemporary reasoning. If Charles II ought not to dispense with penal statutes in ecclesiastical matters but would be well-advised to proceed in a parliamentary way by bill, then the king was not the sole law-maker in parliament; and the legislative power was shared. No other conclusion was possible in light of what had transpired, as both Charles and Shaftesbury recognized. Faced with the unity of the two houses, the king admitted defeat four days after the peers' response when, on March 8, he withdrew the controversial declaration of indulgence, causing the great seal to be torn from it. Before the month was out the first test act was law, and the humiliation of the Stuart monarchy was complete.[58]

The withdrawal of the declaration of indulgence has been described with justification as the most striking surrender ever made by the Stuart kings.[59] Despite an explicit royal appeal, the peers had supported the house of commons on the question of the legislative power; and the withdrawal of the declaration seemed to signify Charles II's acceptance of their interpretation. Faced by the two houses united in support of a particular view of the legislative power, the king had retreated; and this fact, as much as any other that may be adduced, explains why James II's resumption of the indulgence policy in the late 1680s aroused indignation and resentment. Englishmen familiar with the indulgence controversy of 1672–73 could be forgiven for concluding that the constitutional issue involved in the independent exercise of the dispensing power in ecclesiastical matters had been thoroughly threshed out and completely settled here with the final decision against the king. They would have viewed a broad exercise of that power, on the scale of 1672, as simply out of the question. There may well have been all kinds of political facts in the 1670s on which Englishmen differed; but to those mindful of the events of February and early March, 1673, and willing to take the lead supplied by the two houses, the nature of the legislative power was not one of them. The forthright statement in the second Powle committee's address had been accepted by both houses and ratified by Charles II's acquiesence. As a definitive judgment on a substantive matter, the sequence of events had an authority only less than that of a statute. That came in 1689.

One side effect of the episode requires mention. The dramatic scenes in the house of lords, to which the duke of York was a personal witness, could only have left him with a strong sense that the monarchy had been dealt a crippling blow. Even more than Charles II, he must have interpreted the conflict as a struggle between the order theory of kingship and the community-centered view of government. Perhaps the observation sounds strange in light of James' powerful interest in religious toleration, which makes it unlikely that he was as concerned about ideology as the failure of the indulgence policy. But he was at least as interested in the position of the monarchy, and he was keenly aware of the political implications of the struggle over the declaration of indulgence and the subsequent passage of the test acts of 1673 and 1678, which barred Roman Catholics from political office under the crown and from sitting in parliament. According to J. R. Jones, James 'believed that the test acts had been the work of the politically factious who, on the pretence of defending Protestantism, had diminished the power of the crown by restricting the sovereign's choice of ministers and officers'. To him the tests were an invasion of the prerogative.[60]

His interpretation of the indulgence controversy similarly ran on legal and constitutional lines, at least in part. A comment in the semi-authoritative *Life* suggests the depth of James' bitterness with regard to the outcome in 1673. Referring to the manner in which Shaftesbury first upheld the prerogative and then afterwards became the most envenomed enemy to Charles II and the duke of York, his biographer wrote: 'As to his [Shaftesbury's] last change some thing might be said for his excuse, that he deserted not the king till his majesty deserted himself by recalling the declaration for liberty of conscience; so that finding he could not be supported at Whitehall, he was resolved to seek it [support] at Westminster.'[61] Another observer commented on advisers who encouraged James, after he became king, to rest a policy of religious toleration on his dispensing power rather than on parliament. Harking back to Charles II's indulgence policy, these advisers referred scathingly to his unpardonable error in consulting the two houses about the validity of the dispensing power. He had given them 'a title to interpose in a branch of prerogative which was inherent in the crown and independent of them'.[62] Not surprisingly, the year 1673 saw one of the few occasions when James seriously contemplated a military coup as a means of restoring royal authority.[63]

In short, the constitutional and ideological factor was very much in evidence whenever the later Stuart kings considered a religious toleration based on the dispensing power. Admittedly, much of the opposition flowed from religious fervor. Whatever the willingness to grant relief to Protestant dissenters, it did not extend to Roman Catholics; and the fear of popery guaranteed that the declaration of indulgence would be wholly unacceptable to most members of the political nation. Indeed, it might be argued that had Charles II refrained from using the dispensing power in this particular way, it would have remained non-controversial. But this is unlikely. As has been seen, opposition to that power in 1673 was by no means purely religious but was founded as well in the belief that its exercise violated existing constitutional arrangements. While taking expressions of opinion at face value is risky, there seems to have been no pressing reason for Englishmen to couch religious objections in a constitutional guise at this juncture of their history. After all, no shame or opprobrium attached to arguments based on a dislike of Roman Catholicism; in fact, as the popish plot later revealed, arguments of this type might well be the means of attaining popularity and building a political career. Clearly, then, opposition to a royal toleration went beyond religious considerations. Both houses had opposed the royal indulgence policy as contrary to their view of the constitution; and they had done so on the ground that law-making, the highest act of sovereignty, resided in king, lords, and commons in parliament. Their ideological case was that Charles II had no legal or constitutional power to dispense with a statute because he was not the sole law-maker in parliament. Granting the need for a discretionary authority somewhere in the government, a few speakers implied that such a power resided in parliament, but not in the king alone. In other words, parliament was possessed of *gubernaculum*.

Certainly no recorded speaker explicitly rejected the order theory of kingship and substituted the community-centered view of government. But the commons had come sufficiently close to adopting the co-ordination principle for Shaftesbury to consider a charge to this effect creditable, as did Charles II. If that particular principle were present, the idea that the community constituted the human source of political power and authority was not far distant. The co-ordination principle as applied to the legislative power had been consistently linked in civil-war controversial writing with the assertion that the community was the human source of political authority. As one of Herle's associates put it, 'God's ordination is conveyed to the particular magistrate by the consent of the community',[64] and the contention was a commonplace in Charles II's reign. As was earlier pointed out, Locke, writing in the early 1660s, noticed the progress being made by the parliamentarian formula,[65] and it was in active use during the exclusion crisis in political literature and in parliament.[66] Exemplifying the trend is the anonymous *Dialogue at Oxford between a Tutor and a Gentleman, formerly his Pupil, concerning Government* (1681), which summarized succinctly the two divergent views of society and kingship prevalent in late Stuart England.[67] The influence of this tract is apparent. Singled out for attack by George Hickes, the high tory controversialist, it was important enough to be in the private libraries of the two leading whig theorists – Locke and Petyt.[68]

## IV

Much attention has been appropriately devoted to the indulgence controversy of the early 1670s and the whig attempts to exclude the duke of York from the throne; but no less significant for the kingship, if less traumatic in its effects, was the systematic attempt to circumscribe royal authority that was present whenever parliament altered the wording of statutes with the aim of limiting the dispensing power. The procedure, which reflected the theory of a legal sovereignty in king, lords, and commons, was applied both to ecclesiastical and non-ecclesiastical matters and was in evidence when the two houses departed from traditional statutory forms and employed an uncommon wording to render a particular statute non-dispensable. As early as 1666 an obvious attempt was made to limit the dispensing power in this way during the passage of the Irish cattle bill. This measure, which prohibited the importation of Irish cattle, was prompted by fear lest competition ruin the country gentry of England's northern and western counties and Wales. Not trusting Charles to execute the law, the house of commons labeled the importation of Irish cattle a nuisance with the intention thereby of circumventing the dispensing power. The king could not dispense with a nuisance since it was presumed to be of interest to the subject.

The attack upon the dispensing power gave rise to a protracted struggle between the two houses when the peers insisted on removing the word 'nuisance' from the measure. It ended only when Charles II asked the peers to withdraw their opposition; and enough of them, including the duke of York, stayed away from the third reading in the house of lords for the measure to become law. The adamantine manner in which the peers resisted the house of commons on this occasion perhaps explains Shaftesbury's subsequent willingness to turn to the lords as a counterweight to the commons in the later indulgence controversy. In any event, the history of the Irish cattle bill reveals that the dispensing power was subjected to a sustained and ultimately successful assault on the part of a house of commons that was resolved to have its own way without regard for any damage to the dispensing power.[69]

What happened is quickly recounted. The Irish cattle bill passed the house of commons in the fall of 1666, though not without difficulty, as a few members voiced doubt about including the word 'nuisance'. But the house voted, 165 to 104, on October 13, to pass the bill with the offending term; and two days later Seymour carried it up to the house of lords. There it encountered much hostility; and the ensuing debate was disorderly, indeed unparalleled, it was said, since the expulsion of the bishops in 1642.[70] To some peers the measure was wholly unacceptable because of the clauses derogatory to the prerogative, and many thought it disrespectful to the king even to admit them into debate. The word 'nuisance' was particularly objected to as constituting a precedent that might be used thereafter to prevent the king from dispensing with statutes.[71] But the peers would accept the bill if the objectionable clauses were discarded. The sense of the house was 'that it might have no other style than had been accustomed in all the penal acts of parliament which were in force, it being ... presumed that the king would never dispense with any violation of it, except in such cases as the benefit and good of the kingdom required it'.[72] A few peers took a different stand, conspicuous among them the duke of Buckingham and Lord Ashley (later the earl of Shaftesbury). The latter was nothing if not inconsistent with regard to the dispensing power. Buckingham and Ashley were determined to retain the word 'nuisance' : in the absence of this language, given the king's well-known inclination to protect Irish trade, the measure was tantamount to none at all. It was also said that the house of commons was the fittest judge of the people's necessities and grievances. The unwillingness to trust Charles II with a dispensing power where Irish cattle were involved drew from one observer the stinging comment that such a derogation of the king's honor and his prerogative had been heard in the lords only in time of rebellion.[73]

Attention soon centered on making the language less offensive. Ashley proposed, for example, that the statute be rendered nondispensable by labeling the importation of Irish cattle a 'felony' or 'praemunire', drawing from Clarendon the sarcastic retort that the action might as reasonably be called adultery. The decision was finally taken to substitute for 'nuisance' the words 'detriment and mischief' with the idea that this language had no legal standing and would not be interpreted, therefore, as derogating the prerogative.[74]

But the house of commons was opposed to the change and proved equally adamant when the peers proposed another alternative to the 'nuisance' clause. This was to proceed by way of a petition to Charles II not to dispense with the Irish cattle bill. The new proposal was defeated on January 4, 1667, by a vote of 116 to 58; and the deadlock between the two houses was complete. It was broken when the king, concerned as usual about supply, which was threatened by the developing crisis, and fearful of other tactics envisaged by the house of commons for getting its way, sent the duke of York to ask the peers to yield. The Irish cattle bill passed the house of lords ten days later, on January

14, 1667, the final version proscribing the importation of Irish cattle as a 'public and common nuisance'. The house of lords had given way with deep reluctance, and eight peers registered a protest asserting that the house of commons had designed the word 'nuisance' to restrain and limit a just and necessary prerogative that was inherent in the crown for the good and safety of subjects.[75]

One other feature in the bill is of analogous interest. The penalty levied for an offense against the statute was seizure of the imported cattle, one half of it assigned to the poor in the parish where the seizure occurred and one half to the person who seized the cattle. No part of the penalty accrued to the king.[76] It was a highly unusual division. The customary practice was to divide the penalty between king and informer although on occasion it might be shared with the poor in the community where the offense was committed.[77] The failure to grant the king a specific financial interest in the statute was no accident but rather a means of shutting out his dispensing power. In abandoning the usual wording of penal statutes, the house of commons intended, so one historian wrote, 'to take no notice of that branch of the royal prerogative . . . fearing that his majesty might abate his part of the forfeiture, and indulge a reasonable liberty to his own subjects in that part of his dominions'. Its members, accordingly, had 'divided the penalties, assigning one half to the informer, and the other to the parish where the goods were taken'.[78]

This policy, once undertaken, was steadily pursued in subsequent measures dealing with Irish cattle. Although the duration of the act of 1667 was set at seven years, the difficulties of enforcement led in 1668 to another measure designed to implement the terms of the earlier statute, and once more the financial interest of the king was ignored. Whenever a port official failed to seize imported Irish cattle, he was to be fined £100, the whole sum to be assigned to the house of correction in the particular county. Moreover, the ships that carried the cattle were to be seized and sold, with one half the proceeds going to the poor in the parish and the other half to the informer who brought the action.[79] In 1680, still a third statute dealing with Irish cattle was passed. It renewed the statute of 1667 and declared it 'continued forever'. As with the first and subsequent measure, no part of the penalty went to the king.[80] The passage of the statute of 1680 occasioned little debate, so far had the two houses come from the scenes over the Irish cattle act of 1667.

Valuable testimony to the purpose underlying this activity was supplied by Serjeant John Maynard, who addressed himself briefly to the question of Irish cattle in April, 1679, at a time when the popish plot dominated the parliamentary scene. He summarized the approach that had been taken when he stated that if the importation of Irish cattle was a 'nuisance', the king could not legally dispense with it. Properly a nuisance was *malum in se*; and the king, in Maynard's words, might 'not pardon the thing when it is done, nor dispense with the doing it'.[81] As has been seen, the same result could be achieved by not dividing penalties between the king and the informer; and it may be concluded that by these departures from customary practice, post-1660 legislators had made doubly certain that the dispensing power would not be applied to Irish cattle.

Thus opponents of the dispensing power devised in Charles II's reign novel methods of limiting it. In effect, they cramped the absolute prerogative by distorting the traditional rules that defined the conditions under which the king might disregard positive law; and they did this by expanding the concept of the community's interest to include *gubernaculum*, that is, affairs of government such as the importation of Irish cattle. This approach was adopted at other times, too, notably in the *habeas corpus* act of 1679 and in the test acts of 1673 and 1678; and the practice continued even after the Glorious Revolution.[82] Such tactics, suggesting that the two houses shared with the king a responsibility for the public welfare, make possible the insistence that the ideological and political climate differed in cardinal respects from that of sixteenth and early seventeenth-century England, where it is difficult to conceive of their being employed.

By the end of Charles II's reign a substantial majority of the political nation had abandoned the order theory of kingship for the community-centered view of government. The attitude displayed consistently and stubbornly by the political nation, acting through parliament, was one of insisting that the two houses, because they shared the legislative power, might legally deny the free use of the dispensing power to the king both in ecclesiastical matters, as in 1673, and in non-ecclesiastical matters, as in the Irish cattle bills enacted between 1667 and 1680. Despite the absence of explicit references to co-ordination in the surviving parliamentary records, it was as if the cavalier parliament had stated that there was such a principle in the legislative power. Moreover, about the same time, speakers in the second exclusion parliament (October 7, 1679 – January 18, 1681) repeatedly expressed the idea that the legislative power was shared and referred to the overriding power of parliament in dealing with the succession to the throne.[83] The community was also described as the human source of political authority, the parliamentarian formula to this effect being explicitly evoked in an exclusion speech in the house of lords.[84]

This pattern of political thought, displayed repeatedly over a long period of time, can hardly have been submerged by the monarchical sentiment flowing out of the exclusion crisis. Indeed, at virtually the same time as Charles II's triumph over the whigs, there came the carefully formulated and coherent common-law argument with which Petyt reinforced his party's deeply held conviction that a co-ordination in the law-making power was the prime principle in the government. His writings played a conspicuous role in the political literature of the exclusion crisis, to which it is helpful now to turn.

# 7

## Co-ordination and coevality in exclusion literature

### I

The whig attempt to bar the duke of York from the throne combined with the lapse of censorship in 1679 to let loose a veritable flood of tracts, their number and variety unmatched since the civil war. Running through exclusion literature were the civil-war ideologies so noticeable earlier in the century. New tracts were written on the lines charted by Herle and Hunton; and although the *Fuller Answer* was not reprinted, the co-ordination principle was patently in the mainstream of political thought. Hunton's *Treatise of Monarchie* appeared in new editions, in 1679 and 1680, and the Answer to the Nineteen Propositions continued to work its old magic. It became readily available once more with the publication of Charles I's collected works in two editions (1662 and 1687), and the *Political Catechism,* based squarely on the Answer, was reprinted in 1679. That tract was frequently noticed in contemporary literature; and as late as March, 1683, copies were discovered at the Crown and Angel tavern that Titus Oates and his friends frequented.[1] Equally to the point was the republication in 1679 and again in 1685 of the Parker society's papers on the antiquity of parliament, that work providing an intellectual mainstay for an immemorial house of commons.

Anti-co-ordination forces were just as zealous. Heylyn's *Stumbling-block of Disobedience* was reprinted in the clergyman's collected writings, this time with a subtitle drawn from the body of the work. Whereas it was initially named *The Stumbling-block of Disobedience and Rebellion Cunningly laid by Calvin in the Subjects Way, Discovered, Censured, and Removed,* the revised title read *The Stumbling-block of Disobedience and Rebellion, Proving the Kingly Power to be neither Co-ordinate with nor*

*Subordinate to any other upon Earth* – a small but significant change. Also conspicuous on the scene was the *Freeholders Grand Inquest*, as well as such other earlier anti-co-ordination tracts as those written by Jenkins, Sheringham, Ussher, and John Maxwell, bishop of Tuam. Maxwell's *Sacro-Sancta* (1644) was reprinted in 1680 with a dedication to Ormonde, the cavalier duke governing Ireland for Charles II. Such tracts as these were familiar to Dr Brady – the acknowledged leader of the tory historians in the early 1680s and the greatest historical talent on the side of the court – who cited both *Sacro-Sancta* and the *Stumbling-block of Disobedience* in his own writings.[2] To the swelling volume of anti-co-ordination political literature he now made a distinctive contribution when, taking up Prynne's lead, he launched a massive assault on the idea that the house of commons was coeval with the king and house of lords. This was the aspect of his scholarship that so frightened the whigs. For if no coevality marked the relationships of king, lords, and commons, how was it possible to insist on a co-ordination in law-making? And if there was no co-ordination in that process, how could it be said that king, lords, and commons shared legal and political sovereignty on equal terms? These considerations, centering on the legislative power, explain contemporary interest in the antiquity of the house of commons and justify what may seem at times an inordinate amount of attention in the following pages to the Brady controversy.

## II

The controversy began with the publication of William Petyt's *Antient Right* (1680). This tract, reflecting the community-centered view of government, requires extended consideration; but it should be noted here that it was a full-scale argument of unprecedented scope on behalf of an immemorlial house of commons, a house rendered independent of the king and the house of lords by the workings of prescription. Since legal coevality for the house of commons with the king and the house of lords led straight to a legal sovereignty in king, lords, and commons, Petyt was bold to the point of recklessness in making his *Antient Right* public. But he was not alone in defying the court, although his was clearly the most important of the anti-court tracts now published. Before the year was out his pupil and disciple, William Atwood, later chief justice of New York, published his *Jani Anglorum Facies Nova.*[3]

These two tracts drew into the political arena the formidable forensic talents of Dr Brady, court physician, master of Caius College, Cambridge, and doyen of the tory historians whose researches benefited from the patronage of Charles II and James II. This was extended even before Brady's reputation was made, literally overnight, with his celebrated *Full and Clear Answer to a Book lately written by Mr. Petyt* (1681), which was reprinted in the collection of Brady's tracts known as *An Introduction to the Old English History* (1684). There followed the first volume of the *Complete History* (1685), dedicated to James II. These researches, as in Prynne's case, harbored a distinctive political message with which contemporaries had to reckon, one so service-able to the court as to lead to the tory's appointment in 1686 as keeper of the tower records.[4] Brady's writings were substantially completed with the post-Revolution publication of his *Historical Treatise of Cities, and Burghs or Boroughs* (1690), which went through numerous editions in the eighteenth century.

His view of legal sovereignty was at the opposite pole from Petyt's. The high tory wrote to advance two distinct but interre-lated propositions : (1) that the Norman conquest provided an unusually striking illustration of the extremely important fact that William I and his immediate successors were the human source of the law in a period of time long before legal memory began; and (2) that legal sovereignty resided in the Stuart kings of Brady's own day because the Norman kings, before legal memory began, had wielded the law-making power by themselves, in no way sharing it with either the lords or commons. This was Brady's meaning in writing that his *Complete History* contained 'a clear demonstration, that all the liberties and privileges the people can pretend to [including a limited role in law-making], were the grants and concessions of the kings of this nation, and were derived from the crown'.[5] If these propositions held good, the supporters of the common-law argument for early parliaments must abandon their view that England was a mixed monarchy, in which legal sovereignty resided in king, lords, and commons. For the whig writers only one response was possible. Their mounting concern with regard to the law-making power made them treat Brady and writers like him as men of modern and arbitrary principles who would establish a despotism modelled on the French example. Tyrrell could see no other design in those who had written 'so highly against the antiquity of parliament, and especially of the house of commons . . . but to give a just pretence to some arbitrary prince . . . to reduce our mixed and limited monarchy into the like absolute and despotic tyranny that is now exercised in France'.[6]

The main lines of the controversy are in a variety of tracts[7] although Petyt himself was soon out of it for reasons that can only be conjectured. Whether he became discouraged by the court's hostility towards his party or was actually sidelined by the court is not clear. What is clear is that he wrote only a short tract to answer Brady and then fell silent,[8] leaving the field of historical writing to his antagonist. Brady considered that his own case for a legal sovereignty in the crown depended upon destroying the common-law argument for an immemorial house of commons. This kind of writer, he noted indignantly, traced the origin and authority of government to the electors of the house of commons, who were told of their power to set up and pull down governments at will, the common law having 'invested them with uncontrollable privileges and sacred rights'.[9] But these propositions would have to be abandoned and the authority of that house derived from the king if Brady could demonstrate that the knights were summoned for the first time in 1265 and the citizens and burgesses on a regular basis not until a generation later. According to one whig writer, Brady had drawn a scurvy pedigree for the house of commons by showing that it was added only in Henry III's reign. The effect was to make of that house an upstart authority, created by the king.[10] If subordination and not co-ordination characterized this set of relationships, the first casualty must be the theory of a legal sovereignty in king, lords, and commons, this on Petyt's own premises.

That Brady's reasoning ran on such lines appears from his repeated criticisms of prescription as a governing principle in popular politics. His *Answer to Petyt* condemned out of hand two sorts of turbulent men 'who under plausible pretences have appeared for the liberty of the people, or indeed the change of the government'. One sort preached that all power and government

G

had originated with the people so the king was only their servant, accountable for maladministration to the point of deposition and even death. Another sort of turbulent men, of whom Petyt was chief, worked for the same ends when they held forth to the people 'ancient rights and privileges, which they have found out in records, and histories, in charters, and other monuments of antiquity' and taught them to 'prescribe' against the government for many things they miscalled fundamental rights.[11] Chief among them, it may be premised, was the right to representation in parliament. Brady's dislike of prescription as the basis for parliamentary representation was likewise displayed in his *Historical Treatise of Cities*, which was plainly indebted on key points to Prynne although the two polemists were by no means always in agreement. The subtitle revealed Brady's aim of establishing the origins of cities and boroughs and the source from which their liberties, privileges, and immunities were derived. That source was none other than royal charters: the authority of which cities and boroughs boasted in his day flowed initially from the bounty of early English kings and their successors, notwithstanding any other confirmations or acquired rights. Certainly no claim was possible that prescription constituted such a source, not when there were written records to the contrary. In his words, 'Prescription, and pretended immemorial customs or usages avail not, when there are charters or other records which show, that in this case . . . they are mere conjectures.' Brady reported that his interpretation was rare. Earlier accounts of cities and boroughs revealed 'little else but prescription, and pretended usage and possession time out of mind, vouched for the great independent rights they have claimed'. The agreement with Prynne is unmistakable: the principal enemy within the gates was the common-law argument for early parliaments. Brady borrowed directly from *Brevia Parliamentaria Rediviva* and referred explicitly in another passage to that tract.[12]

The ground-breaking tracts of the 1650s and 1660s were equally well-known to Petyt, who referred to them in his own printed works. That he was familiar with, and deeply disturbed by the *Register of Parliamentary Writs*, studying carefully, for example, *Brevia Parliamentaria Rediviva*, appears from the Petyt manuscripts in the Inner Temple Library. As an antiquary, he took much interest in historical records such as the rolls of parliament and chancery records, but the persistence displayed in seeking out parliamentary writs unknown to Prynne was equally due to his ideological zeal. His concern deepened with the publications of Sir William Dugdale, another historian of the Brady school. In Dugdale's opinion the social and political conditions created by feudalism made a house of commons unlikely before 49 H.3, and his discussion was the more provocative because he attributed the extant writ of summons of 1265 to Simon de Montfort.[13] The house of commons was not only a late arrival at Westminster, its coming was due to a baronial revolt against a lawful king. The description was resented as a slur on the good name of the house, but the sense of outrage was insufficient to compel Petyt to make public his own researches; and the publication of the *Antient Right*, when it came, was sparked by the reappearance of the *Freeholders Grand Inquest*. A passage particularly troubling to Petyt was the one belittling the role of the house of commons in the national councils of the kingdom with the statement that it was not called 'to have any part of the legislative power'.[14] The blow was too great to be endured in silence, and the champion of a shared law-making power now made his own views known.

### III

The *Antient Right* struck, undeniably, a strongly sympathetic chord in late Stuart England. In all probability the most influential piece of political writing made public in the decade ending with the Glorious Revolution, its influence was due to Petyt's systematic use of common-law concepts in relationship to early English history. The tract was in three parts : a 'Preface', a 'Discourse', and an 'Appendix', the first two containing the main lines of the common-law argument for early parliaments. The central essay was the 'Discourse',[15] aimed primarily at Prynne, to which Petyt had devoted several years of effort prior to publication, whereas the 'Preface' was a hastier product, put together in an alarmed response to the republished *Freeholders Grand Inquest*. That his house of commons was from its inception an active participant in the law-making process was evident from the tract as a whole, but beyond this the 'Discourse' and the

'Preface' had certain distinctive themes reflecting Petyt's common-law background and the community-centered view of government. Thus the argument in the 'Discourse' placed the founding of the house of commons in the period before 1189 so that 'the commons of England [were] ever an essential part of parliament',[16] while the 'Preface' furnished the requisite corollary that the house of commons, once established, had steadily and continuously shared the law-making power. These points permitted the vital conclusion that prescription had made the Stuart house of commons a fitting partner with the king and house of lords in sharing legal sovereignty. King, lords, and commons were coeval and therefore co-ordinate. Two consequential tests had been met. The house of commons was founded before the time of legal memory; and once it was in being, customary usage and enjoyment had governed the practice of representation. That is, the house of commons was the place where the commons of England – the boroughs and counties – had exercised regularly through the centuries their ancient right to representation in parliament.

But what about the Norman conquest? Did it not stand in the way of this conclusion? How could one urge that the house of commons was coeval when 'modern' writers insistently wrote of William the conqueror that he had totally subdued and crushed the nation, including the nobility and the gentry, from whom the two houses were drawn? The co-ordination principle, with its stress on the house of commons as an independent estate, must receive irreparable harm if this version of the Norman conquest were allowed to prevail. It was necessary, then, to affirm the constitutional nature of that event because of its implications for the powers and functions of the Stuart house of commons. The needed supportive argument was supplied in the 'Preface', where Petyt minimized the elements of compulsion and subjugation at the conquest while making much of William's affirmation of Edward the confessor's laws. Admitting that the conqueror's severity increased as the reign went on, he was firm, nevertheless, that the law-making parliament had survived the storm. Notwithstanding William's great power, Petyt declared, 'We meet with some general councils or parliaments in his reign, whereby it appears, that the freemen or commons of England, were there, and had a share in making of laws.' What could 'the promised restitution of the laws of Edward the confessor signify, if their witenagemot, or parliament . . . was destroyed and broken?'[17]

This argument, it must be stressed, was essentially juridical in nature despite the trappings of historical data; and the case for a legal sovereignty in king, lords, and commons rested not on historical precedent, as one might be tempted to conclude, but on the binding quality of prescription at common law.[18] Nowhere is this better seen than in the 'Discourse', with its constant evocation of prescription to support the ancient right of the English people to representation in parliament. An immemorial right of this kind meant an immemorial house of commons. Petyt's argument in this portion of his tract was in two stages: the first consisted of discrediting Prynne's emphasis, supported by Dugdale, on 49 H.3 as marking the first appearance of the house of commons, and the method was to prove its existence under King John (1199–1216). An attempt was then made to place its beginnings even earlier, to go 'higher' than Richard I, as Petyt put it.[19] The developing argument relied heavily on the case of the burgesses of St Albans, who had successfully petitioned Edward II (1307–27) for recognition of their prescriptive right to parliamentary representation; and this case was said to demonstrate that it was believed in the fourteenth century to be 'a general custom, or law, time out of mind, that the cities and boroughs had sent members to parliament', as the petition set forth.[20] Petyt frequently cited the case of St Albans as he insisted that surviving evidence supported the existence of a house of commons within the express prescription of that borough. He worked from a variety of materials: from references in historical records to what he thought must have been the house of commons, the testimony of earlier historians and such distinguished judges as Bracton, and expressions in medieval statutes that he equated with the common law. In the last category were such statutes as 5 Rich. 2, s.2. c.4, which Lambard had stressed, as well as a statute from the second year of Henry VI's reign, stating, in Petyt's words, 'that the commons had ever been a member of the parliament, and that no statute or law could be made without their assent'.[21]

The burgesses of St Albans had petitioned to send two burgesses to parliament with the claim that they and their predecessors had always been accustomed to doing so in all former ages (*totis retroactis temporibus*), not only in the time of Edward I but also in that of his 'progenitors'. They had sent representatives to parliament *sicut caeteri burgenses regni* (just as other burgesses of the kingdom had). The phrase 'in all former ages' could be made to yield a golden harvest, but Petyt's preference for the moment was to follow the route marked out by the reference to Edward I's progenitors, which permitted the conclusion that the burgesses of St Albans had been represented in King John's parliaments, that king being Edward I's grandfather and 'so before H.3'. The whig historian now found in the fifteenth and sixteenth years of King John's reign the records required for reinforcing this conclusion as he called attention to an assemblage that had met in London *convocatum parliamentum de toto clero et tota secta laicali*. To Petyt this was a parliament convoked of all the clergy and all the laity, including citizens and burgesses, and within the express prescription of the borough of St Albans.

The vital proposition could now be pressed home that the house of commons had existed before King John, indeed even before 1189, the year of Richard I's coronation. Petyt had discovered another statute, this one from Henry III's reign (51 H.3) with that king's promise to maintain the good laws of his 'progenitors'. Assuming that such laws had been made with the consent of the house of commons, he found in the statute a very large prescription of right.[22] In identifying Henry III's progenitors, Petyt was generous : he would construe that statute narrowly even though the law-makers who had enacted this statute had intended otherwise. It would have to be granted that statutes enacted in Richard's and John's reign – uncle and father respectively to Henry III – had received the house of commons' assent. So far so good. Yet an important gap remained since Petyt was still short of his main goal; that is, convincing proof of such a house prior to Richard I. To complete his legal case, he now turned to Bracton, writing : 'The word "progenitors" in the statute must I conceive go higher than Rich. I.' Since Bracton's reputation was at its height in Henry III's reign, it could be assumed that his lifetime spanned the preceding reigns of Richard and John. Moreover, and here was the clincher, the learned judge had left posterity a record of the rule by which laws were made not only in his time but also 'in ages before'.[23] This was his rule concerning the authority by which laws were ordained 'in old times'. A measure had the force and power of a law if it were 'justly declared and approved of by the council and consent of the great men [the house of lords] and by the general agreement of the commonwealth [expressed in the house of commons], the authority of the king preceding'.[24] This rule made possible another conclusion, equally important to seventeenth-century Englishmen: the 'original of the laws' was legally king, lords, and commons.[25] The decisive statement had come from the admired Bracton, and Petyt was deeply chagrined at Brady's failure to deal squarely with it. By taking no notice of this authority, Brady had ignored the central point in the *Antient Right*.[26]

Petyt now took up a related line of thought, equally indispensable to the common-law argument. The house of commons had met steadily and regularly as a constituent member of early parliaments with a share in the law-making power. This was true under the Britons and Anglo-Saxons, and the situation remained the same despite the Norman conquest. Notwithstanding William's high power, parliaments had persisted; and the commons of England had a share in making laws under him and his successors. Petyt's conclusion was that the commons had possessed 'votes and a share in the making and enacting of laws for the government of the kingdom' under the British, the Anglo-Saxons, and the Normans. They formed an essential part of the government before and after the Norman conquest, and the generalization was equally applicable to the house of lords.[27]

The repeated statements about a shared law-making power reveal that Petyt believed in the principle of a co-ordination in the legislative power and in the theory of mixed monarchy (and legal sovereignty), to which it was always central. Moreover, in insisting that king, lords, and commons shared the law-making power, he turned to evidence other than that drawn from the past. His private papers reveal that his ideas on law-making owed much to the Answer to the Nineteen Propositions, where Charles I had declared, in Petyt's words, that 'in this kingdom the laws are jointly made by a king, by a house of lords, and a house of commons chosen by the people, all having free votes and particular privileges'.[28] There was also the act for the king's preservation which 'by declaring that both houses of parliament nor either of them have a legislative power without the king hath admitted that all in conjunction have'.[29] The point was settled to Petyt's satisfaction when the second Powle committee of the cavalier house of commons, on February 26, 1673, at the height of the indulgence controversy, declared that 'the legislative power hath always been acknowledged to reside in his majesty and the two houses of parliament'.[30] Finally, it appears from his private correspondence that he was familiar with the long-lasting controversy over the membership of the three estates.[31]

Sentiments and political ideas of this variety, it has been urged here, led to the theory of a legal sovereignty in king, lords, and commons; and once more Petyt provides the example *par excellence*. That he held a high view of parliamentary power and authority became unmistakable when he quoted with approval Sir Thomas Smith's far-reaching statements on this subject and then added this sentence : 'By this we may sufficiently be informed, what entire, plenary, and absolute authority, pre-eminence and jurisdiction, were inseparably annexed, united, and belonging to parliaments.'[32] Another passage implied that an unlimited power to make laws resided in the joint consent of king, lords, and commons when Petyt denied that the judges at Westminister could legally determine the acts of parliament that were binding or void. His modern outlook was again displayed in the comment that differences of opinion among lawyers with regard to important and weighty points in the common law were settled, not by the judges at Westminster, but by the law-making power.[33] As for the dispensing power, Petyt's language reflected the conventional wisdom of his day. Laws could be legally dispensed with only 'by common consent of the promulgators thereof'.[34] In sum, the unmistakable note echoing through his writings, both before and after the Glorious Revolution, was that a legal sovereignty residing in king, lords, and commons commanded, unchallenged, the very heights of power in the kingdom.

## IV

On first sight the tory historians seem much more alert to historical change than their whig counterparts and much less likely to seek support for their theory of legal sovereignty in the records of the past. Certainly, in some respects they were superior, notably in appreciating the scholarship of Sir Henry Spelman, who had earlier called attention to the close relationship between political feudalism and post-conquest institutions. Yet it ought to be noted that the whig historians were much more handicapped by their view of legal sovereignty than Brady and his friends, their stress on the high power of king, lords, and commons standing squarely in the way of an interpretation of early English history that would pass muster with twentieth-century scholars. The high prerogative views of the tories, by contrast, made them naturally receptive to findings by which the crown was aggrandized and eased the way for accepting the fact of conquest in 1066 and the subsequent introduction of political feudalism. If their findings were in accord on such crucial points with modern scholarship, they too were rigid in outlook and present-minded in interpreting the past, more so than modern accounts of Brady's scholarship allow.

Working from Spelman's article on parliament in his *Archae-ologus* (1664) and from Prynne's critique of the common-law argument for an immemorial house of commons, Brady called attention to the constitutional and legal situation after the Norman conquest. Although he was noticeably reticent in drawing political conclusions, their sense was obvious to contemporaries. The events of 1066 had led to a strong king, who governed England with the aid of Norman military men, they being automatically subordinate to him as his tenants in chief. There was no place in the political scheme of things for a house of commons that shared the law-making power since most Englishmen were serfs and the Anglo-Saxon freeholder was virtually extinct. These circumstances ruled out a prescriptive right to representation and a co-ordination principle in law-making. The requisite social conditions were plainly missing for a house of commons, to say nothing of a house of lords, and so were the political understandings needed for that principle to be operative. Early parliaments were best described as tenurial councils composed of tenants in chief, to which elements of the house of commons were added for the first time in 1265, at the summons of the usurper Simon de Montfort. The origins of that house were lowly, its arrival late on the parliamentary scene. To be sure, knights were summoned by writ to the parliament of 49 H.3, but the regular summoning of citizens and

burgesses came later. They had been summoned by writ for the
first time in 1295 and then only to grant money at the royal
demand, certainly not to share the law-making power as the whigs
believed. And Brady took up Prynne's claim that it was in this
year that the discretionary clause first appeared by which the
sheriffs took so much upon themselves with regard to borough
representation. Cities and boroughs were earlier too humble and
unimportant for that house to assume the weight in the nation
assigned by the whig historians although possibly citizens and
burgesses were present in the parliament of 49 H.3.[35]

Despite the incisive use of feudalism to establish the subordination of the two houses to the king at this time, Brady's conception
of the kingship itself as a legal and constitutional institution in
these centuries owed little to it. His early English monarch was a
Bodinian law-giver of the type esteemed by the conservative
political thinkers of Stuart England. That is, Brady's historical
writings were in the tradition established by modern-minded
royalists like Sir John Spelman, Heylyn, and Holbourne; but he
went well beyond them when, borrowing from a suggestion in
Heylyn, he added a conquest theory of royal power by which the
law and the constitution were dated from the events of 1066.[36]
They revealed that William the conqueror was the human source
of the law by which England was governed in the late eleventh
century; and the introduction of political feudalism meant, as
mentioned above, that neither the conqueror nor his successors
had companions in the law-making power. Nor had they subsequently relinquished this great power, which had passed intact to
their descendants, including presumably Charles II, who was as
a consequence the sole law-maker in parliament. If these propositions were valid, the whig use of common-law principles to support a shared legal sovereignty in king, lords, and commons must
go by the board, the argument from prescription undermined
and subverted. Brady's conquest theory of kingship had the
further merit in conservative opinion of denying that the Stuart
government was traceable either to Anglo-Saxon foundations or
to an original contract, as exponents of mixed monarchy claimed.
These theorists had, in Brady's view, infused dangerous notions
of sovereignty and power into the people's heads which the latter
had never possessed and were incapable of managing in any

government whatsoever. His *Introduction to the Old English History* was intended to show the people that they had not possessed anciently either the pieces of sovereignty or a share in the government such as restless and tumultuous men were trying to make them believe they had earlier possessed and still ought to have.[37]

That the tory historian had set out to depict William the conqueror in the fashion described above may be seen in a number of ways. One way is to glance at the title of Brady's major work, the *Complete History*, which reveals that he had written an historical account of England from the first entrance of the Romans to the establishment of the Norman kingdom and in doing so had demonstrated, in Brady's words, 'the original of . . . English laws'. By 'original' he meant the human source of the law or laws, and to Brady this was none other than William. How could this be seen? The answer was both pointed and illuminating. It appeared first of all from the fact that William had brought in a new law and imposed it upon the people. As Brady stated, ' 'Tis clear he did so.'[38]

Moreover, Brady's 'preface to the Norman History', of about fifty pages, had the musty smell of an old law office, conveying overwhelmingly a sense of preoccupation with the introduction of new law at the conquest. That this had happened could be seen from the dominant position held by Norman land law after 1066, the adoption of Norman legal practices such as ordeal by battle and writs of right, the influx of Norman military men into high legal and political offices as justiciars, lord chancellors, and lord keepers of the seal, and the subsequent use of Norman French in pleadings and judgments that continued without abatement until Edward III's reign. Equally to the point was Brady's reliance on a medieval French law book known as the *Grand Coutumier*, which he viewed as a code of Norman laws and customs that had been transported wholesale to England at the conquest. Recognizing that the Normans had at the time no written laws, he equated customs with laws and insisted that the conqueror had imposed those in the *Grand Coutumier* on his new subjects.[39]

A case having been made for a legal sovereignty in William, Brady undertook to demonstrate that this high power had continued under the conqueror and his successors despite the great

charters. The kings were the sole legislators. No claim was possible
that the people (the two houses) were at this time law-makers, as
some troublesome men claimed. For one thing, no counterpart
existed to the freeholders of the seventeenth century. The land was
on the whole controlled by Norman military men, who owed
military service for their tenures and from whom large numbers
of dependent tenants held by servile tenure. This was the condition of most Englishmen; and despite the erosion of manorial
institutions in the course of time, it was not these men who contended in the interval for the liberties provided in the royal
charters. No, indeed. The *liberi homines*, who received charters
from Henry I, King John, and Henry III, were Norman military
men; and their subvassals and the liberties for which they contended were best understood in terms of feudal laws. As the sole
law-maker the king had the responsibility for adjusting or correcting feudal law, if it proved, for example, too severe for the military
men who held of him. The liberties amounted only to the relaxation of laws and tenures, these being related in turn to the fees
and estates which their ancestors had received from the conqueror
without the easier terms and abatement of the law's strictness
that they required.[40] That Brady was thinking in terms of legal
sovereignty was also evident from his attack on the subvassals at
Runnymede, who were the heroes of the whig writers of his own
day. They were only followers in the rebellion for Magna Carta –
'no law-makers, as this gentleman [Petyt] fondly imagines'. It was
impossible that the men who ruled the nation would permit men
of small reputation to share with them in law-making. Indeed,
the situation was the reverse. 'Those that had the power of this
and other nations *de facto*', Brady continued, 'always did give
laws, and tax the people. And so did the tenants in capite tax
themselves, and all other tenants and freemen of England, in
those times we are writing of.'[41]

Given these themes in his writings, Brady may be termed a
political theorist of Bodinian leanings who made skillful use of
the records of early English history in the service of a greater
cause, namely, the high power of the later Stuart kings. To this
cause his historical scholarship was subordinate. Whatever admiration may be felt for Brady as a pioneer in modern historiography,
he formed part of a dwindling minority in the political nation to

which he belonged, his scholarly findings about early history an imposing barrier to the intellectual acceptance of a theory of legal sovereignty in king, lords, and commons. This was particularly so for those who travelled the common-law route. That this was the case goes far to explain the intensity of emotion that attended Brady's scholarship. The reaction ran deep and strong, comparable only to that provoked by the *Freeholders Grand Inquest*. From these two quarters came the opinions categorized by the whig writers as modern and arbitrary; and if these opinions went unrefuted, there could be no prescriptive right to a representation in parliament nor a house of commons with a share in the legislative power. This was the reasoning of the whig writers; and this line of thought, not that of the high tory writers, commanded the sympathy of the political nation when James II ascended the throne. That is, the political nation believed the law-making power to be a shared power even if its members were unwilling to accept the more radical whig propositions rising out of this premise. But if they accepted the co-ordination principle at all, they had embarked upon an intellectual voyage that must take them further than they ever intended to go.

## V

The manner in which Petyt and Brady approached political problems illuminates the ideological biases of the political nation in the latter half of the seventeenth century and tells much, of course, about the ideological struggle that underlay the Glorious Revolution, a few short years ahead. Their political arguments were the badges of their respective political parties, each receiving handsome rewards for his party services. Thus Petyt, one of the most learned of the whig lawyers, built a career on his intimate acquaintance with the public records that culminated in the publication of the *Antient Right*. Its success appears from Northleigh's acrimonious assault on Petyt as a laborious drudge of sedition, one of the 'factious roll and record mongers' who while seemingly seeking only to prove the antiquity of the house of commons and parliament were actually pursuing researches with the aim of making their political power exorbitant and free of the king's control.[42]

The assessment had a hard core of truth. Petyt's political activities and associates certainly point to a substantial role in the network of opposition to Charles II and later James II. For one thing, his learning brought him the patronage and even the friendship of so substantial a whig leader as Arthur Capel, earl of Essex, who after services as lord lieutenant of Ireland and at the treasury moved from being Charles II's trusted minister to becoming his political enemy and a supporter of Monmouth. One of Shaftesbury's closest associates, Essex was imprisoned because of an alleged complicity in the supposed rye house plot (1683) but committed suicide before the trial. There were links in these years between Petyt and the Capel family. In 1673 Essex wrote to Petyt about his being appointed clerk of the peace for Hertfordshire, where the former had earlier been lord lieutenant;[43] and seven years later the *Antient Right* was published with a dedication to Essex. Petyt was Essex's barrister and handled business matters for him; and that the two men were on intimate terms appears from the presence of Essex's letterbook of 1677, when he was lord lieutenant of Ireland, in the Petyt manuscripts in the Inner Temple Library. Petyt was mentioned by name at that time in the correspondence between Essex and his brother Sir Henry Capel, who would be appointed commissioner of the treasury at the Revolution.[44]

Petyt's circle widened after the *Antient Right* was published. Between 1681 and 1683 he was quietly engaged in searching London's archives for documents to buttress the city's defense of its charter against Charles II's *quo warranto* proceedings. He supplied the city's counsel – Sir George Treby and Sir Francis Pollexfen – with the raw materials for their legal arguments; but his further contribution is difficult to assess. There are in the Petyt manuscripts three stout volumes of materials from which the defense was derived, but not papers written for Treby and Pollexfen. On the other hand, the city's plea sounds like Petyt, particularly in the invocation of prescription and Magna Carta as the bases for London's ancient rights and liberties; and his influence may perhaps be discerned when that helpful word 'progenitors' in a statute from Edward III's reign was used to support the city's case.[45] This relationship with Treby is a milestone in Petyt's career. The former was the recognized leader in London's opposition to Charles II and James II, and he is said to have made the city safe for William of Orange after his entrance into England. One of the counsel for the seven bishops in the famous trial of 1688, Treby was for a time chairman of the committee in the convention house of commons that prepared the declaration of rights.[46] That document, with some additions, became the Bill of Rights. As for Pollexfen, he too was a member of the bishops' counsel in 1688 and of the committee that wrote the declaration of rights. Appointed attorney general at the Revolution, he was later chief justice of common pleas.

If Petyt can be associated with political figures like Essex, Treby, and Pollexfen, he also had a relationship with the most radical whig publicists. Henry Neville, an old associate of James Harrington, referred approvingly to Petyt's and Atwood's defense of the house of commons;[47] and Petyt can be linked directly with the radical lawyer known as 'Postscript' Hunt, whose writings were commonly grouped with Neville's and Algernon Sidney's. On one occasion Petyt supplied Hunt with materials to defend London's rights against the crown. The latter reported that Petyt, whose researches into the records had ferreted out whatever was notable in them, had given him access to unprinted statutes.[48]

Petyt's contribution to his party was recognized when the convention house of lords consulted him at the Revolution, along with Sir Robert Atkyns. Even more to the point was his appointment to be keeper of the tower records. Before the convention assembled, William had recognized the need for a change; and Petyt was given free access to the tower records prior to the formal appointment on July 25, 1689. His elevation signalled a major ideological shift to the leftward in politics, its significance transcending the individuals involved. As Pocock pointed out, 'in the microcosm of the tower records office the Revolution meant the fall of Brady and the substitution of Petyt, who reigned there as a respected scholar to the end of his days'.[49]

For Brady, the Revolution spelled the end of a political career unmatched by any other polemist of his day. He now surrendered the tower records office and retired into the obscurity from which he had emerged with a dazzling display of historical scholarship in the early 1680s. He had been in some ways a more conspicuous figure than Petyt because of his association with Charles II and

James II. One sign of the value that the court attached to his services came when he was given access to the records in the tower of London before his appointment as keeper in 1686.[50] Another appears from the fact that he frequented the court in the years when his historical writings were under way : he was there for almost five months in 1683 and seven in 1684, at Windsor, New-market, etc. He was acquainted with ministers like Sir Leoline Jenkins and Lord Sunderland and may well have been on familiar terms with them. Sunderland, the secretary of state, included Brady's name in a list of notables who were to be given information that no parliament was to be summoned. Brady was also a member of the Oxford parliament and the only parliament of James II's reign. In the latter he was on two committees especially congenial to him : one was to expunge seditious resolutions from the journals of the house of commons, the other to prepare a clause forbidding members to propose an alteration in the succession to the throne.[51]

The zenith of his career came in James II's reign when he was made physician extraordinary to the king and keeper of the tower records with an annual salary of £300 and was even summoned to attend the birth of the prince of Wales in the summer of 1688. There is another unusual sign of a cordial relationship with the king. Brady seems to have been one of the last persons in England to see James II before he left for France. At the instance of Bishop Francis Turner – Sancroft's protégé and later a Jacobite and non-juror – Brady made a last-ditch effort to keep the king in England.[52] This failed, and the sequel is well-known. The order theory of kingship died to all intents and purposes, on February 12, 1689, when the two houses agreed on the declaration of rights; and exactly one month later Brady was ordered officially to deliver the tower records to Petyt. The latter's appointment as keeper followed shortly afterward. When the transfer had taken place, one ideological facet of the Revolution was complete.[53]

But that the decade would end this way was by no means clear in the early 1680s, and it is fair to ask how influential the community-centered ideology actually was at the time of exclusion. How powerfully did it affect the political nation? Had its influence, so pervasive when the restoration was under way and so prominently displayed during the indulgence crisis of the early 1670s, contracted when the political nation rallied to Charles II in the last years of his reign? Was its influence confined to a small circle of radical writers and their readers – a William Disney,[54] the anonymous author of the *Dialogue at Oxford*, a Petyt? Or was that ideology still broadly based, reaching deep into the political nation and perhaps even beyond it? If its influence was broad and deep, did a setback follow the exclusion crisis? Had a wave of conservatism swept the nation, engendered by the dread of '1642' once more, and had that wave submerged the partiality felt by so many Englishmen for the community-centered view of their government?

These questions are not easily answered, in part at least because the Stuart censorship was reimposed after the failure of exclusion. But the evidence is ample, surely, for the conclusion that the community-centered ideology was widely accepted in Charles II's reign and deeply imbedded in the country's political thought at James II's accession. So much was this the case that there can be no thought of its being swept away in Charles II's last years. Perhaps the point requires elaboration since modern historians have written so little about the community-centered ideology of these years. Here Hickes' testimony is pertinent. Writing after Oxford University had publicly condemned major tenets of that ideology and burned tracts where it was expressed,[55] he set out to expose what he viewed as obvious contradictions in the co-ordination principle. These would be apparent to 'the most vulgar understandings among common country people and citizens' if it were not for the influence of republican writers, by which Hickes meant mixed monarchists. He compared their control over the people, whom they managed and directed, to that which priests exerted over the common people among the Roman Catholics. This was striking testimony about the general acceptance of the co-ordination principle, to Hickes the product of traitorous pens.[56]

Also in vogue, as his further remarks reveal, was the view that the community constituted the human source of political authority. The popish doctrine, as Hickes denominated it, circulated to the effect that the king was the people's trustee, his office being described as so purely ministerial in nature that his primary responsibility was to execute laws when parliament was not in session. Such ideas were 'implied in the style of most of the seditious pamphlets'.[57] Although comments from so conservative a quarter

are rightfully treated with caution, still it is notable that Hickes'
findings are compatible with those of a modern scholar who inves-
tigated the pamphlet literature excited by the exclusion crisis.[58]
Moreover, the very prevalence at the Revolution of this version of
the origins of government supports the proposition that it was
widely held earlier in the decade. It was as if the ideology singled
out for condemnation by Hickes and his fellow conservatives had
gone underground in Charles II's last years, only to break out
once more at the Revolution.

That the community-centered ideology was popular also
appears from the aspects of restoration politics discussed earlier
in this study. There was, for example, Shaftesbury's language at
the climax of the indulgence controversy, inspired by Charles II
himself. At that time a majority in the cavalier house of commons
had voted, without a trace of self-consciousness, that the legislative
power resided in the king and the two houses; and Charles II had
even assigned to the co-ordination principle the onus of having
caused the civil war. Clearly the king considered the statement
credible enough to embarrass the house of commons. In this
connection it might be noted that Lord Halifax, writing at the
end of the century, referred to the term 'co-ordination' as 'unman-
nerly'.[59] Doubtless this was a judgment with which the king and
the cavalier parliament could agree, but the house of commons
had proceeded nevertheless to advance a claim regarding the
legislative power that came perilously close to co-ordination and
in doing so received the support of the house of lords.

By mentioning that principle Charles II had run the risk of
enhancing its popularity, a consideration apparently brushed
aside. Yet he could hardly have avoided pondering the consequences since signs are plentiful that the court and its supporters
took the radical principle very seriously, their activity attesting to
its potency and pervasiveness. Deep concern was manifested at
key points in the reign, not only during the indulgence controversy of 1672–73, midway through the reign, but also in such
indicative matters as L'Éstrange's appointment as censor at the
beginning of the reign and Oxford University's condemnatory
decree near its close. L'Éstrange also wrote a host of anti-co-
ordination tracts. Warwick wrote his *Memoires* some time between
1667 and 1675, and his *Discourse of Government* was completed

by 1678. Then there was the outpouring of anti-co-ordination tracts represented by Assheton, Mackenzie, and Hickes and the republication of important royalist writings of this genre from the civil-war and interregnum years. Some tory writers in the 1680s were men of substance, this being notably true of Mackenzie and Hickes; and the association with Ormonde makes Assheton important. Others such as Northleigh and L'Éstrange were hack writers, riding the crest of a trend from which they could hope to profit. Even this evidence is not to be disdained. Hack writers published for an anti-co-ordination market, and their writings are evidence of such a market. To cap it all, there was the intense and serious commitment of Dr Brady and his fellow historians to discredit by means of political feudalism the common-law argument for the co-ordination principle. Building on Prynne's foundation, they worked with court encouragement in two reigns.

Also to be mentioned in this connection is Archbishop Sancroft, said to have been the most single-minded servant of the house of Stuart in the late seventeenth century, with an outlook compounded almost equally of a mystical reverence for the monarchy and a passion for the church of England. The comparison with Archbishop Laud comes quickly to mind. Ambitious to serve the church of England by means of a strengthened prerogative, Sancroft aligned himself with the court and proved immovable in James' cause during the exclusion struggle. Thereafter he united with the Hyde brothers (the earls of Clarendon and Rochester) to build a strong Yorkist party. Part of Sancroft's contribution was to sponsor Brady in his contest with Petyt, and he was also responsible for Hickes' writing *Jovian*, a major tract in the tory wing of the controversy over the legislative power. Sancroft can also be linked with Nalson, another prominent anti-co-ordination writer in this period, and was, in fact, directly involved in Nalson's correction of the definition of estates, to which Charles I had given his sanction. The archbishop's encouragement probably explains the long passage hostile to co-ordination in Nalson's introduction to his *Impartial Collection of the Great Affairs of State* (1682–83).[60]

One other question, phrased in terms of the Brady controversy, should be asked about the presence of co-ordination and coevality themes in exclusion literature. To what extent were Petyt and

Brady genuinely representative of their respective political parties? There is, in Petyt's case, no problem. His insistence on a long-standing legal sovereignty in king, lords, and commons reflected by and large the views of his party even if some of its members, such as Locke, reached their conclusions by a different route. The common-law argument carried conviction to whig writers of all kinds, and to others as well. It is more difficult to assert flatly that Brady spoke for the bulk of the tories in placing legal sovereignty in the king alone. Certainly the idea had support in high tory quarters; and if Charles II and James II are treated as the leaders of that party in their respective reigns, then Brady's conclusion had the most august sponsorship. Whether it was acceptable to a more ordinary tory, as, for example, the member in parliament, is another problem, in some ways a very puzzling one. The tone of the debates in the cavalier house of commons during the indulgence crisis of 1672–73 – a few years before the formation of political parties – makes it very unlikely that the conservatism of the tory party went so far, as does the position on the dispensing power taken formally by the two houses. There was also the practice of altering the wording of statutes to limit the dispensing power, approved by parliamentary majorities in both houses. Such a practice, evident in the years from 1667 to 1680 when it was applied not only to the Irish cattle bills but also to the *habeas corpus* act of 1679 and the test acts of 1673 and 1678, certainly suggests that a tory member of parliament had little respect for the idea of a dispensing power in the king and hence for the proposition that he was the sole law-maker in parliament. Finally, observers in the late seventeenth century frequently stated that the men of the long robe, whose members were often found in parliament and could belong to either party, considered the king to be one of the three estates. To move from this position to one of perceiving a co-ordination principle in law-making was only a short step.

On the other hand, there were conservatives of a moderate hue who found no difficulty in accepting a conclusion like Brady's. Among them was Hale, one of the few genuinely independent-minded judges of Charles II's reign. Hale asserted of the king: 'In him resides the power of making laws. The laws are his laws enacted by him.' Although this great power was exercised in parliament, still it was the king's alone. 'The legislative power be in the king, so that none but he can make laws obliging the subjects of this realm', Hale wrote. Yet a certain solemnity and qualification attached to that power: it had to be exercised with the advice and assent of the two houses of parliament, without which no law could be made.[61] And at the height of the indulgence controversy such political figures as Sir Edward Seymour, Sir Henry Coventry, and Heneage Finch – later prominent in the tory party – described Charles II's power and authority in terms of the order theory of kingship.

Here the events of James II's reign are crucial. In light of the later tory participation in the Glorious Revolution, it may be reasoned that those among the moderate tories who held views like Hale's were torn from these moorings when James II's policies threatened established interests in church and state. This is what happened to Sancroft, and to Ormonde and Mackenzie as well; and they were high tories.[62] Not even a publicist like Hickes, whose high prerogative writings set the tone of Charles II's last years, could accept the declaration of indulgence of 1672. If he was the author of the anti-co-ordination tract attributed to him in the account in the *DNB* of his life, this was where he drew the line. The future leader of the non-jurors repudiated a declaration that suspended so many acts of parliament at once. Charles II's action was lawless. Fortunately, the two houses had persuaded the king to revoke his declaration and 'take upon him the bridle of the law again'.[63] This was strange doctrine for an order theorist of Hickes' standing, and the pronouncement contradicts the tenor of the tract, which supports the dispensing power. Clearly, even among the most stalwart defenders of the Stuart kingship there were those who could not condone the declaration of 1672. They would only go so far and no further.

## VI

A final aspect of the Brady controversy requiring consideration may be phrased as a series of questions. Was the co-ordination principle as understood in Charles II's reign significantly different from what many parliamentarians meant by that principle during the civil war? Were there Englishmen in the 1680s who went beyond an equality in king, lords, and commons to the supremacy of the two houses, their will ultimately to determine all? Or had the co-ordination principle by the early 1680s shed the extremism of the earlier period and settled into the more conservative mold of Petyt's writings – a version stressing the equal partnership of king, lords, and commons in law-making? In short, were there two versions of the co-ordination principle in circulation during the exclusion crisis, one of them more radical than the other and reminiscent in tone of the civil war? If there was a more radical version, how radical was it, and how important was it?

One answer is unequivocal. If the idea of an ultimate supremacy in the two houses is interpreted as a demand for ordinance-making, no such demand was being made. It was discredited as a result of the events of the 1640s. But if what is meant is that the king, after the two houses had approved a bill, must accept it without regard for his own wishes, this is another matter. Such an idea – accepted by Herle at a later stage in his writings and pushed to its limits by Prynne – had exercised much influence during the civil war;[64] and its circulation on a significant scale in the 1680s, buttressed by civil-war arguments, would signal a continuing civil-war extremism. The effect was to place a practical supremacy in the two houses as the principal law-makers even though its advocates were firm that king, lords, and commons, as three co-ordinate estates, made law. It is urged here that there indeed existed in this sense a more radical version of the co-ordination principle during the exclusion crisis than Petyt's writings reveal and, further, that it has to be deemed influential in whig ranks because its advocates included not only the more extreme elements in that party but also leading whigs in the party's mainstream. Even though the latter did not make their views publicly known until the Revolution, they actively combated court policies in the 1680s; and presumably their views matured in the earlier period.

It is unlikely, however, that the radical version of co-ordination was as popular in the whig party as the more moderate one. Nor did it have a wide basis of support in the political nation. After all, the second Powle committee, on February 26, 1673, had stopped short of the word 'co-ordination' in setting forth the position of the cavalier house of commons; and this fact alone is a reminder that the political climate of restoration England was

inhospitable to extremist political ideas. Perhaps it is only surprising that a radical version of co-ordination flourished at all
after the monarchy was restored.

Yet a note of caution is in order. A situation may look one way
to an historian but very different to a contemporary. Englishmen
in the late seventeenth century often treated the distinction
between the two versions of co-ordination as meaningless, concluding that it did not exist at all, either by definition or as a
practical matter. After all, two estates were more than one; and
this political arithmetic meant that a co-ordination in king, lords,
and commons was readily translatable into the supremacy of the
two houses. The two political ideas were often assimilated – either
by equating the co-ordination principle with a supremacy in the
two houses or treating it as an irreversible step in that direction.
Under these circumstances it might be more appropriate to speak
of the two faces of co-ordination. The practice was by no means
confined to conservative writers, who might be thought to have a
vested interest in putting the worst possible interpretation on a
co-ordination in king, lords, and commons. A relatively disin-
terested observer such as Edward Stillingfleet, who would be made
bishop of Worcester at the Revolution, declared in 1680 : 'If there
be three estates in parliament, and the bishops be none, then the
king must be one of the three. The natural consequence from
hence seems to be a co-ordination or that two joining together
may overrule the third.'[65] Three years later Oxford University
reached much the same conclusion in a public condemnation of
this proposition : 'The sovereignty in England is in the three
estates, viz., king, lords, and commons. The king has but a co-
ordinate power, and may be overruled by the other two.'[66] There
was also the tract of an anonymous writer concerned to deny it
was treason, as the conservative Hickes had asserted, to describe
the king as a third estate. The latter had bitterly denounced the
idea that the recently deceased Denzil Holles had employed this
definition of estates in a contemporary tract. 'This may be false',
wrote the anonymous author, 'but surely no treason, except he
[Holles] had said, "the king had but a co-ordinate power, and
might be overruled by the others" .'[67]

Nor can it be stated with assurance that one version of co-ordination proved in practice more radical than the other, not if effect

on the prerogative is the test. Either could have provided a driving force in the process by which the center of political gravity, in a little more than a generation, moved away from the king and perceptibly closer to the two houses. Each was applicable, and contemporaries hostile to the co-ordination principle often failed to distinguish between them in assessing their impact. This appeared when Charles II, in a successful attempt to protect his brother's claim to the throne, exercised freely his powers of sum-moning, proroguing, and dissolving parliament. After he post-poned the second exclusion parliament – prorogued before it met, it did not sit until October 21, 1680 – the whigs mounted a mammoth petitioning campaign calling for an immediate assembly of the new parliament, while their pamphleteers claimed that parliament ought properly to meet annually, or even semi-anually, and asserted openly that the king had no legal right to dismiss a parliament, once in session, unless its business was com-pleted. Tory writers found the prime source of these doctrines in the co-ordination principle and said so. Hickes remarked in 1684 : 'The king, as supreme head, doth adjourn, prorogue, and dissolve parliaments, as it seemeth good to his royal wisdom, which is so inconsistent with the new notion of co-ordinate power, that the traitorous pens of late have been seen to insinuate, as if it were an encroachment of the crown.'[68]

The signs are plentiful that the two versions of co-ordination were in circulation early in Charles II's reign. That this was the case appears, for example, from the comments of Whitelocke, writing about the time of the restoration, and of Vane during the state trial of 1662. It may be supposed that a passage to this effect in Hale's 'Rights of the Crown' was written somewhere near this period of time, but it is difficult to date Hale's manuscripts firmly. A modern authority believes that this particular one was written before the restoration but after 1641. It was unfinished when Hale died in 1676. It would of course be helpful to know just when the passage was written, but an argument can be made for the propo-sition that it dates from the interregnum when Hale was seeking to evolve his own answers to the controversial issues of the day. Pondering the precise location of the law-making power in parlia-ment, he had cast around for a consensus but found it non-existent. His poll revealed :

Some would have the power originally to reside in the commons, and the consent to be only in the lords and king as a convenient ceremony or formality, which if it may be had, will do well, if not, it may be spared. Some would have this power in the lords radically and the commons to be only petitioners or proposers. Some would have it in the king, lords, and commons co-ordinately, but yet so that either two should outbalance the third and carry the law.[69]

Dismissing such views as false and frivolous, Hale described two others: that the legislative power was 'radically and co-ordinately in all three but so that all their concurrence is requisite in the making of a law', and that the legislative power was 'solely in the king but yet so qualified as he cannot enact without the advice of the lords and commons in parliament assembled'.[70] It will have been noticed that Hale listed two versions of co-ordination. The first, and the more radical, allowed for a situation in which the king, aligned with one house, might overrule the other;[71] but practically, the allusion is to the two houses carrying the law.

That the radical version of co-ordination, noticed by Hale, persisted during Charles II's reign appears from the findings of the modern scholar, O.W. Furley, who studied the political litera- ture of the exclusion controversy. His account of the whig concept of monarchy has special value because his language reflects faith- fully that party's political arguments. Setting out to prove parlia- ment capable of regulating the succession, the whigs invoked the pertinent Henrician and Elizabethan statutes but also found parliamentary power unlimited in such matters because parliament represented the whole nation. As the voice of the people it could decide who should be king. Furley's description of the whigs continues: 'Although they admitted that an act of parliament required the sovereign's consent as well as that of the two houses, they held that the people, through parliament, had this funda- mental right which the present king could not ignore.'[72] In short, Charles II was not to exercise his veto if the two houses voted for exclusion. Here was a community-centered view of government that assigned the two houses the central role in law-making, leav- ing the king in a subsidiary position.

But it is time now to examine exclusion literature for overt signs of the more radical version of co-ordination, and the essential preliminary is to determine what constitutes such signs. Here the

declaration of the long parliament, on November 2, 1642, is
invaluable. Noted earlier in this study, it has numerous elements
that foreshadow the whig position of the 1680s. The two houses
had reached the fundamental position that they constituted 'the
collective body of all the kingdom' as they asked :

And are we not also two estates and two estates comprising the
persons of all the peers, and the representative body of all the
commons of England? And shall the collective body of all the
kingdom have nothing to do to look into the discharge of that trust
[the king's duties and responsibilities] that is only for the use and
benefit of the kingdom?[73]

To support this position, it will be recalled, they advanced a set
of arguments urging that the king – *singulis major* but *universis
minor* – was subordinate to them in parliament; that Bracton
(and Fleta) had testified to the superiority of the two houses vis-à-
vis the king and pointed to their duty to impose upon him the
bridle of the law if he acted illegally; and that he was obliged to
accept their legislative measures if they were agreed upon them.
*Quas vulgus elegerit* in the coronation oath left him no veto.[74]
From these arguments and Herle's co-ordination principle had
come the radical version of co-ordination found in Prynne's
*Soveraigne Power of Parliaments and Kingdomes*, which taught
that the two houses, as two co-ordinate estates, were the principal
law-makers in parliament, their will ultimately to determine all.
Under these circumstances the rise and fall of these arguments
may be rightfully treated as a political barometer, measuring and
recording at a given time the state of opinion in the political nation
so far as parliamentary sovereignty was concerned or indeed the
co-ordination principle.

   Accordingly, the presence or absence of this set of arguments in
the 1680s is an index to the extent and degree to which civil-war
extremism continued to influence political discussion. Yet the
situation was by no means simple, and a word of caution is advisable. The persistence of this particular political vocabulary for
more than a generation produced important side effects that
continued long after overt signs of civil-war doctrines had disappeared. That is, the side effects took on a life of their own and

persisted even after the nomenclature for various reasons disappeared. Nor is generalization easy about political argumentation in the 1680s since the evidence is often inconclusive and at times contradictory. Resort has to be had on occasion to the pamphlet literature of the Glorious Revolution for whatever light it may shed retroactively.

Arguments of this kind should have been at the nadir of their influence in the conservative atmosphere of restoration England. They were, after all, associated directly with the death of Charles I. After Bradshaw, as spokesman for the high court of justice, used the first two to castigate the king, they were discredited; and a debate over the meaning of *quas vulgus elegerit* was out of place once the monarchy had been restored without conditions. But more than this. The vote of the convention parliament, on May 1, 1660, followed by the act for the king's preservation, had confirmed the king's veto and by implication rejected the parliamentarian version of *quas vulgus elegerit*. Yet conservative writers in Charles II's reign assessed the ideological situation differently, as they insisted that *singulis major, universis minor* had found a home with what they called a 'restless party of men' and spoke of the people becoming accustomed to 'the noise of this railing rhetoric'.[75] Such testimony is too often present in conservative writings to be ignored. Thus L'Éstrange, writing at the restoration, condemned *singulis major*, along with the co-ordination principle, as a seditious position that the government must suppress.[76] After censorship was lifted in 1679, he wrote as if the two sets of ideas were once more circulating together. Listing libels against the government a year later, he stated that among them 'the doctrine of co-ordination, and the king's being *singulis major, universis minor* is [sic] common'.[77] Another pamphleteer reported that *singulis major, universis minor* was being applied to the king in the coffee houses,[78] which conservative observers treated as nurseries of sedition and rebellion. And there was the anonymous author of *Protestant Loyalty Fairly Drawn* (1681), an able defense of the king's prerogatives of summoning, dissolving, and proroguing parliament. He felt compelled to criticize the maxim as if it were an integral part of his opponent's political argument.[79] At this time, too, Dugdale published his *Short View of the Late Troubles*, in which he charged that the parliamentarians had tampered with Hooker's *Ecclesiastical Polity* in order to promote the anti-monarchical argument.

What, then, was the situation by the early 1680s? Was *singulis major* widespread in whig political tracts, as the persistent criticism in conservative circles suggests? Or were the old ideological wars still being fought, with reprinted civil-war tracts as their focus or even the suspect *Ecclesiastical Polity*? It has to be said at once that the maxim is not invoked by name in the leading whig pamphlets of the exclusion controversy. The whig pamphleteers make no specific mention of it, and some go out of their way to disavow civil-war principles in the struggle with Charles II. There is no gainsaying that in this sense political language is definitely more moderate than earlier in the century. Yet there are distinct traces of the radical maxim in whig tracts. They contain passages where *singulis major* lurked – either by itself or else in the company of other political ideas traceable to the two houses' declaration of November 2, 1642. Thus Elkanah Settle, one of the best-known whig pamphleteers, pointed to the people of England as the law-makers. This remarkable position was explained in this way: 'Here all our laws and decrees by which we are governed are of the people's choice, first made by the subject and then confirmed by the king.'[80] This was to assign the king a very limited share in law-making with much the larger going to the two houses as the representative voice of the community. Such a distribution of power could be justified in terms of *singulis major, universis minor*; and the same description is applicable to other whig tracts, notably those objecting to the manner in which Charles II summoned, prorogued, and dissolved parliaments. If the two houses were the primary law-givers, as the anonymous author of one such tract stated, then the king's activity was unconstitutional.[81]

Further light comes from L'Éstrange, who dealt with the subject in a tract written before the exclusion crisis began and twice reprinted before it was over. Finding what he described as a suspicious and ill-looking passage in Andrew Marvell's *Growth of Popery and Arbitrary Government* (1677) – reprinted perhaps as early as 1678 and twice at the Revolution, in 1689 and again in 1693 – L'Éstrange attributed to Marvell this question: 'As to matter of government, if to murder the king, be (as certainly it is) a fact so horrid, how much more heinous is it to assassinate the kingdom?' L'Éstrange then went straight to the point. 'Here is first involved in this clause', he wrote, 'the deposing position of '41 [sic], that the king is *singulis major, universis minor.*' The people were being taught that they had a greater prize at stake 'in the hazard of their religion, than in the tie of their civil obedience'. Marvell had also found that in England by comparison with the continent 'subjects retain their *proportion* [italics added] in the legislature'. If the passage seems innocuous to modern scholars, who have praised Marvell's moderate constitutionalism, not so to L'Éstrange. Its effect was to make subjects 'partners of the sovereignty', turning the monarchy into 'a tripartite and co-ordinate government', in which 'any two of the three may destroy the third'. Whatever Marvell's intentions, his doctrine, in L'Éstrange's eyes, was the more radical version of co-ordination, the one to which Hale had called attention.[82]

Any possibility that *singulis major* would be cited by name vanished with the disclosure of an alleged rye house plot to assassinate Charles II and the duke of York on their return from Newmarket. The private papers that convicted Algernon Sidney of high treason in 1683 contained just such an explicit reference;[83] and its presence in his papers explains why conservative pamphleteers now attacked the maxim so strongly. This does not mean, however, that its influence was at an end. It may well have persisted in a more subtle form, as was suggested above. But more than this could be said if Sidney was a representative whig and a spokesman for his party. As the matter now stands, this is not the verdict of modern scholars. A leading authority writes that he seems 'not to have found any general sympathy or support amongst the ruling classes of the day';[84] and the usual practice is to place him, along with Henry Neville, in a special category of radical whigs or disguised republicans with political ideologies too individualistic and even eccentric to be treated as representative of their party. The view may be mistaken. Assheton wrote of Sidney as 'a very authentic author with some men',[85] while Hickes explained that he had written his *Harmony of Divinity and Law* as the direct result of Sidney's speech before his execution being disseminated in Hickes' neighbourhood by 'some birds of his feather'. It was being 'greedily read by the people'.[86] Presumably

Hickes was referring to the paper that Sidney before his execution handed to the sheriff.

Nor was Sidney necessarily alone in a willingness to write in the terms that have been described. If the appearance of *singulis major, universis minor* imparts an ultra-radical tone to his papers, he was writing in the privacy of the study; and there is no way of knowing who shared his outlook or even spoke this political language in the coffee houses, which Charles II's government eyed with so much suspicion. Sidney's case was like Vane's, and the lesson is much the same. Thus Petyt, with his own reasons for sympathizing with Sidney, had in his library both the published proceedings against him and the paper handed to the sheriff before the execution. Who is to say what Petyt thought of Sidney's writings beyond the obvious comment that political language of this variety could not be applied to Charles II's government with impunity?[87] Nor is it irrelevant that the judicial proceedings against Sidney were set aside at the Revolution.

Then there was the quotation from Bracton and Fleta, likewise present in Sidney's papers.[88] It, too, had enjoyed a civil-war vogue after being cited by the long parliament in the declaration of November 2. Although its history was intertwined with that of *singulis major*, unlike that maxim it was surprisingly popular in co-ordination tracts published at the Revolution.[89] This is the more remarkable since its temper was more in keeping with civil-war polemics than with that of post-restoration politics. Bradshaw had found the quotation useful in condemning Charles I, and Vane cited it in his defense of 1662. According to Vane, Bracton had found the king to be below God, the law, and parliament (the two houses). Associated with Bradshaw and the high court of justice, Vane, and Sidney, the quotation must have been well-known indeed. Thus Stillingfleet, writing to Halifax before Sidney's execution, discussed the quotation at length, as if it were a matter of central consideration. After a scholarly discussion of Bracton's and Fleta's meaning, Stillingfleet offered the opinion that force was lawful against the king only if there was a power in the state 'superior to his or co-ordinate with it'. In his view Bracton had denied that any such power existed and Fleta had proved that all jurisdiction was in the king and derived from him.[90] Pertinent comment was also forthcoming from the conservative pamphleteer, William Assheton, who wrote in 1684 : 'There is scarce a pamphlet, pretending either to law or Latin, which doth not triumph in this sentence of Bracton.'[91]

Despite the authentic ring of such testimony Bracton's authority on the point at issue was seldom invoked in the whig tracts included in such standard collections as *Somers Tracts*, the *Harleian Miscellany*, or the *State Tracts* of Charles II's reign. Whenever the quotation was used, it was with caution, in so shortened a form that the main argument is missing.[92] But that the quotation was present at all lends support to Assheton, as does its prevalence at the Revolution. That it should have continued to play a prominent role in political debate is extraordinary in view of the bold claims advanced for the two houses and the explicit language in which they are couched. And this is to say nothing of the association of this quotation with Charles I's execution and with Vane's and Sidney's trials for high treason. If there were no other reason than this, it would have to be concluded that this particular view of law-making – and hence of the co-ordination principle – was consequential in whig ranks as late as the Glorious Revolution. This, despite the abandonment of *singulis major, universis minor* by name during the exclusion crisis and the failure at that time to make a greater use of the quotation from Bracton and Fleta.

This conclusion is strengthened by the persistence of the Latin tag *quas vulgus elegerit* in this period. Its appearance in Stuart political literature made it manifest at a given time that a debate was under way about the king's veto in law-making. The claim for a supremacy in the two houses in this case relied on translating *elegerit* in the future tense, whereas the retention of the veto was associated with the preterperfect tense. Thus Hale recognized that controversy centered on the tense of the verb when he noted that 'whether *elegerit* be the preterperfect or the future tense hath been an occasion of great difference'. He himself preferred the first because of the French and English translations of the coronation oath but believed this to be 'the sense also of the clause'.[93] Dugdale's conclusion was much the same : the parliamentarian version was ungrammatical.[94]

Whether this was so or not, it was present in the writings of whigs like Neville and Sidney. The latter went to the heart of the matter. The king had sworn to assent to such laws 'as shall be proposed'.[95] How representative were they of their party? It can be said that they were clearly speaking for others besides themselves. It will be recalled that Furley assigned this view of the veto to the whig party, and there is important evidence to support him. Sir George Treby, who was conspicuous in the formulation of the Bill of Rights, and Sir Robert Atkyns, also of considerable prominence at the Revolution, translated *quas vulgus elegerit* on the same lines as Neville and Sidney. Moreover, they did so publicly – a fact suggesting that their view was not uncommon in their party. According to Treby, speaking in the convention parliament, the king by the law was 'to administer justice, and to execute his office according to the tenor of these laws [sic]'. Further, 'the coronation oath obligeth him likewise to consent to such laws as the people shall choose'.[96] Given the history of *quas vulgus elegerit*, he could hardly have been more explicit. A similar statement emanated from Atkyns, now lord chief baron of the court of exchequer and speaker of the house of lords. At the swearing in of the lord mayor of London in 1693, Atkyns spoke with obvious disapproval of changes in Charles I's coronation oath, which he attributed to Laud. 'That the king should consent to such laws, as the people should choose', had been replaced by 'saving the king's prerogative royal'.[97]

This comment suggests that the phrase *quas vulgus elegerit* – like *singulis major*[98] – figured in the Brady controversy since Atkyns was an historian in the Petyt wing. Not that Petyt used such language in the manner of the civil-war parliamentarians. He was more careful than this; and his discussion was devoid, at least at first sight, of civil-war extremism. It is Brady's comment, in particular, that points to the currency at this time of a radical version of co-ordination. Both treated the coronation oath within the context of early English history, following out their party biases. Thus Petyt turned to the phrase for evidence of an early house of commons that had long shared the law-making power with the king and house of lords. But to invoke the phrase at all was to run a risk, as he surely knew; and he dissociated himself at once from any attack on the king's veto. '*Elegerit*', he explained, was 'admitted to be of the preterperfect tense.' This was to accept the royalist position, indeed the more scholarly one. But it certainly revealed, he added with less caution, 'that the people's election had been the foundation and ground of ancient laws and customs'. The pronouncement has a radical ring, not surprising since it was taken almost word for word from Henry Parker's *Observations upon some of His Majesties late Answers and Expresses*, which was in Petyt's library. Other civil-war influences are noticeable. Petyt followed the argument of the *Freeholders Grand Inquest* in discussing *quas vulgus elegerit* and may have been inspired by a passage in Prynne's *Soveraigne Power of Parliaments* when he declared :

The term of *justas leges* seems to allow a liberty of debate, reason, and argument, so much as might be of efficacy and force, to demonstrate and convince, that the laws so required by the commons of the king [hardly cautious phrasing] were just and reasonable; the debate and consideration of which certainly was never, nor ever could be intended to be done in the diffusive capacity of all the commons of England *separatim*, but in an entire or in an aggregate body, that is, in their *communia concilia*, or parliaments.[99]

If Petyt at times strayed beyond the limits imposed by translating *elegerit* in a court-approved fashion, this course had been rethought by the time he finished his *Jus Parliamentarium*. There was no reference this time to *quas vulgus elegerit* in his commentary on the coronation oath.[100]

Brady also dealt with the subject, though in reference to Prynne, under the headings *communitas regni* and *elegerit* in his *Glossary*. Despite his recognition that parliament contained its modern elements by the early fourteenth century, he confined the 'community of the kingdom', referred to in Edward II's coronation oath, to the military men who held knights' fees or parts of them and paid scutage. Above all, they were not ordinary freemen, freeholders, the multitude, or the rabble. Nor did the parliamentarian translation of key phrases in the coronation oath have any validity. ' 'Tis impossible', Brady wrote, 'that Mr Prynne's sense of *elegerit* can ever be allowed.' High tory conclusions followed. The coronation oath only signified that the community had received the laws which they sought from their ancient kings and asked the latter to keep and observe. No more was meant or intended. As for customs, these were irrelevant unless presented to the king. If they had been presented 'and received his fiat', Brady

H

added, 'they had been laws, by his concession, and no customs'.[101]

In writing history Brady seems to have intended to combat the co-ordination principle in whatever form it appeared, but it is also likely that in making his work public he was moved by a desire to protect the king's veto. It would be endangered if an exclusion bill passed the two houses, but in the event this contingency was not realized. The whigs came nearest to success in the exclusion parliament of 1680, when the second exclusion bill passed the house of commons, only to meet with a rejection in the house of lords. Since it never reached Charles II, no national crisis arose over the veto. But the whigs, too, had to ponder their position in these years; and some of them, such as Neville and Sidney, found no difficulty in insisting that the coronation oath, as traditionally worded, barred the king from using his veto. That they would reach this conclusion was foreseeable; but so, too, did Treby and Atkyns, although they made their views public at a later date and in a different context. If they were thinking on these radical lines, so were others in their party. There is evidence to this effect. Such whig writers as Samuel Johnson,[102] chaplain to William Lord Russell, who like Sidney died for an alleged participation in the rye house plot, and Robert Ferguson the plotter, Shaftesbury's amanuensis and chaplain, took the same position in tracts published either at the Revolution or shortly afterwards.[103] As is well-known, Ferguson shared Shaftesbury's exile in Holland and was present at his bedside when he died; and he later sailed with William of Orange's fleet in 1688. A daring and clever pamphleteer, he wrote tracts of high quality that at least in one case exerted a great deal of influence. His views on government were carried into the eighteenth century, though not under his name, when a dozen pages of his *Brief Justification of the Prince of Orange's Descent into England* (1689) were incorporated without a word of change into *Vox Populi, Vox Dei* (1709),[104] recently described authoritatively as the most popular whig tract of the post-Revolution generation.[105]

This kind of evidence is flawed. It would be difficult, if not impossible, to demonstrate that Shaftesbury's political views towards the end of his life were reflected in Ferguson's tracts at the Revolution, and the same observation applies about Johnson's writings ten years after Russell's death. Just the same, political and social connections of this kind have meaning, and it is an astonishing fact that a list of this nature can be compiled at all, touching so many facets of the whig leadership. Here, after all, was the most delicate of topics, closely associated with the civil war and its outcome at a time when memories of the 1640s and the martyrdom of the best of kings were vivid in men's minds. Moreover, Johnson and Ferguson received rewards at the Revolution from the new rulers, though in Ferguson's case not nearly at the level anticipated. He later became a Jacobite. And there is the further fact that the political extremism which he so well represented had an audience of readers far into the new century when *Vox Populi, Vox Dei*, so popular in Queen Anne's reign, reproduced his main political arguments.

Despite this support in whig ranks, the radical version of co-ordination found no substantial outlet in 1689. This was true only of the more moderate version of co-ordination expressed by the second Powle committee of 1673 and in Petyt's writings during the exclusion crisis. This was the version that shaped the Revolution settlement. There is no difficulty in reaching this conclusion since the parliamentarian version of *quas vulgus elegerit* did not figure in the recorded debates of the convention parliament, with the exception of the passage from Treby; and there is no sign of its direct influence either on the Bill of Rights or in the revised coronation oath that formed part of the Revolution settlement.

Further light is cast on the subject by the debate of January 26, 1694, in the Williamite house of commons when its members considered at length the king's veto of a place bill that the two houses had approved. It appears from their comments that they believed the king had a veto, which he might rightfully and constitutionally exercise; but it is equally clear that they did not like his exercising it. It was as if they accepted the logic of the parliamentarian version of *quas vulgus elegerit* but not the argument itself. At the time speakers vied with one another in professing support for what they called the king's negative voice.[106] Not to allow it was to violate the constitution, so Charles Montagu declared. Presumably he spoke for the majority of the house when he added: 'It was formerly only, and that in the highest times, and by the highest men [stated] that the king cannot deny us bills of right and justice.'[107] The house of commons voted, nevertheless, to send a representation to William III, reminding him that his predecessors rarely refused their assent to bills passed by both houses and that in the few instances in which this had happened, these had been 'attended with great inconveniences to the crown of England, especially where the same has been withheld by insinuations of particular persons, without the advice of the privy council, thereby creating great dissatisfactions and jealousies in the minds of the people'.[108] The king's answer was ambiguous; but the house of commons decided, 229 to 88, not to pursue the matter further. Yet the minority vote was substantial, and thereafter, with a single exception, William III accepted the bills that came to him from the two houses. He did not exercise the veto again after 1696.[109]

The temper of 1689, so far as the co-ordination principle was concerned, was revealed in another way, one requiring a brief digression. There was published at the Revolution, in 1689, and in an enlarged edition in 1693, the collection of tracts from Charles II's reign known as the *State Tracts* or *Baldwin's Tracts*. Their publisher, Richard Baldwin, brought out a number of tracts at this time reflecting the more radical version of co-ordination. Among them was Ferguson's *Brief Justification of the Prince of Orange's Descent into England* (1689), and Johnson's *Essay concerning Parliaments* (1693).[110] It is the more surprising, then, that he acted as if the political note of Charles II's reign most interesting to contemporaries was the one struck in the second Powle committee's address of February 26, 1673. He called his readers' attention to the pertinent sentence on law-making in that address by prefixing a short publisher's note to both editions of the *State Tracts*. The action was the more meaningful because parliamentary records at the time were sparse and difficult to come by. Charles II had withdrawn his declaration of indulgence in 1673, wrote Baldwin, 'for a very good reason which the house of commons then gave, and we have since found too true "that his majesty's pretended power of suspending the penal laws in matters ecclesiastical might tend to the interruption of the free course of the laws, and the altering of the legislative power, which hath been always acknowledged to reside in his majesty and his houses of parliament" '.

One would like to think that Baldwin had made a deliberate

choice between the two versions of co-ordination in writing his note. This is the more plausible because the *Political Catechism*, now indelibly associated with a radical version of co-ordination, loomed large in the newly published collection. Its appearance is a vivid reminder of civil-war extremism : the reprinted edition had first been published in 1643, with lengthy annotations stressing the outright supremacy of the two houses, and by implication had circulated in this form in Charles II's reign. But whether he acted deliberately or not is less important than the fact that the prefatory note setting the tone of the *State Tracts* has a symbolical rightness, not only for Charles II's reign but also for the Revolution. Whatever the route to this conclusion, Baldwin's judgment cannot be faulted.

# 8

## The law-makers and the dispensing power

### I

To Bishop Burnet, the sudden fall of James II was one of the strangest catastrophes in history : 'A great king, with strong armies and mighty fleets, a great treasure and powerful allies, fell all at once, and his whole strength, like a spider's web, was ... irrecoverably broken at a touch.'[1] Certainly the breakdown of royal authority was rapid when it came and the contrast startling between the king's position on the eve of the Glorious Revolution and his involuntary exile in France by the end of 1688. Yet the change in the ideological sphere was long in the making. Ever since the civil war the Stuart kings and their supporters had adhered to one view of the kingship, while many Englishmen – very probably a majority of the political nation – adhered to another, these views encompassing very different versions of legal sovereignty. Should the later Stuart kings embark upon patently unpopular policies, dependent for their execution on a prerogative exercised independently of the two houses, difficulties must accumulate that were potentially overwhelming. Essentially, this is what happened. James II's reign shattered the good will displayed towards the monarchy after the exclusion crisis and the abortive Monmouth rebellion, replacing it with a disaffection that hardened into opposition with the events of 1688. The catalyst was the king's Catholicizing policy, forwarded by means of the controversial dispensing power; and it is by no means clear which contributed more to the coming of the Revolution. Whether fear of popery surpassed that of arbitrary government, to use contemporary terminology, is not easily decided; but what does seem evident is that the combination destroyed political support for James II as the alienated whig and tory parties united to force him into exile and settle the throne on William and Mary – all this despite the ideological differences separating the political parties.[2]

It was no small feat to engender so far-reaching an hostility. Historians have advanced various explanations for the king's political behavior, ranging from the attribution of a premature senility that led to reckless activity when the situation called for a policy of restraint to the sympathetic portrayal of a king who was too great a libertarian for the century in which he ruled. Another explanation well worth pondering came from a contemporary who compared Charles II with his brother, saying: 'The king could see things if he would: the duke would see things if he could.'[3] The failure to assess the political situation realistically was also due to James II's theory of kingship, which encouraged the free exercise of the dispensing power in ecclesiastical matters when so active a royalism seemed to many both unconstitutional and illegal. Viewing the exercise of this prerogative as intimately related to the larger question of who made law in parliament, few would grant that the law-maker in parliament was the king alone. The royal policy of religious toleration was in itself a cause of distrust, especially as applied to Roman Catholics; and apprehension heightened with Louis XIV's persecution of the Huguenots and the final revocation of the edict of Nantes. The deteriorating relationship between king and subject had important consequences when even the most conservative Englishmen felt obliged to seek in the two houses an effective counterweight to James II. As the numbers of those embracing the community-centered view of government increased, the way opened for national acceptance of a legal sovereignty in king, lords, and commons. Perhaps the most significant convert from the standpoint of his earlier political activity was Archbishop Sancroft, whose abandonment of the order theory of kingship in 1688 for a hostile interpretation of the dispensing power placed him on this point at least in the ranks of adherents to the community-centered ideology. The accession of strength to already converted elements helped create the revolutionary situation of 1688, and the unanimity of opinion with regard to the dispensing power shaped in fundamental respects the Revolution settlement.

But the situation was very different when James II ascended the throne. The community-centered ideology had by no means won unqualified acceptance; and there were, on the surface, encouraging factors for the king. Royalism seemed to be at full tide, and the antithetical theory of order had vigorous advocates. Political propaganda extolling its virtues and supporting the dispensing power thrived with court patronage, the prime example supplied by Brady's career. The first volume of his *Complete History*, dedicated to James II, was printed in 1685; and Brady's enthronement in the tower records office followed as a matter of course. The ideological flavor of the new regime was also communicated in unmistakable terms by two other writers, John Wilson and Dr Nathaniel Johnston, the latter one of the historians closely associated with Brady. Given the heightened censorship now prevailing under L'Éstrange, their tracts would never have seen the light of day unless their arguments were acceptable to the court; and it will be seen that their writings were in fact semi-official. Both polemists received government help, either through patronage or else access to research materials and facilities for publication. They were, moreover, personally known to James II and his leading ministers.

The general picture is well worth delineation. Wilson was a minor dramatist, trained in law at Lincoln's Inn, whose high prerogative views endeared him to James while the latter was still duke of York. James' patronage may have led to an appointment in Ireland under Ormonde, to whom Wilson's *Discourse of Monarchy* (1684) was dedicated. But it was printed for Joseph Hindmarsh, the duke's bookseller; and the personal association endured after James became king. This appears from Wilson's *Jus Regium Coronae* (1688), an elaborate apology in Bodinian terms for the dispensing power which was printed by Henry Hills and sold at his printing house in Blackfriars. This fact suggests that it was authorized on the highest level of government since Hills' name on a tract at this time linked its contents directly with the court.[4] A former Anabaptist converted to Roman Catholicism by James' own confessor, the printer had clearly found the road to royal favor by 1686 when the king defended him vigorously at the council board as a very honest man whatever his past. At the time Lord Chancellor Jeffreys was overheard assuring the printer of his constant friendship.[5] Hills became printer of the king's household and chapel and was engaged in turning out a stream of theological tracts from the king's press in London when he printed Wilson's tract.[6]

The encouragement to Wilson pales by comparison with that extended to Johnston, who was second only to Brady as a semi-official spokesman for James II's government. He received special privileges in the tower records office, where he was to pay no fees, and was given access to the library at St James. Secretary of State Sunderland signed the authorizing warrants. According to Johnston himself, he had written his *Excellency of Monarchical Government* (1686) at Sunderland's express invitation,[7] this mattering the more because the latter was ascendant at court. As secretary of state and president of the council Sunderland exercised a political influence comparable to that of a modern prime minister. Johnston's performance must have been thoroughly satisfactory to the court since rumor had it that his tract, said to ascribe 'very much to the crown', was written with much briskness and was very free from flatness,[8] and this literary success led to the semi-official *The King's Visitatorial Power Asserted* (1688). This time a warrant from Sunderland to Robert Scott, the royal bookseller and stationer, authorized the latter to supply Johnston with a list of books required for his writing and to charge them to James II's account.[9] Another directive from Sunderland – to Sir Joseph Williamson at the paper office – allowed Johnston to search there for commissions of visitation or for any other papers relating to the king's supremacy or other ecclesiastical affairs and to copy whatever was necessary for the king's service.[10] Add to this the fact that his brother was a Roman Catholic, always a recommendation to James II, and that after the Glorious Revolution Johnston, by this time in distress, was rescued from penury by Lords Peterborough and Huntingdon – the first groom of the stole to James II; the other, to Prince George of Denmark – and he is properly viewed as a publicist of more than ordinary consequence.[11]

Wilson's and Johnston's writings, along with Brady's, may be treated, then, as a genuine reflection of the political ideology at James II's court. That ideology, it is here suggested, was drawn from the order theory of kingship as it was shaped during the civil war. At that time such modern-minded royalists as Sir John Spelman and Holbourne – writing under Bodin's influence – had placed legal sovereignty in the king in parliament; and their version was clearly visible after the restoration. It was very much alive, for example, in 1673 when Charles II justified his dispensing power with the argument that the king as the only law-maker in parliament might legally set aside his own statutes, if his wisdom and discretion so dictated. In short, the supreme governor of the Tudor and early Stuart theorists, who as keeper of the kingdom exercised a dispensing power that placed him at times above the law, was fast evolving into a Bodinian law-maker, who exercised that great power on much the same terms as earlier and on similar lines. But if the power was the same, the rationale had changed.

Anyone expounding this particular view of the kingship had the two-fold task of upholding a high prerogative while at the same time striking down the rival community-centered view. Wilson's *Discourse of Monarchy*, published in 1684 when the reaction of Charles II's last years was in full swing and James was the real power behind the throne, reveals that as late as the middle of the 1680s a semi-official spokesman for the court thought it both desirable and necessary to treat at length the vexatious problem of the three estates. Wilson found the king to be 'none of the three states', a truism from the court's standpoint but not that of the political nation. Those who believed the king to be one of the three estates in parliament described the government as a mixed monarchy, inasmuch as in parliament the lower house, where the commons were represented, bore a resemblance to democracy and the house of lords to aristocracy. They also held that king, lords, and commons, assembled jointly as one corporation for legislation, acted as law-giver. The view was mistaken. The supreme authority, Wilson explained, 'resteth neither in the one house, or the other, either jointly, or severally, but solely in the king, at whose pleasure they are assembled, and without whose royal assent, they can make no law, to oblige the subject'.[12]

The idea of a mixed monarchy was now condemned as a contradiction in terms and a novelty in political thought. A government that extended itself to more than one could be no monarchy, as was obvious to anyone who understood the word. Nor had the idea of a mixed monarchy been heard of in England until the civil war. No credibility attached, accordingly, to the claim of a co-ordination in law-making. The principle was false; but more than this, it was insidious. To presume the king to be one of three estates was to make him 'but a co-ordinate power' and as a consequence 'concludible by the other two'. By 'concludible' Wilson seems to have meant that the other two estates could restrain and control the king or perhaps even speak for him, a conclusion against which Selden had earlier warned. This political system must lead to chaos and anarchy since no authority prevailed among equals. Happily for Englishmen, their government was not to be described in these terms. The title of king admitted no superior, nor indeed any equals; and for support on this vital point Wilson turned to Bodin, who had found the English king to be 'next to God, of whom he holdeth his sceptre and . . . bound to no man'. So remote were the two houses from a co-ordination with the king that their power and authority were actually derived from him.[13]

Such a king might legally and constitutionally exercise the dispensing power in the manner of the Tudor and early Stuart kings; and this argument was expounded in Wilson's *Jus Regium Coronae*, published in the year of revolution. The usual preliminary to discussing the royal power and authority was quickly disposed of. English kings were absolute monarchs, their titles as long ago as the Anglo-Saxon Edgar's reign revealing that 'all co-ordinate authority' was excluded. To this kind of evidence should be added present-day practice. Only the king possessed the legislative power because he made laws with the two houses' consent, not they with his consent. An essential corollary rose out of this. 'As the laws are the king's laws', it was explained, 'his also is the interpretation of them and the supreme power of dispensing with them.' No weight should be assigned to the political idea that royal power had originated with the community as the human source of political authority. All government was originally from God, who had never intended that the people share it.[14]

Johnston likewise insisted on the king's lofty position as the supreme law-giver. His political ideas were borrowed directly from Filmer and Brady, but also from such proven conservative writers as Sir John Spelman, Holbourne as author of the indispensable *Freeholders Grand Inquest*, Archbishop Ussher, and Sheringham. Johnston quoted liberally, for example, from the *Case of our Affaires* and borrowed from the original edition of the *Freeholders Grand Inquest*. The *Excellency of Monarchical*

*Government* is, in fact, best described as a mosaic of royalist and high tory political arguments, enunciated over several generations, that faithfully reflected the order theory of kingship as understood by pro-court elements before the Glorious Revolution. As such, its contents provide an exceedingly helpful entrée into the sheltered ideological world within which James II's government functioned. The appearance of the tract was nicely timed. Coinciding with James' policy of proceeding unilaterally with the dispensing power on behalf of his co-religionists, it may well have been designed to secure maximum support for his policy. Johnston found the king to be a sovereign ruler, on Bodinian lines, who possessed numerous prerogative powers that were firmly grounded in law. He alone had these powers, which he exercised at his discretion. Of absolute necessity for the security of the government, they were inseparable from the king and included power to summon and dissolve parliament, assent to laws, command the militia, coin money, pardon felonies and treasons, and dispense with penal laws.[15]

The last prerogative commanded much attention as central to the contention that the king was the only law-maker in parliament and as innately hostile to the contrary proposition that the two houses were co-ordinate with the king. An entire chapter was devoted to the dispensing power, which was described as essential to government because no law could sufficiently answer 'the varieties and unthought on plottings of man's nature'. Since even just laws became unprofitable and harsh in time, the king must be in a position to moderate the law.[16] To describe the dispensing power as an instrument of legal flexibility had been common in Tudor and early Stuart England, and this portion of Johnston's argument would have been deemed unexceptionable in the earlier period.

But the next strand was peculiar to his own generation, that is, it was essentially post-1660. It was, however, the natural corollary of the theory of legal sovereignty, expounded by modern-minded royalists in the later stages of the civil war,[17] and was also highly controversial. That the king alone should exercise the dispensing power flowed out of his relationship with the law. Properly speaking, it was the king who made law : he was 'a living law'. Johnston wrote : 'In all government, the legislative power must be fixed somewhere; and it is the concurrent opinion of all civilians that

all laws do flow from the prince, as from a fountain.'[18] The legislative power also resided in the king alone by the common law.[19]
More than this. Not only the legislative power itself, but also its
very exercise, so far as it was essential to government, was in the
king alone. One sign that he was the law-maker was that he might
issue edicts and proclamations to provide for all necessary occasions and special emergencies not provided for by fixed laws. Such
activity constituted one of the most eminent acts of the legislative
power. The same held true for the dispensing power, which
provided convincing evidence that the king alone, properly speaking, was the law-maker. His possession of this power was undeniable. 'None but strangers to our laws can deny', wrote Johnston,
'that the king hath sole power to dispense with the statutes, and
abate their rigour, where a mischief would otherwise ensue.'[20]

Nor was his law-making power diminished by the fact that he
made and repealed laws only in parliament. This activity constituted no diminution of royal sovereignty. The situation was
otherwise in time of revolution, as could be seen when the long
parliament claimed a co-ordinate power and sought to have its
advice swallowed as commands. Loyal persons should oppose this
assertiveness.[21] Predictably Johnston railed against the 'serpent of
co-ordinate power',[22] the origins of which he traced to Charles I's
Answer to the Nineteen Propositions and the forms of earlier
enacting clauses.[23] Admittedly, he argued, the king must cooperate
with the two houses in making laws. But cooperation was by no
means co-ordination; the king made laws in parliament out of his
gracious condescension, and consequently the role of the two
houses in law-making was plainly subordinate.[24] Johnston struck
another familiar note when he linked the denial of co-ordination
with the insistence that the king, empowered directly by God,
constituted the human source of political authority. 'As the light
of the sun is inherent in its own body, and yet diffused through
the whole world : and so we call it moonshine and starlight, when
all their lights are from the sun', so the 'delegate authority' of the
two houses 'may be called theirs'. But since they were summoned
by the king's writ and dissolved at his pleasure, they could not be
said to have the law-making power radically in themselves and so
there was 'no mixture with the monarchy'.[25]

Had there been no direct links between these writers and James

II's government, it would still appear that the king subscribed to
the version of the order theory of kingship posited in their writings.
His experience with the rival ideology during Charles II's reign –
at the time of the Irish cattle bill, the indulgence controversy of
the early 1670s, and the exclusion crisis – must have strengthened
his attachment to the conservative theory of government. The
tendency to equate Charles I's death with the civil-war advocacy
of co-ordination, found so often in conservative writings, would
have had a similar impact upon his thinking. The fashion in which,
once king, he exercised the dispensing power points in the same
direction. Just as clearly his subjects, as a whole, held to a dia-
metrically opposed theory of kingship, its tenets essentially those
of the parliamentarian ideology in the civil-war years and as such
innately hostile to the royal discretionary authority as defined by
the king. The results were predictable, given James' personality
and character. The persistent and provocative use of the dispensing power to favor Roman Catholicism brought once more to the
forefront of politics the central question of who made law in
parliament; and the question no longer evadable was put to rest
at the Revolution when legal sovereignty was firmly placed in
king, lords, and commons. But until then, the political picture was
one of a headstrong monarch, imbued with a view of kingship
that had become Bodinian during the civil war, plunging ahead
with policies affecting law-making that raised the hackles of those
Englishmen who took an entirely different view of the kingship.
The outcome was predetermined by attitudes, formed in the course
of a generation, over which James had little personal control. It is
arguable that a revolutionary situation was bound to develop
whenever England had a king imbued with a highly conservative
interpretation of the order theory of kingship who was either
unwilling or unable to seek an accommodation with those who
held to the community-centered ideology. In the sense that the
civil war had radicalized Stuart political thought while at the
same time stiffening the view of the kingship taken by conservative
elements, and to the degree that James II's loss of the throne rose
out of a disregard for canons of opinion regarding royal power
and authority, the king was as much a victim of the civil war as
his father before him.

## II

The disregard for opinion was amply displayed in the king's well-known attempts to impose his religious policy unilaterally on an unwilling political nation. The issue was formally joined on November 9, 1685, when the two houses learned from James II that he intended to retain in his service the Roman Catholics who had proved loyal during Monmouth's rebellion, his method one of dispensing with the disabling statutes. The chief of them was the test act of 1673, which had been passed after the indulgence crisis to prevent Roman Catholics from holding either civil or military office under the crown. It was followed, five years later, by a second test act, barring Roman Catholics from parliament. Clearly the king considered his personal policy at stake as he warned parliament not to take exception to officers in the army who were not qualified for their posts under the test act of 1673. 'I must tell you', James stated bluntly, 'the gentlemen . . . are most of them well known to me.' They would retain their posts, no matter what the consequences might be. 'I will deal plainly with you, that after having had the benefit of their service in such a time of need and danger, I will neither expose them to disgrace, nor myself to the want of them, if there should be another rebellion to make them necessary for me.'[26]

Parliament had no desire to anger the king, if this was avoidable, but no intention either of repealing the test act. Its resistance surprised such seasoned observers as John Evelyn, the commissioner of the great seal known for his zealous support of the court in the preceding reign. He reported the hostility in the house of commons at James' promise of an indemnity and dispensation for Roman Catholic officers;[27] and this became unmistakable when that house, despite an overwhelmingly loyalist complexion, departed from the usual practice of voting thanks for the king's speech and resolved instead, 183 to 182, on November 13, to postpone supply and take under advisement the part of his speech in which he had declared a fixed intention of dispensing with the test act.[28] Support was forthcoming from an unusual quarter when some army officers supported the resolution, and even moderate Roman Catholics were said to have voiced disapproval of the king's policy.[29] The vote, despite the closeness, was the more significant because the house of commons, many of its members elected by corporations that Charles II had remodelled, might have been expected to take the king's lead. James is supposed to have remarked that there were no more than forty members but such as he himself desired, and Evelyn expressed a common opinion in describing the house's behavior as a great surprise in a parliament from which compliance was expected in all things.[30]

It is the more remarkable, then, that expressions of the community-centered ideology appeared in such a house. To Sir Thomas Clarges, the protracted use of the dispensing power was a breach of English liberties; and, significantly, Sir Edward Seymour, sometime speaker of the house of commons and a leading tory, concurred. In removing the tests the king was dispensing with all the laws at once.[31] These sentiments were reflected when the house now voted two resolutions: the first asked James to desist from employing Roman Catholics as army officers and the second proposed a committee to consider an indemnification of unqualified persons in the king's service.[32] The latter was probably an attempt to establish parliamentary control over dispensations and licenses of *non obstante*. Nothing came of the resolutions because, as Henry Care wrote, James knew his own authority. He was the sole judge of danger to the kingdom and the means of avoiding it.[33] Doubtless this was a valid assessment of the king's outlook, but such language from this quarter is by no means unexpected and to a degree must be discounted. A former whig polemist, who had crossed over to the court, Care proved in James II's reign to be as strenuous a propagandist for the royal prerogative as L'Éstrange.

Nor did the house of commons hesitate to assert its authority. An address to the king (November 16, 1685) claimed that the penalties of the test acts could in no way 'be taken off but by an act of parliament'. Unless parliament acted, Roman Catholics were legally incompetent to hold office, the dispensing power notwithstanding. The existing situation was disturbing because the continuance of Roman Catholics in their employment could be interpreted as dispensing with the appropriate test act without an act of parliament. The consequence was of the greatest concern to the rights of all the king's subjects and to all the laws made for the security of their religion.[34] James had neither sympathy nor patience for such language, and the prorogation of parliament followed. He may even have thought that the two houses might go so far as to declare the dispensing power illegal, but in any case he took no chances. Parliament did not meet again during the reign, although dissolution was delayed until July 2, 1687.

Admittedly, the display of opposition rested on a variety of grounds. Such considerations as financial loss and diminution of political power could constitute a basis of opposition, and their significance should not be minimized. Anglican members of parliament might well dislike sharing the fruits of the establishment with Roman Catholics and Protestant dissenters; and the holders of military and civil office presumably resented replacement by men who were often their social inferiors.[35] Yet this explanation fails to consider so conspicuously important a component of the situation as political ideology and overlooks, in particular, the role of the community-centered view of government, which may have been decisive in molding the opposition to James II. To assert this is not to ignore religion, which ought not to be underrated in this context, but to insist that as the reign went on the widespread resistance to royal policy was as much constitutional and ideological as religious. After all, given the existence of the established church of England, its privileges dependent on statutory law, even clergymen had to decide ultimately about the law-making power; and the hostility that James II encountered was often rooted in the conviction that his use of the dispensing power violated the constitution as commonly interpreted. Perceiving in law-making a shared power, leading members of the political nation denied categorically that the king, who was in their understanding only a third legislator, could legally and constitutionally set aside statutes that were made by three law-makers. Resentment was the stronger because the dispensing power was being wielded on behalf of unpopular religious minorities to set aside statutes that the majority of the political nation wanted enforced.

The turning point in the reign was the king's decision to continue exercising the dispensing power without concurrent parliamentary acceptance and approval. The decision was daring, the timing bad. At no time in the seventeenth century was the policy so potentially dangerous to the kingship, and it may be wondered that James himself did not recognize the danger and draw back in time. As was earlier suggested, the best explanation is very probably to be found in his personal characteristics and ideological prepossessions; and in this connection James II's reading of past events was critical. The difficulties which had overwhelmed Charles I in the 1640s and beset Charles II during the indulgence controversy and the exclusion crisis were traced to their willingness to appease their political enemies. Above all James was determined to avoid what he deemed their path of unwise weakness. A revealing passage in the king's *Life* describes him as having a 'prepossession against that yielding temper, which had proved so dangerous to the king his brother and so fatal to the king his father', the effect one of fixing him 'too obstinately in a contrary method'. The biographer added: 'He [James] had observed that nothing was more pernicious to them, than their frequent goings back from such councils as had been prudently resolved upon, which determined him not to fall into the same error he had so much preached against in his brother's reign.'[36] Whatever the reason, the king had no intention of permitting the two houses to determine royal policy and once embarked upon a policy of religious toleration based on the dispensing power was tenacious in moving towards his goal despite multiplying signs of discontent. The first sign of the bold new course came when he pardoned some eighty Roman Catholics in his service from the penalties of the test act and then issued numerous licenses permitting his co-religionists to hold civil and military office. Even the church of England felt the weight of the dispensing power as royal grants of *non obstante* enabled Roman Catholic priests to hold ecclesiastical preferments legally.

The momentum of this policy led to the suspension of Bishop Compton and the establishment of an ecclesiastical commission to control the church and the universities, the latter action resting on the controversial royal discretionary authority.[37] James now cast around for a new method of demonstrating the legality of his methods. The necessary affirmation was forthcoming in the case of *Godden v. Hales* (1686), which opened the way for a large-scale use of the dispensing power. No pains were spared in securing a favorable verdict, and to this end the king remodelled the bench. This practice, which went on throughout the reign, replaced twelve judges and several serjeants and other law officials, including Solicitor-General Finch, Justice Creswell Levinz, and Exchequer Baron William Gregory.[38] While the effect was to encourage subservience towards the king, this is by no means the whole story. Some judges subscribed by inclination and temperament to the order theory of kingship, to which the dispensing power was annexed; and there were ample legal precedents for the king. After all, a judge as independent in outlook as Hale had found it possible to place the law-making power undivided in the king, and a description of this type was often the prelude to legitimating the king's discretionary use of the dispensing power.[39]

The most provocative aspect of *Godden v. Hales* was the proposition now explicitly advanced in a court of law that the king as the only law-maker in parliament might rightfully and legally exercise the dispensing power to set aside statutes, although admittedly he must operate within the traditional legal framework in doing so. This was the line taken by Solicitor-General Powys;[40] and, more importantly, by Lord Chief Justice Edward Herbert, whose words became at once the very symbol of the legal judgment in the case, laying, in contemporary opinion, the groundwork for James II's indulgence policy. Herbert went directly to the point. The case before him, though of great consequence, was fortunately of little difficulty, resting as it did on the simple maxim that there was 'no law whatsoever but may be dispensed with by the supreme law-giver'. The way seemed open for an unlimited use of the dispensing power, but Herbert's language was more conventional than this. While the king could not dispense with laws that were *mala in se* nor set aside those laws in which the subject had an interest, still his power was very high. This could be seen from the famous *Sheriff's Case*, in which the dispensing power had been upheld despite the fact that a clause in the statute under consideration prohibited the application of a *non obstante* to its provisions. Herbert's language now took on a strongly ideological cast. 'So if an act of parliament had a clause in it that it should never be repealed', he pointed out, 'yet without question, the same power that made it, may repeal it.' In the absence of such a prohibitory clause in the test act, the lord chief justice concluded that the case before him was in some respects more favorable to royal power than the *Sheriff's Case*, which was cited as good law in the law-books and until now never questioned.[41]

With only Baron Thomas Street dissenting, the judges found for the defendant : Hales' dispensation was good in law. The grounds for this decision may properly be described as a diagrammatic chart of the order theory of kingship, as it had evolved since 1660. It was agreed,

1. That the kings of England are sovereign princes.
2. That the laws of England are the king's laws.
3. That therefore 'tis an inseparable prerogative in the kings of England, to dispense with penal laws in particular cases, and upon particular necessary reasons.
4. That of those reasons and those necessities, the king himself is sole judge : and then, which is consequent upon all,
5. That this is not a trust invested in, or granted to the king by the people, but the ancient remains of the sovereign power and prerogative of the kings of England; which never yet was taken from them, nor can be.[42]

The decision established that a Bodinian version of the order theory of kingship had penetrated the bench, a place where it was not typically to be found. The statement that the laws of England were the king's laws could be interpreted to mean that the king alone made law in parliament;[43] and this proposition led in turn to the conclusion that the king, as the sole law-maker in parliament, possessed the inseparable prerogative of dispensing with laws in particular cases and upon particular necessary reasons. He was the sole judge of those reasons and necessities. The judges also rejected the alternative community-centered ideology with the statement that the dispensing power was not a trust invested in, or granted to the king by the people.

To James, the decision in *Godden v. Hales* was a justification and vindication not only of his earlier activity but also of the indulgence policy that he put forward in 1687–88. This appears from the fact that the semi-official *Life* has lengthy extracts from Herbert's argument, prominent among which was the statement that the law-giver might dispense with any law whatsoever. The phrases occur in a passage devoted to the traditional justification for the dispensing power despite this being an ideological argument that was by comparison a latecomer to the legal scene. To be sure, the lord chief justice in a vindication published at the Revolution separated himself from the indulgence policy and visibly retreated from the position of 1686. Even so, the appearance of these phrases in the king's *Life* indicates that his position is properly equated with Herbert's argument in *Godden v. Hales*, a view reinforced by the king's remodelling the bench and the circumstance that it was Herbert who first suggested to James II that the dispensing power might be legally extended to the test act. Moreover, the chief justice, although he was a Protestant, became the exiled king's lord chancellor at St Germain, a sign surely of continuing royal favor.[44]

The unrest created by so authoritative a voice for the order theory of kingship deepened when Roman Catholics were appointed to the army, privy council, commissions of peace, and the judiciary in the wake of *Godden v. Hales*. So powerful was the assumption by this time that legal sovereignty resided in king, lords, and commons that such appointments seemed to many illegal. Here two whig tracts were representative. Sir Robert Atkyns' *Enquiry into the Power of Dispensing with Penal Statutes* and the *Power, Jurisdiction and Priviledge of Parliament and the Antiquity of the House of Commons Asserted* appeared in January, 1689, in time for the convention parliament that assembled on January 22, after James' flight to the continent. The tracts are notable anyway for the reliance on the common-law principles of legal memory and prescription as Atkyns followed out the lines that Petyt had set. But their contents also illustrate the extent to which the political ideas and principles associated with the community-centered view of government had eroded by the end of the seventeenth century what had been at one time a very wide acceptance of the dispensing power.

To the writing of his tracts Atkyns brought an experience compounded almost equally of political and judicial elements. A notable career in the cavalier house of commons was followed by his becoming judge of common pleas, a position from which he was removed in the early 1680s because of his outspoken political views. By this time an enemy to Charles II's government, he was soon busy behind the scenes in collaboration with other anti-court elements. His hostility to the court became open when he gave energetic support to Prince William in the first phase of his entrance into England. Atkyns was early called upon to advise the new rulers, and he became the speaker of the convention house of lords after being made Baron Atkyns at the Revolution.[45] It matters the more, accordingly, that a legal sovereignty in king, lords, and commons seemed to him the distinctive aspect of the government and that in discussing the dispensing power he affirmed the community-centered ideology at the expense of the order theory of kingship and stressed the high power of parliament. The king's legal inability to dispense flowed out of the nature and essence of the law, which Atkyns – unlike Brady and Johnston, to whom he was responding – held to be an independent entity, the very soul animating the body politic. The law had originated in the community's consent. 'We ourselves of the present age chose our common law, and consented to the most ancient acts of parliament', he wrote. This was so because Englishmen lived in their ancestors of a thousand years ago, as their ancestors lived in them now. The law, accordingly, was made by public agreement; it was not imposed upon Englishmen against their will. Laws were 'articles of agreement, chosen and consented to by prince and people', and as a consequence law was the act and deed of the whole body politic, the rule by which the prince governed and the subject obeyed.[46]

The community being the human source of the law-making power, the government was 'a mixt monarchy'.[47] The description assumed a co-ordination principle in the legislative power; and to Atkyns, the law-makers were in fact the king and parliament (the two houses) working together. Certainly, the king's role in law-making was important. 'It is he that quickens the embryo, and first gives it life', ran the explanation. But he was not the only law-maker: 'The king hath not the sole legislature, such as almighty God hath over his creatures, but the whole kingdom hath a share in that power, . . . as well as the king.'[48] This proposition must be kept steadily in mind when contemplating the dispensing power. 'None but the law-maker', wrote Atkyns, 'can dispense with the law, not he that hath but a share in the legislature.'[49] To an extraordinary degree that single sentence summed up the political conclusions of his generation. For Englishmen like him – and their number was legion in the late 1680s – only the king and the two houses, who represented the whole realm, had full power to dispense with the laws. 'There is no just nor lawful power of dispensing with any act of parliament in any other hands than in those that are the law-makers, that is, in the king and parliament in conjunction.' A related point, also at issue, was who should judge when the discretionary authority was to be used. Here only one answer was possible for Atkyns. The king and parliament, not the king alone, were the proper judges of its exercise. 'The king, the nobles and the commons of the realm present in parliament' could dispense whenever they judged it 'meet and convenient for the wealth [welfare?] of the realm'.[50]

So the dispensing power was not completely ruled out. Such a power existed in the government, but its operation was subject to parliamentary approval and control. Indeed, its very existence was dependent on parliament. To the contrary contention that the dispensing power resided in the king independently of the two houses, this reply was returned. Every legal prerogative had to be so by prescription; that is, it had to have been used time out of mind. But the dispensing power, according to Atkyns, did not meet the test. That prerogative was within time of legal memory, and, since it was not immemorial, was not inherent in the crown and not inseparable from it.[51] Yet it had to be granted that on occasion the king alone might have a dispensing power. He might, for example, suspend the rules requiring the recitation of the precise value of land, statutes regulating the shipping of wool, and acts forbidding the pardoning of murder in imprecise terms. These 'trifling' statutes were amenable to royal dispensation because they gave the penalty and forfeiture to the king; 'they concern the king's profit only'. Even this apparent concession was greatly qualified when Atkyns asserted that the king's right to dispense with such statutes resulted from parliamentary permission. The prerogative was not *jure divino* but derived from the people's grant.[52] Presumably the king possessed no such derivative right with regard to other kinds of statutes. The test acts, for example, differed greatly from those measures with which parliament permitted the king to dispense. They touched 'the safety of the government, and *salus populi*, and the maintaining of the true religion established by law'. Any idea that the king might dispense with a statute made in a case of the highest concern to the public, where religion and the government were so deeply affected, was unwarranted, illegal, and innovative. Not just the king alone but the whole realm had an interest in implementing a statute such as the test act.[53]

There was another urgent reason for deeming illegal an independent dispensing power in the king. The matter had been settled when the two houses declared it so in 1663 and in 1673. Since Atkyns had been appointed to the committee of the cavalier house of commons that had pronounced against such a dispensing power on the first occasion, he was writing from personal experience; and probably he was influenced by the defense during the trial of the seven bishops in 1688. That trial will later receive discussion, but here it should be noted that Atkyns pointed to James II's hesitation about the prerogative in question in attempting in 1685 to secure a parliamentary sanction for its exercise. Two telling questions were raised. If the king's prerogative enabled him to dispense with the test act, why had James proposed that the two houses allow him to do it? And why had the two houses, after long debate, excused themselves from consenting to an action which the king could take without them?[54] Atkyns believed, then, that only the agents of the community might lawfully exercise the dispensing power, that is, the king and the two houses. Charged with the kingdom's welfare, all three together were the proper and only judge of its exercise. In other words, the two houses as well as the king possessed *gubernaculum*.[55]

## III

The breach between king and subject widened abruptly when James II, encouraged by *Godden v. Hales*, went beyond individual dispensations and undertook the total suspension of the ecclesiastical penal laws. The declaration of indulgence in 1687, reissued in 1688, revived Charles II's toleration policy of the early 1670s. On February 13, 1687, a liberty of conscience was granted in Scotland and on April 4 in England, by which all penal laws in ecclesiastical matters were suspended and persons holding places of trust were no longer compelled to take the oaths of supremacy and allegiance. Pardons were promised to Protestant dissenters and Roman Catholic recusants for all previous breaches of the penal laws, etc.[56] Despite the sweeping character of these provisions and the favorable verdict in *Hales Case*, evidently James was still uneasy about his legal position since he now pressed for a statute to abolish the obnoxious penal laws. A commission was empowered to visit the provinces and ascertain the willingness of prospective parliamentary candidates to support his toleration policy in a new house of commons, and at the same time came the dismissal of local officials whose responses were deemed unsatisfactory. The commissions of peace were altered and many deputy lieutenants in the counties turned out,[57] their positions passing to Roman Catholics.

The declaration of indulgence was reissued on April 27, 1688, followed by a provocative order in council of May 4 by which it was to be read in the churches and chapels of London and Westminster on the 20th and 27th of the month and in the rest of the kingdom on the 3rd and 10th of June.[58] This combination brought Sancroft out of semi-retirement to meet with six other bishops at Lambeth Palace to draft a protest, in the form of a petition, against the declaration and the order in council.[59] The petition, said to be in Sancroft's handwriting, was presented on May 18 to James II, its contents revealing that the bishops had swung to the side of the two houses in the ideological controversy over the dispensing power. The archbishop's own position had come full circle. Opposition to the order in council, it was stated, was based on the fact that the declaration of indulgence was itself founded upon such a dispensing power as had often been declared illegal in parliament, particularly in the years 1663 and 1673 and at the beginning of James' own reign.[60]

The king was ill-prepared for the petition, which he described as the strangest he had ever seen. Prior information had led him to expect religious objections to his policy, not constitutional and legal, but in any case he could hardly have foreseen the abrupt abandonment of the order theory of kingship for the community-centered ideology. Sancroft's participation must have seemed to him inexplicable after the archbishop's zeal in combating the co-ordination principle, displayed as recently as the exclusion crisis. Moreover, Sancroft had kept private his misgivings about the ecclesiastical commission. Now, in the greatest crisis of the reign, he broke openly with the king, identifying himself with the co-ordination principle that was associated in contemporary writings with Charles I's death. Little wonder that James II characterized the petition as 'a standard of rebellion' and reproached the bishops with a willingness to uphold the absolute prerogative only when it served their turn. 'The dispensing power was never questioned by the men of the church of England', he declared. To this the bishop of St Asaph, William Lloyd, replied : 'It was declared against in the first parliament called by his late majesty and by that which was called by your majesty.' James would have none of this talk. 'God hath given me this dispensing power and I will maintain it.' This was his final word on the subject.[61]

The sequel was the indictment of the seven bishops for seditious libel. James II's action was not, in legal terms, altogether reckless. Before the trial began, on June 29, the judges were asked about the legal correctness of the king's position regarding the petition; and only after an assurance was forthcoming did the prosecution proceed. Nor is it clear that James had any alternative. According to the Dutch ambassador, Aarnout Van Citters, the bishops had made it exceedingly difficult for him not to take punitive action 'as they openly declare the acts of the king illegal or unlawful, and likewise accuse him of injustice'. To overlook their stand was to encourage the community in its resistance. Van Citters forecast correctly that the king's resentment would fall first and foremost on Sancroft, 'he having made the first movement towards this resolution' and having 'regulated everything with his own hand and pen'.[62]

The proceedings, which took place midst the highest excitement, went badly for the king. To sustain the indictment it had to be demonstrated that the petition was written and published in the county of Middlesex. But Sancroft had not been for many months outside the grounds of Lambeth Palace in Surrey. When this difficulty was overcome, witnesses proved evasive as to whether the bishops had actually delivered the petition to the king, an action constituting publication in the eye of the law. For a time it appeared that the trial would end on this technicality; and Lord Chief Justice Wright prepared to charge the jury, only to be interrupted by Heneage Finch, one of the bishops' counsel. Word then came that Sunderland would provide legal proof of publication, and the trial continued with Finch temporarily very unpopular with the bishops' supporters. But the situation changed abruptly when Wright now erred in permitting argument on the legality of the dispensing power, despite an insistence that it was not at issue. This was a major blunder. According to Sir John Reresby, who was sympathetic to the court, 'The king's power to dispense with the laws was extremely arraigned, and . . . it was wished at court that the thing had never been begun.'[63]

The court's regret was due to the astute defense put forward by the counsel for the bishops, four tories and three whigs. The tories were Sir Robert Sawyer, Heneage Finch, Sir Francis Pemberton, and Sir Creswell Levinz; the whigs, Sir George Treby, Sir Francis Pollexfen, and John Somers. Its bipartisan nature makes it seem the more remarkable that the defense's pronouncements were, in a sense, so radical regarding the legislative power and the royal prerogative. But from another point of view – that of the political nation, which was to an extraordinary degree united on the point – the pronouncements were not radical at all. Observers were unanimous that in opposing James II the best possible ground was rejection of his indulgence policy; and everywhere in political literature is to be seen evidence that the political and constitutional issue, at bottom ideological, loomed large with those prepared to resist the king. Anglican and Protestant dissenter saw alike on this issue, and here perhaps is the main condemnation of James' political campaign to forge a new political alliance for the crown. On this rock the campaign foundered. That is, a central issue in what looks to be a religious struggle was widely said to be one of whether Englishmen were or were not to live under an arbitrary government, one by definition in which the claim could rightfully be made that the king was the sole law-maker in parliament. For Edward Fowler, later bishop of Gloucester – who led the London clergy in opposing James – any vote to uphold or accept the king's policy was tantamount to 'countenancing . . . arbitrary government'.[64] The view was widespread. A contemporary who recognized that the petition had tapped a deep-rooted sentiment was James Johnstone, William of Orange's authorized agent in England. In his opinion the bishops could not have offered resistance on a point more plausible and acceptable to the nation 'than that about the dispensing power'.[65] And one of the London clergy asked : 'Do we intend to make a stand at any time or no?

If we do can we have a more legal cause wherein we may more
clearly justify ourselves by law or that we are more likely to be
unanimous in ?'[66] The bishops' counsel reasoned on the same lines.
From their point of view the received doctrine of a shared legislative power nullified any claim by James II to dispense legally
with penal laws in ecclesiastical matters.

The pertinent statement emanated from what seems at first
sight to be a highly unlikely quarter. It came from Finch, whose
inadvertence was responsible for the continuance of the trial at a
critical point and hence the full discussion of the dispensing
power.[67] An impeccable toryism made his language of special
significance. Formerly solicitor general until he abandoned the
post rather than act for the crown in *Godden v. Hales*, he was the
second son of the earlier Heneage Finch, who, as chairman of a
committee in the cavalier house of commons, challenged successfully the dispensing power in 1663, apparently because of hostility
towards a policy of religious toleration. But there is no reason to
think that his objection was constitutional; and thereafter he was
steadily on record as a staunch defender of the king's dispensing
power, both in the debates on the Irish cattle act of 1667 and
during the indulgence crisis of 1672–73. Ennobled as the earl of
Nottingham, he was for a time lord chancellor. The title passed on
his death to his older son, Daniel Finch, brother to the Heneage
Finch who was a member of the bishops' counsel. The second
earl of Nottingham had a career of considerable distinction.
Secretary of state under two sovereigns, William III and Anne,
he was the author of the toleration act of 1689 and a lay leader
of the Anglicans. No less important, though less noticed about
him, was his contribution to the trial of the seven bishops. He was
active behind the scenes when the crucial decision was taken by
the bishops' counsel to contest publicly James II's use of the
dispensing power. The decision was revolutionary, Nottingham
the most reluctant of revolutionaries. Yet at a meeting of June 14,
1688, he insisted successfully that the counsel go beyond techni-
calities and take up the general principle of the dispensing
power.[68]

The tactic was at first too bold for the younger Finch, but he
was soon won over,[69] and within this context he made a singularly
interesting statement regarding the legislative power. His language

provides an important reminder of the ideological gulf separating James II from the leading members of the political nation, which was fast widening into an unbridgeable chasm. Finch went directly to the point, his choice of words reflecting the parliamentary language of the restoration years as he equated the suspending of laws and their dispensation with the repeal and abrogation of laws. Powers such as these belonged only to the legislature. Who constituted the legislature? To this vital question Finch returned an answer altogether different from his father's. Unmistakably, the son accepted the principle of co-ordination when he stated: 'My lord, in all the education that I have had, in all the small knowledge of the laws that I could attain to, I could never yet hear of, or learn, that the constitution of the government in England was otherwise than thus, that the whole legislative power is in the king, lords, and commons.' If James II's declaration was founded 'upon a part of the legislature, which must be by all men acknowledged not to reside in the king alone, but in the king, lords, and commons, it cannot be a legal and true power, or prerogative'.[70]

A major bulwark for the defense was also found in the fate of Charles II's policy of religious toleration. Insisting that the clerk of the court read for the record the pertinent portions of the parliamentary proceedings in 1662–63 and 1673, the bishops' counsel seized on Charles II's admission in 1662 that he had no dispensing power to carry out his religious policy. He had declared: 'I could heartily wish, I had such a power of indulgence to use upon occasion.' There was also the house of commons' statement that 'laws of uniformity then in being . . . could not be dispensed with but by act of parliament'.[71] Attention was also drawn to the Powle committee's address of February 26, 1673, and to the decisive proceedings in the house of lords.[72] The parliamentary proceedings of 1685 were treated as pertinent, too. In response to James' declared intention of suspending the ecclesiastical penal laws, the house of commons then had insisted that such laws could be taken off only by act of parliament.[73]

By comparison, the retort from James II's law officers seemed feeble. For one thing, out of the many available legal precedents, few were cited to demonstrate the legality of the dispensing power. Nor did Sir William Williams, who directed the prosecution, carry conviction when he belittled the parliamentary proceedings by which the dispensing power had received a public condemnation in Charles II's reign. Indeed, he even seemed to accept the validity of the defense argument when he urged that the parliamentary proceedings proved nothing. What were the addresses of a lone house of commons, he inquired. A genuine declaration of parliament, surely, was a bill passed by king, lords, and commons (three co-ordinate estates?); and no such title could be applied to a measure approved by the house of commons alone, or even by the two houses.[74] The tack taken by the Roman Catholic Justice Richard Alibone was altogether different. The bishops, if they were to petition the king legally, should do so in parliament. That was the guiding rule when an act of government was involved.[75] But it was another Roman Catholic, Serjeant Trinder, who asserted the court's fundamental position. His argument was based on the order theory of kingship: the king had the power to dispense because he was king, so the familiar refrain ran. The bishops' counsel, when it questioned the prerogative by citing earlier declarations in parliament, had 'done that which of late days has been always looked upon as an ill thing, as if the king's authority was under the suffrages of a parliament'.[76] Trinder's statement was, of course, correct. This was precisely what the bishops' counsel was contending.

## IV

By the end of 1688 James II's government was gone, and with his departure for France and the crowning of William and Mary came a host of pamphlets written in terms of the community-centered ideology and aimed at justifying the Glorious Revolution. They sounded the consistent theme that by dispensing with the law James had acted illegally and thus forfeited the right to rule. No dispensing power of the kind that had been claimed resided legally in the king because his authority flowed from the community, which, empowered by God, was the earthly repository of all legitimate political power and authority. Since the community had vested legislative sovereignty in king, lords, and commons, the discretionary authority in the government resided jointly and co-ordinately in all three estates. Acting for the community the two houses of the convention parliament had accepted the for-

feiture, filled the vacancy in the throne, and re-established the
government. Not that all tracts written to support the Revolution
followed these lines. It was also said that the subject's allegiance
and obedience were due to William and Mary because divine
Providence had guided the Revolution to a successful conclusion,
because they were *de facto* rulers in firm possession of the kingdom
and as such capable of giving subjects the protection that the *de
jure* James II could not provide; because William had bested
James II in a military duel, resulting in a just conquest of the
kingdom; and so on. Such arguments were sometimes present by
themselves; at other times they might co-exist with the community-
centered ideology in a given tract or in the writings of an author
such as the prolific Bishop Burnet. But whatever the variety of
the reasons advanced to defend the Revolution, the community-
centered ideology was conspicuous among them, very probably
dominant. Its influence, as will be seen, shaped the handiwork of
the convention parliament; it was in evidence for all to see when
Petyt abruptly replaced Brady in the tower records office; and it
radiated throughout the first volume of the state tracts of William
III's reign, where it was used in defense of the Revolution, the title
of King William and Queen Mary to the crown, and the oaths
enjoined by act of parliament to be taken to them. On the other
hand, a modern scholar has noted that both the conquest and
providentialist theories were relatively short-lived, despite their
usefulness to the tories who found the new situation difficult to
accept. Their problems were greater than those of the whigs in
fitting the events of 1688–89 into their ideological framework
because of their strong support for the principles of non-resistance
and hereditary right.[77]

The community-centered ideology underlay the Bill of Rights,
the cardinal document of the Glorious Revolution and the centerpiece of the Revolution settlement. This assertion can be made
with confidence even though the terms 'co-ordination' and 'mixed
monarchy' are absent from the completed statute and on the
whole from the surviving parliamentary records of its formulation.
It must also be recognized that the language of estates in the Bill
of Rights leaves in doubt its authors' intentions.[78] On the other
hand, the records for the critical months are at best fragmentary,
and there is no way of knowing exactly what was said in the

convention parliament. Further, surviving records, examined from the standpoint of the parliamentarian ideology, yield numerous signs of its acceptance or at least awareness of its existence. Thus, Sir Robert Howard, speaking in the house of commons on January 28, 1689, when a resolution dealing with the contractual nature of the government was under discussion, made contract the basis of political power. 'Compact is the origin of power', he quoted from Grotius; and he also referred to the people as 'part of the legislative power', a sentiment reflecting the co-ordination principle. Working from Bracton, he found God and the law to be above the king; or, as the community-centered ideology held, the king was below the law.[79] On the following day, January 29, when the idea of drawing up a bill of rights (or declaration of rights) was before the house of commons, John Hampden, son of Richard Hampden and grandson of John Hampden of ship money reputation, harked back to the restoration in the language of co-ordination. The convention had voted 'that the government was in king, lords, and commons'. And he asked the house of commons to proceed on the basis of the vote of May 1, 1660, in declaring 'the constitution and rule of the government'.[80] Lord Nottingham's language in the house of lords, on another occasion, was equally pertinent. 'The pretence [the claim] of the late times', he told the listening peers, 'was but the king being co-ordinate'.[81] The reference must have been obvious to them.

One obstacle to the proposition that the community-centered ideology underlay the Bill of Rights is its authors' statements to the effect that they were only acting to restore an older order that the king had disrupted. That document was said to declare existing law. This viewpoint appears to contradict the idea that they had in fact proceeded on the basis of a radicalizing parliamentarian ideology, the product of the civil-war years – an ideology frequently associated by contemporaries with Charles I's death at the end of the civil war and forced in his sons' reigns to run underground for long stretches of time. As recently as 1683, Oxford University had publicly condemned its main tenets. That the political leadership in the Revolution spoke the language of political restoration appears from the parliamentary record of the steps leading to the Bill of Rights. After James II's flight to France, William of Orange summoned the convention parliament, and this irregular body prepared a declaration of rights that William and Mary accepted formally before being proclaimed king and queen. As early as January 29, 1689, the convention house of commons had introduced the idea of such a declaration as the integral accompaniment to settling the succession to the throne and had appointed a committee to draw up the 'heads' of such a declaration.[82] Four days later, on February 2, the committee reported to the house of commons with twenty-three 'heads', which it approved. By adding five more 'heads' the house of commons then brought the total to twenty-eight.[83] The decisive move came on February 4, when the vote was taken to have the committee distinguish between 'such of the general heads, as are introductory of new laws, from those that are declaratory of ancient rights'. The heads introductory of new laws were abandoned and only those 'declaratory of ancient rights' were retained.[84] The declaration of rights was embodied in the more comprehensive Bill of Rights, which contained some additional and very important provisions, including the exclusion from the throne of a Roman Catholic or anyone married to a Roman Catholic; and the expanded document was passed as a statute in the second session of the convention parliament.

It is tempting, then, to treat the Bill of Rights as an essentially conservative document merely declaring the existing law, which by implication James II had violated, and to conclude from the abandonment of 'the general heads . . . introductory of new laws' that the convention parliament had turned away from reform, either running out of steam in the attempt to restrict the new rulers or else failing to achieve this design because of the pressure of time, the resistance forthcoming from Prince William, or whatever. But to accept at face value the language of the parliamentary leaders for the fact that they were only re-enacting an existing constitution[85] is to ignore the extended controversy over lawmaking in which the Stuart government had consistently maintained its own version of who made law in parliament and also to underestimate the importance of the Revolution settlement, in which the court view was effectively replaced by that of the political nation. In short, a striking victory was won in 1689 in the realm of political ideology.

There is no need, of course, to impugn the sincerity of contem-

I

porary statements, but it must be kept in mind that the men of 1689 were in no position to assert categorically the law of the constitution. After all, they were interested parties with their own distinctive view of the constitution, a highly controversial one from the standpoint of the pre-1689 court, that dated from 1642 when Charles I's Answer to the Nineteen Propositions inadvertently gave rise to the co-ordination principle and the closely related theory of a legal sovereignty in king, lords, and commons. That the Answer had, indeed, this kind of effect has been seen repeatedly; and one is reminded once more of the political ideas that it spawned in examining the careers of such prominent parliamentary leaders in 1689 as Henry Powle, Richard Hampden, and Sir Thomas Lee. All three were active in arranging William's arrival in England;[86] and the signs are ample that they believed the government to be a mixed monarchy in which the legislative power, the highest power, was shared. This article of belief more than any other informs the Bill of Rights and the Revolution settlement.

Powle and Lee had made public their theoretical position as early as the indulgence crisis of 1673 when Powle served as chairman of the two committees that prepared notable addresses against Charles II's dispensing power. Lee had lent support to the same cause. The address of February 26, 1673, was said by no less an authority than Charles II himself to embody the co-ordination principle. Powle and Lee were prominent in the emergent whig party, as was Hampden. His career began somewhat later than Powle's and Lee's, but he was one of Shaftesbury's lieutenants in the house of commons during the Danby impeachment and the exclusion crisis and, more to the point, can be linked, with them, directly to the Answer to the Nineteen Propositions. All three were members of the committee of the house of commons known as the Sacheverell committee, its name drawn from one of its leading members, William Sacheverell. That committee, it will be remembered, had used the Answer to the Nineteen Propositions to strengthen the house of commons against Charles II during the Danby impeachment. Relevant portions of the Answer were incorporated in the committee's report, which received wide publicity under the name of *Narrative and Reasons*. The idea of borrowing from the Answer to the Nineteen Propositions was due, however, not to Sacheverell, whose biographer considered him the chief author of the committee's report, but to Hampden, who had brought the royal declaration into the house of commons and read portions of it to the members. These circumstances make possible the categorical statement that the authors of the Bill of Rights were familiar with the Answer to the Nineteen Propositions, a fact of much consequence in determining their ideological outlook.[87] That Hampden also promoted actively the exclusion bills to bar the duke of York from the throne points to his acceptance of a legal sovereignty in king, lords, and commons.

It matters in any assessment of the ideological context of the Revolution that all three parliamentary leaders were of conspicuous importance when the declaration of rights was taking shape and that they subsequently held high office in the Williamite government. Thus Powle was chosen speaker of the convention house of commons; and as such he presented the Bill of Rights to William and Mary for their formal acceptance on December 16, 1689. Appointed to William's privy council, he became master of the rolls in March 1690.[88] His efforts were ably seconded by Hampden as chairman of the committee of the whole house of commons when it adopted the two resolutions of January 28 and 29 that became the cornerstone of the Revolution settlement. According to a modern historian, Hampden's duties were performed skillfully, and he was subsequently appointed a commissioner of the treasury.[89] Lee seems on first sight less important, but he was a representative member of the convention house of commons and was a member of the committee that prepared the declaration of rights. So extensive were his services to the house of commons of his generation that he has been singled out as one of the great parliamentary figures of the second half of the seventeenth century. He was appointed commissioner of the admiralty in 1689.[90]

Moreover, the first chairman of the committee who prepared the declaration of rights was Sir George Treby, a parliamentary leader of the same ideological persuasion. He too had served on the Sacheverell committee, and his leadership during London's attempt to defeat the *quo warranto* proceedings won him contemporary acclaim. In addition, Treby, as a member of the bishops' counsel, had been party to the successful attack on the dispensing power during their trial. These great services to the new order brought political rewards when he was appointed attorney general to William and Mary and lord chief justice of common pleas in 1692.[91]

There were also Sir Robert Atkyns and William Petyt. The first presided over the post-Revolution house of lords, while Petyt was identified with the Capel family and Treby's defense of the London charter. It was no accident that it was Petyt who replaced Brady in the tower records office. As the author of the *Antient Right*, he had particular claims to William's gratitude, as the prince early recognized. Petyt was, after all, at the center of a network of opposition writers who skillfully exploited the public records to embarrass the government of Charles II and his successor. Even if he was a more obscure political figure than those mentioned above, he had contributed largely to pulling together the strands of political thought that converged in the theory of a legal sovereignty in king, lords, and commons. Besides his common-law argument for a house of commons coeval with the king and house of lords and hence independent in its origins, Petyt's private papers strongly suggest that his own thinking about law-making had been shaped fundamentally by such seemingly varied sources as Charles I's Answer to the Nineteen Propositions, the act for the king's preservation passed early in the restoration, and the Powle committee's address of February 26, 1673. To this list should be added the *Narrative and Reasons*, of which he had four copies.[92] This was the Sacheverell committee's report, with which Hampden, Powle, Lee, and Treby, all four, were closely associated.

A document emanating from a convention parliament, where men of this type were in positions of commanding influence, must inevitably reflect the community-centered ideology while displaying an antipathy towards the political theory of order. This can be said confidently: the two went together. That the former was very much in evidence is easily seen from the fate of the dispensing power. Hereafter, the king must exercise a discretionary authority under the control of parliament, where the three co-ordinate estates of king, lords, and commons made law as representatives of the community, the only earthly source of political authority. 'None but the law-maker', had run Atkyns' memorable phrase, 'can dispense with the law, not he that hath but a share in the legislature.' The sentiment was widespread : it was the ideological motto of the Glorious Revolution. Whatever disagreement marked the convention parliament's proceedings, there was singular unanimity that the dispensing power must be placed under parliamentary control. National concern about the dispensing power was manifested when the declaration of rights opened with the charge that James II had sought to subvert the Protestant religion and the kingdom's laws and liberties 'by assuming and exercising a power of dispensing with, and suspending of laws, and the execution of laws, without consent of parliament'. The assertions followed that 'the pretended power of suspending of laws, or the execution of laws, by regal authority, without consent of parliament, is illegal', and that 'the pretended power of dispensing with laws, or the execution of laws, by regal authority, as it hath been assumed and exercised of late, is illegal'.[93]

A distinction had been drawn between a suspending and dispensing power, and only the first was condemned out of hand. The dispensing power, as now defined, was illegal only 'as it hath been assumed and exercised of late'. It seemed to follow that it might be retained in some form, and it appeared for a time that this would, indeed, be the outcome. The denunciation of the royal discretionary authority, on the lines given above, was incorporated in the Bill of Rights : and also a new clause regarding the dispensing power, discussed below, that had not been part of the earlier declaration of rights. Even so there was no thought of amending the declaration of rights so as to allow a dispensing power free of parliamentary control. That was ruled out by the terms of the Revolution. The new clause, added only after much debate and at the stage when the Bill of Rights was taking final form, presupposed a dispensing power thoroughly under parliamentary control. That the clause was added at all was due to the house of lords, whose members proved reluctant to abolish the dispensing power entirely. In passing the Bill of Rights they introduced language to the effect that a statute might be dispensed with under these circumstances : (1) if it expressly allowed for a dispensation or (2) if it fell into the category of statutes for which the convention parliament had made special provision at the time of the Revolution. The acceptance of this clause by the house of commons, on November 25, 1689, signalled that the Bill of Rights had achieved its final form.[94]

The intent was to continue a portion of the dispensing power, but instead the insertion of this clause proved a preliminary to the demise of the royal discretionary authority. That this would be the result was not at first apparent. The two houses were on record as planning to define the boundaries within which the dispensing power might legally operate; and on December 5, the peers discussed a *non obstante* bill that the royal judges had prepared. It contained no elucidation of the kinds of statutes with which the king could dispense. Its framers had proceeded in a different way, towards the abolition of the statutes that were most commonly defeated in practice. The *non obstante* bill did away with the medieval statutes regulating the pardoning power, the acts restraining the granting of certain offices for life or a period of years, the statute requiring that the precise value of conveyed lands be stated in letters patent, and the statutes *mortmain*. But its contents are only of academic interest since the bill, after being committed to the committee of the whole house, was eventually dropped.[95] Parliamentary records are too limited to give reasons for the failure, but it actually mattered very little in historical terms that the persistent attempt to save the dispensing power in some form had ended so abruptly. Its chief interest lies in demonstrating that this power, so much a storm center in two reigns, was no longer a central concern. All that was changed by the Revolution, and it was accepted that the dispensing power must now be exercised in accordance with the will of a sovereign parliament, if at all. The statutory regulations that were advanced were without exception fatal to the essence of that power. But one point that emerged during the debates in the house of commons does deserve mention. It suggests that the ultimate failure to retain the dispensing power in an attenuated form owed much to the conviction that even a remnant of the disputed power must keep alive the question of who made law in parliament, a question that was in process of solution. Surely this was the meaning conveyed by one member of parliament (Mr Ettrick) when he declared 'In *Hales'* *Case* the judges did agree, "that the law was the king's law, and he might dispense with it." ' The risk was too great, he seemed to say.[96]

The Revolution settlement confirmed at every turn the demise of the royal discretionary authority, and with it went automatically the order theory of kingship, which had been so powerful before 1642. The work of the convention parliament marked the final passing of this view of the kingship with its emphasis on an absolute prerogative that operated above the law. At the same time the ideological revolution of the civil-war years achieved a formal respectability; and the co-ordination principle – whether in explicit language or not – was enshrined in the Bill of Rights. The *coup de grâce* was administered to the order theory of kingship when the convention parliament implicitly asserted that kings hold their titles not from God immediately but from God mediately with the community's sanction. This seems to have been the sense of the two houses as manifested in the debates on the original contract.

As was mentioned earlier, tracts and declarations accompanying James' deposition often referred to a contract between king and people which he had broken by dispensing with the penal laws. The tone was set for the pamphleteers when the house of commons voted on January 28, with only one dissentient voice :

that King James the Second, having endeavoured to subvert the constitution of the kingdom, by breaking the original contract between king and people, and, by the advice of Jesuits, and other wicked persons, having violated the fundamental laws, and having withdrawn himself out of this kingdom, has abdicated the government, and that the throne is thereby become vacant.[97]

In the ensuing debates Serjeant Maynard, a friend of Petyt's,[98] asserted flatly that the beginnings of the government were from the people,[99] a sentiment echoed by Sir Robert Howard, an early supporter of William of Orange. Reporting comment that the king's crown rested on divine right, Howard attributed a divine right to the people. A king who broke his pact or covenant with his people, who had elected him, could forfeit the throne.[100]

Greater caution was displayed in the house of lords, where the peers inquiring as to the precise nature of the original contract turned to the judges for advice. According to Atkyns, whose political ideas had just been made public, his lawbooks shed no light on this point; but he believed that the contract in question referred 'to the first original of government'. The king never took any government, he continued, without an agreement with the people. The result was 'a limited monarchy and a body politic, and the king head of it'. Richard Hooker and James I were the prime authorities for this conclusion. The first had found all public government to be by agreement, while James I had recognized that every just king in a settled kingdom was bound to obey the 'paction' made to his people in his laws. There was also the authority of Grotius, who had traced all public government to a contract between the king and people.[101]

The other judges took a similar stand. Despite the absence of this terminology from their lawbooks, Sir Edward Montagu and Justice Dolben conveyed the impression that they themselves believed a contract underlay government. Sir Edward Nevill spoke in terms of conquest. 'In conquests the government puts laws upon them [the governed], yet in a little time that becomes an original contract. It must of necessity be implied by the nature of government.' Lord Chief Justice Holt was more precise. The question was whether this government was by contract. He believed it was. Otherwise one had to conclude that the English monarchy was *jure divino*. If it were, all other monarchies were unlawful. Like Atkyns earlier, Petyt expressed his view at length. Finding the source of the government in Germany, he implied that the original contract had produced a government in which the king had no legal and constitutional rights independent of parliament. These opinions were acceptable to the house of lords, whose members voted, 54 to 45, in favor of the language in the house of commons' resolution affirming a contract between the prince and people.[102] The concept was acceptable, then, to a majority in both houses, though to a greater number in the house of commons.

Yet no reference to the original contract appeared in the final version of the Bill of Rights. It disappeared for reasons other than ideological. After the resolution of January 28, 1689 reached the house of lords, its members proved willing, as has been seen, to adopt the idea of a contract but were opposed to the language which held that the king had abdicated the government and thereby left the throne vacant. Finding the word 'abdicated' too strong, they substituted the softer 'deserted'; and a series of conferences now followed between the two houses, in the first two weeks of February, which resulted in compromise. The reference to the original contract was a major casualty. It was dropped from the resolution and the clause about James' abdication retained, with the result that the language of contract is present neither in the declaration of rights nor in the Bill of Rights.[103]

But times had changed, of that there could be little doubt. Before abandoning the original contract as the basis of government, the convention parliament had given it serious consideration; and other signs point to an opinion moving in this channel. For example, Robert Harley declared in a private letter (July 27, 1689), with regard to a recent judicial case: 'The judge's charge would have been high treason eighteen months ago. The assertion was that kings are made by the people.'[104] The offer of the crown to William and Mary on February 13, 1689, which came immediately after a formal reading of the declaration of rights in their presence, provided a practical demonstration of the idea of contract-monarchy; and this idea rested, in turn, on the premise that the powers of the monarchy were rooted in the community as the human source of political power and authority.[105] There was also the change of personnel in the tower records office as Brady gave way to Petyt. The common-law argument with which Petyt was identified assumed that the community (the commons of England) was the human source of political power and authority; and its exponents championed, in addition, the principle of a co-ordination in the legislative power.

## V

At the Revolution the Bodinian version of the order theory of kingship, which enjoyed the court's sanction after 1660, gave way to the widely held community-centered ideology. This meant the acceptance of the co-ordination principle in law-making and the theory of a legal sovereignty in king, lords, and commons. That the two of them – the co-ordination principle and the concept of a shared legal sovereignty – operated in unison after 1642 has provided a central theme in this study. The changed ideological atmosphere must inevitably affect the king and the parliament. He no longer occupied the lofty position so characteristic of his Tudor and early Stuart predecessors, who, as keepers of the kingdom, had exercised without controversy a dispensing power that placed them at times above the law made in parliament. Nor could the king assert the right to set aside statute law on the ground that he was the single law-maker in parliament, the claim advanced by Charles II and James II and so roundly rejected at the Revolution. The Bill of Rights, by formally abolishing the dispensing power, placed the post-1689 king to all intents and purposes below the law; and any lingering doubt about this important matter was dispelled when the coronation oath was re-written.[106]

It was a momentous change for the kingship even if the process had been at work since 1642 and the erosion of royal authority extended over a long period of time. The demise of this ideologically significant power, and the underlying royal discretionary authority, signalled that *gubernaculum*, formerly the king's province and preserve, had passed officially and formally to the king and parliament together – that is, to king, lords, and commons in parliament. The shift in power carried with it a fundamental alteration of the kingship. With the exception of Anne, James' immediate successors no longer touched for the king's evil, a royal practice symbolic of the old order; and the monarch, now in ideological terms only a third legislator, was on his way to becoming a first magistrate, as radical writers like Algernon Sidney had already claimed. It was, however, a long process.

Conversely, the two houses had gained in important respects. To put the matter in its simplest form, the statute book was now, at long last, in harmony with the radicalization of English political thought that had taken place after Charles I's Answer to the Nineteen Propositions placed law-making in the forefront of discussion. The Answer had made a very substantial contribution, indeed, towards shaping public opinion regarding the role of the two houses in legislation. Certain memorable phrases, on Charles I's authority, coupled with the thoughtless and unplanned language of earlier enacting clauses in statutes, provided the theoretical mainstay of those who urged in the years from 1642 to 1689 that law-making was a shared power. If the king was below the law, as first the parliamentarians and then the whigs, and even many tories, and, finally, the makers of the Revolution settlement insisted, it was a law made jointly by king, lords, and commons.

The three of them were independent estates, the human source of their political authority the community, either by virtue of a contract or else the common-law principle of prescription.

It has been urged at length in this study that the principle of a co-ordination in law-making, which also included the idea of coevality – a principle that has seemed axiomatic and common-place to modern historians discussing the political outlook of restoration England – was actually the storm center of polemical writing until the Glorious Revolution put the matter to rest. Further, that the primary significance of the Revolution is to be found in the court's formal and official acceptance of that principle. On the high importance attached at this time to the legis-lative power, the comments of two contemporaries, both prominent in making the Revolution settlement, may be noticed. One of them was from Treby. Acting as a spokesman for London, in an address of welcome to Prince William on December 20, 1688, two days after he reached the capital, Treby referred to the late danger when church and state were brought to the verge of destruction by the conduct of certain men. That conduct, he explained, had broken 'the sacred fences of our laws, and (which was worse) the very constitution of our legislature'.[107] The other comment was from William Sacheverell, earlier a member of the second Powle committee and subsequently of the Treby–Somers committee and in his own right an important parliamentary leader identified publicly with the Answer to the Nineteen Propo-sitions in the years preceding the Revolution. Exhorting the con-vention house of commons to impose conditions on the new ruler or rulers, he made use of these words: 'Since God hath put this opportunity into our hands, all the world will laugh at us, if we make a half settlement . . . Secure the right of elections, and the legislative power.'[108] The advice was heeded. If the question 'Who makes law?' was the primary one still to be settled between the king and the two houses after the great civil war, and surely it was, that question received a final answer in 1689. Thereafter, even the court agreed that law-making was in king, lords, and commons; and the way had been cleared in all essential respects for the theory of parliamentary sovereignty, of which this was the distinguishing characteristic.[109]

# Appendix: Co-ordination and resistance at the Revolution

The co-ordination principle, and the community-centered ideology generally, gave rise at the Revolution to a distinctive theory of resistance to James II, which legitimated the use of force against him. The details varied from one co-ordination tract to another, but the same line of argument was developed. It was usual to explain the source of government in terms of the parliamentarian formula; that is, government in general was from God but the species from the community. Free to frame its own constitution, the community had erected a mixed and limited monarchy with characteristics often traceable to Charles I's Answer to the Nineteen Propositions. Whoever was invested with the royal dignity had been chosen by the community, and the coronation oath was frequently cited as a visible badge of the contract between the king and his subjects. As Peter Allix, the learned Huguenot scholar wrote: 'This consent of the people, or of the most considerable amongst the people, has constituted the forms of all lawful governments, and has legitimated those empires that were at first obtained by conquest or violence. And we may in particular add, that after this manner things have been carried in England . . .'[1] The king was obliged to protect his subjects and respect and preserve their privileges and liberties.

The surety for their privileges and liberties was the 'shared' legislative power, which all writers of this genre found characteristic of the English government. They were not likely, however, to employ the word 'co-ordination' though both versions of that principle are found in these tracts. Another salient characteristic of this government, stated over and over again, was that the king was under the law. As one writer explained, summarizing:

These being . . . the two main hinges of our government, that all the laws the people of England can be governed by are made in parliament, and that the government itself be administered according to these laws; if either the king alone, or any one, or both, of the houses of parliament take upon them to make laws, the one hinge is broken off; and if . . . the king do not govern according to the laws, the other hinge is broken off also, and then the constitution is at an end; and our legal government does cease.

In his view the dispensing power was to all intents and purposes a legislative power.[2] According to another writer (Robert Ferguson), James II's great crime was that he had 'challenged the whole legislative power to be vested in the king'.[3]

By the use made of the dispensing and suspending powers, James had broken the double hinge. And by attacking the legislative power, he had attacked the species of government rightfully established by the community. At this juncture he became a lawless king, who had divested himself of his royal power, and his private will did not oblige the subject. As one writer pointed out, 'if a king shall set himself against the constitution, and the public good, he is no longer that king to whom the laws oblige us'.[4] Samuel Masters made the same point at greater length : while it might be true that there was an obligation to obey actively whatever the legislative power of the kingdom commanded, if the command was not repugnant to the law of God, yet the same observation could not be made with regard to the king only 'because he having not the whole legislative power, an act of his private will' was 'destitute of that authority which can derive an obligation upon conscience'.[5]

The oath of allegiance was no longer binding, nor were the restoration statutes forbidding the use of force against the king. Some writers found that James had forfeited the government; and they wrote of the two houses as the proper parties to receive the forfeiture[6] or even the community itself.[7] Other writers, willing for subjects to use force against the king either actively or passively or even in both ways, frequently turned at this point in their argument either to Hugo Grotius' sixth book of his famed *De Jure Belli ac Pacis* (1625), published in English as recently as 1682, or to the quotation from Bracton and Fleta, discussed earlier in this study. According to a writer such as Allix, who used both, James

II was a prince who overthrew the laws and preferred to retire himself rather than to part with his resolution to overthrow the state. Yet 'his retirement was not altogether voluntary but rather by a kind of force and constraint'. To explain why a community could lawfully overthrow 'a tyrant' he had recourse to Grotius. The latter was credited with stating :

If a king have one share in the sovereign power, and the people or senate another; if the king entrench upon the power of the people, he may be justly opposed, as extending his power beyond its bounds : and this I judge ought to take place, notwithstanding . . . that the power of waging war is in the king; for that is to be understood with respect to foreign war, it being self-evident, that he who has *a share in the sovereignty* [italics added] must needs have a right to defend and secure the same : and where this happens, it is as plain that the king may lose his share in the government by the law of war.

Basing his position squarely on this doctrine, Allix now summarized it : 'As Grotius has observed . . . *where the sovereign power is shared, as it is in England*, it is always lawful for the party whose share is invaded, to defend their *right by force* [italics added].'[8]

Equally to the point was Edward Stephens. He would deal with this important matter :

Whether by the constitution of the government of England in legislation, or making of laws the . . . regal power, be more than one third part? Or the king's negative voice comprehend any thing more than what each of the houses have? And therefore his assuming as his prerogative, of what belongs to the whole, be not an invasion of the rights, both of the lords and of the commons; and within the sixth case of Hugo Grotius, 1. *de Jure Belli* c.4, section 13, wherein just force may be used against the invader?[9]

Another passage explained that the king was but a supreme officer, a high reeve of the nation like the high shire-reeve of the county 'who in many respects doth truly represent him'. His power was a trust from the community.[10] And the tory, Thomas Long of Exeter, in another tract studded with quotations from Grotius, wrote : 'Much more might be added from Grotius to our purpose, but he is so commonly quoted, that I forbear.'[11]

These tracts also resorted to Bracton's authority on the lines discussed earlier in this study. Thus Long likewise noted that

Bracton 'hath been often quoted, who says L.1, c.17 : "The king
hath for his superiors God, and the law, by which he is made
king, as also his court the earls and barons, who when they see
him exorbitant may restrain him . . ." and c.17 "Let kings therefore temper their power by the law, which is the bridle of
power".'[12] Finally, this useful statement in a conservative tract
is well worth noting. Its author wrote : ' 'Tis true, our parliaments
are taken into the government, and have a share in the highest
acts, as making laws. Whence some have argued, that upon the
prince's breaking in upon the legislative power, the parliament
may take arms against such an invader, as one sovereign may
against another.'[13] Its author would not claim the king to be
absolute, without rules in governing, but denied that parliament's
share in law-making was that of 'a co-ordinate sovereign's'. The
two houses sat with the king in parliament as 'subjects under him
their sole sovereign'.[14]

Of the co-ordination tracts published at the Revolution to
justify resistance to the king, the most famous is of course Locke's
*Two Treatises of Government* (1690). According to Laslett, this
work was first prepared for the exclusion crisis but remained in
manuscript until the Revolution brought William and Mary to
the throne. It was then published with a preface and some emen-
dations of the text that reflected more recent events. Little can be
added to the far-ranging commentary already in print on the
historical importance of the *Two Treatises*, but it ought to be
noted how representative Locke was of the genre of writers
described above.

Unmistakably, the *Two Treatises* expounded the community-
centered ideology while rejecting the order theory of kingship, as
that theory was reflected in Filmer's *Patriarcha*. Despite a distinct
reservation about an unlimited legislative power, a point on which
he differed from other members of the whig party, Locke elevated
that particular power to a position of undoubted supremacy in
the governmental system when he wrote : ' 'Tis in their legislative
[sic] that the members of a commonwealth are united, and combined together into one coherent living body.' It was the soul,
giving form, life, and unity to the commonwealth. Following
Hunton rather than Herle, Locke pointed to a concurrence in the
legislature of 'three distinct persons' – (1) a single hereditary

person having the constant, supreme, executive power; (2) an assembly of hereditary nobility; and (3) an assembly of representatives chosen *pro tempore* by the people. This reference to a concurrence in the legislature made it apparent that the law-making power was shared. There is no reason to conjecture about so important a matter. Locke referred to the supreme executive, meaning the king, 'who has also a share in the legislative' – a clause reminiscent of Charles I.[15]

His stress on the community as the human source of political authority is equally in evidence. Writing in opposition to Filmer's *Patriarcha*, in which the power of kings was treated as analogous to that in the fathers of families, Locke objected to the proposition that God had placed an initial grant of absolute power in Adam that descended by way of Noah's sons and grandsons to the kings of Filmer's own day. He himself favored the idea that God had empowered the community, which might then institute whatever form of government it pleased. The king's title and authority had roots in the community, and his power was totally fiduciary. Indeed, the English constitution as a whole was the manifestation of the popular will : the people had created the kingship and the king held his power as a trust.[16]

In fact, a double trust resided in the king – as part of the legislature and as the supreme executor of the law. If he acted arbitrarily, he put himself into a state of war with the community, which was thereupon absolved from any further obedience. That is, he forfeited the power allowed to him for very different purposes, and the community had the right to resume its original liberty and establish a new government.[17] What were the signs of arbitrary activity? Locke now wrote of James II's attempts to control the legislature. The king acts contrary to his trust, he explained, 'when he either employs the force, treasure, and offices of the society, to corrupt the representatives, and gain them to his purposes; or openly pre-engages the electors, and prescribes to their choice, such, whom he has by solicitations, threats, promises, or otherwise won to his designs; and employs them to bring in such, who have promised before-hand, what to vote and what to enact'. Only one conclusion was possible. 'To prepare such an assembly as this, and endeavour to set up the declared abettors of his own will, for the true representatives of the people, and the law-makers of the society, is certainly as great a breach of trust, and as perfect a declaration of a design to subvert the government, as is possible to be met with.' Whoever had engaged in such a design could no longer be trusted.[18]

If the king or 'the legislative' violated their trust, the government was dissolved; and dissolution might also be the outcome if the legislature was altered. In the following passage Locke may have had in mind James II's tampering with the legislative power, on the lines mentioned above, but perhaps he was referring as well to the king's independent exercise of the dispensing power. As earlier noted, the free use of the dispensing power was easily construed as the claim that the king was the only law-maker in parliament; and there were hostile writers in 1689 who wrote of the dispensing power as a law-making power in its own right. These were Locke's words :

When any one, or more, shall take upon them to make laws, whom the people have not appointed so to do, they make laws without authority, which the people are not therefore bound to obey; by which means they come again to be out of subjection, and may constitute to themselves a new legislative, as they think best, being in full liberty to resist the force of those, who without authority would impose any thing upon them. Every one is at the disposure of his own will, when those who had by the delegation of the society, the declaring of the public will, are excluded from it, and others usurp the place who have no such authority or delegation.[19]

Although Laslett believes that this passage was written in the early 1680s,[20] it bears the imprint of the Revolution. It could have been written by any of the pamphleteers who developed a theory of resistance to James II based on the co-ordination principle in law-making even if many of them stopped short of seeing a dissolution of the government as the final result of James' activity.

# Notes

1. W. H. Greenleaf, *Order, Empiricism and Politics: Two Traditions of English Political Thought, 1500–1700* (London, 1964), 1–156.
2. This idea, well-known long before the English civil war, may actually have been introduced into civil-war polemics by the royalist Dr Henry Ferne. In any event, the formula was occasionally invoked by royalists as well as parliamentarians though royalist conclusions were very different from those of the parliamentarians, indeed antithetical to them. Royalists reasoned that, whatever the role of the community in determining the species of government or choosing the ruler, the king's power and authority were due not to the community but to God. They were of divine institution. See note 41, Chapter 3 of this study and also James Daly, *Sir Robert Filmer and English political thought* (Toronto, 1979), 101–02. After 1643 the formula, in the form favored by the parliamentarians, was an integral part of the community-centered ideology; and the royalists ceased to use it. It was interpreted in radically different ways by the parliamentarians themselves. Cp., for example, William Bridge, *The Wounded Conscience Cured* (London, 1643), 52, and the much more conservative *Opinion of Divers Learned and Leading Dissenters, Concerning the Original of Government. Referring to the Doctrine of the Political Catechism* (London, 1680), *passim.* The pervasiveness of the parliamentarian formula in the seventeenth century is noted – and identified with anti-court elements – in J. W. Allen, *English Political Thought, 1603–1644* (London, 1938, reprinted 1967), 459; B. Behrens, 'The Whig Theory of the Constitution in the Reign of Charles II' *Cambridge Historical Journal, VII* (1941–43), 47–48; and Gordon Schochet, *Patriarchalism in Political Thought* (Oxford,

1975), 48; and its background in Greenleaf, *Order, Empiricism and Politics*, 35–41. But Greenleaf's interpretation of the period generally has to be treated with caution. Conrad Russell, in *Parliaments and English Politics 1621–1629* (Oxford, 1979), takes a very different view of the early seventeenth century.

3. John Northleigh, *Remarks upon the Most Eminent of our Antimonarchical Authors and their Writings* (London, 1685, reprinted 1699), 183. This tract was first published under the title *The Triumph of our Monarchy*. See also the pungent assessment of a high tory clergyman who declared early in the eighteenth century : 'The law tells us that the high court of parliament in which all our statutes are drawn up, and receive their sanction, consists of three estates; which three estates, our atheistic scribblers and penny-politicians impudently tell us, are the king or queen, the house of lords, and the house of commons. From whence, if it were true, it would follow, that the queen, lords, and commons, stand all upon the same level, and if anyone of these three estates should offer to encroach upon another, the other two might act in confederacy, and strip the first of all their [its] power, and divide it between themselves; and if the queen, lords, and commons, are the three estates of this kingdom, are really co-ordinate or upon the [same] level with one another, the consequence may be reasonable enough.' Luke Milbourne, *The People not the Original of Civil Power* (London, 1707), 9. In other editions the appropriate pages are 13–14. The authors of this study are indebted for this reference to Dr Jeffrey M. Nelson, Department of History, Harvard University. There is comment on Milbourne in Geoffrey Holmes, *The Trial of Doctor Sacheverell* (London, 1973), 5, 45, 119.

4. *The Stumbling-block of Disobedience and Rebellion* (London, 1658), Preface, no pagination. Heylyn was writing about 1644. His relationship with Laud is noted in H. R. Trevor-Roper, *Archbishop Laud, 1573–1645* (New York, 1965), 82.

5. *The Freeholders Grand Inquest* (n.p., 1648), 19. For reasons given later in this study, it is assumed that the royalist Sir Robert Holbourne wrote this tract; but this is by no means the received opinion. It is usually ascribed to Sir Robert Filmer. According to Peter Laslett, the *Freeholders* was an expansion and completion of the last five chapters *of Patriarcha* (1680), in manuscript when the *Freeholders* was published. *Patriarcha and Other Political Works of Sir Robert Filmer*, ed. Peter

Laslett (Oxford, 1949), 128, 129–84. Laslett's lead has been taken by Greenleaf, Schochet, J. W. Gough, and J. G. A. Pocock. Dismissing Holbourne's name with the comment that it is no longer even being suggested, Schochet expresses current opinion on the authorship. *Sir Robert Filmer: Some New Bibliographical Discoveries* (London, 1971), 145. The comment on Gough is based on his *Fundamental Law in English Constitutional History* (Oxford, 1955, reprinted 1961), 118, where the assumption is clearly made that Filmer wrote the *Freeholders*. Since then he seems to have rethought his position; there is some hesitation at least in the comment in 'James Tyrrell, Whig Historian and Friend of John Locke', *Historical Journal*, XIX (1976), 584, note 13.

6. *Table Talk of John Selden*, ed. Sir Frederick Pollock (Selden Society, 1927), 64. This work, dedicated to Sir Matthew Hale, was not published until 1689; but Selden's comments were apparently written down between 1654 and 1658. D. E. C. Yale, *Hale as a Legal Historian* (Selden Society, 1976), 18, note 25. Earlier Selden himself had described the king as one of the three estates. *Jani Anglorum Facies Altera* (London, 1610, reprinted 1683), 94. This work was also reprinted in 1681, its popularity perhaps engendered by the ideological controversy discussed in this study. Selden was corrected in Redman Westcot, *The Reverse or Back-face of the English Janus* (London, 1682), 127–28, where the definition of the three estates in parliament to include the king is treated as a fundamental mistake that had caused the civil war : it was *ipsam Majestatem in ordinem redigere*. The argument should be compared with Milbourne's, mentioned in note 3 above. Since Hale, writing between 1641 and 1660, likewise condemned this definition of estates as a great mistake, leading to the erroneous co-ordination principle, it may be surmised that this subject was actively discussed in Selden's circle of scholarship. *The Prerogatives of the King*, ed. D. E. C. Yale (Selden Society, 1976), 13–14.

7. Charles Herle, *A Fuller Answer to a Treatise written by Dr. Ferne* (London, revised edition, 1642), 1.

8. This study does not deal with such sources of radical political thought as the Leveller movement or the Engagement controversy over the oath of allegiance to the commonwealth established in 1649. Instead, the focus is on what may be termed mainstream radicalism, found in parliamentary circles and in such professional groups as the Presbyterian clergy and the

members of the legal profession that contemporaries termed the long robe.

CHAPTER 2 THE KEEPER OF THE KINGDOM

1. *Caudrey's Case*, 5 Coke *Reports* (London, 1826), 8b, 10a, 21a, 39b, 40b. *Magdalen College Case*, 11 Coke *Reports*, 72a. *The Third Part of the Institutes of the Laws of England. Concerning High Treason and other Pleas of the Crown and Criminal Causes*, ed. Francis Hargrave (London, 1797), 18. All cases cited in this study, with the exception of those in the *Year Books*, are in the *English Reports* (London, 166 vols., 1865–1900; reprinted, 176 vols., 1900–30).
2. Henry Finch, *Law, or a Discourse Thereof* (London, 1627), 81.
3. *Hill v. Grange*, Hil. 2 and 3 Ph. and Mary, Edmund Plowden, *Commentaries or Reports* (London, 1816), 177.
4. 'A Reading of the Midle Temple full of excellent good discourse and learninge circa 21 Eliz. R. [1578]', in Edward T. Lampson, 'The Royal Prerogative, 1485–1603' (Ph.D. Dissertation, Harvard University, 1938), fos. 249a–49b.
5. Sir Thomas Elyot, *The Boke named Governor*, ed. S. E. Lehmberg (London, 1962), 7.
6. Charles Butler, *The Feminine Monarchie: or, a Treatise Concerning Bees, and the Due Ordering of Them* (Oxford, 1609), 5, 2–6 *passim*.
7. *De Republica Anglorum*, ed. L. Alston (Cambridge, 1906), 62, 63.
8. William Lambarde, *Archeion, or, A Discourse upon the High Courts of Justice in England*, ed. Charles H. McIlwain and Paul L. Ward (Cambridge, Mass., 1957), 56, 57, 62. *William Lambarde and Local Government. His 'Ephemeris' and Twenty-nine Charges to Juries and Commissions*, ed. Conyers Read (Ithaca, 1962), 101.
9. Edward Forset, *A Comparative Discourse of the Bodies Natural and Politique* (London, 1606), 6, 8.
10. T. B. Howell, *A Complete Collection of State Trials* (London, 1809–28), III, 1226. Similar statements abound. See, for example, Sir Thomas Craig, *De Unione Regnorum Britanniae Tractatus* [1605], ed. C. Sanford Terry (Edinburgh, 1909), 227, 229; Charles Merbury, *A Briefe Discourse of Royall Monarchie, as of the Best Common Weale* (London, 1581), 41–52, especially

43; 'An Exhortation concerning good Order, and obedience to Rules and Magistrates,' in *Certaine Sermons or Homilies Appointed to be Read in Churches in the time of Queen Elizabeth I* (Gainesville, 1968), 69–71; and see the remarks by Attorney-general Sir John Bankes in the *Ship Money Case*, Howell, *A Complete Collection of State Trials*, III, 1023–25, 1026–27; Sir Robert Heath in the *Five Knights' Case, ibid.,* 37; and Sir Edward Crawley, *ibid.,* 1083.

11. Sir William Stanford, *An Exposition of the Kinges Prerogative,* ed. Tottell (London, 1577), 5–6. Stanford was justice of common pleas under Queen Elizabeth.

12. *Case of Non Obstante,* 12 Coke *Reports,* 18. See also Coke's remarks to the same effect in *Calendar of State Papers, Domestic Series 1598–1601,* CCLXXVI, 521; Sir Henry Hobart's speech in the house of commons, *Parliamentary Debates in 1610,* ed. Samuel R. Gardiner (Camden Society, 1962), 90; James Morrice, 'A Reading of the Midle Temple full of excellent good discourse and learninge circa 21 Eliz. R. [1578]', fo. 259; John Cowell, *The Interpreter or 'Booke Containing the Signification of Words'* (Cambridge, 1607), 'Prerogative'; Sir Francis Bacon, *Works,* ed. James K. Spedding, Robert L. Ellis, and Douglas D. Heath (London, 1879), VII, 370; Smith, *De Republica Anglorum,* ed. Alston, 58–63. Bertrand de Jouvenel terms the king's inability to alienate the inseparable prerogative 'the fortunate powerlessness'. In his words, 'Whatever tends to destroy sovereignty is beyond the competence of the sovereign, and estoppel of suicide constitutes no diminution of his authority. The powerlessness is fortunate because it serves the interest of sovereignty itself.' *Sovereignty; An Inquiry into the Political Good* (Chicago, 1963), 205.

13. *Case of the Dutchy of Lancaster,* Plowden, *Commentaries or Reports,* 213; *Willion v. Berkeley, ibid.,* 234; *Sir Thomas Wroth's Case, ibid.,* 457. Ernst H. Kantorowicz deals with the medieval doctrine of the two capacities. As a public person the king was 'expected to consider all issues with regard to the well-being of the *res publica,* and not with regard to his *privata voluntas'. The King's Two Bodies: A Study in Medieval Political Theology* (Princeton, 1957), 95–96.

14. Morrice, 'A Reading of the Midle Temple full of excellent good discourse and learninge circa 21 Eliz. R. [1578]', fo. 248a.

15. See, for example, *Parliamentary Debates in 1610,* ed. Gardiner, 15; and *Proceedings in Parliament, 1610,* ed. Elizabeth Read

Foster (New Haven, 1966), II, 213, and in general the debates over purveyance, *primer seisin*, and the *nullum tempus* clause.

16. Smith, *De Republica Anglorum*, ed. Alston, 16–17.

17. 'View of the Differences in question betwixt the King's Bench and the Council in the Marches', in *The Letters and Life of Francis Bacon*, ed. James Spedding (London, 1861–72), III, 371–74; 'Maxims of the Law', *Works*, ed. Spedding, Ellis, and Heath, VII, 370; 'A Brief Discourse upon the Commission of Bridewell', *ibid.*, 509.

18. 'A brief Discourse upon the Commission of Bridewell', 511; 'The Argument of Sir Francis Bacon, Knight, His Majesty's Solicitor-General, in the *Case of the Post-Nati of Scotland*', in *Works*, ed. Spedding, Ellis, and Heath, VII, 646.

19. 'Of the Dignity and Advancement of Learning', *ibid.* (London, 1877). v, 16.

20. Sir John Davies, *The question concerning Impositions* (London, 1656), 30–32. For similar statements see Sir Benjamin Rudyerd's remarks in Howell, *A Complete Collection of State Trials*, III, 173; and Forset, *A Comparative Discourse of the Bodies Natural and Politique*, 20–21. Francis Oakley perceives the importance of the comparison between the royal absolute power and the miracle-working power of God in 'Jacobean Political Theology : The Absolute and Ordinary Powers of the King', *Journal of the History of Ideas*, XXIX (1968), 323–46. Oakley's study is by far the most illuminating treatment of the subject of the absolute and ordinary royal prerogatives. See also his 'The "Hidden" and "Revealed" Wills of James I : More Political Theology', *Studia Gratiana*, XV (1972), 365–75.

21. 'True Law of Free Monarchies', in *Political Works of James I*, ed. Charles H. McIlwain (Cambridge, Mass., 1918), 63. 'A Speech in the Star Chamber, 1616', *ibid.*, 333. 'Speech to the Lords and Commons . . . xxi March, 1609', *ibid.*, 307.

22. *Archeion*, ed. McIlwain and Ward, 48, 61–63. Here Lambarde was speaking of conciliar courts, which he saw as one particular manifestation of the royal discretionary authority.

23. Howell, *A Complete Collection of State Trials*, II, 389.

24. John Rushworth, *Historical Collections of Private Passages of State, Weighty Matters in Law, Remarkable Proceedings in Five Parliaments* (London, 1721–22), III, 1135. Similar views of the absolute and ordinary prerogatives can be found in the parliamentary debates of 1610, 1621, and 1628, in which many speakers, some of them opponents of royal policies, acknow-

ledged the existence of a royal discretionary authority. See, for example, the remarks of Sir Edward Coke in *Commons Debates, 1621,* ed. Wallace Notestein, Hartley Simpson, and Frances Relf (New Haven, 1935), II, 193, 495; IV, 79; VI, 43; Christopher Brooke, *ibid.*, II, 494; Thomas Crew, *ibid*; Heneage Finch in *Proceedings in Parliament, 1610,* ed. Foster, II, 228, 235, 241–43; Thomas Hedley, *ibid.*, II, 185, 191. There is also relevant material in *ibid.*, 199, 204–06, 249; *Parliamentary Debates in 1610,* ed. Gardiner, 8, 69, 71, 88, 93; and Rushworth, *Historical Collections,* I, 573. See, too, Conrad Russell's helpful discussion of the parliamentary debates in 1628 surrounding the Petition of Right. *Parliaments and English Politics 1621–1629,* Chapter VI *passim,* and especially 363–67 and 371. Of course not every Tudor and early Stuart Englishman who commented on the kingship acknowledged the existence of an absolute discretionary authority vested in the king. Both John Ponet and John Aylmer denied that the ruler possessed such a reserve of power. Ponet. *A Shorte Treatise of politike power* (n.p., 1556), 19, 44, 106. Aylmer, *An Harborowe for faithfule and Trewe Subjectes, agaynst the late Blowne Blaste, concerninge the Government of Women* (Strassburg, 1559), 54–55. A discussion of Ponet's and Aylmer's political thought with regard to the order theory may be found in Janelle R. Greenberg, 'Tudor and Stuart Theories of Kingship : The Dispensing Power and the Royal Discretionary Authority in Sixteenth and Seventeenth Century England' (Ph.D. Dissertation, University of Michigan, 1970), I, 81–89. Dislike of such Stuart policies as impositions, forced loans, tonnage and poundage, imprisonment without cause shown, and ship money provoked discussion over the nature and extent of the royal discretionary authority. Some members of the political nation denied altogether the discretionary nature of the absolute prerogative, insisting that it was bound by common law. For a discussion of the erosion of the royal discretionary authority in the early seventeenth century see *ibid.*, Chapter III; and Russell, *Parliaments and English Politics 1621–1629,* Chapter VI *passim,* especially 347–49, 353, 362–63, and 370.

25. C. H. McIlwain, *Constitutionalism Ancient and Modern* (New York, 1947), 75–111 *passim.,* Chapters V, and VI, and 168, note 29. *Growth of Political Thought in the West* (New York, 1932), 373.

26. See, for example, Margaret Judson, *The Crisis of the Constitu-*

*tion* (New Brunswick, New Jersey, 1949, reprinted, 1964); R. F. V. Heuston, *Essays in Constitutional Law* (London, second edition, 1964), 61–62; Francis D. Wormuth, *The Origins of Modern Constitutionalism* (New York, 1949), 37–38; R. W. K. Hinton, 'Was Charles I a Tyrant?' *Review of Politics,* xviii (1956), 84–85. A critique of McIlwain's view of medieval constitutionalism and Bracton may be found in Ewart Lewis, 'King above Law? *"Quod Principi Placuit"* in Bracton', *Speculum,* xxxix (1964), 240–69; and Brian Tierney, 'Bracton on Government', *ibid.*, xxxviii (1963), 295, 307–08.

27. 'Jacobean Political Theology: The Absolute and Ordinary Powers of the King,' 343–46.

28. 'A Reading of the Midle Temple full of excellent good discourse and learninge circa 21 Eliz. R. [1578]', fos. 247b–48b.

29. 'An Exhortation concerning good Order, and obedience to Rulers and Magistrates', in *Certaine Sermons or Homilies Appointed to be Read in Churches in the time of Queen Elizabeth I,* i, 70.

30. 'The Prince, or Maxims of State', in *Somers Tracts. A Second Collection* (London, 1750), ii, 215.

31. Lambarde, *Archeion*, ed. McIlwain and Ward, 126.

32. Richard Hooker, *Ecclesiastical Polity: Book VIII*, ed. Raymond A. Houk (New York, 1931), 244.

33. There is a recent discussion of Whitelocke's remarks in A. G. R. Smith, 'Constitutional Ideas and Parliamentary Developments in England 1603–1625', *The Reign of James VI and I* (London, 1973), 161–63.

34. Chapter 4, note 52 of this study. James Whitelocke's remarks on law-making may be compared with those of his son, Bulstrode Whitelocke, discussed in Chapter 3 of this study. The comparison provides a reminder of how the view of law-making had altered in a cardinal respect in the course of little more than a generation.

35. Howell, *A Complete Collection of State Trials*, iii, 863. James I made a similar analysis of law-making in 1621. Robert Zaller, *The Parliament of 1621* (Berkeley, 1971), 32.

36. S. B. Chrimes, 'The Constitutional Ideas of Dr. John Cowell', *English Historical Review* lxiv (1949), 461–87.

37. Cowell, *The Interpreter*, 'King', 'Parliament', 'Prerogative'.

38. R. W. K. Hinton, 'The Decline of Parliamentary Government under Elizabeth I and the Early Stuarts', *Cambridge Historical Journal*, xiii (1957), 116–32. J. H. Roskell, 'Perspectives in

English Parliamentary History', *Bulletin of the John Rylands Library*, XLVI (1963–64), 448–75.

39. Judson, *The Crisis of the Constitution*, Chapter III. Gough, *Fundamental Law in English Constitutional History*, 80–84. Smith, 'Constitutional Ideas and Parliamentary Developments in England 1603–1625', 160–64. Conrad Russell, 'The Theory of Treason in the Trial of Strafford', *English Historical Review*, LXXX (1965), 30–50.

40. Judson, *The Crisis of the Constitution*. 361.

41. The dispensing power has received extended attention from only two historians, E. F. Churchill and Paul Birdsall. Churchill, 'The Crown and the Alien from the Norman Conquest down to 1689', *Law Quarterly Review*, XXXVI (1920), 402–28; 'The Dispensing Power and the Defence of the Realm', *ibid.*, XXXVII (1921), 412–41; 'The Dispensing Power of the Crown in Ecclesiastical Affairs', *ibid.*, part I, XXXVIII (1922), 297–316, and part II, *ibid.*, 420–34; and 'Dispensations under the Tudors and Stuarts', *English Historical Review*, XXXIV (1919), 409–15. Birdsall, ' "*Non Obstante*", A Study of the Dispensing Power of English Kings', *Essays in History and Political Theory in Honor of Charles Howard McIlwain*, ed. Carl Wittke, (Cambridge, Mass., 1936), 36–76. Neither Churchill nor Birdsall discusses the dispensing power within its proper ideological context – the political theory of order. See also note 70 of this chapter.

42. The statutes were 2 Edw. 3, c. 2; 14 Edw. 3, c. 15; 10 Edw. 3, s. 1. c. 3; and 13 Rich. 2, s. 2. c. 1.

43. Sir Robert Brooke, *La Graunde Abridgement*, ed. R. Tottell (London, 1586), Patents, 109. See also William Stanford, *Les Plees del Coron, Divisees in Plusors Titles & Common Lieux*, ed. R. Tottell (London, 1574), Lib. 2, Charte de Pardon, 101.

44. David Jenkins, *Eight Centuries of Reports* (London, third edition, 1771), 173.

45. 3 Coke *Institute*, 237. Other pertinent material may be found in Brooke, *La Graunde Abridgement*, Appeal, 150; Jenkins, *Eight Centuries of Reports*, 307. Appeal, which was contrasted to indictment by grand jury, referred to a private accusation and prosecution by which the victim or a relative of the victim brought the offender to justice. This method, while common at one time in the middle ages, was probably infrequently resorted to in the sixteenth and seventeenth centuries.

46. Pasch. 15 Eliz., cited under Hil. 18 Eliz., Plowden, *Commentaries or Reports*, 476. The case, which was heard at the Warwick Assizes in 15 Eliz., did not itself involve a pardon.

47. Brooke, *La Graunde Abridgement*, Appeal, 150; 3 Coke *Institute*, 237.

48. Jenkins, *Eight Centuries of Reports*, III; *Magdalen College Case*, Pasch. 13 Jac. I, 11 Coke *Reports*, 65b–66a; Brooke, *La Graunde Abridgement*, Action Popular, 3; and John Rastell, *Les Termes de la Ley* (London, 1721), 219.

49. Jenkins, *Eight Centuries of Reports*, 198; *Case of Pardons*, Trin. 7 Jac. I, 12 Coke *Reports*, 29–30; Brooke, *La Graunde Abridgement*, Nuisance, 15.

50. Mich. 17 and 18 Eliz., Plowden, *Commentaries or Reports*, 487.

51. *Year Book*, Mich. 2 Hen. 7. 6, ed. Tottell (London, 1555), 1–21. Although the account of the *Sheriff's Case* is somewhat confused, it was generally cited as good law until the late seventeenth century, when opponents of the dispensing power denied its validity.

52. Mich. 5 and 6 Eliz., Sir James Dyer, *Reports of Cases* (London, 1794), II, 225b. See also *Northcote v. Ward*, heard in 1572, cited in *ibid.*, III, 303a–03b.

53. 4 Eliz., Jenkins, *Eight Centuries of Reports*, 225.

54. *Ingram's Case*, cited in *Roy v. Bishop of Norwich*, Sir Henry Hobart, *Reports* (London, 1650), 75. 12 Coke *Reports*, 29–30. For a discussion of *malum in se* and *malum prohibitum* see Sir Thomas Egerton, *A Discourse upon the Exposicion and Understandinge of Statutes*, ed. Samuel E. Thorne (San Marino, California, 1942), 168–69.

55. Churchill, 'The Crown and the Alien', 417.

56. Churchill, 'The Dispensing Power and the Defence of the Realm', 414–17.

57. *Ibid.*, 433–34, 434, note.

58. *Ibid.*, 438–39, notes.

59. *A Bibliography of Royal Proclamations of the Tudor and Stuart Sovereigns*, ed. Robert Steele (Oxford, 1910), I, nos. 507, 1197, 1696. J. R. Jones, 'The Clegate Case', *English Historical Review*, XC (1975), 281–82. The practice of dispensing with as well as suspending statutes seems to have been fairly common under the Tudors. See, for example, *Tudor Royal Proclamations*, ed. Paul L. Hughes and James F. Larkin (New Haven, 1964–69), I, nos. 166, 175, 195, 196, 198, 202, 207, 226; II,

424, 457, 464; and III, 697. There is a helpful discussion in I, xxv–xxxii.

60. Mich. 18 and 19 Eliz., Plowden, *Commentaries or Reports*, 493–504, especially 501–04. In such cases it was not necessary that the grant be made through a license carrying a clause of *non obstante*. The reasons for this are explained in *ibid.*, 502–03. For further discussion of the use of the dispensing power to defeat the statutes of *mortmain* and *quia emptores see* Coke, *Systematic Arrangement of Lord Coke's First Institute of the Laws of England . . . With Annotations of Mr. Hargrave, Lord Chief Justice Hale, and Lord Chancellor Nottingham*, ed. J. H. Thomas (Philadelphia, 1836), 93b–99a.

61. Finch, *Law, or a Discourse Thereof*, 100–02. *Duke of Chandois's Case*, Trin. 4 Jac. I, 6 Coke *Reports*, 55a–56a. *Case of Alton Woods*, Trin. 17 Eliz., 1 Coke *Reports*, 52a. (This entire case is relevant).

62. *Case of Alton Woods*, Trin. 42 Eliz., 1 Coke *Reports*, 52a.

63. Trin. 17 Eliz., William Benloe, *Les Reports de Gulielme Bendloes* (London, 1689), 33. See also *Bozoun's Case*, Mich. 26 and 27 Eliz., 4 Coke *Reports*, 34b–36a for further clarification of the use of *non obstantes* in this matter.

64. Churchill, 'The Crown and the Alien', 425–26.

65. Quoted in *ibid.*, 417, 418, note.

66. *Ibid.*, 418, 426.

67. Churchill, 'The Dispensing Power of the Crown in Ecclesiastical Affairs', 422–26.

68. Churchill, 'The Crown and the Alien', 427.

69. Quoted in Churchill, 'The Dispensing Power of the Crown in Ecclesiastical Affairs', 427.

70. This view of the dispensing power is at odds with that of Birdsall, who bases his interpretation of that prerogative squarely on McIlwain's two spheres of interest, *gubernaculum* and *jurisdictio*. In so doing Birdsall overlooks the discretionary nature of the absolute prerogative and misses the implications of the order theory of kingship.

71. But see the doctrine on these points enunciated by Sir Robert Holbourne, who with St John was counsel for Hampden in the *Ship Money Case* of 1637. Concerned to deny an extra-parliamentary taxing power to Charles I, which seemed to Holbourne the principal issue at stake, he insisted that the king might legally invade the subject's property only in extraordinary cases where danger was so pressing that parliament could not meet.

Only where there was a 'particular appearance of instant and apparent danger', he asserted, must 'particular property . . . yield much to necessity'. No charge could be exacted if the danger were only apprehended and not imminent. Thus Queen Elizabeth at the time of the Armada was justified in ordering the burning of corn only if the enemy landed : she could not command, of her own authority, that the corn be burned 'before an enemy did come'. At another point Holbourne stated to the judges : 'Your lordships know the king may command in case of danger the destruction of all suburbs, rather than an enemy should come in them. But if there be a fear only of wars, if the king should command it, how far that is justifiable, I leave it to your lordships' judgments.' Howell, *A Complete Collection of State Trials*, III, 975, 1012. His language also made it apparent that in his view the king alone could not judge the nature of the emergency. These statements and others of similar import led the modern historian, D. L. Keir, to write of Holbourne that he 'appears to debate the extent to which the realm was really in danger, to reduce almost to vanishing point the king's discretionary power to ensure the safety of the realm, and to assert that kings may fall into error and wrong, and that means of restraining them must be devised'. 'The Case of Ship-Money', *Law Quarterly Review*, LII (1936), 560. How representative were Holbourne's positions? He is generally considered, curiously enough, to have been more extremist than St John, also counsel for Hampden; and the only justice to ascribe fully to the two lawyers' strongest lines was Sir George Croke, justice of king's bench. Sir Richard Hutton, justice of common pleas, likewise insisted on a visible danger before the king might levy a charge outside of parliament. The condemnation of ship money in 1641 (16 Car. 1, c. 14) supported Holbourne, but by that time the political revolution was under way. It is more difficult to state whether his stand was genuinely representative in 1637. W. J. Jones has offered a cautious assessment : 'In fairness to those who voted for the crown it must be said that the arguments made for Hampden could be interpreted as confining the discretion of the king within limits which were too narrow for most contemporaries to digest.' *Politics and the Bench* (London, 1971), 127. Holbourne's arguments were, however, grounded on the assumption that taxation and not defense was the main issue; and it would be easy to overstate his radicalism. He believed, for example, that the king possessed unquestionably a dispensing power – 'The king may dispense with penal statutes, and make them as none. Doth any laws say he shall not do it?' Howell, *A Complete Collection of State Trials*, III, 1014. Other materials to be consulted are in *ibid.*, 971–72, 975, 1011–14, 1149, 1159, 1162, etc. It should be noted that Holbourne was later a royalist in the king's civil-war government at Oxford. He has been described as the author of the anonymous *Freeholders Grand Inquest* (1648), a tract taking a high view of royal power, and to this subject it is necessary to return at a later stage of this study.

72. Sir Simonds D'Ewes, *The Journals of all the Parliaments during the Reign of Queen Elizabeth* (London, 1682), 646. J. E. Neale, *Elizabeth I and Her Parliaments, 1584–1601* (New York, Norton Library, 1966), 376–93.

73. D'Ewes, *The Journals of all the Parliaments during the Reign of Queen Elizabeth*, 645, 649.

74. Neale, *Elizabeth I and her Parliaments, 1584–1601*, 376. But see this account for at least one speech suggesting the superiority of statute law to the dispensing power. There were also members willing to proceed by bill. *Ibid.*, 378, 381–82. See also note 79 of this chapter of this study.

75. Robert Bowyer, *Parliamentary Diary, 1606–07*, ed. David H. Willson (Minneapolis, 1931), 66, 135. For a discussion of Ellesmere's views on the prerogative see Louis A. Knafla, *Law and Politics in Jacobean England. The Tracts of Lord Chancellor Ellesmere* (Cambridge, 1977), 65–76.

76. Bowyer, *Parliamentary Diary, 1606–07*, 143–44.

77. *Ibid.*, 308.

78. This interpretation is somewhat at variance with that of Gough and Holdsworth, who have suggested that the problem raised by the dispensing power, so far as statute law was concerned, was not practical but purely logical. Both believe that in the late Tudor and early Stuart periods the idea of an inseparable dispensing power was analogous to the idea that parliament could not bind its successor. Gough, *Fundamental Law in English Constitutional History*, 46–47; Sir William Holdsworth, *A History of English Law* (London, third edition reprinted, 1966), IV, 204–06.

79. Monopolies were also a source of bitterness in James I's reign, and at its end the statute of monopolies was enacted. This is what happened. A bill against monopolies passed the house of commons in 1621, only to be defeated in the house of lords.

The picture was very different, however, in the parliament of 1624, which enacted the statute of monopolies apparently without contention. Here the key factor was a political alliance between Prince Charles and the duke of Buckingham on the one hand and the opposition leaders in parliament on the other; and even James seems to have been willing for the bill to become law. Robert E. Ruigh, *The Parliament of 1624: Politics and Foreign Policy* (Cambridge, Mass., 1971), 151. Despite the successful attack on monopolies, parliamentary leaders did not deny the king's right to grant them. Judson, *The Crisis of the Constitution*, 289. There is also pertinent comment in Elizabeth Read Foster, 'The Procedure of the House of Commons against Patents and Monopolies, 1621–1624', *Conflict in Stuart England: Essays in honour of Wallace Notestein*, ed. William Appleton Aiken and Basil Duke Henning (London, 1960), 76–77. But Zaller describes an unsuccessful attempt at amending the bill of 1621 that certainly suggests doubt on someone's part about the king's power to set aside a statute. The bill was to be amended to provide that it could be defeated by a *non obstante. The Parliament of 1621*, 129. See also notes 24 and 71 of this chapter of this study for other instances of the erosion of the king's discretionary authority by the 1620s and 1630s. On the other hand, the power of parliament in these years, and its self-consciousness as a political institution apart from the king, ought not to be overestimated. Conrad Russell, 'Parliamentary History in Perspective, 1604–1629', *History*, LXI (1976), 1–27. Russell's ideas are more fully developed in the more recent *Parliaments and English Politics 1621–1629, passim.*

CHAPTER 3 THE NEW AGE OF POLITICAL DEFINITION

1. Edward Gee, 'Preface', *The Divine Right and Original of the Civill Magistrate from God* (London, 1658). For comment on Gee, see note 68 of this chapter. That debate centered on the legislative power appears from the *Freeholders Grand Inquest*, 31. Its author wrote : 'The main question in these our days is, "where this power legislative remains [resides]?" or is placed.'

2. *His Majesties Answer to the XIX. Propositions of Both Houses of Parliament* (London, 1642), 3, 29–30. Corinne Comstock Weston, *English Constitutional Theory and the House of Lords, 1556–1832* (London, 1965), 26–27. The Answer is further dis-

cussed in Chapter 4 of this study. The royal veto was also rejected in the two houses' declaration of May 19. *Journals of the House of Commons*, II, 580. Perez Zagorin, *The Court and the Country* (London, 1969), 310.

3. *His Majesties Answer to the XIX. Propositions of Both Houses of Parliament*, 17–18. This particular definition of estates was used repeatedly, the king treated as the first estate. *Ibid.*, 12, 13, 18, 20, 21, 22. Another royal declaration (June 17) defined the three estates to include the king, the purpose one of defending the royal veto. Edward Husband, *An Exact Collection of all Remonstrances, Declarations . . . and other Remarkable Passages between the Kings most Excellent Majesty, and His High Court of Parliament* (London, 1642), 363.

4. *His Majesties Answer to the XIX. Propositions of Both Houses of Parliament*, 18–22.

5. *Calendar of State Papers, Domestic Series, Charles I*, XIX (1641–43), 343. *Journals of the House of Lords*, V, 153. *Journals of the House of Commons*, II, 635. The warrant is dated June 18, 1642.

6. Weston, *English Constitutional Theory and the House of Lords*, 32, note 43.

7. *Journals of the House of Commons*, II, 637. The outbreak of the civil war meant that no response was made to the Answer.

8. *Ibid.*, X, 35. Weston, *English Constitutional Theory and the House of Lords*, 92–123. For comment on the Answer in a different context, see J. G. A. Pocock, *The Machiavellian Moment: Florentine Political Thought and the Atlantic Republican Tradition* (Princeton, 1975), 361–66 and *passim*.

9. *His Majesties Answer to the XIX. Propositions of Both Houses of Parliament*, 13.

10. *Ibid.*, 29. In another passage the king insisted on being admitted as 'a part of parliament'. *Ibid.*, 13.

11. Later commentators on the Answer inclined towards a theory of planned concession. Thus Lord Chancellor Nottingham (Sir Heneage Finch), writing during the Danby impeachment of 1679, concluded that it was penned to appeal to the common people and keep them from entering into a war but not 'as a treatise and argument of law'. *A Treatise on the King's Power of Granting Pardons in Cases of Impeachment* (London, 1791), 18. The high tory Dr Nathaniel Johnston was specific : Charles I's definition of estates represented a policy of deliberate concession because he and his party employed this line of argument

K

so frequently in defending his cause. *The Excellency of Monarchical Government, Especially of the English Monarchy*
(London, 1686), 302–03, 304. This observation about royalist
writings holds good, however, only for the opening years of the
civil war, before the king's party recognized how damaging the
Answer was to his cause. Edward Stillingfleet offered a somewhat different interpretation. 'The penner of that Answer was
so intent upon the main business, viz. that the two houses could
do nothing without the king, that he did not go about to dispute
this matter with them, whether the king were one of the three
estates or not; but taking their supposition for granted, he
shows that they could have no authority to act without the
king's concurrence.' *The Grand Question, concerning the
Bishops Right to Vote in Parliament in Cases Capital* (London,
1680), 173. As for the expression 'legislative power', Heylyn
implied that it was new. *The Stumbling-block of Disobedience*,
273. This is not to state that there was no earlier usage before
the Answer appeared. It was used, for example, by St John
during the proceedings against Strafford in the spring of 1641
and in the autumn of that year when the Grand Remonstrance
was in course of preparation. Howell, *A Complete Collection of
State Trials*, III, 1478, 1508, 1512. Derek Hirst, 'The Defection
of Sir Edward Dering, 1640–41', *Historical Journal*, xv (1972),
207. Nathaniel Fiennes even claimed for the house of commons,
the representative body of the commons of England, 'a share in
the legislative power'. *A Second Speech . . . in the Commons
House of Parliament. Touching the Subjects Liberty against the
late canons and the new oath* (London, 1641). 6–7.

12. *The Maximes of Mixt Monarchy* (London, 1643), A3.
13. Elton's writings on this topic are extensive. See, for example,
    *England under the Tudors* (London, 1955, reprinted 1963),
    165–68, 400–03; *The Tudor Constitution: Documents and
    Commentary* (Cambridge, 1962), 228–34; and, in particular,
    *Studies in Tudor and Stuart Politics and Government* (Cam-
    bridge, 1974), II, 27–37, 53, 215–35.
14. Vernon F. Snow, *Parliament in Elizabethan England: John
    Hooker's 'Order and Usage'* (New Haven, 1977), 136, 146, 181.
    The question of the membership of the three parliamentary
    estates prior to 1642 is a complicated one. Chrimes demon-
    strated that by the late fourteenth and early fifteenth centuries
    the definition of the three estates as consisting of lords spiritual,
    lords temporal, and commons had received official sanction.

*English Constitutional Ideas in the Fifteenth Century* (Cambridge, 1936), 100–26. The extent to which this view permeated sixteenth and early seventeenth-century political thought is problematic. On the one hand, authorities as different as Coke and Cowell reiterated the late medieval definition. Coke, *The Fourth Part of the Institutes of the Laws of England: Concerning the Jurisdiction of Courts,* ed. Francis Hargrave (London, 1797), B,1. Cowell, *The Interpreter,* under 'Parliament'. The *Fourth Institute* was completed as early as 1628 though not published until 1644. Speaking through the earl of Salisbury, James I likewise used this definition in the controversy over the *Interpreter,* apparently without challenge from the two houses. Chrimes, 'The Constitutional Ideas of Dr. John Cowell', 471–72, 483–84. On the other hand, such authorities as Lambarde and Ellesmere wrote of the three estates as consisting of king, lords, and commons. Lambarde, *Archeion,* ed. McIlwain and Ward, 123, 126, 128–29, 139–40; Ellesmere, 'Speciall Observations Touching All the Sessions of the Last Parlement Anno 7 Regis and Etc.', in Knafla, *Law and Politics in Jacobean England. The Tracts of Lord Chancellor Ellesmere,* 254. Finally, some writers occasionally expanded the membership of the estates from three to four or six. See, for example, the anonymous *Modus tenendi Parliamentum,* a tract written in the fourteenth century and deemed influential in the sixteenth and seventeenth centuries; and Hooker's *Order and Usage.* These are discussed in Snow, *Parliament in Elizabethan England: John Hooker's 'Order and Usage',* 102–03, 152. The membership of the three estates may have been a peripheral issue in a dispute in 1581 between Arthur Hall and the house of commons. Hall had written a tract in which he denied the antiquity of the lower house and also described the three estates as king, lords, and commons. Forced by the house to retract his statement concerning its antiquity, Hall in his apology did an about-face on the composition of the three estates, which he now defined as lords spiritual, lords temporal, and commons. It is not clear, however, whether this second definition was motivated by pressure from the lower house, the members of which were more concerned with Hall's denial of its antiquity. See Hall, *An admonition to the Father of F. A. to him being a Burgesse of the Parliament, for his better behaviour therein* (London, 1579), no pagination; H. G. Wright, *The Life and Work of Arthur Hall of Grantham* (London, 1919), 68–75,

190–91. For another interpretation of Hall's retraction see Snow, *Parliament in Elizabethan England: John Hooker's 'Order and Usage'*, 106–08. The membership of the three estates became an issue of political significance in the years 1640 and 1641 as hostility to the bishops grew into a movement for their exclusion from the house of lords. There is relevant material in William Cobbett, *Parliamentary History of England: From the Norman Conquest in 1066 to . . . 1803* (London, 1806–38), II, 802, 810, 919–22; *Proceedings of the Short Parliament of 1640*, ed. Esther S. Cope and Willson H. Coates (Camden Society, 1977), 235–36; and William Laud, *The Works of the Most Reverend Father in God, William Laud, D.D.* (Oxford, 1847), VI, Part I, 223–33. Still, it was not until the publication of Charles I's Answer to the Nineteen Propositions that the membership of the three estates became inextricably linked to theories of kingship and hence an explosive issue, engaging widespread interest and penetrating seventeenth-century political thought. See notes 13 and 15, Chapter 4 of this study.

15. S. R. Gardiner, *History of the Great Civil War, 1642–1649* (London, 1910–11), I, 292, note 1. The note is not present in earlier editions. See also Gough, *Fundamental Law in English Constitutional History*, 87, note 1. For contemporary comment see Heylyn, *The Stumbling-block of Disobedience*, 264. George Bate, *The Regal Apology, or the Declaration of the Commons, Feb 11, 1647. Canvassed* (London, 1648), 52. This tract should not be confused with Sir Kenelm Digby, *The Royal Apology* (Paris, 1648).

16. *The Maximes of Mixt Monarchy*, title page.

17. *The Stumbling-block of Disobedience*, 226–27, 230–31, 263–64. Heylyn did not know whether the king's advisers were aware of the dangerous consequences of his definition of estates.

18. Dudley Digges, *The Unlawfulnesse of Subjects taking up Armes against their Soveraigne* (n.p., 1644), 67–68. Northleigh, *Remarks upon the most Eminent of our Antimonarchical Authors*, 365–66. David Jenkins, *Lex Terrae* (London, 1647), 18. Heylyn's *The Rebells Catechisme* (n.p., 1643), 21–22 has the admission that the two houses under certain circumstances might lawfully oppose the king with force if indeed there was a co-ordination in law-making. See also note 10, Chapter 6 of this study.

19. William Assheton, *The Royal Apology: or, An Answer to the*

*Rebels Plea* (London, second edition, 1685), 16; Henry Neville, *Plato Redivivus: or, A Dialogue concerning Government* (London, second edition, 1681), 211. See also Sir Henry Vane's defense in Howell, *A Complete Collection of State Trials*, VI, 158ff. Other pertinent materials are in Richard Baxter, *A Holy Commonwealth* (London, 1659), 477–78; George Hickes, *Jovian, or, An Answer to Julian the Apostate* (London, 1683), 236; Weston, *English Constitutional Theory and the House of Lords*, 41–42 (Thomas Hobbes' view). Heylyn's view, in note 17 above, ought also to be noted.

20. This is the key passage : 'The experience and wisdom of *your ancestors* [italics added] hath so moulded this [government] out of a mixture of these [monarchy, aristocracy, and democracy], as to give to this kingdom . . . the conveniences of all three, without the inconveniences of any one, as long as the balance hangs even between the three estates, and they run jointly on in their proper channel.' *His Majesties Answer to the XIX. Propositions of Both Houses of Parliament*, 18. See also *ibid.*, 1 and 23 for another statement in which Charles I referred to 'that trust which God, nature, and the laws of the land have placed in us'.

21. Husband, *An Exact Collection of all Remonstrances*, 514. Since the difference in the two positions turned on the presence or absence of the letter 'y', perhaps an error had crept into the Answer's text before the printing.

22. It was used against the king in *A Political Catechism, or Certain Questions concerning the Government of this Land, Answered in His Majesties own words, taken out of His Answer to the Nineteen Propositions* (London, 1643). This is reprinted in Weston, *English Constitutional Theory and the House of Lords*, 267–79. *Ibid.*, 270. A new edition of the much-reprinted *Political Catechism* appeared as late as 1710, doubtless prompted by the Sacheverell trial. Some modern historians have assigned the tract to Henry Parker, but Fabian Philipps named John White as the author. *The Established Government of England, Vindicated from all Popular and Republican Principles and Mistakes* (London, 1687), 735. White is discussed in Valerie Pearl, *London and the Outbreak of the Puritan Revolution* (Oxford, 1961), 169, 194–95, and 213. Jones, 'The Clegate Case', 275–77. For other tracts reflecting Charles I's remarks on the human source of the government, see *A Friendly Debate between Dr. Kingsman, A Dissatisfied Clergy-man, and Grati-*

*anus Trimmer, A Neighbour Minister* (London, 1689), 28, and Samuel Johnson on a standing army in Howell, *A Complete Collection of State Trials*, XI, 1341–48, especially 1344. Also eminently worth noting are the remarks of the marquess of Halifax recorded in a newly found manuscript on the prerogative. It is printed in Mark N. Brown, *The Works of George Savile, Marquis of Halifax* (forthcoming). Brown has described the manuscript in 'The Works of George Savile Marquis of Halifax : Dates and Circumstances of Composition', *Huntington Library Quarterly*, XXXV (1972), 156. Recalling how Charles I had granted that 'the original of government' was 'from the people', Halifax wrote : 'Ch[arles] I. in his declarations acknowledgeth himself to be a part of the parliament.' This was the king's language in the Answer. Note 10 above. Since Halifax also referred explicitly to the Answer to the Nineteen Propositions, he must have been aware of the relationships discussed in this study. The king had referred to the political system that he was describing as an 'ancient constitution', and this language, too, became part of the discussion. Roger Acherley, *The Britannic Constitution: or, the Fundamental Form of Government in Britain* (London, second edition, 1759), 142. This tract contains an unequalled summary of the political ideas discussed in this study as a community-centered ideology.

23. Heylyn, *Aerius redivivus, or, The History of the Presbyterians* (Oxford, 1670), 447.

24. Gough, *Fundamental Law in English Constitutional History*, 84–85. An eminently practical reason, not mentioned by Gough, which helps explain the emphasis placed by the two houses at this time on the judicial capacity of parliament, is that the king was admittedly bound by judgments in the lower courts although he himself was not present.

25. *Ibid.*, 27.

26. Heylyn, *The Stumbling-block of Disobedience*, 226–27, 230–31, 262. *Aerius redivivus*, 446.

27. *A Holy Commonwealth*, 465. For tracts asserting the arbitrary power of parliament in these years, see Gough, *Fundamental Law in English Constitutional History*, Chapters VI–VIII. See, in particular, the remarks attributed to William Walwyn, *ibid.*, 108–09. Note 107 below has pertinent comment. It is clear, however, that many Englishmen continued to insist on limitations on parliamentary power and that attachment to fundamental law remained strong.

28. For the statement of October 23, see Husband, *An Exact Collection of all Remonstrances*, 655–57; for that of November 2, *ibid.*, 701–03.

29. 'To the Reader', *The Royall and the Royalists Plea* (London, 1647), no pagination. Hudson was familiar with the Answer to the Nineteen Propositions.

30. J. H. M. Salmon, *The French Religious Wars in English Political Thought* (Oxford, 1959), 82–86. See also Herle, *A Fuller Answer*, 1.

31. This description of Herle is based primarily on the distinction that he drew between giving law and declaring law. *A Fuller Answer*, 8. Co-ordination was the hallmark of the first, and it was the highest power. *Ibid.*, 2.

32. Husband, *An Exact Collection of all Remonstrances*, 727.

33. See the discussion in Allen, *English Political Thought, 1603–1644*, 443, 448. Allen has chosen the alternative description.

34. See note 86 below.

35. Anthony Wood, *Athenae Oxonienses: An Exact History of all the Writers and Bishops who have had their Education in the University of Oxford*. ed. Philip Bliss (London, 4 vols., 1813–20), III, 478.

36. *A Fuller Answer*, 1–3, 8. *An Answer to Dr. Ferne's Reply, Entitled Conscience Satisfied* (London, 1643), 20. Also to be consulted is the revised *Oxford English Dictionary* for a discussion of the first appearance of the words 'co-ordination' and 'co-ordinative' in a political context. The example for 'co-ordination' is from *Maximes Unfolded* (1643), written under Herle's influence, while that of 'co-ordinative' comes from a 1689 edition of Philip Hunton's *A Treatise of Monarchie* (1643). In fact, Hunton had borrowed this particular language from Herle. The idea of co-ordination is present in Herle's sermon, *A Payre of Compasses for Church and State* (London, 1642), 11–12, which antedates the *Fuller Answer*.

37. *An Answer to Dr. Ferne's Reply*, 29–31, 35. The execution of the laws was the main area where he had sought to demonstrate in his *Fuller Answer* that the two houses were co-ordinate with the king and that supply therein was the end of that co-ordination. *Ibid.*, 31.

38. *A Fuller Answer*, 5.

39. *Ibid.*, 1, 4, 6–9. Judson found a genuinely modern theory of legal sovereignty in Herle's tracts. *The Crisis of the Constitution*, 423–24, 429–33. See also Donald Hanson, *From Kingdom*

*to Commonwealth: The Development of Civic Consciousness
in English Political Thought* (Cambridge, Mass., 1970), 311–17,
and Weston, 'Concepts of Estates in Stuart Political Thought',
*Representative Institutions in Theory and Practice*, 107–10,
including note 46, found on 109–10. This article is in
Vol. xxxix of *Studies Presented to the International Commission for the History of Representative and Parliamentary Institutions* (Brussels, 1970), 87–130. Herle's doctrine of supply was
foreshadowed in the two houses' declaration of May 19, and
his comment that he had found 'the contrivement of this co-
ordination to this supply' in the Answer to the Nineteen Propositions is in his *Answer to Dr. Ferne's Reply*, 33–35. His maxim
*'co-ordinata invicem supplent'* was remembered in this context
as late as the 1680s in John Nalson, *An Impartial Collection of
the Great Affairs of State* (London, 1682), i, xv and in the
anonymous *The Primitive Cavalerism Revived* (London, 1684),
9. The author of the latter associated it with ordinance-making.
Converts to Herle's doctrine of the king's virtual presence at
Westminster included the anonymous author of *The Subject of
Supremacie: the Right of Caesar* (London, 1643), 29; John
Bellamy, *A Justification of the City Remonstrance and its
Vindication* (London, 1646), 34–38. Valerie Pearl discusses
Bellamy in 'London's Counter-Revolution', *The Interregnum:
The Quest for Settlement 1646–1660*, ed. G. E. Aylmer (Lon-
don, 1972), 33, 37, 50, 217. A wealthy publisher, Bellamy
published and sold Hunton's works at his shop at the sign of the
three golden lions in Cornhill near the royal exchange.

40. *A Fuller Answer*, 2–3. The argument calls to mind the statement attributed to Charles I before his death in January, 1649.
He is supposed to have stated publicly that the happiness of the
people was not in sharing government, 'subject and sovereign
being clean different things'. His words have led modern
historians to discern in him a steadfast attachment to absolutism
that prevented practical arrangements for ending the civil war.
Disregarding his private opinions one is tempted to conclude
that the problem has been misstated. Surely, Charles was strug-
gling with the issue of sovereignty. He and his party assigned
sovereignty, admittedly a term with variant meanings, to the
king alone and with it the law-making power. His words on the
scaffold sound like a last riposte to advocates of co-ordination,
who contended that king, lords, and commons shared the
sovereignty. Thus Herle had insisted that subject and sovereign

were on occasion the same : they were not clean different things. It seems an ill usage to condemn the king for not accepting the opposition's theory of the constitution on a matter of such high importance even if he had inadvertently contributed to its formulation. Influential hostile analyses of the king's words are in Gardiner, *History of the Great Civil War*, IV, 322, 326–27; Godfrey Davies, *The Early Stuarts, 1603–1660* (Oxford, second edition, 1959), 33–34; and H. R. Trevor-Roper, 'The Myth of Charles I : A Tercentenary Occasion', *Historical Essays* (New York, 1966), 207. Their view of Charles' last words has even penetrated the textbooks. William Willcox, *The Age of Aristocracy* (Lexington, Mass., second edition, 1971), 130. For the fact that Charles' statement was representative of royalist political thought, see Sir Philip Warwick, *Memoires of the Reigne of King Charles I* (London, 1701), 345; Sir John Spelman, *The Case of our Affaires, in Law, Religion, and other Circumstances briefly examined and Presented to the Conscience* (Oxford, 1644), 2; Robert Sheringham, *The Kings Supremacy Asserted* (London, 1660), 14, and Nalson, *An Impartial Collection of the Great Affairs of State*, I, xvi. Nalson's remarks are apposite. Queen Elizabeth – whom he was using to illustrate his point – could not be 'both sovereign and subject too, as she must be, if one of the three estates of this realm'. The anti-coordination views of Warwick, Spelman, and Sheringham are discussed in Chapter 4 of this study.

41. *A Fuller Answer*, 2–4, 8, 13–15, 17. For the argument that St Peter's statement also supported submission to the king, see *Great Britain's Vote: or, God Save King Charles* (London, 1648), 16; and there is pertinent comment in Northleigh, *Remarks upon the most Eminent of our Antimonarchical Authors*, 378. The parliamentarian formula seems to have appeared first in the royalist camp when Ferne replied to Henry Parker in *The Resolving of Conscience, upon this Question, Whether upon such a Supposition or Case, as is now usually made (the King will not discharge his trust, but is bent or seduced to subvert Religion, Laws, and Liberties) Subjects may take Arms and resist? and whether that Case be now* (Cambridge, 1642), 14–18. Yet Ferne wrote of the king's power as 'itself of God originally and chiefly' and denied that the people were 'the fountain and original' of the government. Even so, other passages opened the door wide to the parliamentarian insistence that the government was a creation of man and not

of God. Thus Ferne wrote that the qualification of the governing power according to the several forms of government and the offices in them was 'from the invention of man'; that forms of government, including monarchy, were not *jure divino*; and, further, that God 'now . . . designs his vicegerents on earth mediately, as by election of the people, by succession or inheritance, by conquest, etc'. *Ibid.*, 15–18. It was to this tract that Herle's *Fuller Answer* was addressed, and he embraced wholeheartedly Ferne's description of the human source of political power. *Ibid.*, 3, 13–15. See also Hunton, *A Treatise of Monarchie, Containing Two Parts: 1. Concerning Monarchy in generall; 2. Concerning this particular Monarchy* (London, 1643), 4; Bridge, *The Wounded Conscience Cured*, 52–56. By the fall of 1643 Ferne was in retreat, as can be seen in his *A Reply unto Severall Treatises Pleading for the Armes now taken up by Subjects in the pretended defence of Religion and Liberty* (Oxford, 1643), 13. He was explicit : government was 'not the invention of man, but the institution of God' and those who ruled over men as God's vicegerents had their power 'not from the people . . . but from God, by virtue of his institution of government'. There is, of course, a parallel between the Presbyterian system of church government and the political ideology of the Presbyterian pamphleteers. Both assumed that political authority flowed from the community to the government, from the governed to the governor. Some light is shed on the manner in which the community viewed the magistrate, as the community-centered ideology spread, by Richard Tuck, '*Power* and *Authority* in Seventeenth-Century England', *Historical Journal*, XVII (1974), 43–61. See *ibid.*, 46, note 12, 51, 55, for a distinction between the positions of Herle and Hunton.

42. Wood, *Athenae Oxonienses*, ed. Bliss, IV, 50. William Nicolson, *The English Historical Library* (London, 1699), III, 19.

43. *A Treatise of Monarchie*, 25–26, 39–40.

44. *Ibid.*, 39–41, 48, 61. *A Vindication of the Treatise of Monarchy* (London, 1644), 38. See also Judson, *The Crisis of the Constitution*, 400–01.

45. *A Treatise of Monarchie*, 42. *A Vindication of the Treatise of Monarchy*, 39–40. There is discussion of the contemporary use of enacting clauses in Weston, 'Concepts of Estates,' 91–92.

46. *A Treatise of Monarchie*, 1–4, 17, 24–25, 43–44, 45, 48, 49, 64.

47. *Ibid.*, 47–48, 62–63. It was Charles' hope, he stated at Newmarket, that the two houses would not use any other power

than what the law had given them. He always intended, he added, that the law should be the measure of his own power and expected it to be the rule of his subjects' obedience. *His Majesties Declaration to both Houses of Parliament . . . in Answer to that presented to Him at New-market the 9th of March 1641 [1642]* (London, 1642), 12–13.

48. McIlwain, *The High Court of Parliament and its Supremacy* (New Haven, 1910), 154. Prynne, 'To the Reader', *The Treachery and Disloyalty of Papists to their Soveraignes, in Doctrine and Practise* (London, second edition, 1643), no pagination. This work is in four parts.

49. Husband, *An Exact Collection of all Remonstrances*, 703–15. Note 67, Chapter 4 of this study. In making use of *singulis major* the parliamentarians were probably influenced by two Huguenot theorists, Hubert Languet and Philippe Du Plessis–Mornay. They argued in *Vindiciae contra Tyrannos* that the community could discipline and even depose its ruler. Salmon, *The French Religious Wars in English Political Thought*, 7–8, 82. The maxim entered civil-war political thought by way of Henry Parker's *Observations upon some of His Majesties late Answers and Expresses* (1642). For earlier uses of *singulis major, universis minor* see Quentin Skinner, *The Foundations of Modern Political Thought* (Cambridge, 1978), II, 133, 181, 182, 342, 347, and *passim*.

50. *The Treachery and Disloyalty of Papists to their Soveraignes, in Doctrine and Practise. Together with The First Part of the Soveraigne Power of Parliaments and Kingdomes* (London, second edition, 1643), 34–35, 39–41, 45–49, 105–07. Prynne cited Bodin as an authority for parliament as a sovereign body. *Ibid.*, 39, 46. The king's assent was in no way essential to the very being of the laws 'but rather a complemental ceremony'. *Ibid.*, 50. See also *The Fourth Part of the Soveraigne Power of Parliaments and Kingdomes* (London, second edition, 1643). 14–15. Prynne's ideas are discussed in Allen, *English Political Thought, 1603–1644*, 436–48.

51. *The Treachery and Disloyalty of Papists to their Soveraignes . . . with The First Part of the Soveraigne Power of Parliaments*, 41–42, 51. Cp. Herle, *A Fuller Answer*, 1. Salmon, *The French Religious Wars in English Political Thought*, 93.

52. L'Éstrange, *The Free-born Subject: or, The Englishman's Birthright* (London, 1679), 5.

53. Husband, *An Exact Collection of all Remonstrances*, 268–70,

705–15. There is a brief but useful description of the appearance of this clause in the coronation oath in B. Wilkinson, *The Coronation in History* (London, 1953), 13–15.

54. Husband, *An Exact Collection of all Remonstrances*, 289–90.

55. Prynne, *The Soveraigne Power of Parliaments and Kingdomes, or, Second Part of the Treachery and Disloyalty of Papists to their Soveraignes* (London, second edition, 1643) 74, 75. Archbishop Laud was charged during his impeachment with having removed *quas vulgus elegerit* from the coronation oath so as to strengthen the prerogative. The charge, due to Prynne, and Laud's defense, are in the *Works of William Laud*, iv, 211–19. See also Corinne Comstock Weston, 'Legal Sovereignty in the Brady Controversy', *Historical Journal*, xv (1972), 428–30.

56. *Brief Animadversions on, Amendments of, and Additional Explanatory Records to, the Fourth Part of the Institutes of the Lawes of England; Concerning the Jurisdiction of Courts. Compiled by the late Famous Lawyer, Sir Edward Cooke Knight* (London, 1669), 129.

57. *The Treachery and Disloyalty of Papists to their Soveraignes . . . with The First Part of the Soveraigne Power of Parliaments*, 35–36, 39, 49. Cp. William Lamont, *Marginal Prynne 1600–1669* (London, 1963), 100–01.

58. The *Observations* is readily accessible in the second volume of *Tracts on Liberty in the Puritan Revolution, 1638–1647*, ed. William Haller (New York, 1934). The influence of the Answer to the Nineteen Propositions may be seen in *ibid.*, 21–23. Margaret Judson concludes that Parker was the first parliamentarian writer to expound the modern theory of parliamentary sovereignty, Herle the second. 'Henry Parker and the Theory of Parliamentary Sovereignty', *Essays in History and Political Theory in Honor of Charles Howard McIlwain* ed. Carl Wittke (Cambridge, Mass., 1936), 144–45, 147, 153, and 166, note 77. Yet Parker wrote of parliament as a high court and only incidentally as a legislature and urged a controlling power in the two houses in an emergency but not as normal practice, whereas Herle applied the co-ordination principle unhesitatingly to the law-making power, both in ordinary times and in the unusual circumstances of 1642. He, not Parker, was the prophet of the new age. There is another discussion of Parker's *Observations* in Ernest Sirluck, Introduction : Chapter 1, *The Complete Prose Works of John Milton* (New Haven, 1959), ii, 1–52. See also Gough, *Fundamental Law in English Constitutional History*, 86.

59. *Reliquiae Baxterianae: or, Mr. Richard Baxter's Narrative of the most Memorable Passages of his Life and Times,* ed. Matthew Sylvester (London, 1696), I, 41.

60. Baxter, *A Holy Commonwealth,* 458. Geoffrey Nuttall has published a transcript of Baxter's library catalogue. *Journal of Ecclesiastical History,* III (1952), 74–100. The items directly related to this study include Nathaniel Bacon's *An Historical Discourse of the Uniformity of the Government of England* (1647); Dudley Digges, *The Unlawfulnesse of Subjects taking up Armes against their Soveraigne* (1644); Edward Gee, *The Divine Right and Original of the Civill Magistrate from God* (1658); and George Lawson, *An Examination of the Political Part of Mr Hobbes his Leviathan* (1657) and *Politica Sacra et Civilis* (1660).

61. McIlwain, *Constitutionalism and the Changing World* (Cambridge, Mass., 1939), 196–230. Judson, *The Crisis of the Constitution,* 397–409.

62. *The Freeholders Grand Inquest,* 11–13, 19, 45–48. There is comment on Holbourne as a royalist in note 64, Chapter 4 of this study, and on the authorship of the *Freeholders* in note 80 of the same chapter.

63. Hickes, *Jovian,* 238. Robert Brady, 'Glossary', *An Introduction to the Old English History* (London, 1684), 35–36.

64. *Calendar of State Papers, Domestic Series, July 1 to September 30, 1683,* 359.

65. *Ibid., January 1 to December 31, 1682,* 608.

66. Ferne's *Conscience Satisfied* (Oxford, 1643) was a reply to the *Fuller Answer.* Other royalist tracts to be consulted are Digges, *The Unlawfulnesse of Subjects taking up Armes against their Soveraigne,* 138–46; Heylyn, *The Stumbling-block of Disobedience,* 262–67; Sheringham, *The Kings Supremacy Asserted,* 12–15, 80, *passim.* For the swiftness with which Prynne seized on Herle's invention of the co-ordination principle, see note 67, Chapter 4 of this study. See also note 104, Chapter 8.

67. Herle, *An Answer to Doctor Ferne's Reply, Entitled Conscience Satisfied* (London, 1643), *Ahab's Fall by his Prophets Flatteries: Being the Substance of Three Sermons, Upon 1 King. 22.22* (London, 1644).

68. William Stafford, *The Reason of the War,* (London, 1646), 4, 94–96. A passage on co-ordination, which looks like an answer to Herle, is in Robert Sanderson, *Ten Lectures on the Obligation of Humane Conscience,* translated by Robert Codrington

(London, 1660), 248–49. These lectures were delivered at Oxford in 1647. Herle's influence is also apparent in the early stages of the controversy over taking an engagement to be faithful to the commonwealth. Edward Gee, *An Exercitation concerning Usurped Powers* (London, 1650), 1–9. *The Exercitation Answered* (London, 1650), 8–9. See also Gee, *The Divine Right and Original of the Civill Magistrate from God*, 140–41. A Presbyterian clergyman, Gee was rector of Eccleston in Lancashire and at one point Herle's curate. His living was in the gift of Lord Saye and Sele (mentioned in note 79 below), who let the congregation choose the minister. Consult the *DNB* for Gee and also J. E. Bailey, *The Life of a Lancashire Rector* [Herle] (Leigh, 1877), 6, 14. Herle's influence is also apparent in the regicide trials of 1660 and in Sir Henry Vane's trial, discussed in Chapter 6 of this study; and the co-ordination principle is found everywhere in post-restoration political literature.

69. *The Vindication of Judge Jenkins Prisoner in the Tower, the 29 of Aprill, 1647* (London, 1647), 5–6, 8. *Lex Terrae*, 5–7, 18, 20. Jenkins denied vehemently that the king was virtually with the two houses at Westminster.

70. Nalson *An Impartial Collection of the Great Affairs of State*, I, xv. See also Heylyn, *Aerius Redivivus*, 446–47; the Sanderson reference in note 68 of this chapter of this study; Charles Leslie, *Cassandra. (But I hope not) Telling what will come of it. Num. 1* (London, 1704) 9–24, 39, 40 and *The Constitution, Laws, and Government of England, Vindicated* (London, 1709), 7–8; and Luke Milbourne, *The Traytors Reward: or, A King's Death Revenged* (London, 1714), 13–14, reprinted in *The Royal Martyr Lamented, Preach'd on the thirtieth of January* (London, 1708–20). This collection of sermons was preached on the anniversary of Charles I's death. There is pertinent comment on both Leslie and Milbourne in J. P. Kenyon, *Revolution Principles: The Politics of Party, 1689–1720* (Cambridge, 1977). See, in particular, 80, 110.

71. The quoted statement is from *Vindiciae Veritatis* (London, 1654), 6, completed as early as 1648. The authors are said to have been Fiennes and his father Lord Saye and Sele; and the tract has been described as the political testament of a larger group in the long parliament that also included Oliver St John, Samuel Browne, John Crewe, William Pierrepoint, and Sir John Evelyn. Valerie Pearl. ' "The Royal Independents" in the

English Civil War', *Transactions of the Royal Historical Society,* fifth series, XVIII (London, 1968), 72–96. St John had come a long way since 1637. Crewe and Pierrepoint, along with Fiennes, were named to the committee of the house of commons that was to prepare a reply to the preamble of the Answer to the Nineteen Propositions.

72. Clement Walker, *The Compleat History of Independency. Upon the Parliament begun 1640. Continued till . . . 1660* (London, 1660, 1661), Part II, 55.

73. These sermons, recently printed by Cornmarket Press, are discussed in Trevor–Roper, 'The Fast Sermons of the Long Parliament', *Religion, the Reformation and Social Change* (London, 1967), 294–344.

74. Herle's description of himself as a stranger in London in the fall of 1642 is in a preliminary note to his published sermon, *A Payre of Compasses for Church and State.* See also Bailey, *The Life of a Lancashire Rector,* 1–8. *Journals of the House of Commons,* II, 824, 870.

75. *Ibid.* M. F. Keeler, *The Long Parliament, 1640–1641* (Philadelphia, 1954), 277. Moore's invitation to Herle may have reflected a rivalry between the earl of Derby (Herle's former patron) and Moore in Lancashire that spilled over on the London scene. Derby was the leading royalist in Lancashire during the civil war, and Herle was earlier his tutor.

76. J. H. Hexter, *The Reign of King Pym* (Cambridge, Mass., 1941), 112.

77. *Journals of the House of Lords,* VI, 85, 99.

78. *Journals of the House of Commons,* III, 121. See the account of Sedgwick in the *DNB* and also in Wood, *Athenae Oxonienses,* ed. Bliss, III, 441–44. It was Sir William Masham, member for Essex in the house of commons from 1640 to 1653, who thanked Marshall and Sedgwick for preaching in the emergency. His ties with the middle group are undoubted. Married to Barrington's sister, he served on important committees such as that on privileges and worked regularly with Pym. Keeler, *The Long Parliament, 1640–1641,* 266–69. *Journals of the House of Commons,* III, 130. Hexter, *The Reign of King Pym,* 87.

79. *Journals of the House of Lords,* VI, 85, 97. The peers were as hasty as the house of commons; the decision to invite Calamy and Herle was taken on the day of their vote for a public thanksgiving. It is not possible to state which peer extended the invita-

tion, but there may have been a link between Herle and Lord Saye and Sele. See note 68 of this chapter.

80. *Journals of the House of Commons*, III, 138. The ordinance (June 12, 1643) is in the *Journals of the House of Lords*, VI, 92–94.

81. C. V. Wedgwood, *The King's War 1641–1647* (London, 1966), 208. *Journals of the House of Commons*, III, 688. Keeler, *The Long Parliament, 1640–1641*, 285.

82. *Journals of the House of Commons*, IV, 526, 556; V, 344.

83. *Ibid.*, V, 697.

84. Hexter believes that Hunton represented the constitutional outlook of the middle group. 'Appendix B : A Constitutional Basis for the Middle-Group Policy', *The Reign of King Pym*, 214–16. Although Herle's and Hunton's political ideas are related, it was the former who coined the magic phrase with his invocation of 'co-ordination'. Nor does Hunton seem to have enjoyed a relationship with the leaders of the long parliament comparable to Herle's.

85. Gardiner, *History of the Great Civil War*, IV, 116, 124. The two houses made a similar statement on May 6. On October 23, 1646 a group of peers opposed legislating by ordinance in a matter affecting their house. The ground was that 'things that are to be perpetual' ought to 'be settled in the old way by the three estates'. *Journals of the House of Lords*, VIII, 543.

86. That parliament was commonly described as a body where three co-ordinate estates made law may be seen in Thomas Edwards, *The Third Part of Gangraena* (London, 1646), 216. James Cranford, *Plain English, or, The Sectaries Anatomized* (London, 1646), 17 and 22; and Bellamy, *A Justification of the City Remonstrance and its Vindication*, also published in 1646, 34–38. Bulstrode Whitelocke provided a helpful statement on the word 'government' in his *Notes Uppon the Kings Writt for Choosing Members of Parliament . . . Being Disquisitions on the Government of England by King, Lords, and Commons*, ed. Charles Morton (London, 1766), Writing about the time of the restoration, he stated : 'In the government of England (whereby I mean not the executive part of government, which is in the king and his subordinate officers), but in the supreme legislative and judicial power in government there are these distinct parts, different qualities, sounds and voices, which yet being moderated, tempered and mixed together, do make a pleasing harmony and concord of government.' *Ibid.*, II, 55.

This definition is the more helpful because he wrote within the context of parliamentarian ideology, and even the tract's title is significant. That the house of commons' vote was unacceptable to a royalist may be seen in Charles Dallison's *The Royalist's Defence: Vindicating the King's Proceedings in the late Warre made against Him* (n.p., 1648), 83–86. He equated government with *gubernaculum* but was also hostile to the idea of a shared law-making power. See also Heylyn, *Certamen Epistolare* (London, 1659), III, 243–44. The main elements of the parliamentarian position may be seen in more tracts than those cited to this point. See, for example, 'The Vindication of the Parliament, and their Proceedings [1642]', in *The Harleian Miscellany: A Collection of Scarce, Curious, and Entertaining Pamphlets and Tracts . . . Selected from the Library of Edward Harley, Second Earl of Oxford*, ed. Thomas Park (London, 1811), VIII, 58; *The Subjects Liberty Set Forth in the Royall and Politique Power of England* (1643); Robert Austine, *Allegiance not impeached: viz. By the Parliament's taking up Arms* (1644); Walter Mantell, *A Short Treatise of the Lawes of England* (1644); Samuel Rutherford, *Lex, Rex, or, The Law and the Prince. A Dispute for the Just Prerogative of King and People* (1644); and William Ball, *The Power of Kings Discussed* (1649).

87. Digges, *The Unlawfulness of Subjects taking up Armes against their Soveraigne*, 66. Abednigo Seller, *The History of Passive Obedience since the Reformation* (Amsterdam, 1689), 56.

88. Thus Heylyn found the co-ordination principle dangerous 'because so universally admired and harkened to'. *The Stumbling-block of Disobedience*, 263. There is pertinent comment in Filmer, 'The Anarchy of a Limited or Mixed Monarchy', *Patriarcha and Other Political Works*, ed. Laslett, 279, and in Sir Roger Twysden, *Certaine Considerations upon the Government*, ed. John Mitchell Kemble (Camden Society, 1849), 127–28, which was apparently written in the 1650s. There is a comparable statement for the 1680s in Henry Care, *English Liberties* (London, fourth edition, 1719), 116, first published in 1680. Other signs of the widespread acceptance of the community-centered view of government are in Weston, 'Theory of Mixed Monarchy under Charles I and After', *English Historical Review*, LXXV (1960), 431–32, 436–37. Weston, *English Constitutional Theory and the House of Lords*, 41–43, Chapter II, *passim*.

89. Edward Bagshaw, *The Rights of the Crown of England, as it is established by Law* (London, 1660), 3–5, 69–72. See note 13, Chapter 4 of this study. Johnston offered a similar appraisal in the late 1680s when looking back to civil-war literature he declared : 'The first and principal topic they [parliamentarian writers] used, was, that the monarchy of England was in its constitution allayed, and the power of the two houses, in making laws, had such a copartnership, and radical mixture, that they had something more than a consultive and assenting part; and that the king was obliged in the duty of his office, and by his coronation oath, to grant what they desired.' And he wrote in the margin : 'The monarchy of England not mixed.' *The Excellency of Monarchical Government*, 304–05.

90. Bagshaw, *The Rights of the Crown of England*, 66. See also Stafford, *The Reason of the War*, 4; Rutherford, *Lex, Rex*, 140; Heylyn, *Aerius Redivivus*, 447.

91. Clement Walker, *Anarchia Anglicana: or, the History of Independency. The Second Part* (London, 1661), 22.

92. Salmon, *The French Religious Wars in English Political Thought*, 135, note 18.

93. William Dugdale, *A Short View of the Late Troubles in England* (Oxford, 1681), 38–39. See also Izaak Walton, *The Life of Mr. Richard Hooker* (London, 1665), 171, for an account of the concern displayed by Robert Sanderson (bishop of Lincoln) and Fabian Philipps (a high tory historian in the later Brady controversy) about this aspect of the *Ecclesiastical Polity*. There is pertinent information about Walton's *Life* in note 95 below. See also *Reliquiae Baxterianae*, I, 41. Dugdale considered that the tampering had come during the civil war.

94. Richard Hooker, *Of the Laws of Ecclesiastical Politie: the Sixth and Eighth Books* (London, 1648), Eighth Book, 153, 155. A prefatory note states that the publication was intended to counteract the effect of 'some erroneous, if not counterfeit copies' in circulation. Thomason's copy was dated June 17 and could have been the first issue. There were two others in 1648 and another one in 1651. *Hooker's Ecclesiastical Polity: Book VIII*, ed. Houk, 116–17.

95. *Ibid.*, 87. It is possible to authenticate the portion of the eighth book with the reference to *singulis major* by comparing the text with the Dublin manuscript, a copy of that book known to have been at one time in the possession of Archbishop Ussher. It has been suggested that desirous of promoting an accommo-

dation between Charles I and the long parliament, Ussher may have brought out the edition of 1648 in the belief it would have this effect. It is difficult to believe, however, that he would have brought out a work so manifestly injurious to Charles I. *Hooker's Ecclesiastical Polity: Book VIII*, ed. Houk, 118–19. The authors of this study are indebted to W. Speed Hill, the modern editor of *The Folger Library Edition of the Works of Richard Hooker* for advice and counsel on the critical issue of whether in fact tampering took place in the 1648 edition. Professor Hill writes : 'There is no evidence that people unsympathetic to Charles "corrupted [those very books] in sundry places, omitting diverse passages . . . unsuitable to their purposes;" etc. The text of [Book] VIII is complicated but deliberate tampering is mythical.' He adds : 'There is strong, if indirect, evidence that the Laudian church was responsible for discrediting those "three last books" in the seventeenth century, presumably because of the very Elizabethan radicalism you mention. So Charles is simply reciting received, if royalist, views when he says that "those three books were not allowed to be Mr. Hooker's" '. W. Speed Hill to C. C. Weston, June 21, 1979. For a sense of the complexities surrounding the authorship of the last three books, see Hill, 'Hooker's *Polity* : The Problem of the "Three Last Books" '. *Huntington Library Quarterly*, XXXIV (1971) 317–36, and, in particular, 326–30, for a discussion of the Gauden edition of the *Ecclesiastical Polity* of 1662, which illuminates the attitude of the Laudian church to the last three books. Apparently Archbishop Sheldon played an important role in bringing out the Gauden edition, only to discover that the publication of the posthumous books was less than wise. It is curious that the mistake was made in the first instance since he could hardly have been unaware of the stand taken by Charles I on the isle of Wight. He was one of the royalists close to the king in the late stages of the civil war although he was not present during the negotiations at Newport. Be that as it may, he commissioned Walton to write a life of Hooker, calculated to undo the blunder, which was thereafter fixed to successive editions of the *Ecclesiastical Polity*. Until recently Walton's *Life* discredited the last three books. As Hill notes : 'It has remained for modern scholarship to rebut Walton, if not to vindicate Gauden.' 'Hooker's *Polity* : The problem of the "Three Last Books",' 329. There is also pertinent information in C. J. Sisson, *The Judicious Marriage* of Mr. Hooker and the Birth of the 'Laws of Ecclesiastical Polity' (Cambridge, 1940), 108. See also note 93 above in this chapter of this study and Dugdale, *A Short View of the Late Troubles in England*, 39–40. The most recent and authoritative discussion of the eighth book is in Volume III of *The Folger Library Edition of the Works of Richard Hooker*, ed. P. G. Stanwood (Cambridge, Mass., 1980).

96. Trevor-Roper writes of Peter: 'What Marshall was to Pym, Hugh Peter is to Cromwell . . . If Marshall holloa'd the parliamentary pack onwards into war in 1642, Peter in 1647, would holloa the army onwards into revolution.' *Religion, the Reformation, and Social Change*, 323–24. See also the *DNB* article on Hooker and *Hooker's Ecclesiastical Polity: Book VIII*, ed. Houk, 130–32. Professor Hill supplied information about Peter and the surviving Hooker manuscripts. Letter to C. C. Weston, June 21, 1979.

97. J. G. Muddiman, *The Trial of King Charles the First* (Edinburgh and London, 1928), 115.

98. Husband, *An Exact Collection of all Remonstrances*, 703.

99. 'Reflections upon the Opinions of Some Modern Divines'. *A Collection of State Tracts, Publish'd on Occasion of the late Revolution in 1688, and during the reign of William III* (London, 1705–07), I, 507.

100. Peter Allix, *An Examination of the Scruples of Those who Refuse to Take the Oath of Allegiance* (London, 1689), 22. See Vane's defense at his trial for high treason in 1662, described in Chapter 6 of this study. Algernon Sidney wrote: 'Bracton saith, that the king hath three superiors, to wit, "Deum, legem, and parliament".' *The Arraignment, Tryal and Condemnation of Algernon Sidney, Esq., for High Treason* (London, 1684), 23. As early as 1644 Griffith Williams, bishop of Ossory, was referring to this particular argument as 'the sectaries' chiefest argument out of Bracton'. *Jura Majestatis, The Rights of Kings both in Church and State* (Oxford, 1644), 131, marginal note. See also Sir John Spelman, *The Case of our Affaires*, 10–12; *The Freeholders Grand Inquest*, 9–10; Thomas Tomkins, *The Rebels Plea, or, Mr. Baxter's Judgment, concerning the Late Wars* (London, 1660), 14.

101. *A Fuller Answer*, 1.

102. Muddiman, *The Trial of King Charles the First*, 115.

103. *Journals of the House of Commons*, V, 352.

104. David Underdown, *Pride's Purge: Politics in the Puritan Revolution* (Oxford, 1971), 200–01. See also Chapter v.
105. *The Freeholders Grand Inquest*, 45–48. Weston, 'Legal Sovereignty in the Brady Controversy', 429.
106. *Pride's Purge: Politics in the Puritan Revolution*, 296.
107. *Whitelocke's Notes Uppon the Kings Writt*, ed. Morton, ii, 43–44, 50, 308–11, 339–43. Unmistakably, Whitelocke believed in a parliamentary sovereignty in the modern sense of the term. *Ibid.*, ii, 331–35. See also note 27 of this chapter. Whitelocke can also be associated with the Answer to the Nineteen Propositions since he was chairman of the committee of the house of commons charged in 1642 with replying to its preamble. Weston, 'The Theory of Mixed Monarchy under Charles I and After', 441–43.
108. The clash between the parliamentarian ideology and advancing Leveller democracy may be seen in Edwards, *The Third Part of Gangraena*, 195, 200–03, 215–18. The Levellers seem to have been a minority even in the lower ranks of the new model army. Ivan Roots, *The Great Rebellion, 1642–1660* (London, 1966), 138–40. It appears that the parliamentarian ideology penetrated the royalist party after the king's death. See the discussion in Chapter 6 of this study of the famous resolution (May 1, 1660) of the convention parliament, which brought back the monarchy, and of the equally well-known act for the preservation of the king (13 Car. 2, s. 1. c. 1.).
109. J. P. Kenyon, *The Stuart Constitution, 1603–1688: Documents and Commentary* (Cambridge, 1966), 353. J. G. A. Pocock, 'James Harrington and the Good Old Cause : a study of the ideological context of his writings', *Journal of British Studies*, x (1970), 39. Ivan Roots has described a quarrel over the legislative power in the period just before the adoption of the *Humble Petition*. 'Cromwell's Ordinances : The Early Legislation of the Protectorate', *The Interregnum: The Quest for Settlement*, ed. Aylmer, 144–45, 159–64.
110. Lawson, *An Examination of the Political Part of Mr. Hobbes his Leviathan*, 31.
111. John Locke, *Two Tracts on Government*, ed. Philip Abrams (Cambridge, 1967), 231.
112. 'Patriarchalism, Politics and Mass Attitudes in Stuart England', *Historical Journal*, xii (1969), 414, 424, 425, 435. Despite an emphasis on the illiterate masses of Stuart England, the article has references to members of the politically conscious classes.

*Ibid.*, 438. The failure to consider the implications of the parliamentarian formula for the human source of political authority raises doubt about Schochet's conclusions and also those of Gerald Straka, 'The Final Phase of Divine Right Theory in England, 1688–1702', *English Historical Review*, LXXVII (1962), 638–58.

113. D. D. Raphael, *Problems of Political Philosophy* (London, 1970), 10. In this connection, see the description of law-making in the broadside *No King but the Old King's Son, or, A Vindication of Limited Monarchy, as it was Established in this Nation, before the late War between the King and Parliament* (London, 1660) and also Hickes' recognition that appearances told against the king in the great struggle over the legislative power. *The Harmony of Divinity and Law, in a Discourse about not Resisting of Soveraign Princes* (London, 1684), 43–44.

114. Baxter, *A Holy Commonwealth*, 457–59, 461–62.

115. *Ibid.*, 462–65, 477–78, 479. See the statement: 'The laws in England are above the king: because they are not his acts alone, but the acts of king and parliament conjunctly, who have the legislative (that is, the sovereign) power. This is confessed by the king in the forecited Answer to the 19 Propositions.' *Ibid.*, 470. Consult as well note 8, in the Appendix to this study.

CHAPTER 4 THAT 'POISONOUS TENET' OF CO-ORDINATION

1. Richard Mocket, *God and the King, or, A Dialogue. Shewing that our Soveraigne Lord King James being immediate under God within his Dominions, Doth Rightly claim whatsoever is Required by the Oath of Allegiance* (London, 1615, reprinted 1616), 2–3. There is discussion in David Harris Willson, *King James VI and I* (London, paperback edition, 1966), 294–95; Greenleaf, *Order, Empiricism and Politics*, 48–49; Schochet, *Patriarchalism in Political Thought*, 88–90.

2. Digges, *The Unlawfulnesse of Subjects taking up Armes against their Soveraigne*, 84.

3. Jean Bodin, *The Six Bookes of a Commonweale: A Facsimile reprint of the English translation of 1606*, ed. Kenneth Douglas McRae (Cambridge, Mass., 1962), introduction, A14, 84, 96, 155, marginal note, 159. Richard Knolles edited the English translation of 1606.

4. *Ibid.*, 98, 162–63.
5. Greenleaf, *Order, Empiricism and Politics*, 132–34.
6. Heylyn, *The Stumbling-block of Disobedience*, 264, 267, 289.
7. *Calendar of State Papers, Domestic Series, November 1, 1673 to February 28, 1675*, 220–21. The comment was by Thomas Turner, describing a civil-war manuscript of his father-in-law, Judge William Morton, which Turner wanted Charles II's government to publish. See also note 26 of this chapter.
8. *The Excellency of Monarchical Government*, 157. Johnston was borrowing from Sheringham's *The Kings Supremacy Asserted*, 25–26.
9. *Life of Edward Earl of Clarendon . . . written by himself* (Oxford, 1827), I, 155.
10. Heylyn, *The Stumbling-block of Disobedience*, 231–32.
11. Initially, Hyde's primary objection may have been to the bishops' exclusion from membership in the three estates. He was specific in his comment : the church 'was principally concerned in that mistake'. *Life of Edward Earl of Clarendon*, I, 155. The question of who comprised the three estates of parliament was bound up in the seventeenth century not only with the issue of the king versus the two houses but also with the question of the status of the bishops in the house of lords. That status was bound to suffer if Charles I's definition of estates became popular. In this sense Hyde's comment is pertinent. But that the relationship between the Answer and the contemporary controversy over legal sovereignty long eluded him became clear when he was able to write, as late as 1646, that the two houses ought to grant the king 'his share in the legislative power'. Edward Earl of Clarendon, *History of the Rebellion and Civil Wars in England begun in the year 1641*. ed. W. Dunn Macray (Oxford, 1888), II, 176. Hyde was summarizing at this time the contents of the Answer to the Nineteen Propositions for inclusion in his *History*; and although he elided Charles I's description of the constitution, he retained this part of the Answer. To keep the king's share in the legislative power, without asking for more, was his highest goal as the civil war went on. *Calendar of the Clarendon State Papers*, ed. O. Ogle and W. H. Bliss (Oxford, 1872), I, 434, item 2860. A generation later Hyde expressed objection to Thomas Hobbes' view that in the co-ordination principle was to be found a major explanation for the coming of the civil war. Hyde argued

that the opinion that power was divided in England among king, lords, and commons was never put forward until after the rebellion was underway. *A Brief View and Survey of the Dangerous and Pernicious Errors to Church and State in Mr. Hobbes Book, Entitled Leviathan* (Sheldonian Theatre, 1676), 54.

12. Philipps, *The Established Government of England*, 666. This is probably a reference to the post that carried the Answer to the Nineteen Propositions to the two houses at Westminster. In this connection see the discussion later in this chapter of the earl of Southampton and Lord Hertford.

13. *Life of Edward Earl of Clarendon*, I, 154–56. The lawyers from whom Colepeper received information may have been reading Lambarde's *Archeion*, written as early as 1591 but published for the first time in 1635, when it appeared in two editions. For repeated uses of the term three estates to signify king, lords, and commons, see *Archeion*, ed. McIlwain and Ward, 123, 126, 128–29, 139–40. A. F. Pollard cites other Tudor precedents in *The Evolution of Parliament* (London, 1920), 70. See also note 14 in Chapter 3 of this study, and that chapter itself, for further discussion of the terminology of estates prior to the civil war. Material relevant to Hyde's view can be found in Weston, *English Constitutional Theory and the House of Lords*, 27–28. M. J. Mendle in 'Politics and Political Thought, 1640–1642', *The Origins of the English Civil War*, ed. Conrad Russell (London, 1973), 219–45, seems to attribute the popularity of Charles I's definition of estates to earlier parliamentary usage in the short parliament and in the first years of the long parliament. That it was used before 1642 is unquestionable, and the same statement is possible about other phrases and expressions in the Answer that had great influence after 1642. This matter has been briefly discussed in Chapter 3 of this study. This is not to agree with Mendle, however, that the widespread use of this definition of estates in Stuart England was due to the language to which he calls attention. Rather, it was the Answer to the Nineteen Propositions that made this definition widely known – not only because the definition appeared in a royal declaration, published by authority, a fact of cardinal importance – but also because it was present in a context that encouraged Herle to formulate the parliamentarian ideology. One other point should receive mention. Mendle's examples reflect the hostility of parliamentary speakers towards

the bishops; and, despite Gardiner's interpretation, which Mendle cites, it is by no means clear that they had considered the implications of this definition of estates for the kingship. On this point, see Mendle's description of Bagshaw's speech concerning episcopacy (February 9, 1641), where the latter explicitly defined the three estates as kings, lords, and commons. 'Politics and Political Thought', 228. Despite this usage Bagshaw seems to have had no designs on royal power. It is true that he was at this time part of the opposition to Charles I. Yet his speech only objected to the presence of the bishops in parliament, not to the traditional powers of the kingship; and he even described episcopacy as 'trenching upon the crown'. *Mr. Bagshaw's Speech in Parliament, February the Ninth, 1640, concerning Episcopacy and the London Petition* (London, 1641), 2–6. Writing in the years 1644 to 1646, Bagshaw, now a royalist, set down once more his opinion regarding the membership of the estates of parliament. The appearance of the co-ordination principle, which he repudiated, had given him pause; and he now dissociated himself from his earlier definition of estates, saying: 'in truth the king be more than an estate'. *The Rights of the Crown of England*, 70–71. His larger discussion is pertinent. *Ibid.*, 69–75.

14. *Life of Edward Earl of Clarendon*, I, 155. Weston, *English Constitutional Theory and the House of Lords*, 27–28.

15. *Memoires of the Reigne of King Charles I*, 183–84, 194–98. Warwick attributed the error to the inexperience of the royal advisers, who were expected to understand all at once a court, a camp, and a council-board. *Ibid.*, 198. See Mendle's suggestion that Colepeper used the language of estates in the Answer with deliberation and in full awareness of its implications. Mendle, 'Politics and Political Thought', *Origins of the English Civil War*, 245. As was noted earlier, Colepeper apparently did believe the king to be one of the three estates, but that he used the term with an awareness of its implications is another matter. The suggestion that he did so is at variance with Warwick's and Hyde's comments and the interpretation in this study.

16. *Memoires of the Reigne of King Charles I*, 75.

17. *Ibid.*, 75, 184.

18. Smith may have come to value Warwick's writings about the time of their composition. The orientalist was a chaplain to Sir Joseph Williamson, one of the secretaries of state, when War-

wick was finishing his writing. Smith performed much drudgery for Williamson and as a noted bibliophile must surely have been involved in the secretary's responsibility to license books on politics and history.

19. Warwick, *A Discourse of Government, as Examined by Reason, Scripture, and Law of the Land* (London, 1694), 10, 19. The Preface, which lacks pagination, states that the *Discourse* was intended as an appendix to the *Memoires*. See also 'Introduction,' *Memoires of the Reign of King Charles* (Edinburgh, 1813), ix, for the statement that Dr Smith also published the *Memoires.* The *DNB* article on Smith is helpful.

20. *A Discourse of Government*, 6, 20–21, 45.

21. *Ibid.*, 45, 47–49. Other statements about the membership of the three estates are in *ibid.*, 3, 42.

22. The details of Warwick's career are in Sir Charles Firth's *DNB* article. G. E. Aylmer, *The King's Servants: The Civil Service of Charles I, 1625–1642* (London, 1961), 77, 204, 321, 348, and Stephen Baxter, *The Development of the Treasury, 1660–1702* (London, 1957), 174–78, 258. Wood also commented on Warwick's relationships with politically influential royalists. *Fasti Oxonienses*, ed. Bliss, II, 505–06. On the night before he died, Charles I spoke of Warwick to Archbishop Juxon, saying 'My lord, I must remember one that hath had relation to you and myself : tell Charles he hath been an useful and honest man unto me.' Warwick, *Memoires*, 331. See, also, *ibid.*, 197–98, 213. Other leading royalists with whom Warwick was associated and who receive mention later in this study include the marquess of Ormonde, Dr Robert Sanderson, Gilbert Sheldon, James Ussher, Sir Orlando Bridgeman, Sir Robert Holbourne, and Sir Geoffrey Palmer.

23. Sir William Dugdale, *A Short View of the Late Troubles in England*, 95. *The Works of King Charles the Martyr: With a Collection of Declarations, Treaties and other Papers* (London, second edition, 1687), 27. *Journals of the House of Lords*, v, 153. *Journals of the House of Commons*, II, 635. Hertford and Southampton, at a later date, were closely involved with the first printing of the *Eikon Basilike* (1649), like the Answer highly influential in the propaganda warfare of the period. Francis F. Madan, *A New Bibliography of the Eikon Basilike of King Charles the First* (Oxford, 1950), Appendix I, paras. 2 and 7, notes 37–38. See also item no. 221, *ibid.*, 160.

24. Philipps, *The Established Government of England*, 666. That

the Oxford parliament took up a position condemnatory of the co-ordination principle also appears from the declaration cited in note 69 of this chapter.

25. Herle's comments are in *Ahab's Fall*, 42. Thomason's copy was picked up on May 30, about six weeks after the first session of the Oxford parliament and well before the second one. Although *Ahab's Fall* was published anonymously, the tract was easily identified with Herle by this listing of his major sermons. He was later named as its author in William Assheton, *Evangelium Armatum: A Specimen: or Short Collection of several Doctrines and Positions destructive to our Government Both Civil and Ecclesiastical* (London, 1663), 28.

26. *The Stumbling-block of Disobedience*, 262. Two other anti-co-ordination tracts of this period were *Sacro-Sancta Regum Majestas: or; The Sacred and Royall Prerogative of Christian Kings* (Oxford, 1644), written by John Maxwell, bishop of Tuam, and *The King's Cause Rationally, briefly, and plainly debated, as it Stands Defacto* (n.p., 1644), by John Doughty, formerly chaplain to the earl of Northumberland. See *Sacro-Sancta*, 4–5, 68, and 103–04; *The King's Cause*, 27–28. Mention should also be made of a manuscript entitled 'Jus Regium, sive jus Monarchiae Anglicanae', written by Justice Sir William Morton, who became king's serjeant soon after the restoration and subsequently a justice of king's bench. A royalist who had served as lieutenant colonel in Lord Chandos' regiment of horse, Morton was governor of Chandos' castle at Sudeley, Gloucestershire, when it was surrendered in June, 1644, to Sir William Waller. Morton was sent to the tower and while there wrote the manuscript. Never published, it was the subject of a discussion between his son-in-law, Thomas Turner, and the earl of Arlington in 1674. The manuscript was described as anti-co-ordination in tone, and it follows that Morton had reached this position before his imprisonment, that is, by 1644. Given the date of composition, the manuscript attests to the widespread nature of the anti-co-ordination sentiment in royalist circles at this stage of the civil war. By the same token its existence is another reminder of the great influence of the community-centered ideology, which had taken shape at the hands of the Presbyterian clergy. Morton's manuscript is described in *Calendar of State Papers, Domestic Series, November 1, 1673 to February 28, 1675*, 220–21.

27. *Calendar of State Papers, Domestic Series, Charles I, 1644*, 20.

The reference is in a letter from a John Jones to Lord Hopton, February 20, 1644. Bagshaw's views are described in Chapter 3 of this study.

28. Philipps, *The Established Government of England*, 666.
29. Note 80 of this chapter.
30. *The Freeholders Grand Inquest*, 18–19.
31. Howell, *A Complete Collection of State Trials*, v, 988–92, 1227.
32. See note 11 of this chapter.
33. Ferne, *Conscience Satisfied, that there is no warrant for the Armes now taken up by Subjects*, 6. See also note 41, Chapter 3 of this study for what royalists must surely have seen as another bad slip on Ferne's part.
34. *Conscience Satisfied*, 13, 14, 25–26.
35. *Ibid.*, 14. *A Reply unto Severall Treatises*, 29–30.
36. *Ibid.*, 32.
37. Spelman, *The Case of our Affaires*, 1. Heylyn, *The Stumbling-block of Disobedience*, 252–54. Howell, *A Complete Collection of State Trials*, v, 989–91.
38. *Conscience Satisfied*, 15.
39. *Ibid.*, 7–13, 15. *The Resolving of Conscience*, 15–23. *A Reply unto Severall Treatises*, 21–30.
40. Williams, *Jura Majestatis*, 149–50. Digges, *The Unlawfulnesse of Subjects taking up Armes against their Soveraigne*, 88, 139. The latter tract reached a large audience. Printed in two editions in 1644, it was reprinted in 1647, 1662, 1664, and 1679. It was known to Locke. *Two Treatises of Government* ed. Peter Laslett (Cambridge, 1960, revised 1963, published as a Mentor Book, 1965), 152 (Appendix B); and the whig lawyer, William Petyt, had three copies. See note 28, Chapter 7 of this study.
41. *The Stumbling-block of Disobedience*, 264.
42. *The Royalist's Defence*, 2, 7–10. The royalist also wrote : 'The lords and commons put together . . . have no commission to make laws.' The legislative power is 'in the king'. 'He alone' is 'properly law-maker'. *Ibid.*, 34. Dallison's tract created a considerable contemporary stir. William Petyt, *Jus Parliamentarium: or, the Ancient Power, Jurisdiction, Rights and Liberties, of the Most High Court of Parliament, Revived and Asserted* (London, 1739), 66–67.
43. *The Royalist's Defence*, 75. See also *ibid.*, 88 : 'When the two houses have passed a bill for a new law, and have presented

it to the king, they have performed their duty. It then rests in the king, whether to make it a law, or not.'

44. *Ibid.*, 10, 43, 78.
45. *Ibid.*, 78.
46. *Ibid.*, 43–44. The royal prerogatives were frequently described as flowers of the crown. J. W. Gough, 'Flowers of the Crown', *English Historical Review*, LXXVII (1962), 86–93. Dallison's interpretation of the dispensing power should be compared with Robert Sanderson's. See note 86 of this chapter.
47. *The Royalist's Defence*, 39–40, 48, 70–72, 83–86, 89, and 135–36.
48. *Ibid.*, 12–13, 77–78.
49. M. J. C. Vile has described Dallison's pamphlet as representing perhaps the clearest and most comprehensive statement that had been made up to this time about the relationship between the ideas of separating the functions of government and balancing the parts of government. But he had some reservations about the pamphlet as expressing the pure doctrine of the separation of powers in its modern form. *Constitutionalism and the Separation of Powers* (Oxford, 1967), 45–47. Vile's statement was cautiously framed, but perhaps did not go far enough in this direction. Admittedly Dallison divided the three governmental functions – executive, legislative, and judicial – in form at least among king, parliament, and the courts. Yet his political thought was more conventional than Vile has recognized. Thus the royalist believed that the king alone made law in parliament and that as the sole law-maker he could dispense on occasion with the law. In other words, two-thirds of what would now be thought of as the legislative body, if it is assumed that parliament consisted of king, lords, and commons, had only a tenuous hold on legislation. Moreover, a king who could dispense on occasion with statute law, had much more than an 'executive' power. If he was also the human source of political authority, as Dallison's theory presupposed, the legislative and judicial branches of government were in theory at least dependent upon the king. In short, Dallison's whole system was aimed at checking the legislative power, which he saw as falling under the control of the two houses of parliament; and he accordingly downgraded the importance of this power while leaving it essentially in the hands of the king with the additional safeguard that judicial review would provide.

50. Another royalist to be mentioned is the Welsh judge, David Jenkins, best known for *Lex Terrae* (1647). Although he understood the idea of parliamentary sovereignty, he preferred that of fundamental law 'in a form that approached more closely than hitherto to the modern legal doctrine in which it is a definite alternative to legislative sovereignty'. Gough, *Fundamental Law in English Constitutional History*, 103–05.

51. *Patriarcha and Other Political Works of Sir Robert Filmer*, ed. Laslett, 105.

52. *A View of a Printed Book Intituled Observations upon His Majesties late Answers and Expresses* (Oxford, 1643), no pagination. The tract is paged erratically. Spelman wrote in another passage : 'The legislature is the most sovereign power, *jus dare* is somewhat more than *jus dicere*.' The power to give law was solely in the king. *Ibid.*, 19. Spelman also cited the well-known comment on parliamentary sovereignty in Sir James Whitelocke's speech on impositions in 1610 as perfectly compatible with the royalist theory of a legal sovereignty in the king and indeed supportive of such a theory. The king in parliament made the statutes that controlled the regal power out of parliament. Spelman wrote : 'The sovereign power (sayeth he) is agreed to be in the king, but in the king is a twofold power, the one in parliament, the other out of parliament, the correcting of the errors of the ordinary courts is by him, acts of parliament be they law's grounds, or whatsoever, the act and power is the king's, but with the assent of the lords and commons, which maketh it the most supreme power, not controllable by any, but controlling the regal power out of parliament, so he.' *Ibid.*, 19. Even if the law-making power was in the king in parliament, Spelman found some areas where no act of parliament could prevail. Thus a statute could not lawfully depose a king, or deprive him of his right or authority or any necessary part thereof. Nor could it take away the king's duty of protection or the subject's of service, these being due by the law of nature. The dispensing power also lay outside parliament's jurisdiction. Spelman wrote : 'A statute that the king by no *non obstante* shall dispense with it is void, because it would take a necessary part of government out of the king.' *View of a Printed Book*, 8–9. This material is on pp. 8–9, but the printer made a mistake and the paging appears as 8–7. It is noticeable that the list of areas free of parliamentary control was much reduced in the *Case of our Affaires*. Only a divine

right of succession to the throne remained outside parliament's jurisdiction. Wood, relying on Dr Thomas Barlow, bishop of Lincoln, assigned the two tracts to Spelman, and their contents are internally consistent. Wood, *Athenae Oxonienses*, ed. Bliss, III, 62. Thomason dated a London reprint of the *Case of our Affaires* January 29, 1644. The Oxford printing may have been January 20. Falconer Madan, *Oxford Books* (Oxford, 1912), II, 310–11. There were at least two London reprints. The Council Register (October, 1640–August, 1645) is in the Public Record Office, P.R.O. P.C. 2./53.

53. Heylyn, *The Stumbling-block of Disobedience*, 255–58, 262. Williams, *Jura Majestatis* 133, 149. Tomkins, *The Rebels Plea*, 20. The passage about courts of ministerial jurisdiction in the *Freeholders Grand Inquest*, 44, comes from the *Case of our Affaires*, 7. Also compare *ibid.*, 6–9, with Johnston's *Excellency of Monarchical Government*, 300–01, and the *Case of our Affaires*, 2, with the *Excellency of Monarchical Government*, 128. It is very possible that Spelman's exposition shaped Bridgeman's presentation in the regicide trials.

54. J. G. A. Pocock, *The Ancient Constitution and the Feudal Law* (Cambridge 1957) 182–228. Salmon, *The French Religious Wars in English Political Thought*, 90–96. Heylyn, *The Stumbling-block of Disobedience*, 34. Spelman was one of the royalist writers who advocated a theory of legal sovereignty in the king, at least at first, without reference to the co-ordination principle. His *View of a Printed Book*, reflecting Bodin's influence, was written in response to Henry Parker's *Observations*, which appeared before the *Fuller Answer*. But the *Case of our Affaires* contains an elaboration of a theory of legal sovereignty in the king that comes close to the modern theory. As was mentioned earlier (note 52 of this chapter), Spelman in the *Case of our Affaires* placed fewer areas beyond the control of the king in parliament than earlier in his *View of a Printed Book*. This means, it may be urged, that his exposition of a legal sovereignty in the king in parliament became progressively more sophisticated and more elaborate in response to the parliamentarian advocacy of the co-ordination principle. See also note 55 of this chapter for another difference between the two tracts.

55. *The Case of our Affaires*, 1–2, 15. Spelman earlier accepted uncritically the royal definition of estates. *A View of a Printed Book*, 16, 21.

56. *The Case of our Affaires*, 2–3.
57. *Ibid.*, 5–6.
58. *Ibid.*, 8–9.
59. *Ibid.*, 9, 11–12.
60. *A View of a Printed Book*, 11–13.
61. *Ibid.*, 13.
62. *Ibid.*, 16–18.
63. *The Case of our Affaires*, 14. Bodin is mentioned by name in *A View of a Printed Book*, 10, 21. There is further discussion of Spelman's political ideas in Weston, 'Concepts of Estates', 111–18. See also note 54 above.
64. Like other members of the king's party, Holbourne was earlier a member of the opposition. But his anti-court ardor cooled after serving as Hampden's counsel and early in the long parliament he turned against Pym. Part of the small minority who voted against Strafford's attainder, he delivered a learned speech in the bishops' behalf in November, 1641 and by June of the following year left to join the king. Known to contemporaries as a great lawyer, he rose rapidly at Oxford, where his name was coupled with men such as Sir John Bankes and Sir Robert Heath as legal advisers to the crown. 'Justice Bankes, and Justice Heath, and Holbourne', wrote a contemporary pamphleteer, would 'advise his majesty how to punish subverters of the laws of the land'. *The Oxonian Antippodes, or, The Oxford Anty-Parliament* (London, 1644), 16. He was knighted and appointed attorney general to the prince of Wales on the eve of the Oxford parliament and subsequently served as a leading member of the administrative council that conducted the prince's business affairs after the latter was made the titular commander of the king's military forces in the west of England. This administrative council worked with the privy councillors who accompanied the prince, including Colepeper, Hyde, and Southampton. Holbourne was at Uxbridge early in 1645, and Charles I asked for him at the time of the treaty of Newport. It is likely that he was by that time dead. After the fall of Oxford he had returned to London, where he compounded for his estates; and he lived out his life there, barred from the inns of court although he had earlier been a counsellor of Lincoln's Inn and a lent reader in 1641. As a dying man he sent a last legacy to Charles I in the form of a letter of advice. There is helpful material on Holbourne in Warwick, *Memoires*, 156–57; Mary Coate, *Cornwall in the Great Civil War and*

*Interregnum, 1642–1660* (Oxford, 1933), 27, 166–68; *The Life, Diary and Correspondence of Sir William Dugdale*, ed. William Hamper (London, 1827), 59, 437–38. Dugdale seems to be mistaken in believing that Holbourne was on the isle of Wight during the treaty of Newport. *A Short View of the Late Troubles*, 289. See also note 80 of this chapter and note 71 of Chapter 2.

65. 'The Argument', *The Freeholders Grand Inquest*.
66. *Ibid.*, 30–31, 38. See also note 53 of this chapter of this study.
67. Cp. *The Freeholders Grand Inquest*, 19, with p. 20, first edition of volume 1 of the *Soveraigne Power of Parliaments* (published under the title *The Treachery and Disloyalty of Papists to their Soveraignes*). The latter was licensed for publication on January 13, 1643, approximately two weeks after Thomason picked up the *Fuller Answer*. This means that this section was added to the *Soveraigne Power of Parliaments* at a very late stage in its composition, pointing to a rapid appreciation in parliamentarian ranks of the great advantages posed by the co-ordination principle. The discussion of Prynne's political ideas in Chapter 3 of this study is based on a later edition of the *Soveraigne Power of Parliaments*.
68. *The Freeholders Grand Inquest*, 4–5, 31–38.
69. *A Declaration of the Lords and Commons of Parliament Assembled at Oxford* (Oxford, 1644), 15. Charles I, on March 19, 1644, ordered that the declaration be read by the parsons, vicars, and curates in every church and chapel in England and Wales. For earlier signs of a discussion at Oxford about royal writs as the basis of the relationships between the king and the two houses, see Spelman, *A View of a Printed Book*, 5; *The Case of our Affaires*, 1, marginal note. Also to be consulted is *The Freeholders Grand Inquest*, 1, 17.
70. *The Freeholders Grand Inquest*, 4.
71. *Ibid.*, 5. Cp. Herle, *A Fuller Answer*, 2–3.
72. *The Freeholders Grand Inquest*, 4–6. The distinct parallels between this tract and Heylyn's *Stumbling-block of Disobedience* suggest that both authors were present in Oxford, where there must have been lively discussions of the relationship between the king and the two houses and the co-ordination principle in law-making. See *The Stumbling-block of Disobedience*, 256, for a discussion of the royal writs of summons to the house of commons and the report that the house, because of its limited role in law-making, was being compared with the

L

grand inquest of a general sessions 'whose principal work it is to receive bills, and prepare businesses, and make them fit and ready for my lords the judges'. The reference has special interest in view of the title *The Freeholders Grand Inquest.* Heylyn referred his readers to Dudley Digges, *A Review of the Observations upon some of His Majesties Late Answers and Expresses* (Oxford, 1643), 22. See also *The Stumbling-block of Disobedience*, 256, note. q

73. Pocock, *The Ancient Constitution and the Feudal Law*, 153.
74. *The Freeholders Grand Inquest*, 24–25, 29.
75. *Ibid.*, 35.
76. *The Freeholders Grand Inquest*, 30, 38, 39. Heylyn's comment on the writs of summons to the peers is on the same lines. *The Stumbling-block of Disobedience*, 255.
77. *The Freeholders Grand Inquest*, 31.
78. *Ibid.*, 34–35.
79. *Ibid.*, 34.
80. Given the circumstances mentioned above, one wonders whether the list is to be taken at face value; and there are substantial reasons for doubting Filmer's authorship, notwithstanding the conclusions of Laslett and other modern scholars. *Sir Robert Filmer: Patriarcha and Other Political Works*, ed. Laslett, 6–7. First of all, there is the fact that so experienced an observer as Wood, with access to contemporary information, assigned the *Freeholders* to Holbourne. He did so as a matter of deliberate choice since he was writing at a time when the tract was circulating as part of Filmer's collected writings. Secondly, there is evidence of a related kind. Heylyn, an intimate of Filmer's, despite an undoubted success in identifying certain anonymous tracts as Filmer's, never assigned the *Freeholders* to Filmer. *Certamen Epistolare*, Part III, 208–09. Moreover, according to Schochet, the private papers of the earl of Shaftesbury and John Locke in the 1670s listed all but two of Filmer's writings with accuracy, leaving out only the *Freeholders* and extracts from Bodin (probably the *Power of Kings*). 'Sir Robert Filmer: Some New Bibliographical Discoveries', 154. Surely it is significant that observers as perceptive and knowledgeable as Heylyn, Shaftesbury, and Locke were not in the habit of associating the *Freeholders* with Filmer in the years before its inclusion in his collected writings introduced an extraneous and distracting element into the problem of authorship. Thirdly, the striking parallels between Heylyn's

*Stumbling-block of Disobedience* and the *Freeholders* suggest that both tracts were written in civil-war Oxford. See notes 72 and 76 of this chapter. Such a description fits Holbourne, a political figure of the second rank, acquainted with Warwick and the leading royalists, whereas Filmer in the same period of time was a prisoner in Leeds castle, Kent. He was in prison from late 1643 to at least 1645, perhaps as late as April, 1647. Fourthly, one of the gravest doubts concerning Filmer's authorship rises out of the treatment accorded the definition of estates in the *Freeholders* by comparison with that in the *Anarchy of a Limited or Mixed Monarchy* (1648), which no one denies was Filmer's. The two tracts were published within months of one another, the first in print by January 31, 1648, the other by April of that year. Despite the dates of publication, it is probable that both were written in the middle years of the civil war. The *Anarchy*, a critique of Hunton's *Treatise of Monarchie*, accepts uncritically the parliamentarian's language of estates though not his argument. On the other hand, the *Freeholders*, written to refute Prynne's *Soveraigne Power of Parliaments*, excoriates the contention that the king was but one of three estates in parliament. Despite its Bodinian overtones, the *Anarchy* is not an anti-co-ordination tract, unlike the *Freeholders*, which certainly is. It is exceedingly difficult to believe that Filmer, fearful of co-ordination, published the *Freeholders* in January, 1648, only to publish three months later a second anti-parliamentarian tract, in which he displayed indifference towards the definition of estates in the *Treatise of Monarchie* and no awareness that the terminology was related to ideas about the distribution of political power in the state. It looks as if Filmer, in prison in the critical period, was simply out of circulation when the royalists discovered, either late in 1643 or early in 1644, that they had to deal with Charles I's definition of estates. By contrast, Holbourne is said to have denounced the royal definition of estates in the Oxford parliament. These are not all the points that can be made about the authorship of the *Freeholders*, but it may suffice to note in conclusion that there are aspects of Holbourne's career before the civil war that point to him as the author of the *Freeholders*. In this connection the episode discussed in Esther Cope's 'The Short Parliament of 1640 and Convocation' is suggestive. *Journal of Ecclesiastical History*, xxv (1974), 167–84. The case for Holbourne's authorship of the *Freeholders Grand Inquest* is more fully developed in '*The Authorship of the* Freeholders Grand Inquest', *English Historical Review*, xcv (1980), 74–98, written by C. C. Weston. There is biographical comment on Holbourne in note 64 of this chapter of this study.

81. *Athenae Oxonienses*, ed. Bliss, iii, 1046–47. See also the comment on Sheldon's attitude to the *Ecclesiastical Polity* in note 95, Chapter 3 of this study. Surely it was colored by anti-co-ordination sentiment.

82. Tomkins, *The Rebels Plea*, 11.

83. *Ibid.*, 12, 15, 17–19.

84. *Ibid.*, 16–17. Laurence Womock (bishop of St Davids) cited this pamphlet in his *Answer to the Gentleman's Letter to his Friend, Shewing that Bishops may be Judges in Causes Capital* (London, 1680), 3.

85. James Ussher, *The Power Communicated by God to the Prince, and the Obedience required of the Subject* (London, 1661), 13, 20–21, 27–36, 49, 54–57, 66, etc.

86. Sanderson, 'The Preface to the Reader', *The Power Communicated by God to the Prince*, no pagination. See also Chapter 3, notes 68 and 93 of this study. Sanderson's earlier *Ten Lectures on the Humane Conscience* has a valuable section on law-making, which is assigned to the king alone even though laws were made with the people's consent in parliament, and also on the royal dispensing power, which placed the king above the law. The dispensing power was 'an arbitrary power' – a 'sovereign power' – in the king by which he as law-maker acted above the law, remedying deficiencies whenever needed and even setting aside laws for a while when domestic or foreign enemies threatened the realm. For the king as law-maker, see *ibid.*, 241–46, 249, and 263–68. For the dispensing power – exercised above the law on the maxim *salus populi supreme lex* – see *ibid.*, 351–58. This is one of the few royalist tracts in the civil-war years to give attention to the dispensing power, and Sanderson's discussion, carried on in the context of law-making, constitutes a noteworthy foreshadowing of the line of argument in post-1660 conservative writings. It differed in key respects from Dallison's, cited earlier in this study, since Sanderson's discussion of the dispensing power was that of a modern-minded royalist relying on Bodin, whereas Dallison was representative of the more traditionalist elements in that party. One other point ought to be made. Much has been written about

the manner in which the church of England after 1660 sponsored doctrines of non-resistance and passive obedience in enjoining obedience to the king. Though this is an accurate description of the church's ideological position, as enunciated by its leadership, surely it does not go far enough. The strain of anti-co-ordination in conservative political thought, so often accompanied by a stress on the law-making power as the king's alone, meant that spokesmen for the church of England took up a position much more aggressive and positive than the usual description allows. It was the tendency of the church of England to be identified with Bodinian statements about the law-making power in the king, along with expressions of anti-co-ordination sentiment, that made the turnabout in the early summer of 1688 so astonishing. Much more was involved than the breakdown of passive obedience when Sancroft and his fellow bishops petitioned not to read James II's declaration of indulgence from the church's pulpits. This subject is discussed at greater length in Chapter 8 of this study. It was especially difficult for the church to take up the position of 1688 since to accept the co-ordination principle was to lend credence to the related idea that the bishops could not properly be denominated one of the three estates in parliament. This subject requires more attention than can be given here, but there is brief comment in note 11, Chapter 3 of this study and note 78 of Chapter 8.

87. Ussher, *The Power Communicated by God to the Prince*, 29.
88. William Nicolson, *The English Historical Library*, Part III, 204. See also Sir Robert Poyntz, *A Vindication of Monarchy* (London, 1661), *passim*, but especially, 136–41. A native of Iron Acton, Gloucestershire, Poyntz went to Bristol when it was a garrison for Charles I and compounded for his estates after the city's fall. He was uncle to the marquess of Ormonde, who visited him and corresponded with him. See note 92 below.
89. *The Stumbling-block of Disobedience* was republished in 1681, with a new subtitle, as part of Heylyn's collected works. Another sign of the tract's continuing usefulness to the anti-co-ordination movement is in Schochet, 'Sir Robert Filmer : Some New Bibliographical Discoveries', 143. It was known to such whigs as William Petyt and James Tyrrell at the end of the century as well as to the high tory historian, Dr Robert Brady. New editions of Sheringham's *The King's Supremacy Asserted* and Ussher's *Power Communicated by God to the Prince* appeared

in 1682 and 1683 respectively; and Johnston, writing with court patronage, made generous use of their arguments in 1686. Ussher's tract was reprinted in 1710, at the time of the Sacheverell trial.

90. This is an outstanding example of an occasional tract written to make the anti-co-ordination movement popular. The full title is *The Absurdity of that New devised State-Principle (Viz.) That in a Monarchy, The Legislative Power is Communicable to the Subject, and is not radically in Soveraignty in one, but in More* (London, 1681). Trained at Lincoln's Inn, Brydall was secretary to Sir Harbottle Grimstone, master of the rolls, and wrote a number of anti-co-ordination tracts.

91. For the relationship between Sancroft and Hickes, see Robert Beddard, 'The Commission for Ecclesiastical Promotions, 1681–84: An Instrument of Tory Reaction,' *Historical Journal*, x (1967), 26–30.

92. This tract is of more than ordinary interest because it summarized so well the anti-court position in the early 1680s as a preliminary to rejection and also because Assheton was chaplain to Ormonde, when he was governing Ireland for Charles II. It is unlikely that its high tory sentiments displeased his powerful patron. Their association was of long standing, extending over a decade when the *Royal Apology* was published. In April, 1684, Assheton wrote to Ormonde of its success and his plans to bring out an amended edition. Wood, *Athenae Oxonienses*, ed. Bliss, iv, 606–07. H.M.C., *The Manuscripts of the Marquess of Ormonde*, new series, vii, 217.

93. David Ogg, *England in the Reigns of James II and William III* (Oxford, 1955, reprinted 1966), 171. *Jus Regium: or, the Just and Solid Foundations of Monarchy in General; and more especially of the Monarchy of Scotland: Maintained against Buchanan, Naphtali, Dolman, Milton, etc.* (London, 1684), 2, 4, 13–19, 36, 40–41, 47, 54–55, 67–75.

CHAPTER 5 THE CURIOUS CASE OF WILLIAM PRYNNE

1. The main tracts are *A Plea for the House of Lords, and House of Peers* (London, 1648, reprinted in a much expanded form in 1658, 1659); *The First Part of an Historical Collection of the Ancient Parliaments of England* (London, 1649); *An Exact Abridgement of the Records in the Tower of London . . . Collected by Sir Robert Cotton* (London, 1657); *A Brief Regis-*

*ter of Parliamentary Writs* (London, 4 vols., 1659–64). The
third volume, in many ways the most interesting, was published
as *Brevia Parliamentaria Rediviva* (London, 1662). *Brief Animadversions on . . . The Fourth Part of the Institutes of the
Lawes of England*, published in 1669.

2. 'To the Ingenuous Reader', *A Plea for the Lords, and House
of Peers* (London, 1658), no pagination.
3. *The First Part of an Historical Collection of the Ancient Parliaments of England* (London, 1649), 3.
4. *A Treatise of the True and Ancient Jurisdiction of the House
of Peers* (London, 1699), 3. The main lines of Atkyns' career,
sketched later in this study, may be seen conveniently in
Michael Landon, *The Triumph of the Lawyers* (Alabama,
1970), *passim*. Atkyns' collected works were published under
the title *Parliamentary and Political Tracts* in 1734, with a
second edition in 1741.
5. 'To the Ingenuous Reader', *A Plea for the Lords*, no pagination.
See also Gough, *Fundamental Law in English Constitutional
History*, 125–29.
6. 'To the Reader', *The Second Part of a Brief Register and
Survey of the Several Kinds and Forms of Parliamentary Writs*
(London, 1660), no pagination. *A Plea for the Lords*, 37. See
also the comment on Prynne in Pocock, *The Ancient Constitution and the Feudal Law*, 155–61.
7. 'To the Ingenuous Reader', *A Plea for the Lords*, no pagination. See also *ibid.*, 164, 183–8, 386–87.
8. 'To the Ingenuous Reader', *A Plea for the Lords*, no pagination. *Ibid.*, 183–85, 188, 345, 374.
9. The antiquary, Francis Hargrave, believed that Prynne's
comments on the late appearance of the house of commons in
parliament, as expressed in his *Plea for the Lords* and in the
second volume of his *Parliamentary Writs*, gave rise to the
grand controversy over the origin of the house of commons
that haunted late Stuart and early Georgian England. This
conclusion is correct though properly more of Prynne's writings ought to be considered. Nor did Hargrave give attention
to the co-ordination principle as applied to the legislative
power and to the common-law argument, based on what is
called the rule of 1189, which forms the subject matter of this
chapter. See his preface to *Lord Chief Justice Hale, The Jurisdiction of the Lords House, or Parliament* (London, 1796),
lxxix, lxxx, cciii. Prynne's activity in the 1650s is discussed

with a somewhat different emphasis by Lamont. *Marginal Prynne*, Chapter VIII. The historical argument excited by Prynne's scholarship seems to have had no direct connection with the well-known case of Arthur Hall in late Elizabethan England. See note 14, Chapter 3 of this study and E. Evans, 'Of the Antiquity of Parliaments in England: Some Elizabethan and Early Stuart Opinions', *History*, XXIII (1938), 219–21. Evans thinks Hall's argument was completely suppressed and, noting that only a few copies of his book survive, writes that 'no one seems to have read it in the seventeenth century'. *Ibid.*, 221. One exception is, however, William Petyt, who certainly perused Hall's argument.

10. Pocock, *The Ancient Constitution and the Feudal Law*, Chapter VIII. There is pertinent material, too, in Pocock, 'Robert Brady, 1627–1700. A Cambridge Historian of the Restoration', *Cambridge Historical Journal*, X (1951), 186–204.

11. Weston, *English Constitutional History and the House of Lords*, 27, note 34.

12. James Tyrrell, *Bibliotheca Politica: or, An Enquiry into the Antient Constitution of the English Government . . . Wherein all the Chief Arguments both for and against the Late Revolution, are Impartially Represented and Consider'd* (London, second edition, 1727), 271–72. To Tyrrell, Lambarde was 'a person whom all the learned own extremely knowing in the English Saxon government'. Atkyns, *The Power, Jurisdiction and Priviledge of Parliament; and the Antiquity of the House of Commons Asserted* (London, 1689), 18.

13. Samuel Squire, *An Enquiry into the Foundation of the English Constitution* (London, 1745), 262–65.

14. *Brief Animadversions on . . . The Fourth Part of the Institutes*, 1–10. *The Second Part of a Brief Register and Survey of the several Kinds and Forms of Parliamentary Writs* (London, 1660), 3. Prynne also singled out for hostile scrutiny the preface to Coke's *Ninth Report*, where the *Modus tenendi* was invoked to support the existence of a house of commons long before the Norman conquest. Modern scholars believe the controversial document was written in the early 1320s.

15. Evans, 'Of the Antiquity of Parliaments in England', 206–07.

16. This was Prynne's opinion. *The Second Part of a Brief Register*, 3. According to Evans, however, they viewed Henry I as the restorer but not the originator of modern parliaments. 'Of the Antiquity of Parliaments in England', 208. The pertinent tract

is John Dodderidge, *The several Opinions of Sundry learned Antiquaries: . . . Touching the Antiquity, Power, Order, State, Manner, Persons and Proceedings of the High-Court of Parliament in England* (London, 1658).

17. Prynne, *The Second Part of a Brief Register*, 3–4. *The Freeholders Grand Inquest*, 6. William Petyt, 'A Discourse', *The Antient Right of the Commons of England Asserted* (London, 1680), 67–69.

18. 'To the Ingenuous Reader', *The First Part of a Brief Register, Kalendar and Survey of the Several Kinds [and] Forms of all Parliamentary Writs* (London, 1659), no pagination.

19. 'Preface to the Reader', *An Exact Abridgement of the Records in the Tower of London*. A contemporary publication as influential with Prynne as the *Freeholders* was *Cottoni Posthuma* (1651), attributed to Sir Robert Cotton. For the suggestion about the *Freeholders*, see Pocock, *The Ancient Constitution and the Feudal Law*, 155–61. There is pertinent material in Prynne, *A Plea for the Lords*, 37, 182–83.

20. The tory reaction is apparent in Philipps, *The Established Government of England*, 148, 663. His denunciation of Coke's use of the *Modus tenendi* is explicable in the terms discussed in this chapter. *Ibid.*, 673–74, 688–89, 690–91, etc. See also note 45 below. Another tory writer who drew on Prynne's scholarship was Dr George Hickes, chaplain to Charles II, dean of Worcester, and later a leader of the non-jurors. *The Harmony of Divinity and Law*, 33. The whig reaction may be seen in Tyrrell, 'Preface to the Appendix', *General History of England* (London, 1704), III, Part II, ii–iii. Tyrrell acknowledged his intellectual debt to Petyt. *Ibid.*, 213. There is comment on the writers whom Tyrrell was answering in Leslie, *The Constitution, Laws and Government of England*, 116. Atkyns, also prominent in the whig camp, included in *The Power Jurisdiction and Priviledge of Parliament*, 14, a list of innovating writers who would 'destroy foundations, and remove our ancient land-marks, and the ancient and just limits and boundaries of power and authority'. Prynne is listed with such highly conservative writers as Heylyn, Filmer, and Dugdale. See also Atkyns, *A Treatise of the True and Ancient Jurisdiction of the House of Peers*, 13.

21. Tyrrell, *Bibliotheca Politica*, 421, 423, 425–26. Atkyns, The *Power, Jurisdiction and Priviledge of Parliament*, 23, 34; *An Enquiry into the Power of Dispensing with Penal Statutes*

(London, 1689), 21. The concept of a legal memory limited by the date of Richard I's coronation is due to the statute of Westminster (1275), where it is applied to land law. Much remains to be learned of the process by which it came to be used for other purposes and the way in which it entered Stuart political controversy. Probably a key role was played by Rolle's *Un Abridgment des plusiers cases et resolutions del common ley* (1668), which Hale edited. Alan Wharam, 'The 1189 Rule : Fact, Fiction or Fraud?' *Anglo-American Law Review*, I (1972), 262–78; the *DNB* account of Rolle, a legal luminary second only to Hale; and note 16, Chapter 7 of this study. See, in particular, Wharam, *ibid.*, 266–67.

22. *Bibliotheca Politica*, 414–18, 421. Tyrrell, *General History*, III, Part II, 213. Petyt, 'Discourse', *Antient Right*, 3, 7–12, 21. Atkyns, *The Power, Jurisdiction and Priviledge of Parliament*, 24. Acherley, *The Britannic Constitution*, 24, 116, 119. See also the discussion under 'parliament' in Giles Jacob, *A New Law-Dictionary* (London 1729). Pocock has explained how the common-law mind worked. *The Ancient Constitution and the Feudal Law*, Chapter II.

23. *Bibliotheca Politica*, 390, 414. Pocock, *The Ancient Constitution and the Feudal Law*, 42–43, 53–54.

24. *Brevia Parliamentaria Rediviva*, 230.

25. *Bibliotheca Politica*, 390, 414. *General History*, III, Part II, 'Appendix', 1.

26. *Ibid. Bibliotheca Politica*, 390, 435.

27. *The Antient Right of the Commons of England Asserted, or, A Discourse proving by Records and the best Historians, that the Commons of England were ever an Essential Part of Parliament.* Page 5 in the 'Discourse' has a reference to the 'commons of the land'. Much light is shed on his argument by the Petyt manuscripts in the Inner Temple Library in London, used in Chapter 7 of this study, where Petyt's views on prescription and the house of commons are more fully developed. See, for example, note 16, Chapter 7, which makes unmistakable his reliance on the rule of 1189. The use of the Petyt manuscripts was made possible by the courtesy of the Masters of the Bench of the Inner Temple.

28. 'Epistle to the Candid Reader', *An Introduction to the Old English History*, no pagination. See in particular Brady's reference to two sorts of turbulent men. Wilfred R. Prest has concluded from studying the common-law mind before the

civil war that it 'did not have an exclusively parliamentarian orientation'. *The Inns of Court under Elizabeth I and the early Stuarts* (Totowa, New Jersey, 1972), 221. It would be difficult to insist that the common-law mind after the appearance of the co-ordination principle had 'an exclusively parliamentarian orientation'; but that it was anti-court in the second half of the Stuart century seems undoubted. By this time the common law was in the service of the theory of a legal sovereignty in king, lords, and commons; and its contribution was very great.

29. Lambarde, *Archeion*, ed. McIlwain and Ward, 132–33.
30. *Ibid.*, 133–34.
31. *Ibid.*, 134–35.
32. *Ibid.*, 128–29, 138–40.
33. There is confusion in the references to this statute. Lambarde, in the McIlwain and Ward edition, assigned it to the first year of Richard II, the citation reading 1 Rich.2, s.2. c.4, whereas the whig writers agree that the statute was enacted in the fifth year of Richard II. The mistake is in Lambarde. There is also an error in Tyrrell, who gives 'cap. 5'. Compare *Bibliotheca Politica*, 434, and Petyt, 'Discourse', *Antient Right*, 20–23. Tyrrell also quoted Lambarde's interpretation of enacting clauses. *Bibliotheca Politica*, 236.
34. *Ibid.*, 434.
35. 'To the Reader', *Ninth Part, The Reports of Sir Edward Coke, Knt. in English, in Thirteen Parts Complete*, ed. George Wilson (London, 1777), v, *v, *vi.
36. Prynne, *Second Part of a Brief Register and Survey of Parliamentary Writs*, 174.
37. *Ibid.*, 175.
38. *Ibid.*, 177.
39. 'The Epistle Dedicatory', *Brevia Parliamentaria Rediviva*, no pagination. Prynne viewed this tract as a supplement to the second volume of parliamentary writs. It is not clear exactly when he was appointed keeper of the tower records, at £500 a year; but since his predecessor, William Ryley, was in charge of the records as late as December, 1660, Prynne's appointment probably came during the first half of 1661. *Calendar of State Papers, Domestic Series, Charles II, 1660–1661*, 402, 419.
40. *Brevia Parliamentaria Rediviva*, 223.
41. *Ibid.*, 223–26. There is an error in Prynne's figures. *Ibid.*, 226.
42. *Ibid.*, 231–32.

43. *Ibid.*, 234. See also the following page, which is not numbered.

44. *Ibid.*, 235. See also the following page, which is not numbered.

45. William Blackstone, *Commentaries on the Laws of England* (Oxford, 1765), I, 50, 145; Atkyns, *The Power, Jurisdiction and Priviledge of Parliament*, 13–14. Fabian Philipps steadfastly denied that the house of commons constituted a third estate co-ordinate with the king and the house of lords. *The Established Government of England*, I, 393, 656–59, 663, etc. And there is the comment of the non-juror Charles Leslie in *The Rehearsal* 338 (July 7, 1708), in *A View of the Times* (London, second edition, 1750), V, 122. Insisting that the authority of the two houses in law-making was derived solely from the crown, he warned : 'If they held it independently of the crown, they would be co-ordinate powers'. See also Brydall, *The Absurdity of that New devised State – Principle*, 6–7, and note 47 below. The political ideas ascribed to the whig writers in this chapter are fused with the Answer to the Nineteen Propositions in Acherley, *The Britannic Constitution*, 116–21, 139–45.

46. Atkyns, *The Power, Jurisdiction and Priviledge of Parliament*, 23.

47. *Whitelockes Notes Uppon the Kings Writt*, ed, Morton, II, 111. Whitelocke was referring to Prynne's *Plea for the Lords*, reprinted in a much expanded edition before the restoration. He also noted the appearance of the Parker society's papers on the antiquity of parliament. *Ibid.*, II, 130–31. See Atkyns' condemnation of Prynne and the conservative writers who had concluded 'that . . . all the power and privilege the house of commons claims, is not by prescription, but . . . depend upon the king's royal will and pleasure, and had their original by his mere concession, and not by ancient inherent right, nor original constitution, and therefore may be resumed at pleasure'. *The Power, Jurisdiction and Priviledge of Parliament*, 14. There is also pertinent comment in Tyrrell, 'Preface to the Appendix', *General History*, III, Part II, i–iii; *Bibliotheca Politica*, 431, 433, 435–36.

48. Hickes, *The Harmony of Divinity and Law*, 33–34, 37.

49. Herle, *A Fuller Answer*, 1. Contemporaries had by no means forgotten the link between the Answer to the Nineteen Propositions and the concept of a shared legislative power. Lawson, *Politica Sacra et Civilis: or, A Modell of Civil and Ecclesiasticall Government* (London, 1660), 102. Thomason had a copy on May 16, 1660, about a fortnight before Charles II entered

London in triumph. The same point is made in Lawson's earlier *Examination of the Political Part of Mr Hobbes his Leviathan,* 100.

### CHAPTER 6 THE IDIOM OF RESTORATION POLITICS

1. *Journals of the House of Commons,* VIII, 7–8. By 'government' the convention parliament seems to have meant the legislative power, this being the interpretation later offered by contemporaries. It is also suggested by their preoccupation with the legislative power as the cardinal feature of the government. There is comment on similar language used by the two houses during the civil war in note 86, Chapter 3, of this study. For a royalist gloss, see Warwick, *Memoires,* 434. The resolution stated, so he said, 'that by the ancient and fundamental laws of the kingdom the government ought to be administered by the king with the lords and commons'. A tract reflecting the changing view of the legislative power among the royalists is *The Primitive Cavalerism Revived,* 7–9.

2. David Ogg, *England in the Reign of Charles II* (Oxford paperbacks, 1963), I, 30–31. George R. Abernathy, Jr., *The English Presbyterians and the Stuart Restoration, 1648–1663* (Philadelphia, 1965), 50–55. Godfrey Davies, *The Restoration of Charles II, 1658–1660* (London, 1955), Chapter XVI. For later references to the convention parliament's resolution, see Anchitell Grey, *Debates of the House of Commons, from . . . 1667 to . . . 1694* (London, 1769), II, 67–68; 'Some Short Considerations relating to the Settling of the Government [1689]', *Somers Tracts. A Second Collection,* IV, 256; and note 51 of this chapter.

3. The statute is reprinted in *English Historical Documents, 1660–1714,* ed. Andrew Browning (New York, 1953), 63–65. It underwent a rigorous scrutiny during its passage. Thus the pertinent clause on the legislative power was amended in the house of commons by substituting 'to the same effect' for 'to such, or the like effect'. Moreover, its substance was repeated elsewhere in the statute. *Journals of the House of Commons,* VIII, 252. See *ibid.,* 249 for the heavily royalist membership of the pertinent committee. Ironically, it was Warwick who reported the committee's proposed amendments to the house of commons. See also the comment on 12 Car. 2, c. 30 in note 10 below.

4. *The Arraignment of Co-ordinate Power* (London, 1683), 13.

There is shrewd comment in Acherley, *The Britannic Constitution*, 145.

5. Betty Kemp, *King and Commons, 1660–1832* (London, 1957), 7.

6. This conclusion is consonant with J. R. Tanner, *English Constitutional Conflicts of the Seventeenth Century* (Cambridge, 1928, reprinted 1961), 217 ff. and Gough, *Fundamental Law in English Constitutional History*, Chapters VI–IX. The latter points out that the extreme tories in the name of the king's inseparable prerogatives denied the omnipotence of parliament when they invoked fundamental law to protect his rights. *Ibid.*, 145. This was hardly necessary if the king was the law-maker in parliament, as they also thought. The radical whig lawyer, Thomas Hunt, expressed the whig view of fundamental law when he wrote that 'no laws of men are so fundamental but they are alterable'. *Mr. Hunt's Postscript for Rectifying some Mistakes in some of the Inferiour Clergy, Mischievous to our Government and Religion* (London, 1682), 130. Pocock has made the idea of the ancient constitution familiar but has a tendency to equate it with an overriding fundamental law that is a barrier to the full assertion of parliamentary sovereignty. *The Ancient Constitution and the Feudal Law*, 49–50; 229–31. See also Baxter, *A Holy Commonwealth*, 462–65, 482, and Acherley, *The Britannic Constitution*, 142–45, and *passim*, the latter for the identification of the ancient constitution with the Answer to the Nineteen Propositions and for the combination of elements that produced the theory of a legal sovereignty in king, lords, and commons.

7. Howell, *A Complete Collection of State Trials*, VI, 134.

8. At this time there was a close relationship between Charles II's government and the judges. Ogg, *England in the Reign of Charles II*, II, 522. Alfred Havighurst, 'The Judiciary and Politics in the Reign of Charles II', Part I, *Law Quarterly Review*, LXVI (1950), 65–68. But the situation was very different by the time of the indulgence crisis of 1672–73. In this connection it may be noted that Charles I's definition of estates, according to contemporary publicists, had made great inroads in so influential a class as the lawyers and judges whom contemporaries called the long robe. See, for example, *The Honour of the Lords Spiritual Asserted: and their Priviledges to Vote in Capital Cases in Parliament Maintained by Reason and Precedents* (London, 1679), 31. See also Hickes, *The Harmony of*

*Divinity and Law*, 28–29, and Baxter's comment with regard to what lawyers had told him about the legislative power. The latter is in Richard Schlatter, *Richard Baxter and Puritan Politics* (New Jersey, 1957), 149. Sir John Vaughan, who died a lord chief justice of common pleas, was said to have defined the three estates as king, lords, and commons in the presence of others of the long robe who made no effort to correct him. British Library, Lansdowne MS. 737, fos. 32v.–33.

9. *Lex Terrae*, 5, 8–10, 18. See also note 39, Chapter 3 of this study.

10. Howell, *A Complete Collection of State Trials*, v, 989, 992, 1144. 'If the king be supreme', the lord chief baron added in another passage, 'then there is no co-ordination.' *Ibid.*, 1227. The assertion was also explicit that 'no authority, no single person, no community of persons, not the people collectively, or representatively, have any coercive power over the king of England'. *Ibid.*, 989, 1226. For a critique of Bridgeman's argument, expressed in terms of the more radical version of co-ordination, see Edmund Ludlow, *A Voyce from the Watch Tower: Part Five: 1660–1662*, ed. A. B. Worden (Camden Society, 1978), 201–05. After 1660 the idea of coercing the king and the co-ordination principle were viewed as closely associated. Weston, *English Constitutional Theory and the House of Lords*, 100. The idea of coercive power, on the lines indicated by Bridgeman, was formally renounced at the restoration in the statute 12 Car. 2, c. 30. According to Leslie, that statute 'was made on purpose against the traitorous principles and pretences of forty-one, particularly this of making the king co-ordinate with the two houses of parliament, and one of the three estates'. *Cassandra. (But I hope not) . . . Num. 1*, p. 15. To Leslie, such language was 'jargon'. *Ibid.*, 11. Bridgeman's condemnation of the opinion of the Spencers was conservative orthodoxy during the rest of the century. Seller, *The History of Passive Obedience*, 58. See also *ibid.*, 13, for comment on the famous non-resistance oath imposed on office holders and the clergy in the corporation act (1661) and the act of uniformity (1662). They were to swear that it was not 'lawful upon any pretence whatsoever to take arms against the king'. Seller wrote of the declaration as aimed at the doctrines of the early civil war, including the principle that 'the king was co-ordinate with the states'.

11. Howell, *A Complete Collection of State Trials*, v, 992. Charles

I's last words on the scaffold are discussed in note 40, Chapter 3 of this study.

12. Howell, *A Complete Collection of State Trials*, v, 989.
13. *Ibid.*, 1030.
14. *Ibid.*, 1025. Surprisingly little attention was given to either Leveller or Engager doctrines even if the regicides were cautious in advancing their political ideas. Cp. Harrison's remarks, for example, with the account of regicide argument in C. V. Wedgwood, *The Trial of Charles I* (London, 1965), 85, 134–35, 159–61. The judges' remarks were aimed squarely at Herle's community-centered ideology.
15. Weston, *English Constitutional Theory and the House of Lords*, 83–86. Howell, *A Complete Collection of State Trials*, vi, 158–59. See also note 22, Chapter 3 of this study.
16. Howell, *A Complete Collection of State Trials*, vi, 157–59, 162, 168.
17. *Ibid.*, 163–64. Vane had also placed the king below the law.
18. *Ibid.*, 187–88, note.
19. Ogg, *England in the Reign of Charles II*, i, 179–80.
20. *The Secret History of the Court and Reign of Charles the Second, by a Member of his Privy Council* (London, 1792), i, 127. Although this work is attributed to Clarendon in the British Library Catalogue, the attribution is doubtful. Contemporaries often cited the courage with which Vane died, and his political ideas aroused much interest. Mrs Pepys, who thought him 'to have been a very wise man', read the whole trial to her husband. *The Diary of Samuel Pepys*, ed. Henry Wheatley (London, 1903), ii, 262, 264, 271–72; iii, 37. There is pertinent comment in Ludlow, *A Voyce from the Watch Tower*, ed. Worden 310–11. L'Éstrange's *Considerations and Proposals in order to the Regulation of the Press* (London, 1663), 18, 21, condemned the radical *People's Cause, Stated, in the [Pretended] Trial of Sir Henry Vane* (1662) as supporting the idea that the two houses had sovereignty in emergencies. In fact, its author went further than this, justifying supreme power in the house of commons alone under such circumstances. The argument was based on the co-ordination principle, which was said to explain the civil war. The king and the two houses had become 'standing powers, co-ordinate and distinct parts of the supremacy . . . hence sprang the war'. *The People's Cause, Stated* was part of the larger *Tryal of Sir Henry Vane Kt. at the King's Bench, Westminster, June the 2d. and 6th, 1662* (n.p., 1662). See *ibid.*,

102, 108–09. The former was reprinted in 1689. Sir Charles Firth, writing in the *DNB*, treats the *People's Cause, Stated* as reflecting Vane's creed regarding civil government, but its argument was more radical than the defense of 1662.

21. *Considerations and Proposals in order to the Regulation of the Press*, 8, 17. L'Estrange wrote in the same vein in the 1680s. *The Dissenters Sayings, in Requital for L'Éstrange's Sayings* (London, third edition, 1681), 26. The licensing act was in force until 1679 when a proclamation ordering the seizure of anti-court libels temporarily took its place. Renewed in 1685, the act lasted another decade. Ogg, *England in the Reign of Charles II*, II, 515–16. For recognition in the seventeenth century that Herle wrote *Ahab's Fall*, see note 25, Chapter 4 of this study.

22. Owen Ruffhead, 'Preface', *The Statutes at Large, from Magna Charta to the End of the Last Parliament* (London, 1769), xvi. Commenting on this enacting clause, Leslie wrote : 'The enacting part is attributed only to the king.' *The Rehearsal* 338, 122. It is no coincidence that the well-known law dictionary associated with John Rastell contained in the edition of 1685, for the first time, the term 'parliament'. Under the term were these words : 'See the Lord Coke's 4th Institutes, and Mr. Cowell's Interpreter, title parliament.' Whoever followed these directions encountered the court-approved version of the three estates. *Les Termes de la Ley* (London, 1685), 529. The edition is said to have been prepared by Thomas Blount, a friend of Dugdale's.

23. British Library, Lansdowne MS. 737, fo. 33. See also Assheton, *The Royal Apology*, 18.

24. *Book of Common Prayer* (Cambridge, 1663), no pagination. The passages should be compared with *Prayers and Thanksgiving to be used by all the Kings Majesties loving Subjects, for the happy deliverance of his Majestie, the Queene, Prince, and States of the Parliament . . . the 5 November 1605* (London, 1620). The pertinent articles on the revision of the book of common prayer are G. J. Cuming, 'The Making of the Durham Book,' *Journal of Ecclesiastical History*, v (1955), 60–72, and 'The Prayer Book in Convocation, November, 1661', *ibid.*, VIII, #2 (1957), 182–92. See in particular 'The Prayer Book in Convocation, November, 1661,' 188, 192. There is comment on Sanderson's political ideas in notes 68 and 93, Chapter 3 of this study, and in note 86, Chapter 4. A contemporary response

to the revised service of November 5 is in *An Answer to Dr. Stillingfleet's Sermon, by some Nonconformists* (London, 1680), 11. Another reaction to the co-ordination principle, early in Charles II's reign, comparable to the revision of the state services, was Sheldon's sponsorship of Walton's *Life of Hooker.* Note 95, Chapter 3 of this study.

25. *An Impartial Collection of the Great Affairs of State*, I, xv; Hickes, *The Harmony of Divinity and Law*, 31. See also North-leigh, *Remarks upon the most Eminent of our Antimonarchical Authors*, 178, and Milbourne, *The People not the Original of Civil Power prov'd from God's word, the Doctrine and Liturgy of the Established Church and from the Laws of England*, 9. The latter expounded his anti-co-ordination views at length in *The Royal Martyr Lamented, Preached on the thirtieth of January, passim.* See also Kenyon, *Revolution Principles: The Politics of Party, 1689–1720*, Chapter 5, and note 70, Chapter 3 of this study.

26. *A Bibliography of Royal Proclamations of the Tudor and Stuart Sovereigns*, ed. Steele, I, nos. 3414, 3499, 3508.

27. Churchill, 'The Dispensing Power and the Defence of the Realm', 422–23.

28. *Ibid.*, 423–24.

29. *Ibid.*, 424. Lawrence A. Harper, *The English Navigation Laws* (New York, 1964), 72. The whole discussion is of interest. *Ibid.*, 68–74.

30. The fullest treatment of the declaration of indulgence of 1672 is in Frank Bate, *The Declaration of Indulgence, 1672* (London, 1908). The text is in *English Historical Documents, 1660–1714*, ed. Browning, 387–88. Although he recognizes that a change in the theory of the constitution had affected the royal dispensing power, Bate does not discuss its nature. *Ibid.*, 84. There is perceptive comment in T. B. Macaulay, *The History of England from the Accession of James II* (New York, n.d.), I, 207.

31. Cobbett, *Parliamentary History of England*, IV, 503.

32. Sir Edward Dering, *Parliamentary Diary, 1670–1673*, ed. Basil Duke Henning (New Haven, 1940), 115.

33. *Journals of the House of Commons*, IX, 251. Besides Powle, the committee included Colonel John Birch, Sir John Bramston, Sir Robert Carr, a Mr Cheney, Henry Coventry, Sir William Coventry, Thomas Crouch, Sir Edward Dering, Attorney-General Finch, William Garraway, Sir Robert Howard, Sir Thomas Lee, Sir Thomas Littleton, John Milward, Sir Thomas

Osborne, Sir Edward Seymour, a Serjeant Seys, Colonel Giles Strangeways, Sir Richard Temple, Colonel Silas Titus, Sir John Vaughan, and Mr Edmund Waller. It has been said that the committee was packed with courtiers. D. T. Witcombe, *Charles II and the Cavalier House of Commons, 1663–1674* (Manchester, 1966), 133. Biographical sketches of almost all the membership are in Witcombe, 196–210. In the later stages of preparing this study its authors had access to the draft biographies for the period 1660–1690 that are being prepared for the History of Parliament Trust. The editor for this period is Professor Basil D. Henning. This is cited below as 'draft biographies for the History of Parliament Trust', ed. Henning.

34. 'Henry Powle', in 'draft biographies for the History of Parliament Trust', ed. Henning. Witcombe, *Charles II and the Cavalier House of Commons*, 207. Landon, *The Triumph of the Lawyers*, 44, 83. J. R. Jones, *The Revolution of 1688 in England* (London, 1972), 225. The relationship between the Sacheverell committee of 1679 and the committee that prepared the Bill of Rights is discussed in Weston, *English Constitutional Theory and the House of Lords*, 95–123.

35. *Journals of the House of Commons*, IX, 251, 252, 257. The members of the second Powle committee are listed in note 47 of this chapter.

36. Grey, *Debates of the House of Commons*, II, 13–14. Cobbett, *Parliamentary History of* England, IV, 518. Witcombe, *Charles II and the Cavalier House of Commons*, 205. Meres was appointed to the committee of the house of commons that shaped the act for the preservation of the king, as were Lee and John Swinfen, who are mentioned below.

37. Cobbett, *Parliamentary History of England*, IV, 519. Grey, *Debates of the House of Commons*, II, 15. Witcombe, *Charles II and the Cavalier House of Commons*, 207.

38. Cobbett, *Parliamentary History of England*, IV, 520. Grey, *Debates of the House of Commons*, II, 17. Strangeways, who usually opposed any degree of toleration, was typically found in the group who opposed Shaftesbury on a given issue. As a young man, the latter had burned the Strangeways house during the civil war. K. H. D. Haley, *The First Earl of Shaftesbury* (Oxford, 1968), 318. It was, however, a more complex situation than this. Attempting to have his son returned from Dorset in a bye-election, Strangeways suffered a sharp setback

as a result of Shaftesbury's political interest there and had come to Westminster in a great rage. 'Colonel Giles Strangeways', in 'draft biographies for the History of Parliament Trust', ed. Henning.

39. Grey, *Debates of the House of Commons*, II, 17.

40. *Ibid.*, 24. There is comment on Lee in Witcombe, *Charles II and the Cavalier House of Commons*, 203. Appointed to both Powle committees in 1673, he was also a member of the Sacheverell committee and the committee that prepared the Bill of Rights. He, along with Powle, formed part of a clandestine system of correspondence and intelligence that functioned prior to the Glorious Revolution. So did Richard Hampden, another prominent leader of the anti-court elements. See note 86, Chapter 8 of this study.

41. Cobbett, *Parliamentary History of England*, IV, 522. Grey. *Debates of the House of Commons*, II, 19.

42. *Ibid.*, 16–17. Cobbett, *Parliamentary History of England*, IV, 520. Witcombe, *Charles II and the Cavalier House of Commons*, 138.

43. Grey, *Debates of the House of Commons*, II, 18. Cobbett, *Parliamentary History of England*, IV, 521.

44. *Ibid.*, 522–23. Grey, *Debates of the House of Commons*, II, 19–20. Dering, *Parliamentary Diary*, 115–16.

45. Cobbett, *Parliamentary History of England*, IV, 526–28, 533–34, 538.

46. *Ibid.*, 546–47. Grey, *Debates of the House of Commons*, II, 54–55.

47. *Ibid.*, 62. Cobbett, *Parliamentary History of England*, IV, 551. Dering, *Parliamentary Diary*, 131–33. *Journals of the House of Commons*, IX, 256–57. The second Powle committee was much like the first one. See above, note 33. The members of the second Powle committee, who served on the first, are marked with an asterisk in the following list. Beside Powle himself, it included Carr*, Henry Coventry*, Sir William Coventry*, Sir John Downing, Sir John Duncombe, Finch*, Garraway*, Howard*, Lee*, Sir William Lowther, Sir Thomas Meres, Sir Philip Musgrave, Francis North, William Sacheverell, Strangeways*, John Swinfen, Vaughan*, Waller*, and Brome Whorwood. *Ibid.*, 257.

48. Grey, *Debates of the House of Commons*, II, 62–63. The Latin phrase used by Finch was translated by Sir John Spelman, writing earlier in the century, to read 'The legislative power is

solely in the king, although not in the king being sole.' *A View of a Printed Book*, 19. It was originally from Bracton.

49. Grey, *Debates of the House of Commons*, II, 67. North was later attorney general and lord chief justice of common pleas.

50. See note 8 of this chapter.

51. Grey, *Debates of the House of Commons*, II, 67–68. Swinfen sat in the convention parliament of 1660 and was also a member of the committee of the cavalier house of commons that prepared the act for the king's preservation. Like Powle and other members of the two committees of 1673, he was subsequently a member of the Sacheverell committee that invoked the Answer to the Nineteen Propositions against Charles II in the Danby case. For more complete detail, see Douglas Lacey, *Dissent and Parliamentary Politics in England, 1661–1689* (New Brunswick, New Jersey, 1969), 443–47. John Hampden, Jr. – son of Richard Hampden and grandson of John Hampden – also recalled the convention parliament's resolution when he asked the convention house of commons of 1689 to consider the vote of May 1, 1660, as the necessary preliminary to declaring 'the constitution and rule of the government'. Grey, *Debates of the House of Commons*, IX, 36. Lacey, *Dissent and Parliamentary Politics in England*, 229.

52. Grey, *Debates of the House of Commons*, II, 69.

53. Haley, *The First Earl of Shaftesbury*, 320. W. D. Christie, *A Life of Anthony Ashley Cooper, First Earl of Shaftesbury* (London, 1871), II, 132–35. Christie printed a pertinent paper, entitled 'Reasons for referring the declaration of indulgence to the house of peers, 1673', which he attributed to Shaftesbury. It is in the Public Record Office. P.R.O. 30/24/6B. Shaftesbury's adoption of this policy may have been due to his experience during the passing of the Irish cattle bill of 1666–67, discussed later in this chapter.

54. *Journals of the House of Lords*, XII, 539–40.

55. Haley, *The First Earl of Shaftesbury*, 321.

56. *Journals of the House of Lords*, XII, 542.

57. *Ibid.*, 543. The *Journal* has this account: 'The house took into consideration the advice to be given his majesty, concerning the addresses made to him from the house of commons. The addresses of the house of commons, and his majesty's answer, were read. And after a long debate, the question being put, "whether that the king's answer to the house of commons, in referring the points now controverted to a parliamentary

way by bill, is good and gracious, that being a proper and natural course for satisfaction therein?" it was resolved in the affirmative.' See also Witcombe, *Charles II and the Cavalier House of Commons*, 135, note 7, where the peers are described as refusing to intervene. They had, in fact, intervened, and in the most decisive fashion. Gerald R. Cragg, *Puritanism in the Period of the Great Persecution, 1660–1688* (Cambridge, 1957), 21, has pertinent comment on the factors motivating the two houses.

58. An anonymous pamphleteer, writing after the Revolution, looked back to the indulgence crisis for an explanation of that momentous event and found it in these terms. 'Here was there a plain conquest, and indeed triumph over the dispensing power of our kings', he wrote, 'and yet James the Second, taking the throne resumes the same, and persists in it with that obstinacy, as we all know, [that] hath occasioned our present revolution.' *A Glance on the Ecclesiastical Commission* (London, 1690), 8. Comment on Charles II's acquiesence is in *Calendar of State Papers and Manuscripts, Relating to English Affairs Existing in the Archives and Collections of Venice, and in other Libraries of Northern Italy*, ed. Allen B. Hinds (London, 1947), xxxviii, (1673–75), the entries of March (item 31); March 10 (items 35, 36); March 17 (item 40); March 20 (item 43); and March 24 (item 44).

59. Ogg, *England in the Reign of Charles II*, 1, 368.

60. *The Revolution of 1688 in England*, 100–01.

61. James S. Clarke, *The Life of James the Second King of England, etc. Collected out of Memoirs writ of His Own Hand* (London, 1816), 1, 689. See also *The Continuation of the Life of Edward Earl of Clarendon* (Oxford, 1759), iii, 721; *Calendar of State Papers . . . Relating to English Affairs Existing in the Archives of Venice*, xxxviii, (1673–75), the entries of March 17 (item 40); March 24 (item 44); and December 8 (item 251). Witcombe, *Charles II and the Cavalier House of Commons*, 133, 135.

62. John Dalrymple, *Memoirs of Great Britain and Ireland* (London, 1790), ii, Part i, Book iv, 68.

63. John Miller, 'Catholic Officers in the later Stuart Army', *English Historical Review*, lxxxviii (1973), 39.

64. Gee, *The Divine Right and Original of the Civill Magistrate from God*, 136–43. Baxter held the same view, as did many others. *A Holy Commonwealth*, 122, 124, 461.

65. John Locke, *Two Tracts on Government*, ed. Abrams, 231.
66. *The Opinion of Divers Learned and Leading Dissenters, Concerning the Original of Government, Referring to the Doctrine of the Political Catechism*, entire. That the formula was useful as late as 1716, if not much later, may be seen from Thomas Burnett, *An Essay upon Government* (London, 1716), 28–30. See also note 84 in this chapter of this study and note 109 in Chapter 8.
67. *A Dialogue at Oxford*, 2–3, 10. This tract has been attributed to Richard Janeway, who published a number of radical tracts. By this time exponents of the community-centered ideology were recommending annual meetings of parliament and restrictions on the king's power to summon, dissolve, and prorogue parliament. *Ibid.*, 10–13.
68. *Jovian*, 237. *The Library of John Locke*, ed. John Harrison and Peter Laslett (Oxford, 1965), no. 1296. Petyt's library is described in note 28, Chapter 7 of this study.
69. Carolyn A. Edie's *The Irish Cattle Bills: A Study in Restoration Politics* (Philadelphia, 1970) is the authoritative account of the Irish cattle act of 1667 and its implications. Passage of this legislation marked, in her view, 'a turning point in the conflict between Stuart kings and their parliaments, and offered a key to the character and intentions of the parliamentary rule which shortly was to achieve domination, if not control, of English politics'. *Ibid.*, 6. She also concludes that the peers, 'who stubbornly blocked the bill until directed by the king to withdraw, did so not from any considerations of English, or Irish, commerce, but because they saw in its clauses a threat to the royal prerogative'. *Ibid.*, 53–54, and, in particular, 56.
70. *Ibid.*, 24–26. *The Diary of John Milward, Esq., Member of Parliament for Derbyshire, September, 1666 to May, 1668*, ed. Caroline Robbins (Cambridge, 1938), 14–15, 17. *Journals of the House of Commons*, VIII, 635. Andrew Browning, *Thomas Osborne, Earl of Danby and Duke of Leeds, 1632–1712* (Glasgow, 1951), I, 43. Thomas Carte, *An History of the Life of James Duke of Ormonde* (London, 1736), II, 322–23. The excitement caused by the passage of the Irish cattle bill through the house of lords was attested when the duke of Buckingham, a strong supporter, attended the debates, an almost unheard of practice for him. The exchange became so heated at one point that Lord Ossory, son of the duke of Ormonde, challenged

Buckingham to a duel. The former was known for his duelling talents; and Buckingham, rather than decline, accepted; but he then came to a field other than that appointed by the seconds. The house of lords committed both of them. *The Continuation of the Life of Edward Earl of Clarendon*, III, 711–18 and A. S. Turberville. 'The House of Lords under Charles II', *English Historical Review*, XLIV (1929), 407–08.

71. *Ibid.*, 408, note 4. Edie, *The Irish Cattle Bills*, 27–28. *The Diary of Samuel Pepys*, ed. Wheatley, VI, 126–27. Pepys was reporting the arguments in a conference between the two houses, held early in January, 1667. *The Continuation of the Life of Edward Earl of Clarendon*, III, 712, 720.

72. *Ibid.*, 721.

73. *Ibid.*, 713, 721–22.

74. Haley, *The First Earl of Shaftesbury*, 190–91. According to Edie, Lord Keeper Bridgeman influenced the language of the proposed amendment. *The Irish Cattle Bills*, 28.

75. *Ibid.*, 30–34. *Journals of the House of Commons*, VIII, 671. The attitude of leading spokesman for the house of commons was expressed at a conference of the two houses, on December 14, 1666. *Journals of the House of Lords*, XII, 48–50. One of the speakers was Sir Robert Atkyns, whose views on the dispensing power are discussed later in this study. He actively pressed the retention of the word 'nuisance'. *Ibid.*, 50. Among the managers for the house of commons were parliamentarians who subsequently opposed the second declaration of indulgence. The list is in *Journals of the House of Commons*, VIII, 669–70. They included, besides Atkyns, such later members of the two Powle committees as Carr, Garraway, Howard, Lee, Meres, Strangeways, and Swinfen. Consult also *The Complete Works in Verse and Prose of Andrew Marvell*, ed. Alexander B. Grosart (n.p., 1875), II, 202–03. For the lords' protest, see *Journals of the House of Lords*, XII, 74, and Edie, *The Irish Cattle Bills*, 34.

76. *Statutes of the Realm*, (London, 1963), V, 597 (18 and 19 Car. 2, c. 2).

77. Statutes where the penalty was divided between king and informer are in *Statutes of the Realm*, V, 246–50 (12 Car. 2, c. 18); 266–68 (12 Car. 2, c. 25); 293–96 (12 Car. 2, c. 32); 364–70 (14 Car. 2, c. 4); 378–79 (14 Car. 2, c. 7); 410–12 (14 Car. 2, c. 18); 575 (17 Car. 2, c. 2). This was also the form of earlier penal statutes. See, for example, *Statutes of the Realm*,

II, 287 (11 Hen. 6, c. 14); 332–34 (23 Hen. 6, c. 7); 396–98 (3 Edw. 4, c. 4); 534–35 (4 Hen. 7, c. 10). *Statutes of the Realm,* III, 760–63 (32 Hen. 8, c. 14); 836 (33 Hen. 8, c. 7). *Statutes of the Realm,* IV, Part I, 243–44 (1 and 2 Ph. and Mar. c. 5); 414–22 (5 Eliz. c. 4). See also in this connection the account in Edie of an earlier Irish cattle bill, this one in 1621, in which the penalty was 'forfeiture of ship and cattle, dimidium to the king, dimidium to the informer'. *The Irish Cattle Bills,* 7.

78. *Life of Ormonde,* II, 322–23. Carte also notes that statutes had been customarily phrased differently : he states that penalties typically went to the king, although a part thereof was sometimes given to the prosecutor or informer for his encouragement. In 1681 a similar bill limiting the importation of Scottish cattle also labelled such importation a 'public and common nuisance', and the penalty was divided between the informer and the poor. H.M.C. *Eleventh Report, Appendix, Part II. The Manuscripts of the House of Lords, 1678–1688,* 266–67. The bill passed the house of commons and was given a first reading in the house of lords but dropped with the session. Also relevant is Halifax's comment on the dispensing power. 'When any act of importance is made', he stated, 'care will be taken to give the whole penalty to the informer.' The comment is in his observations on the prerogative, a manuscript described in note 22, chapter 3 of this study. It may be noted, however, that two statutes passed early in Charles II's reign declared an offense a nuisance or felony and gave half the penalty to the king. See st. 14 Car. 2, c. 7 and st. 14 Car 2, c. 18.

79. *Statutes of the Realm,* V, 641–42, (19 and 20 Car. 2, c. 12).

80. *Ibid.,* 941–42 (32 Car. 2, c. 32).

81. Grey, *Debates of the House of Commons,* VII, 90–91. Edie, *The Irish Cattle Bills,* 47. See also Atkyns' discussion in 1666, *Journals of the House of Lords,* XII, 50.

82. The *habeas corpus* act and the test acts, considered vital to the welfare and liberty of the subject, assigned the entire penalty for violations to the informer. James II's opponents later argued that he was incapable of dispensing with the test acts because of this provision. Tyrrell, *Bibliotheca Politica,* 597. Noting that no part of the fine for violating the test act was to go to the crown, Bishop Burnet wrote 'so carefully was this act penned that the king should be bound by it, and not be able to break through it'. *Some Sermons Preach'd on Several*

*Occasions* (London, 1713), iv–v. There is also pertinent comment in 'An Enquiry into the Present State of Affairs', *A Collection of State Tracts Publish'd on Occasion of the late Revolution*, I, 130. The practice of altering statutory language to limit the dispensing power continued after the Revolution. See the act for abrogating the oath of supremacy in Ireland and appointing other oaths. *Statutes of the Realm*, VI, 254–57 (3 Gul. and Mar. c. 2). One clause reads : 'Provided always and be it enacted that this act shall not be dispensed with by any warrants or letters patent under the great seal of England or Ireland.' *Ibid.*, 257. Moreover, the entire penalty was assigned to the informer. The altered view of the dispensing power is reflected in *Thomas v. Sorrell*, which was heard in the late 1660s in king's bench and the exchequer chamber. The case is reported in Joseph Keble, *Reports in the Court of Kings-Bench* (London, 1685), Parts II and III, and in Sir John Vaughan, *Reports and Arguments* (London, 1677). For helpful comment on *Thomas v. Sorrell*, see Yale's introduction to Hale's *The Prerogatives of the King*, li–liv.

83. Cobbett, *Parliamentary History of England*, IV, 1182, 1209. See also the account of the exclusion debates of 1680 in the house of commons in Clarke, *The Life of James the Second*, I, 601–11. Thomas Bennet is described as stating that the lawmaking power was unlimited. *Ibid.*, 605. Sir William Hickman found it 'a strange argument to doubt whether the legislative power of the nation could make laws to bind its subjects'. *Ibid.*, 610. Sir Francis Winnington asked : 'Does not the thirteenth of Queen Elizabeth make it treason to say that the parliament cannot alter the succession?' *Ibid.*, 611. It is significant that debates of this type were included in James II's memoirs and that the king, prior to his accession to the throne, should have been quoted as referring in 1680 to 'the disorderly pretensions of . . . parliament' in urging Charles II to resist exclusion. Clarke, *The Life of James the Second*, I, 614.

84. H.M.C. *Report on the Manuscripts of the late Reginald Rawdon Hastings, Esq. of the Manor House, Ashby-de-la-Zouche*, ed. Francis Bickley (London, 1928–47), IV, 302–05. The notes on this speech are in the handwriting of Lord Huntingdon, at this time a whig leader but later a Jacobite. The speech was given on November 15, 1680.

CHAPTER 7 CO-ORDINATION AND COEVALITY
IN EXCLUSION LITERATURE

1. Robert Sheringham, *The Kings Supremacy Asserted* (two editions, 1660; 1682) was a response to Herle and Hunton. *Ibid.*, 12–15, 80–81, 86–90, 93–106. Herle was 'the Fuller Answerer'. Sheringham's work was used in turn by Hickes in *Jovian*, 213, and by Johnston in *The Excellency of Monarchical Government*, 305–07. Since Hickes relied on *Evangelium Armatum*, he must have associated Herle by name with the co-ordination principle. See *A Sermon Preached before the Lord Mayor, Aldermen, and Citizens of London, at Bow-Church on the 30th. of January, 1681/2* (London, 1682), 21. The Answer to the Nineteen Propositions was given new prominence during the Danby impeachment. Weston, *English Constitutional Theory and the House of Lords*, 92–123. See also *ibid.*, 105–09 for references to the *Political Catechism* and consult *Calendar of State Papers, Domestic Series, January 1 to June 30, 1683*, 129–30 and note 22, Chapter 3 of this study.
2. See note 26, Chapter 4 of this study and note 36 of this chapter.
3. In 1681 Atwood published another anti-Brady tract, this one with the revealing title *Jus Anglorum ab Antiquo: or, a Confutation of an Important Libel against the Government by King, Lords, and Commons* (London) He had demonstrated in this tract, and in his *Jani Anglorum Facies Nova* (London, 1680), he wrote, 'that the king has not the legislative exclusive of others'. Howell, *A Complete Collection of State Trials*, xi, 1282. Other writings of Atwood's receive mention in notes 67 and 87 below.
4. Pocock, the modern authority on Brady, believes him to have been made keeper *de facto*. 'Robert Brady', 197–98. But a warrant, issued by Sunderland on May 31, 1686, to Laurence Halsted (chief clerk of the records in the tower of London), suggests that Brady received a formal appointment. *Calendar of State Papers, Domestic Series, James II,* (January, 1686–May, 1687), 147. The Brady controversy is described at length in Chapter viii of the *Ancient Constitution and the Feudal Law.*
5. Brady, 'Preface to the Reader', *Complete History*, no pagination.
6. Tyrrell, 'Preface to the Appendix', *General History of England*, iii, Part ii, i–ii.

7. See Atwood, *Jus Anglorum ab Antiquo*, and two other polemists lent further support – Sir Robert Atkyns, a judge of the
court of common pleas, recorder of Bristol, lord chief baron
of the exchequer after the Revolution, and for a few years
speaker of the house of lords, and Tyrrell, grandson to Archbishop Ussher, friend and neighbor to Locke in Buckingham-
shire, and disciple as well to Petyt. Atkyns brought out his
*Power, Jurisdiction and Priviledge of Parliament and the Anti-
quity of the House of Commons Asserted* in 1689, while Tyrrell
provided substantial support, first with his *Bibliotheca Politica*
(1694) and then his three-volume *General History* (1696–1704),
in which half a volume was devoted to the vexed question of
the antiquity of the house of commons. The impact of the
whig argument was long-lasting, as was the tory response.
Petyt's *Antient Right* and Brady's *Answer to Petyt* were invoked repeatedly in the polemical literature of the early eighteenth century, a second edition of Tyrrell's *Bibliotheca Politica*
was published in 1727, and Atkyns' collected tracts were
printed in 1734 and again in 1741. There is a helpful account
of Tyrrell in Gough, 'James Tyrrell, Whig Historian and
Friend of John Locke', 581–610. For Locke's own interest in
the Brady controversy, see *ibid.*, 588, note 30.

8. William Petyt, *The Pillars of Parliament struck at by the Hands
of a Cambridge Doctor* (London, 1681), 12–13. Very few copies
of this tract made their way into libraries. Pocock, *The Ancient
Constitution and the Feudal Law*, 211, note 1. They are incomplete, as are the numerous copies in the Petyt MSS, suggesting
that Petyt pulled the tract from the press before the
printing was completed. *Catalogue of Manuscripts in the
Library of the Honourable Society of the Inner Temple*, ed.
J. Conway Davies (London, 1972), I, 14; Weston, 'Legal Sovereignty in the Brady Controversy', 413, note 8. Petyt had reason
to fear the government's hostility on another ground. When
Charles II instituted *quo warranto* proceedings against London
in 1681, he helped prepare the city's case against the crown.
*Ibid.*, 21. This subject is discussed later in this chapter. According to Samuel Johnson, writing shortly after the Glorious
Revolution, Petyt was dismayed by the reception given by the
loyal clergy to Brady's scholarship and in particular by the
applause in Hickes' *Jovian*. Johnson wrote : 'Mr. Petyt found
the tide so strong against him, as not to venture on a reply,
though to my knowledge he was furnished with a very good

one.' *An Argument Proving that the Abrogation of King James by the People of England from the Regal Throne, and the Promotion of the Prince of Orange, one of the Royal Family, to the Throne of the Kingdom in his stead, was according to the Constitution of the English Government, and Prescribed by it* (London, 1692), 4. Hickes, writing in 1683, had indeed singled Petyt out by name for attack. *Jovian*, 235. See also Northleigh, *Remarks upon the Most Eminent of our Antimonarchical Authors and their Writings*, 190, 254–55, 562–66.

9. 'Probi Homines', in the 'Glossary', Brady, *An Introduction to the Old English History*, 63–64.

10. Samuel Johnson, *An Argument Proving that the Abrogation of King James . . . was according to the Constitution*, 4.

11. 'Epistle to the Candid Reader', *An Introduction to the Old English History*, no pagination.

12. *An Historical Treatise of Cities, and Burghs or Boroughs* (London, 1690), i–iv, 51–60, 79. That Brady followed Prynne closely also appears from Tyrrell, *General History*, III, Part II, 'Appendix', 188–202.

13. Petyt to Sir John Cotton, December 13, 1676 (Copy), MS. 538, Vol. 17, fo. 482. See also Petyt MS. 512, Vol. T, fos. 175–78v; MS. 533, Vol. 15, fos. 112–13. *The Pillars of Parliament*, 5, 10, 11. Dugdale's preface to his *The Baronage of England* (London, 1675), no pagination. Pocock, *The Ancient Constitution and the Feudal Law*, 182–87. For Petyt's references to Prynne, see, for example. 'Discourse', *Antient Right*, 7, 23, 40, 55, 56, 57, 63, and 68. Consult *Catalogue of Manuscripts in the Library of the Honourable Society of the Inner Temple*, ed. Davies, I, 19–20, 30, 281–82, 298. Volume IV of the *Brief Register of Parliamentary Writs* is in the Petyt MSS. Miscellaneous MS. No. 152.

14. 'Discourse', *Antient Right*, 125. Petyt was especially hostile to the author of the *Freeholders Grand Inquest* and to James Howell, appointed historiographer royal to Charles II early in the restoration. The Petyt MSS reveal that he objected to Howell's *Some Sober Inspections made into the Cariage and Consults of the late-long Parliament* (London, 1655), a thinly veiled paraphrase of the *Freeholders*. *Some Sober Inspections*, 11–50. That Petyt had read the *Freeholders* with much care appears from his *Miscellanea Parliamentaria* (London, 1680), published shortly after the *Antient Right*. Cp. *Miscellanea Parliamentaria*, 66–67, 70–72, Appendix, and the *Freeholders*,

4, 5, 22, 24, 34–35, 51, 55. Petyt MS. 512, Vol. N, fos. 1–43, 46, 56–71, and others.

15. 'Preface', *Antient Right*, 74.
16. This is the heading used throughout much of the 'Discourse'. For further light on Petyt's common-law approach to political problems, see the draft entitled 'The Antient Rights of the Commons of England Reasserted, in Reply to a Book, written by Robert Brady Dr. of Physick against a Discourse', in Petyt MS. 512, Vol. L, fos. 49–49v., 73v.–75, 92–93. and 103–103v. Working from Henry Rolle's *Abridgment des plusiers cases et resolutions del common ley*, he wrote 'From those so solemn declarations and resolutions must it not now be agreed and confessed on all hands that prescription is 1. time before R. 1, uncle to H. 3, son of King John; 2. the contrary of which no memory of man can prove; 3. beyond all testimony and evidence; 4. without any limitation?' Further, it was 'the general ground and foundation of the joint right both of the lords and of the representatives of the commons to be constituent parts of parliament'. He would show that parliament was 'a body politic or corporation by prescription' and 'a court by prescription'. It was Brady's failure to understand prescription that vitiated his history. In this connection Petyt wrote : 'The true knowledge of which Dr. Brady was so far from understanding that it never so much as entered into his head : the ignorance whereof hath made his whole book [*Answer to Petyt*] stand upon no stronger supports than the tottering basis of new and improbable conjectures [and] bold and daring affirmations without any solid proofs for what he says.' *Ibid.*, fos. 49v., 73–75. Petyt MS. 512, Vol. T, fos. 1–2, 51–54. See also Howard Nenner, *by colour of law: Legal Culture and Constitutional Politics in England, 1660–1689* (Chicago, 1977), 83.
17. 'Preface', *Antient Right*, 17–18, 39–40.
18. See also Tyrrell, *General History*, III, Part II, 213, where he writes of supplying 'an additional proof of the constant claim the commons have made before the king and lords in parliament, of their being therein represented of common right of the realm, that is, by prescription'. Whatever he knew about prescription and representation he had learned from Petyt. There is material on Petyt in Weston, 'Legal Sovereignty in the Brady Controversy', *Historical Journal*, XV (1972), 409–31.
19. 'Discourse', *Antient Right*, 44.
20. Tyrrell, *Bibliotheca Politica*, 416.

21. 'Discourse', *Antient Right,* 22, 39–43. He described 5 Rich. 2, s. 2. c. 4 as 'a mighty authority to prove that both the lords and commons had had writs of summons to come to parliament long before Rich. the 2nd, and that they were bound and had been accustomed so to do of old time, *i.e.* by general prescription'. Petyt MS. 512, Vol. T, fos. 124–26v. For the continued importance attached to this statute in whig writings, and to Petyt's argument generally, see Acherley, *The Britannic Constitution,* 116–19. Although Petyt is not named, the debt is unmistakable.

22. 'Discourse', *Antient Right,* 42–43. Petyt was indebted to Lambarde for this style of argument. *Archeion,* ed. McIlwain and Ward, 124–25.

23. 'Discourse', *Antient Right,* 43–44. *The Pillars of Parliament,* 14.

24. *Ibid.* Petyt, *Jus Parliamentarium,* xiii; xiii, note; xiv. 'Discourse', *Antient Right,* 44.

25. *Jus Parliamentarium,* xiii–xiv. This should be read in conjunction with 'Discourse', *Antient Right,* 43–44, and *The Pillars of Parliament,* 14.

26. *Ibid.* See the marginal comment.

27. 'Preface', *Antient Right,* 1–12, 40, 54–58, 73–74. See also 'The Epistle Dedicatory', *ibid.,* no pagination, and Atwood, 'Preface', *Jus Anglorum ab Antiquo,* no pagination. Petyt's references to a shared law-making power in early English history, an idea replete with implications for Stuart England, link him to the principle of a co-ordination in the legislative power that was at the heart of the theory of mixed monarchy and the accompanying view of a legal sovereignty in king, lords, and commons. The comment of Petyt's disciple, Tyrrell, is helpful in this matter. He had a participant in a political dialogue, who was upholding a legal sovereignty in the king, declare 'I cannot comprehend how the two houses can have any share (properly speaking) in the legislative power, without falling into that old error of making the king one of the three estates, and so co-ordinate with the other two.' *Bibliotheca Politica,* 237. Petyt referred explicitly to the co-ordination principle in expressing sarcastic bewilderment as to why the barons, if they had actually usurped the sovereign power in 49 H. 3, should have proceeded so easily and speedily to 'divide and share it with the commons, constitute a new court of parliament, and make them [the commons] essential and co-ordinate with them-

selves in the legislative power'. 'Discourse', *Antient Right*, 61–62.

28. Petyt MS. 512, Vol. N, fo. 68v. Petyt's familiarity with the great ideological controversy over law-making, which drew its fire from Charles I's Answer to the Nineteen Propositions, appears from *A Catalogue of the Petyt Library at Skipton, Yorkshire* (Gargrave, 1964), which lists more than 2,000 tracts sent to Skipton by William's brother Silvester in the years from 1708 to 1715. The first transmittal came in the year that followed William Petyt's death, and a comparison of the *Catalogue* with the references to pamphlet literature in the Petyt MSS leaves little doubt that the library was his. More than nostalgia explains the decision to send the library to Yorkshire, where he and Silvester had been scholars in Skipton grammar school. The distribution took place amidst the uncertainty engendered by the war of the Spanish succession, which threatened the permanence of the Glorious Revolution. If it were to be undone, the retention of the library in London must be a source of acute embarrassment, but the destruction of so extensive a collection could hardly have been contemplated with equanimity. The solution, it may be surmised, was to place Petyt's tracts where they would be secure and safe, that is, in Skipton. Any estimate of his political thought must now be made not only on the basis of the Petyt MSS in London, and Petyt's printed works, but also of this library in Yorkshire. A word about the library's contents is called for. All the works cited earlier in this study as civil-war sources of the community-centered ideology are represented here although not necessarily in their entirety nor in civil-war editions. The representation is striking. Thus Petyt owned Herle's *Fuller Answer* (1642) and Stafford's *Reason of the War* (1646), which borrowed from it; Hunton's *Treatise of Monarchie* (1680 and 1689) and the anonymous *Dialogue at Oxford between a Tutor and his Pupil* (1681), written under Hunton's influence; the *Political Catechism* (1643), a very radical tract distinguished by its close analysis of the Answer to the Nineteen Propositions; two volumes of Prynne's *Soveraigne Power of Parliaments and Kingdomes* (1643); and Nathaniel Bacon's *An Historical Discourse* (1689). Also of interest are Dodderidge's *The Several Opinions of Sundry learned Antiquaries . . . touching the Antiquity . . . of the High-Court of Parliament* (1658); Baxter's *Holy Commonwealth* (1659); and the exceedingly radical

*Cause of the People of England, Stated* (1689), first published in 1662 and circulated in conjunction with the proceedings in Vane's trial. Quoting from the Answer to the Nineteen Propositions in the Petyt MSS, Petyt gave as his source the collected works of Charles I, published in 1662, but he also had in his possession Husband's *Exact Collection* (1642), which has the declarations and counterdeclarations of 1642, including the Answer. Petyt may have been reminded of the Answer's importance when the house of commons made use of it during the Danby impeachment. There are four editions of the *Narrative and Reasons* in the Petyt library. Equally zealous in collecting anti-co-ordination literature, he had Ferne's *Conscience Satisfied* (1643); Digges, *The Unlawfulnesse of Subjects taking up Armes* (1644, 1647, 1679); three copies of Dallison's *Royalist's Defence*; two copies of *The Freeholders Grand Inquest* (1648); Heylyn's *Stumbling-block of Disobedience* (1658), and also his *Historical and Miscellaneous Tracts* (1681), which contained the *Stumbling-block* with a new subtitle; Sanderson's *Ten Lectures on the Obligation of Humane Conscience* (1660); two copies of Tomkins' *Rebels Plea*; Ussher's *The Power Communicated by God to the Prince* (1660); two copies of the regicide trials; three copies of Assheton's *Evangelium Armatum*; the 1663 edition of Mocket's *God and the King*; Brydall's popularly written *Absurdity of that New Devised State – Principle* (1681); Maxwell's *Sacro-Sancta* (1644, 1680); Mackenzie's *Jus Regium* (1684), etc. Petyt also had the decree of Oxford University of 1683. The most important royalist tract missing from the *Catalogue* is Spelman's *Case of our Affaires* (1644), although his *View of a Printed Book* is listed. If a selection of Leveller and Engager tracts is added to this list, an exceedingly interesting political library emerges. To know fully what Petyt possessed, it is necessary to use the *Catalogue* in conjunction with the Petyt MSS.

29. Petyt MS. 512, Vol. N, fo. 68v.
30. *Ibid.*, fo. 69.
31. Petyt MS. 538, Vol. 17, fo. 291. Ralph Cudworth to Petyt, October 16, 1679. Cudworth discussed the definition of estates as if in response to an earlier statement by Petyt and related the definition to the legislative power.
32. 'Appendix', *Antient Right*, 146–47. Petyt MS. 512, Vol. N, fos. 64v.–65v. *Jus Parliamentarium*, 10–12. There is a similar view of parliamentary power in *Mr. Hunt's Postscript*, 41–42, 130–

M

31; and in Care, *English Liberties*, 120–21. Of equal interest are Algernon Sidney's comments in *Discourses concerning Government* (London, second edition, 1704), 412–13, 414, section XLVI. Pocock has a different interpretation of Petyt's political thought. *The Ancient Constitution and the Feudal Law*, 191–92, 229–31, 235.

33. *Jus Parliamentarium*, 45, 66–67.

34. *Ibid.*, xiv. Petyt's comment on the Anglo-Saxon kingship suggests that he considered the king below the law in all important respects. 'Preface', *Antient Right*, 12–13. The whigs also advocated frequent parliaments. *Ibid.*, 42. *Jus Parliamentarium*, 4. Atwood's remarks are in Howell, *A Complete Collection of State Trials*, XI, 1283.

35. *An Historical Treatise of Cities*, 24–26, 32–35, 59. 'Preface to the Reader,' *A Complete History*, no pagination; 'General Preface', *ibid.*, xxv–xxx.

36. Brady recommended to his readers Heylyn's *Stumbling-block of Disobedience*, which has numerous references to Bodin. *Ibid.*, 233, 259, 266, 278. The recommendation is in *Introduction to the Old English History*, 343. In doing so Brady called attention to chapter 6, among others, in the *Stumbling-block*, which discusses such topics as 'the king of England always accounted heretofore for an absolute monarch', 'no part of sovereignty invested legally in the English parliaments' 'the three estates assembled in the parliament of England, subordinate unto the king, not co-ordinate with him', and 'the legislative power of parliaments is properly and legally in the king alone'. Brady expressed admiration for another civil-war tract hostile to co-ordination, Maxwell's *Sacro-Sancta*, which like the *Stumbling-block* was republished in the early 1680s. *An Introduction to the Old English History*, 349. Heylyn's remarks on the Norman conquest are in *The Stumbling-block of Disobedience*, 267–71. There is an interesting if brief comment on Brady's enterprise by William Atwood (Petyt's colleague) in Howell, *A Complete Collection of State Trials*, XI, 1309, note p.

37. 'Epistle to the Candid Reader', *An Introduction to the Old English History*. Tyrrell, 'Introduction', *The General History of England* (London, 1700), II, xxx.

38. *An Introduction to the Old English History*, 13–14. See also *ibid.*, 252, for Brady's statement that he was not claiming either that William abolished all the law he found in England or that

he changed the whole frame and constitution of the government. What Brady was claiming was that William had brought
in a new law by which he governed the nation. See Weston,
'Legal Sovereignty in the Brady Controversy', *passim* for
much of the following treatment of Brady's political
thought.

39. 'Preface to the Norman History', *A Complete History*, 181.
See also *ibid.*, 143, 150, 151–56, etc. 'General Preface', *ibid.*,
xlvii. According to Brady, the whole feudal law consisted of
customs, including 'laws of fees'. There is pertinent material in
*An Introduction to the Old English History*, 13–14.

40. 'General Preface', *A Complete History*, xxiv–xxviii, lxviii.
'Preface to the Reader', *An Introduction to the Old English
History*, 17–18, 252, 255, 266.

41. 'Glossary', *An Introduction to the Old English History*, 51.
Petyt, *The Pillars of Parliament*, 4–5. This aspect of Brady's
thought is further discussed in Weston, 'Legal Sovereignty in
the Brady Controversy', 422–31.

42. Northleigh, *Remarks upon the Most Eminent of our Anti-
monarchical Authors*. 190, 254–55. See also *ibid.*, 562–66.
Pocock, *The Ancient Constitution and the Feudal Law*, 186–
88.

43. Lord Essex to Petyt, October 18, 1673. British Library Add.
MS. 34513, fo. 129v.

44. Petyt MS. 538, Vol. 17, fos. 293, 296; Miscellaneous MS. No.
61. Henry Capel referred to Petyt in a letter to Essex, May 15,
1677. *Ibid.*, fo. 56.

45. Petyt MS. 535, Vols. 1–3. The materials collected by Petyt are
conveniently listed in *Catalogue of Manuscripts in the Library
of the Honourable Society of the Inner Temple*, ed. Davies, II,
528–47. The city's plea sounds like Petyt, as do the references
to the statute 1 Edw. 3. Howell, *A Complete Collection of
State Trials*, VIII, 1041–50, 1228–29. Discussing this statute,
Pollexfen referred to the records of the exchequer. *Ibid.*, 1229.
No one was more familiar with such records than Petyt. *Catalogue of Manuscripts in the Library of the Honourable Society
of the Inner Temple*, ed. Davies, I, 20. Petyt MS. 533, Vol. 15,
fos. 112–13.

46. 'Sir George Treby', in 'draft biographies for the History of
Parliament Trust', ed. Henning. See also the references to
Treby in Chapter 8, note 91 of this study.

47. *Plato Redivivus*, 108–09.

48. Thomas Hunt, *A Defence of the Charter, and Municipal Rights of the City of London* (London, 1683), 42–43. Petyt was also well acquainted with Samuel Johnson. See note 8 above in this chapter. So were Hunt and Johnson. Hunt is supposed to have contributed to Johnson's *Julian the Apostate* (1682), the well-known attack on passive obedience; and Johnson testified to this effect before the privy council. *Calendar of State Papers, Domestic Series, July 1–September 30, 1683*, 432. For the close relationship between Petyt and James Tyrrell, see note 20, Chapter 5 of this study and note 18 of this chapter.

49. Pocock, *The Ancient Constitution and the Feudal Law*, 229. That Petyt enjoyed a contemporary reputation was also attested, indirectly, when a report circulated during the Oxford parliament (1681) that the house of commons was contemplating an attack on Brady's *Answer to Petyt*. *The Life and Times of Anthony Wood*, ed. Andrew Clarke (Oxford, 1891–95), II, 533. Petyt's situation at the Revolution is described in *Catalogue of Manuscripts in the Library of the Honourable Society of the Inner Temple*, ed. Davies, I, 14–15. According to Davies, Petyt was recommended to Prince William by an 'F. Jephson'. He may have meant William Jephson, a whig who had lived at The Hague since 1683 and was the prince's private secretary during the invasion and afterwards secretary of the treasury. He was named to the committee of the convention house of commons that drew up the Bill of Rights. Stephen Baxter, *William III* (London, 1966), 277. The continuing influence of the Petyt school of historians may be seen in George St Amand, *An Historical Essay on the Legislative Power of England* (London, 1725) and Paul de Rapin-Thoyras, *A Dissertation on the Government, Laws, Customs, Manners, and Language, of the Anglo-Saxons*, trans. N. Tindal (London, 1730). See also D. W. L. Earl, 'Procrustean Feudalism. An Interpretative Dilemma in English Historical Narration, 1700–1725,' *Historical Journal*, XIX (1976), 33–51. Discussing the writers mentioned above, Earl makes no mention of Petyt and at one point remarks on what he sees as the absence from the whig political argument of any reference to the rule of 1189. *Ibid.*, 42, note 36. The article follows Pocock's interpretation of the Brady controversy.

50. Pocock, 'Robert Brady', 196–98. *Calendar of State Papers, Domestic Series, James II*, 14.

51. Pocock, 'Robert Brady', 197.

52. Clarke, *The Life of James II*, II, 270–71. According to Clarke, Brady served as intermediator between the king and those who wanted him to remain in England; and Pocock named Turner as one of the group. 'Robert Brady', 202. There is a revealing account of the bishop's career in Beddard, 'The Commission for Ecclesiastical Promotions, 1681–84', 26–30.

53. Pocock, 'Robert Brady', 202.

54. Disney, executed for his part in the Monmouth rebellion, wrote *Nil dictum quod non dictum prius, or, the Case of the Government of England Established by Law* (London, 1681). Apparently little known, it was representative, nevertheless, of the whig party when relying on the Answer to the Nineteen Propositions as the authoritative statement of the constitution, Disney assigned legal sovereignty to king, lords, and commons. The king was below the law, but there was nothing that a parliament could not do. It had an unlimited and unerring power, and its authority was above the law. *Ibid.*, 49–51, 54, 70, 97, 134–35, 173, 176.

55. *The Judgment and Decree of the University of Oxford Past in their Convocation July 21, 1683, Against Certain Pernicious Books and Damnable Doctrines Destructive to the Sacred Persons of Princes, their State and Government, and of all Human Society* (Oxford, 1683). The decree, 'published by command', was practically official. Ogg, *England in the Reigns of James II and William III*, 510. Materials shedding light on the decree – its authorship, support for it in the University, its direct relationship to the controversy over the legislative power, etc. – are in the following : *The Life and Times of Anthony Wood*, ed. Clarke, III, 61–64, 68–72; *An Account of Mr Parkinson's Expulsion from the University of Oxford in the late Times* (London, 1689), 4–5; *University Loyalty: or, the Genuine Explanation of the Principles and Practices of the English Clergy, as Established and Directed by the Decree of the University of Oxford, past in their Convocation 21 July, 1683 and Republished at the Trying of Dr. H. Sacheverell* (London, 1710), 4–5, 15–19, 25–27. See also Weston, *English Constitutional Theory and the House of Lords*, 112, and note 62 below.

56. Hickes, *The Harmony of Divinity and Law*, 33, 36. In 1685 Dugdale wrote to Brady after receiving a copy of the first volume of the *Complete History* : 'I heartily wish that all our nobility, gentry, and lawyers, would seriously read your book, and consider whereby they might be better seasoned with loyal

principles than they are'. *The Life, Diary and Correspondence of Sir William Dugdale,* ed. Hamper, 463. The letter is not dated. See also *ibid.,* 459–60.

57. Hickes, *A Sermon Preached before the Lord Mayor, Aldermen, and Citizens of London, at Bow Church,* 29. See also the marginal note. *A Discourse of the Soveraign Power, in a Sermon Preached at St. Mary Le Bow, November 28, 1682, Before the Artillery Company of London* (London, 1682), 16–24. *The Harmony of Divinity and Law,* 57, 58, 61. A moderate statement of the problem is in the anonymous *The Opinion of divers Learned and Leading Dissenters, concerning the Original of Government. Referring to the Doctrine of the Political Catechism, passim.*

58. Such a view of government, sometimes on the lines of John Locke's *Second Treatise of Government* (1690), was widely expounded in whig pamphlets. O. W. Furley, 'The Whig Exclusionists : Pamphlet Literature in the Exclusion Campaign, 1679–81', *Cambridge Historical Journal,* xiii (1957), 29–30. Since both tory and whig beliefs were 'rooted in a God-centred view of the universe', Furley may have encountered the parliamentarian formula. J. R. Western, *Monarchy and Revolution: The English State in the 1680s* (London, 1972), 45. The formula is explicitly noticed in Schochet, *Patriarchalism in Political Thought,* 48, and in Behrens, 'The Whig Theory of the Constitution in the Reign of Charles II', 47–48. There is interesting comment in *Protestant Loyalty Fairly Drawn, in an Answer to A Pair of Scandalous and Popish Pamphlets. The First Intituled A Dialogue at Oxford between Tutor and Pupil, etc.* (London, 1681), 7, 10, 11–18.

59. See the reference to Halifax's observations on the prerogative in note 22, Chapter 3 of this study.

60. Nalson, 'Introduction', *An Impartial Collection of the Great Affairs of State,* i, vi–xvi. See, in particular, the reference to Sancroft in the text and in the margin. *Ibid.,* vi and xiv–xvi. That he was interested in Nalson's work is borne out by the existence of what seems to be an unpublished 'Preface to Dr. John Nalson's Collection of the Great Affairs of State' in Sancroft's papers in the Bodleian Library. Tanner MS. 103, fo. 245. The government also expedited Nalson's research. H.M.C., *Thirteenth Report, Appendix, Part I. The Manuscripts of . . . the Duke of Portland, preserved at Welbeck Abbey* (London, 1891), i, iii. Other materials to be consulted

are Beddard, 'The Commission for Ecclesiastical Promotions', 33, note 104; Pocock, *The Antient Constitution and the Feudal Law*, 195. There are other signs of Sancroft's activity in combating the co-ordination principle. The Tanner manuscripts reveal that he received letters from a host of conservative writers – not only Brady, Hickes, and Nalson, but also Assheton, Brydall, Dugdale, L'Éstrange and Mackenzie. He also went to much trouble and effort to see that a correct version of Filmer's *Patriarcha* was published and may have been responsible for reprinting his tracts. *Patriarcha and other Political Works*, ed. Laslett, 36, 45; Schochet, 'Sir Robert Filmer: Some New Bibliographical Discoveries', 156–59. Even if it was written before the co-ordination principle entered political discussion, the *Patriarcha* was obviously useful to the Yorkist party.

61. 'Reflections by the Lrd. Cheife Justice Hale on Mr. Hobbes: His Dialogue of the Lawe', in Holdsworth, *A History of English Law*, v, 508.

62. Keith Feiling, *A History of the Tory Party 1640–1714* (Oxford, 1924, reprinted 1965), 221. After their acquittal, Mackenzie expressed sympathy for the bishops and their cause. Since the constitutional issue had been clearly delineated, he had abandoned the position in *Jus Regium*. John Gutch, ed. *Collectanea Curiosa* (Oxford, 1781), I, 384. Even Dr William Jane, regius professor of divinity at Oxford and author of the University's decree in 1683, discarded passive obedience as James' Catholicizing tendencies became more apparent and, for a time at least, was willing to join William of Orange in 1688. See the *DNB* account. There is a useful account of moderate toryism in Mark N. Brown, 'Trimmers and Moderates in the Reign of Charles II', *Huntington Library Quarterly*, xxxvii (1974), 311–36. See, in particular, the comment on Francis North, who became Lord Keeper Guilford. *Ibid.*, 329–30. As early as the indulgence crisis of 1672–73, North was on record as believing that the legislative power was in king, lords, and commons.

63. Hickes, *The Harmony of Divinity and Law*, 42. Consult *ibid.*, 37, for support of the dispensing power, and *ibid.*, 49, for comment on the king as the sole law-maker. The tract was written, in part at least, under the influence of the *Freeholders Grand Inquest*.

64. It was expressed in the long parliament's declaration of November 2, 1642. Husband, *An Exact Collection of all Remonstrances*, 703–15, 727.

65. Stillingfleet, *The Grand Question, concerning the Bishops Right to Vote in Parliament in Cases Capital*, 163.
66. See note 55 above.
67. *A Letter of Remarks on Jovian, by a Person of Quality* (London, 1683), 6. This tract has been attributed to Atwood, Petyt's friend and colleague. See also Hickes, *Jovian*, 236.
68. Hickes, *The Harmony of Divinity and Law*, 36. The difficulty in drawing a line between the two versions of co-ordination may be seen in the case of Herle himself. In the important *Fuller Answer*, he strenuously advocated a co-ordination in king, lords, and commons and drew back from what he saw as an extremist position in the use made by the long parliament of the quotation attributed to Bracton. Yet he equated his view that one estate was less than three with the maxim *singulis major. A Fuller Answer*, 1. See also Behrens. 'The Whig Theory of the Constitution in the Reign of Charles II', 60–61; J. R. Jones, *The First Whigs: The Politics of the Exclusion Crisis, 1678–1683* (London, 1961, reprinted 1966), 115–20; and the tracts mentioned in note 81 below.
69. Quoted in D. E. C. Yale, 'Hobbes and Hale on Law, Legislation and the Sovereign', *Cambridge Law Journal*, 31 (1). (1972), 141. *Ibid.*, 122, note 7. See also *The Prerogatives of the King*, ed. Yale, 170–71 and Yale, 'Hale as a Legal Historian', 13.
70. Yale, 'Hobbes and Hale on Law, Legislation and the Sovereign', 141.
71. This was one of L'Estrange's favorite arguments by the late 1670s. The aim was to discredit the co-ordination principle as destructive not only of the kingship but also of parliament. See, for example, his *The Free-Born Subject, or, The Englishman's Birthright*, 5.
72. Furley, 'The Whig Exclusionists: Pamphlet Literature in the Exclusion Campaign', 27. Behrens, 'The Whig Theory of the Constitution in the Reign of Charles II', 50, note 20, 55–63.
73. Husband, *An Exact Collection of all Remonstrances*, 703.
74. *Ibid.*, 703–15.
75. *Protestant Loyalty Fairly Drawn*, 3, 5, 36. Hickes, *A Discourse of the Soveraign Power*, 19–20.
76. L'Éstrange, *Considerations and Proposals in order to the Regulation of the Press*, 19–20.
77. L'Éstrange, *The Free-born Subject, or, The Englishman's Birthright*, 5. L'Éstrange, *A Short Answer to a Whole Litter of Libels* (London, 1680), 15.

78. *A Letter to a Friend in the Country, Touching the present Fears and Jealousies of the Nation, and from whence they arise* (London, 1680), 1, 4, See also *A Letter to a Friend, Shewing from Scripture, Fathers and Reason, how false that State Maxim is, Royal Authority is Originally and Radically in the People* (London, 1679), 9; *The Primitive Cavalerism Revived*, 7.

79. *Protestant Loyalty Fairly Drawn*, 36. There is critical comment on the coffee houses in 'The Present Great Interest of King and People' [1679], *A Collection of Scarce and Valuable Tracts, . . . selected from . . . Libraries, particularly that of the Late Lord Somers*, ed. Walter Scott (London, 1809–15), VIII, 119–20.

80. 'Character of a Popish Successor' [1681], *State Tracts: Being a Collection of Several Treatises relating to the Government* (London, 1689), 158, 159, 162.

81. *A Dialogue at Oxford*, 7. According to the anonymous author, the two houses were 'representatively the whole body of the kingdom, having commission by the original constitution to make new laws, or to guard and repair the old ones'. By contrast, the king's power was derivative : the two houses had set him up as the chief magistrate. *Ibid.*, 5, 7. See also 'Vox Populi : or, the Peoples Claim to their Parliament's Sitting, to Redress Grievances, and to provide for the Common Safety' [1681], *State Tracts: Being a Collection of Several Treatises relating to the Government* (London, two volumes in one, 1693), II, 219, 222–23.

82. *An Account of the Growth of Knavery, under the Pretended Fears of Arbitrary Government and Popery* (London, 1678), 44–45. A friend of John Milton, Marvell was member for Hull for twenty years in the parliament of Richard Cromwell, the convention parliament of 1660, and the cavalier parliament. Charles II's government, alarmed by the tract in question, issued a warrant for its seizure. For more information about the political reasoning that L'Éstrange and conservative thinkers associated with *singulis major*, see his *Considerations and Proposals in order to the Regulation of the Press*, 19. He also condemned pertinent parts of the long parliament's declaration of November 2, 1642. *The Dissenters Sayings, in Requital for L'Éstrange's Sayings*, 27–28.

83. *The Arraignment, Tryal and Condemnation of Algernon Sidney*, 23.

84. Caroline Robbins, *The Eighteenth-Century Commonwealth-man* (Cambridge, Mass., 1961) 42. Behrens agrees. 'The Whig Theory of the Constitution in the Reign of Charles II', 50. J. P. Kenyon struck a somewhat different note in 'The Revolution of 1688 : Resistance and Contract', *Historical Perspectives: Studies in English Thought and Society in Honour of J. H. Plumb*, ed. Neil McKendrick (London, 1974), 60. But he too thinks Sidney's ideas were running against the general tide of accepted political thought. *Ibid.*, 60. See note 86 below.

85. Assheton, *The Royal Apology*, 39.

86. 'Preface', *The Harmony of Divinity and Law*, no pagination. L'Éstrange wrote to Secretary Jenkins : 'Great stress is laid on Mr. Sidney's last paper and they say the *Haarlem Courant* has it at length. Abundance of manuscript copies of it are up and down the town, and inferences drawn from the suppressing of the paper, as they call it, to the dishonour of the government . . .' He also reported : 'There is much discourse of the strength of Sidney's defence of the popular cause in his Essay on a reply to Patriarcha [that is, in the *Discourses*].' *Calendar of State Papers, Domestic Series, October 1683 to April 1684*, 150–51.

87. Petyt's library is described in note 28 above. See Atwood's opinion on Sidney's fate in his *Fundamental Constitution of the English Government* (London, 1690), xvi. And see note 100 below.

88. *The Arraignment, Tryal and Condemnation of Algernon Sidney.* 23.

89. It appeared in these tracts : Peter Allix, *An Examination of the Scruples of Those who Refuse to take the Oath of Allegiance*, 22 and 'Reflections upon the Opinions of Some Modern Divines', *A Collection of State Tracts, Publish'd on Occasion of the late Revolution*, I, 507; Robert Ferguson, *A Representation of the Threatening Dangers, Impending over Protestants in Great Britain, Before the Coming of His Highness the Prince of Orange* (n.p., 1689), 25; Thomas Long, *The Historian Unmask'd: or, Some Reflections on the late History of Passive Obedience* (London, 1689), 42; *A Friendly Debate between Dr. Kingsman, a Dissatisfied Clergy-man, and Gratianus Trimmer, a Neighbour Minister*, 22; *A Full Answer to all the Popular Objections that have yet Appeared, for not taking the Oath of Allegiance to their Present Majesties* (London, 1689), 37; *The New Oath of Allegiance Justified, from the Original Constitution of the English Monarchy* (London, 1689), 9 and

17; *Obedience due to the Present King, Notwithstanding our Oaths to the Former* (London, 1689), 3; and *Sidney Redivivus* (London, 1689), 3. The quotation was popular in Queen Anne's reign. See, for example, *Vox Populi, Vox Dei: Being True Maxims of Government* (London, 1709), 16–17 : *The Manager's Pro and Con: or, An Account of what is said at Child's and Tom's Coffee-Houses For and Against Dr. Sacheverell* (London, 1710), 27–28; *A Prelude to the Tryal of Skill between Sacheverellism and the Constitution of the Monarchy of Great Britain* (London, 1710), 21; and John Shute Barrington, *The Revolution and Anti-Revolution Principles Stated and Compar'd* (London, 1714), 55–56. Barrington, a liberal disciple of Locke's, implied that the nation had been obliged in 1689 'to bridle the lawless king'. See note 104 below for comment on *Vox Populi, Vox Dei*. According to the British Library Catalogue, *The Manager's Pro and Con* went through five editions in 1710. By comparison, *singulis major* rarely appears in the political literature of the Revolution, at least by name. It is cited in 'The Proceedings of the Present Parliament Justified by the Opinion of the Most Judicious and Learned Hugo Grotius', *A Collection of State Tracts, Publish'd on Occasion of the late Revolution,'* 1, 180–81 and see note 92 below.

90. The letter is dated August 8, 1683. Tanner MS. 34, fos. 102–03. Dr Joel Fishman supplied this reference.

91. Assheton, *The Royal Apology*, 25.

92. Disney, *Nil dictum quod non dictum prius*, 70. Samuel Johnson, 'Of Magistracy, of prerogative by divine right, etc.', *State Tracts: Being a Collection of Several Treatises relating to the Government* [1693], II, 272; 'An Impartial Account of the Nature and Tendency of the late Addresses' [1682–83], *State Tracts: Being a Collection of Several Treatises relating to the Government* [1689], 429. See also William Denton, *Jus Regiminis: Being a Justification of Defensive Arms in General* (London, 1689), 37. The author was also familiar with *singulis major, universis minor. Ibid.*, 29. Although the tract was licensed for publication on June 17, 1689, the preface states that it was written before the Revolution.

93. Hale, *The Prerogatives of the King*, ed. Yale, 67.

94. Dugdale, *A Short View of the Late Troubles in England*, 94.

95. Sidney, *Discourses concerning Government*, 417–18, 419. Neville, *Plato Redivivus*, 126–27. See also Disney, *Nil dictum quod non dictum prius*, 52, and *Mr. Hunt's Postscript*, 30; and consult

Northleigh, *Remarks upon the Most Eminent of our Anti-monarchical Writers*, 385, 392–93, 400–01, for comment on Hunt.

96. Cobbett, *Parliamentary History of England*, v, 81.

97. *The Lord Chief Baron Atkyns' Speech to Sir William Ashhurst, Lord Mayor Elect of the City of London* (London, 1693), 4.

98. Dugdale, *A Short View of the Late Troubles in England*, 38–39. See also note 93 in Chapter 3 of this study.

99. Petyt, 'Discourse', *The Antient Right*, 58–61. Parker, *Observations*, 5. Prynne, *The Soveraigne Power of Parliaments and Kingdomes, or, Second Part of the Treachery and Disloyalty of Papists to their Soveraignes*, 75.

100. Petyt, *Jus Parliamentarium*, 163. Atwood moved in the opposite direction. His language in the preface to his *Jus Anglorum ab Antiquo* is studiously moderate, given his frame of reference; but he was willing to invoke the radical quotation from Bracton and Fleta in his *Fundamental Constitution of the English Government. Ibid.*, 35.

101. Brady, 'Glossary', *An Introduction to the Old English History*, 34–36.

102. Samuel Johnson, *An Essay concerning Parliaments at a Certainty* (London, third edition, 1694), 26–27. This was first published in 1693.

103. Ferguson, *A Representation of the Threatening Dangers*, 30. Ferguson, *A Brief Justification of the Prince of Orange's Descent into England, And of the Kingdoms Late Recourse to Arms* (London, 1689) 13. Other tracts at the Revolution citing *quas vulgus elegerit* include 'Good Advice before it be too late', *Somers Tracts*, x, 201; *A True Relation of the Manner of the Deposing of King Edward II* (London, 1689), 13–14. The first of these is attributed to John Humphrey, a prominent dissenter who wrote frequently on controversial topics.

104. Cp. pp. 3–10 of *Vox Populi, Vox Dei* with pp. 5–17 of *A Brief Justification of the Prince of Orange's Descent*. Also, *Vox Populi*, 15, 16, with *A Brief Justification*, 26, 29.

105. Kenyon, 'The Revolution of 1688: Resistance and Contract', 47, 62–64. *Vox Populi* went through eight editions in 1709 and six more in 1710. *Ibid.*, 64. There is a fuller description of this tract in Kenyon's more recent *Revolution Principles: The Politics of Party, 1689–1720*, 123–24, 142, 209–10. By concentrating almost exclusively on the relationship between the theory of contract and the idea of deposing the king, Ken-

yon has seriously underestimated the importance of contract theory in this period. 'The Revolution of 1668 : Resistance and Contract', 48, 49, 66. It is contended in this study that the prime importance of contract theory lies in its relationship to the human source of political power and authority, this being related in turn to the concept of a shared legislative power and the theory of a parliamentary sovereignty in king, lords, and commons. Read in this light, Nicholas Lechmere's argument in the Sacheverell trial looks very different from Kenyon's description. *Ibid.*, 65–66. In this connection see the remarks of Benjamin Hoadly, quoted in note 109, Chapter 8 of this study.

106. Grey, *Debates of the House of Commons*, x, 375–86.
107. *Ibid.*, 379.
108. *Ibid.*, 380–81.
109. *Ibid.*, 381–86. Consult also Kemp, *King and Commons*, 26–27; David Ogg, *England in the Reigns of James II and William III*, 391–92, 496–97. The last English monarch to use the veto was Queen Anne, in 1708, but the practice was rare after Charles II's restoration. Despite the king's withdrawal in this sense from the law-making process, theorists continued to maintain that he had a veto. Even the so-called real whigs, described by Caroline Robbins, took this view. W. B. Gwyn, *The Meaning of the Separation of Powers* (New Orleans, 1965), 82–99. There are other signs in the immediate post-Revolution years that the two houses were becoming supreme in law-making, a process pointing in turn to the importance of the co-ordination principle. See Kenyon's comments on the demise of the crown act (1696). *Revolution Principles: The Politics of Party, 1689–1720*, 42, and cp. Warwick, *A Discourse of Monarchy*, 47.
110. There is information about Baldwin as a radical publisher in Blair Worden, 'Edmund Ludlow : the Puritan and the Whig', *The Times Literary Supplement* (January 7, 1977), 15–16.

CHAPTER 8 THE LAW-MAKERS AND THE DISPENSING POWER

1. Quoted in Tanner, *English Constitutional Conflicts of the Seventeenth Century*, 250.
2. Geoffrey Holmes, *British Politics in the Age of Anne* (London, 1967), 58–64.
3. Quoted in the *DNB* article on James II.
4. See Jones, *Revolution of 1688 in England*, 88, for the importance to be attached to Hills' name on a tract.

5. See Roger Morrice, 'The Entring Book : Being an Historical Register of Occurences from April An : 1677 to April 1691'. The authors of this study are grateful to the trustees of Dr Williams' Library in London for permission to make use of this Entry Book. It is cited in Dr Williams' Library as the Roger Morrice Collection MSS P, Q, and R, and the comment on Hills, given above, is based on Morrice MSS, P, 520–21.

6. Macaulay, *History of England*, II, 107–08.

7. *The Excellency of Monarchical Government*, 2. He would not have undertaken this work, Johnston explained, unless 'invited to it by a great and wise minister of state'; and a marginal note reveals that the invitation came from the lord president, *i.e.* Sunderland.

8. Morrice MSS, P, 522.

9. *Calendar of State Papers, Domestic Series, James II*, III (June, 1687–February, 1689), 14. The warrant is dated June 20, 1687.

10. *Ibid.*, 99. Henry Hills also published one of Johnston's tracts : *The Assurance of Abby and other Churchlands in England to the Possessors* (London, 1687). It was to be sold at Hills' printing house on the ditch-side in Blackfriars.

11. Peterborough was one of the few high ranking Englishmen whom James won over to Catholicism. Macaulay, *History of England*, II, 181–82. There are numerous references to Johnston in the *Hastings Manuscripts*, II, 232, 237, 245–49, 253–55, 256, 282, etc. Also involved in the discussions about helping him was the bishop of St Davids, viewed by the seven bishops who went on trial in 1688 as too close to the court to share their deliberations. Johnston's brother Henry is described in the *DNB*. Appointed clerk to Dugdale at Johnston's request, he was later the prior of the English Benedictines in Paris, where he died.

12. John Wilson, *A Discourse of Monarchy, More particularly of the Imperial Crowns of England, Scotland, and Ireland, According to the Ancient, Common, and Statute-Laws of the Same* (London, 1684), 138–40, 145–50.

13. *Ibid.*, 140–41, 150–52.

14. John Wilson, *Jus Regium Coronae: or, The King's Supream Power in Dispensing with Penal Statutes* (London, 1688), 7, 9, 10–11.

15. *The Excellency of Monarchical Government*, 126, 153.

16. *Ibid.*, 138–39.

17. This kind of argument had begun to appear in the late stages

of the civil war, so it appears from Sanderson's lectures in the divinity school at Oxford in 1647. See note 86, Chapter 4 of this study.

18. *The Excellency of Monarchical Government*, 139, 145, 152.
19. *Ibid.*, 151.
20. *Ibid.*, 152–53, 306–07.
21. *Ibid.*, 155.
22. *Ibid.*, 157.
23. *Ibid.*, 301, 302–03.
24. *Ibid.*, 127–28, 152, 306.
25. *Ibid.*, 12–15, 127, 155–56, 305.
26. Cobbett, *Parliamentary History of England*, IV, 1370–71. Grey, *Debates of the House of Commons*, VIII, 353–54.
27. *The Diary of John Evelyn*, ed. E. S. de Beer (Oxford, 1955), IV, 488, 489.
28. *Journals of the House of Commons*, IX, 757.
29. F. C. Turner, *James II* (London, 1948), 292, 292, note.
30. Grey, *Debates of the House of Commons*, VIII, 343. *The Diary of John Evelyn*, ed. de Beer, IV, 489.
31. Cobbett, *Parliamentary History of England*, IV, 1373, 1374.
32. *Ibid.*, 1377. Among those who were to prepare the appropriate address to be sent to James were Clarges, Seymour, Meres, Hampden, and Maynard. *Journals of the House of Commons*, IX, 757.
33. 'An Answer to a Paper importing a Petition of the Archbishop of Canterbury and Six Other Bishops to his Majesty', *A Third Collection of Scarce and Valuable Tracts . . . selected from . . . [tracts in possession of] Lord Somers* (London, 1751), III, 496. Henry Hills published the tract.
34. Grey, *Debates of the House of Commons*, VIII, 361–62. Cobbett, *Parliamentary History of England*, IV, 1378–79.
35. There is contemporary comment in 'Observations upon the Late Revolution in England', *Somers Tracts*, X, 337. A modern scholar associated with this view of the coming of the Revolution is Lucile Pinkham. *William III and the Respectable Revolution* (Cambridge, Mass., 1954). Cp. Jones, *The Revolution of 1688 in England*, 10, 253.
36. Clarke, *The Life of James the Second*, II, 157.
37. *A Letter to the Author of the Vindication of the Proceedings of the Ecclesiastical Commissioners concerning the Legality of that Court* (Oxford, 1688), 13–15. The tract was a reply to Care's *A Vindication of the Proceedings of His Majesties*

*Ecclesiastical Commissioners, against the Bishop of London and the Fellows of Magdalen College* (London, 1688). Pertinent materials are also in *A Glance on the Ecclesiastical Commission,* 8–9. Edward Stillingfleet, *A Discourse concerning the Illegality of the late Ecclesiastical Commission . . . Wherein . . . an Account is given of the Nature, Original, and Mischief of the Dispensing Power* (London, 1689). Atkyns, *The Power, Jurisdiction and Priviledge of Parliament,* 66–74. Sancroft was named to the ecclesiastical commission but asked not to serve, ostensibly on the ground of age and infirmities; but the refusal was due to his belief that the ecclesiastical commission was illegal and unconstitutional because of the statute of 1641 abolishing the court of high commission and forbidding the establishment of similar courts. It foreshadowed the more forthright opposition displayed in the case of the seven bishops. George D'Oyly, *The Life of William Sancroft* (London, 1821), I, 229.

38. Also dismissed were Baron Neville, Justice Powell, and Serjeant Holloway. Cobbett, *Parliamentary History of England,* v, 308–13. A. F. Havighurst, 'James II and the Twelve Men in Scarlet', *Law Quarterly Review,* LXIX (1953), 522, 530–31. Henry Horwitz, *Revolution Politicks: The Career of Daniel Finch, Second Earl of Nottingham, 1647–1730* (Cambridge, 1968), 43–44.

39. Hale's outlook puzzled Holdsworth. *A History of English Law,* VI, 204–07. The ample legal precedents for the dispensing power are discussed in Chapter 2 of this study.

40. Howell, *A Complete Collection of State Trials,* XI, 1193. Powys replaced Heneage Finch as solicitor general when he resigned rather than become involved in *Godden v. Hales. Ibid.,* 1192. Landon, *The Triumph of the Lawyers,* 208.

41. Howell, *A Complete Collection of State Trials,* XI, 1195–97. Havighurst, 'James II and the Twelve Men in Scarlet', 532.

42. Howell, *A Complete Collection of State Trials,* XI, 1199. The basis of Street's dissent is not recorded, but there is helpful comment in Sir John Reresby, *Memoirs,* ed. Andrew Browning (Glasgow, 1936), 429, note 3, and in Havighurst, 'James II and the Twelve Men in Scarlet', 532.

43. Hale interpreted this phrase in this way, as did such tory writers as Wilson, Johnston, and Hickes. Hickes explained their view : 'The legislative power is strictly, and properly taken for the power of sanction, or for that commanding ordaining power,

which giveth life, and being to the law, and force to oblige the conscience of the subject, and this is radically and incommunicably in the king, as sovereign . . . And from the legislative power thus properly taken, the laws are properly called the king's laws.' *The Harmony of Divinity and Law*, 49. Ogg noticed that the judges' decision was based on ideology. *England in the Reigns of James II and William III*, 168.

44. Clarke, *The Life of James II*, ii, 80–85. See *ibid.*, 83, for Herbert's remark that 'there is no law whatever, but what may be dispensed with, by the lawgiver', etc. In this part of the *Life* Clarke seems to have been working from papers compiled by the king himself. The margin reads : 'King Jam. Loose Papers, pag. 2.' *Ibid.*, 80. But Herbert's tone was much more moderate when he wrote a vindication of the judges' decision in *Godden v. Hales*. The ideological position was abandoned that the king as lawmaker might dispense with all the laws and stress placed on Chief Justice Vaughan's discussion of the dispensing power in *Thomas v. Sorrell* (1674). Sir Edward Herbert, *A Short Account of the Authorities in Law, upon which Judgement was given in Sir Edward Hales His Case* (London, 1688), 7, 19–21, 28, and 37. The vindication appeared on the day (December 11) on which James fled from Whitehall and Herbert himself left for France. *Thomas v. Sorrell* receives mention in note 82, Chapter 6 of this study, and there is a useful summary statement in Tanner, *English Constitutional Conflicts of the Seventeenth Century*, 290.

45. More may be said than this about Atkyns' political ideas and their influence. Thus he was a member of two Cromwellian parliaments and active in the cavalier house of commons. When he became judge of common pleas (April, 1673), he had served on more than 400 committees of the cavalier house of commons and delivered some 50 speeches. His political ideology was early in evidence when he helped pass the act for the preservation of the king and served as member of the committee of the house of commons whose members challenged successfully Charles II's early use of the dispensing power in ecclesiastical matters. Consistently with this record Atkyns urged the retention of the words 'public nuisance' in the Irish cattle bill. He was turned out of his judgeship and the recordership of Bristol at the time of the exclusion crisis, but his political activity seems to have been undiminished. He was soon busy helping Russell with his legal defense in the wake of the rye house plot. Atkyns' political

views were much like Russell's if the latter's were reflected in the writings of Samuel Johnson, Russell's chaplain and a well-known whig pamphleteer of the day, with whom Atkyns was in close touch. As was stated above, Atkyns was early at Prince William's side in 1688, and he along with Petyt was conspicuous among the judges who advised the convention house of lords. He was created lord chief baron of the exchequer at the Revolution and was for four years the speaker of the house of lords. 'Sir Robert Atkyns', 'draft biographies for the History of Parliament Trust', ed. Henning. *Calendar of State Papers Domestic, Charles II, July–September, 1683*, 127. Landon, *The Triumph of the Lawyers*, 48–50. 170, 220–23. Edward Foss *The Judges of England* (London, 1864), vii, 306–10. Pinkham, *William III and the Respectable Revolution*, 170. Henry Horwitz, 'Parliament and the Glorious Revolution', *Bulletin of the Institute of Historical Research* xlvii, (1974), 49. This study has comment on Atkyns in note 75, Chapter 6 and Section vi, Chapter 7. He seems to have subscribed to a radical view of co-ordination, one more like Prynne's than Herle's.

46. Atkyns, *An Enquiry into the Power of Dispensing with Penal Statutes* (London, 1689), 6–7.

47. Atkyns, *The Power, Jurisdiction and Priviledge of Parliament*, 33.

48. *An Enquiry into the Power of Dispensing,* 39–40.

49. *Ibid.*, 20.

50. *Ibid.*, 18, 21. He was confining himself to dispensations with acts of parliament, so he stated. See also *ibid.*, 20, for the further observation : 'Now, a law being made by consent of all, should not be dissolved again, but by the like consent; that is, by authority of the king and parliament, who have the legislature.' For the explicit denial that the king was the sole legislator, as Herbert had said, see *ibid.*, 23.

51. *Ibid.*, 16, 21, 27. See also p. 50, which is in a tract appended to the larger work. The additional material, which is numbered consecutively with *An Enquiry into the Power of Dispensing with Penal Statutes*, is entitled *Postscript: Being Some Animadversions upon a Book Writ by Sir Edward Herbert, Lord Chief Justice of the Common Pleas, Entituled, a Short Account of the Authorities in Law*, etc.

52. *Ibid.*, 28, 31, 50–53.

53. *Ibid.*, 28, 31, 50, 52.

54. *Ibid.*, 27.

55. *Ibid.*, 20–21, 51–53. Atkyns was severely critical of Vaughan's decision in *Thomas v. Sorrell* that the king might dispense with a particular statute because as supreme governor he was more concerned in the act than any subject. Arguments resembling Atkyns' are in Samuel Johnson, 'Several Reasons for the Establishment of a Standing Army and Dissolving the Militia', printed in Howell, *A Complete Collection of State Trials*, xi, 1348.

56. 'By the King, A Proclamation for a Toleration in Scotland', in Gilbert Burnet, *A Collection of Eighteen Papers, relating to the Affairs of Church and State, during the Reign of King James the Second* (London, 1689), 18–24. James also issued a proclamation proroguing the English parliament from November 22 to February 13 that contained an embarrassing error. Sir John Bramston thought it unprecedented. The proclamation referred to 'lords' rather than to the usual 'lords spiritual and temporal'. Once the error was recognized a new proclamation was issued. *The Autobiography of Sir John Bramston of Skreens*, ed. Lord Braybrooke (Camden Society, 1845), 246–47. The government's concern was rooted, surely, in the knowledge that the inclusion of the lords spiritual and temporal under the single heading 'lords' would be treated by the public as a signal of the co-ordination principle. Its appearance in a proclamation issued by James II would not do.

57. Narcissus Luttrell, *A Brief Historical Relation of State Affairs from September 1678 to April 1714* (Oxford, 1857), i, 426.

58. *His Majesties Gracious Declaration to all his Loving Subjects for Liberty of Conscience* (London, 1688), 4.

59. Gutch, *Collectanea Curiosa*, i, 335–37. A. Tindal Hart, *William Lloyd, 1627–1717, Bishop, Politician, Author, and Prophet* (London, 1952), 93–96.

60. For an account of how the bishops strengthened the statement on the dispensing power that had come from the London clergy, see Thomas, 'The Seven Bishops and their Petition', 64–65. Sancroft's interest in the events of 1672–73 appears from Tanner MS. 28, fo. 65. The only reservation common to the dissenters who thanked the king for his declaration was that they 'tried to avoid pronouncements in favor of the dispensing power'. Western, *Monarchy and Revolution: The English State in the 1680s*, 227. This account owes much to Thomas. See the importance attached to the bishops' petition in Peter Allix, *An Examination of the Scruples of Those who Refuse to take the*

*Oath of Allegiance,* 24–25. He wrote : 'The seven bishops by their remonstrance made to the king, openly avowed, that the king had no power to dispense with the laws, for as much as that power had been declared illegal by the parliaments of 1662 and 1672, which shows their renouncing of that notion, that the laws, being of the king's own making, he may, when he pleases, dispense with them.'

61. *The Correspondence of Henry Hyde, Earl of Clarendon, and of His Brother, Laurence Hyde, Earl of Rochester,* ed. Samuel W. Singer (London, 1828), II, 479–80. Gutch, *Collectanea Curiosa,* I, 338–40. See note 37 of this chapter.

62. British Library, Add. MS. 34512, fos. 83, 83v. The exiles at St Germain referred to Sancroft with aversion and disgust. Macaulay wrote : 'The sacrifice of the first place in the church, of the first place in the peerage, of the mansion at Lambeth and the mansion at Croydon, of immense patronage and of a revenue of more than five thousand a year, was thought but a poor atonement for the great crime of having modestly remonstrated against the unconstitutional declaration of indulgence.' *History of England,* IV, 446–47. Yet the attitude at St Germain seems less extravagant if one considers the ideological shock to the king. Sancroft had gone far beyond a modest remonstrance against an 'unconstitutional' declaration of indulgence.

63. Reresby, *Memoirs,* ed. Browning, 501. According to James Johnstone, Lord Chief Justice Wright was much blamed at court for allowing a debate on the dispensing power. British Library, Add. MS. 34515, fo. 86 (July 2, 1688). Johnstone added : 'The truth is, the argument was so plain, that nothing was to be said to it.' *Ibid.,* fo. 86v.

64. Morrice MSS, Q, 256. Fowler's importance at the Revolution appears from Thomas, 'The Seven Bishops and their Petition', 61. It is of interest that Samuel Johnson, who was imprisoned under James II, is said to have received money from Fowler, the more so since Johnson made use in his writings of the Answer to the Nineteen Propositions. Weston, 'Concepts of Estates', 126–28. 'Some Memorials of the Reverend Mr. Samuel Johnson', *Collected Works* (London, 1713), viii. Mr James Hendricks of New York City supplied this information.

65. British Library, Add. MS. 34515, fo. 66 (May 23, 1688).

66. Morrice MSS, Q, 258.

67. Macaulay, *History of England,* II, 344, 350–51.

68. Feiling, *A History of the Tory Party*, 223, note 1. Horwitz, *Revolution Politics*, 51. Gutch, *Collectanea Curiosa*, I, 358–59. Edward Harley, who was there, wrote an account. H.M.C. *Fourteenth Report, Appendix, Part II. The Manuscripts of . . . the Duke of Portland, Preserved at Welbeck Abbey* (London, 1894), III, 412–13. There is further comment on Nottingham's attitude, to which Feiling makes reference, in Thomas 'The Seven Bishops and their Petition', 59, 59, note 5. According to Morrice, the nobleman most trusted by the London clergy was Nottingham. Morrice MSS, Q, 255.

69. Gutch, *Collectanea Curiosa*, I, 359.

70. Howell, *A Complete Collection of State Trials*, XII, 367. Finch also declared that 'to suspend law is all one as to abrogate laws . . . but the abrogation of laws is part of the legislature [and] that legislative power is lodged . . . in king, lords, and commons'. *Ibid.*, 395. Solicitor general from 1667 to 1686, he was a member of James II's parliament and represented Oxford University in a number of parliaments beginning in 1689. His career is described in Millicent Rex, *University Representation in England, 1604–1690* (London, 1954), 266–72.

71. Howell, *A Complete Collection of State Trials*, XII, 378, 382.

72. *Ibid.*, 385–88.

73. *Ibid.*, 391.

74. *Ibid.*, 410–12. Williams had moved from an earlier support of exclusion to a willingness to uphold the unpopular royal policy of religious toleration. Yet he took the same view of the legislative power as anti-court elements. That this was so may help explain why the judges, probably equally ambivalent in their outlook, decided to let the jury decide whether the king had a dispensing power. It was a matter that ordinarily would have fallen to the judges. Tanner, *English Constitutional Conflicts of the Seventeenth Century*, 294.

75. Howell, *A Complete Collection of State Trials*, XII, 427–29.

76. *Ibid.*, 420–21.

77. Kenyon, *Revolution Principles: The Politics of Party, 1689–1720*, 22, 24–32. Kenyon is skeptical about the providentialist theory, suggesting that it was no more than a pious platitude. In this connection, see also note 112, Chapter 3 of this study. He concludes that 'the strict *de facto* theory' was left 'in possession of the field; that is, the theory that the Revolution, whatever its motives, and the conduct of James II, whatever its precise nature, had resulted in an ineluctable situation in which

the king *de jure*, without prejudice to his long-term right, had simply been replaced by a king *de facto*, to whom a qualified and limited allegiance was owing, but who enjoyed no legal rights'. But Kenyon says nothing of the community-centered ideology discussed in this study, which stands squarely in the way of his conclusion. He does write at one point that the whig view of the Revolution was based firmly on English history, but there is no attempt made to link the whig interest in medieval history with the subject of a parliamentary sovereignty in king, lords, and commons. *Ibid.*, 35–37. Nor can it be stated that the community-centered ideology was confined to the whigs, increasingly described by modern scholars as a minority in the late seventeenth century, since whig and tory alike accepted the Bill of Rights. That statute, as will be seen, reflected the community-centered ideology. No move was ever made to rescind it, despite the more conservative political atmosphere at times in Queen Anne's reign. Moreover, at the height of the Sacheverell affair, the house of lords ordered that the Oxford decree of 1683, which explicitly condemned the community-centered ideology, be burned publicly by the common hangman, an action reaffirming the acceptance of that ideology. Another sign of its continuing influence was the defense by Dr Sacheverell's counsel. H. T. Dickinson, *Liberty and Property: Political Ideology in Eighteenth-Century Britain* (London, 1977), 49–50. Cp. Holmes, *The Trial of Doctor Sacheverell*, 140, 181–84. And then there was the continued use of the parliamentarian formula regarding the human source of political power and authority. On this point an anonymous pamphleteer was instructive when he declared: 'All government is from God, that is certain; but the different forms of government are of human stamp, and suitable to the genius and inclinations of the people. But there being so many tracts lately printed upon this subject, it would be tautology to proceed.' *Some Modest Remarks on Dr. Sherlock's New Book about the Case of Allegiance due to Sovereign Power, etc.* (London, 1691), 4. A very interesting tract reflecting the community-centered ideology and thoroughly representative of this genre, is *A Friendly Debate between Dr. Kingsman, a Dissatisfied Clergy-man, and Gratianus Trimmer, a Neighbour Minister*, 6, 13–16, 18, 22, 23, 28–29, 35, 39, 42, 47, 50, 56–57, 61, 70–71, 77. The first volume of the state tracts published at the Revolution includes numerous pertinent tracts such as 'The

Desertion Discussed', *A Collection of State Tracts Publish'd on Occasion of the late Revolution,* I, 110; 'An Enquiry into the present State of Affairs', *ibid.,* 130, 131; Ferguson, 'A Brief Justification of the Prince of Orange's Descent into England', *ibid.,* 135–40, especially 138; 'Some Remarks upon Government', *ibid.,* 152–53, 158, 162; 'Four questions Debated', *ibid.,* 163, 165; Edward Stephens, 'Important Questions of State, Law, Justice, and Prudence, Both Civil and Religious, upon the Late Revolutions and Present State of these Nations', *ibid.,* 167–74; 'Some Short Considerations relating to the Settling of the Government', *ibid.,* 175, 176; 'The Proceedings of the Present Parliament Justified by the Opinion of the most Judicious and Learned Hugo Grotius, with Considerations thereupon', *ibid.,* 178–84; 'A Defence of their Majesties King William and Queen Mary', *ibid.,* 191–92, 206; 'A Word to the Wise for Settling the Government', *ibid.,* 227–28; 'Reflections upon the Late Great Revolution', *ibid.,* 254–59, 261; 'The Advantages of the Present Settlement', *ibid.,* 269, 272; 'A Brief Account of the Nullity of King James' Title, and of the Obligation of the Present Oath of Allegiance', *ibid.,* 280–85; Peter Allix, 'An Examination of the Scruples of Those who Refuse to take the Oath of Allegiance', *ibid.,* 301–18; Samuel Masters, 'The Case of Allegiance in our present Circumstances considered', *ibid.,* 318–33; 'The Doctrine of Passive Obedience and Jure Divino disprov'd', *ibid.,* 368–71; Thomas Long, 'A Resolution of Certain Queries concerning Submission to the present Government', *ibid.,* 450–51; Allix, 'Reflections upon the Opinions of some Modern Divines concerning the Nature of Government in General, and that of England in Particular', *ibid.,* 466–514; and 'An Historical Account of some Things relating to the Nature of the English Government and the Conceptions which our Forefathers had of it', *ibid.,* 575–97. See also 'Plain English', *ibid.,* II, 85–86; and Matthew Tindal, 'An Essay concerning Obedience to the Supreme Powers [1694]', *ibid.,* 432–34, The relationship between the co-ordination principle and the idea of resistance at the Revolution is discussed in the Appendix of this study. The tracts described there provide further signs of the large-scale influence of the community-centered ideology. Two recent articles consider the conquest theory : Mark Goldie, 'Edmund Bohun and *Jus Gentium* in the Revolution Debate, 1689–1693', *Historical Journal,* xx (1977), 569–86; M. P. Thompson, 'The Idea of Conquest in Controversies over the 1688 Revolution', *Journal of the History of Ideas*, XXXVIII (1977), 33–46.

78. The Bill of Rights begins 'whereas the lords spiritual and temporal and commons assembled at Westminster, lawfully, fully and freely representing all the estates of the people of this realm.' The language – unlike that in the book of common prayer, discussed in Chapter 6 of this study – is somewhat ambiguous. Its authors could have worked from the definition of estates in the Answer to the Nineteen Propositions since the idea that the lords spiritual, lords temporal, and commons represented 'fully . . . all the estates of the people of this realm' left the way open for a king who was an estate of parliament if not 'of the people of this realm'. Some light is cast on the subject by the pamphlet literature at the time of the Danby impeachment. Those who treated the king as one of the three estates described the clergy as one of the estates of the kingdom but not of parliament. Stillingfleet, *The Grand Question, concerning the Bishops Right to Vote in Parliament in Cases Capital*, 161–62, 171. For conflicting interpretations of the language of estates in the Bill of Rights, see British Library, Lansdowne MS. 737, fo. 33v., and Henry Maddock, *An Account of the Life and Writings of Lord Chancellor Somers* (London, 1812), 263. There were leading members of the convention parliament who invoked Charles I's definition of estates. This appears to have been true, for example, of Sir Robert Sawyer, earlier a member of the bishops' counsel; it can be stated confidently about Colonel John Birch. Both were appointed to the committee that prepared the Bill of Rights. Maddock, *ibid.*, Appendix, No. 1 ('Notes of Debates in the Convention Parliament'), 3, 11. These are Somers' notes of the debates in the convention house of commons, January 28 and 29, 1689, reprinted from the *Hardwicke State Papers (Miscellaneous State Papers from 1501 to 1726)*, ed. Philip Yorke (London, 1778), II, 401–25. These are cited hereafter as Somers, 'Notes of Debates in the Convention Parliament.' The doubt about Sawyer rises out of the report of the same speech in the recently published 'A Jornall of the Convention at Westminster begun the 22 of January 1688/9', ed. Lois Schwoerer, *Bulletin of the Institute of Historical Research*, XLIX (1976), 252. Charles I's definition of estates was used in the convention house of lords. Morrice MSS, Q, 460. Maddock, *ibid.*, 263–71, has a list of the 'great names . . . at variance on this very embroiled affair'.

79. Somers, 'Notes of Debates in the Convention Parliament', 3; 'A Jornall of the Convention at Westminster', ed. Schwoerer, 250–51. Howard was a member of the two Powle committees of 1673. See Chapter 6 of this study, notes 33 and 47. See also Hugh Boscawen's speech, 'A Jornall of the Convention at Westminster', ed. Schwoerer. 254–55. The 'Jornall' reveals that of those present in the convention house of commons, three voted against the resolution in committee and only one in the full house. *Ibid.*, 247, 261. But see *ibid.*, 247, note 2, for the comment that there was actually more opposition to the resolution than this vote suggests. Howard had used an incomplete statement of the quotation from Bracton and Fleta, discussed earlier in this study. It may be supposed that the references to 'arbitrary government' in the debates are to the Bodinian version of the order theory of kingship.

80. Grey, *Debates of the House of Commons*, IX, 36. Somers, 'Notes of Debates in the Convention Parliament', 17. Note 51, Chapter 6 of this study.

81. Horwitz, 'Parliament and the Glorious Revolution', 50. Nottingham seems to have opposed the idea that the king was one of the three estates. See his speech in the debate on the word 'abdicated' where he rejected the policy of declaring the throne vacant, on the ground apparently that the effect was to make the king a member of the three estates. Cobbett, *Parliamentary History of England*, V, 105.

82. Grey, *Debates of the House of Commons*, IX, 29–37. Somers, 'Notes of Debates in the Convention Parliament', 11–20.

83. *Journals of the House of Commons*, X, 17.

84. *Ibid.*, 19, 20, 21–22. Grey, *Debates of the House of Commons*, IX, 51–52,

85. It has often been noted that the men of 1688–89 viewed themselves as conservatives, correcting revolutionary tendencies on the part of their monarchs, in particular, James II. E. N. Williams, *The Eighteenth-Century Constitution, 1688–1815: Documents and Commentary* (Cambridge, 1960), 3. Western, *Monarchy and Revolution*, 326–28. Robert Frankle, 'The Formulation of the Declaration of Rights', *Historical Journal*, XVII (1974), 265–79. If contemporary comment is accepted with regard to the antiquity of a shared law-making power and the subsequent illegality of the dispensing power, an interpretation of the Bill of Rights emerges like that of Frankle, who describes it as 'a mere declaration of existing rights' and as 'the non-

binding recitation of traditionally claimed liberties'. *Ibid.*, 269–70. Jennifer Carter agrees. Finding in the provision for the succession to the throne the major constitutional change, she follows Ogg in calling attention to the revised coronation oath by which William and Mary were sworn to govern according to 'the statutes in parliament agreed on, and the laws and customs of the same'. Since this clause in the coronation oath is of a piece with the fate of the dispensing power, it is difficult to understand her perfunctory attention to its disposition and her conclusion that the Bill of Rights imposed restrictions on royal power only to a very limited degree. 'The Revolution and the Constitution', *Britain after the Glorious Revolution 1689–1714*, ed. Geoffrey Holmes (London, 1969), 39–43, 55. A different impression is conveyed by the account in Horwitz, 'Parliament and the Glorious Revolution', where it is suggested that those around William, and perhaps even William himself, viewed the stipulations in the Bill of Rights as usurpations on the crown. But if he entertained any idea of opposing the Bill of Rights for such a reason, he quickly abandoned it. *Ibid.*, 47–49. See also Clayton Roberts' discussion of 'The Constitutional Significance of the Financial Settlement of 1690', *Historical Journal*, XX (1977), 59–76. Ogg's comments on the coronation oath are in *England in the Reigns of James II and William III*, 235–39. His conclusion that the clause mentioned above was 'an obvious and non-controversial change' requires no comment. *Ibid.*, 236. It is not intended to imply here that only the provisions regarding the dispensing power were new in 1689. Schwoerer has concluded that 'so far as the standing army issue is concerned, the Bill of Rights was a revolutionary document'. By no means ancient law, the pertinent clause 'was a revolutionary assertion, which reflected parliamentarian and republican thinking since 1641–42'. *'No Standing Armies!': The Antiarmy Ideology in Seventeenth-Century England* (Baltimore, 1974), 151. Since those objecting to this prerogative did so in terms of mixed and balanced government, one is reminded once more of the influence of the Answer to the Nineteen Propositions. See also her account of the parliamentary leaders who kept the issue of a standing army alive in Charles II's cavalier parliament. There is a helpful list in *ibid.*, 96.

86. At the Revolution, William Bentinck, the most important of William of Orange's advisers in Holland, worked closely with

Henry Sidney and James Johnstone in England. Powle's name is on the list of Bentinck's correspondents, and Johnstone was in close touch with both Hampden and Lee. British Library, Add. MS. 34515, fos. 80–81 (June 18, 1688). Jones, *The Revolution of 1688 in England*, 169–70, 225, 235–36. There is an account of Powle's activities shortly after the prince landed in 'Henry Powle', 'draft biographies for the History of Parliament Trust', ed. Henning. See also Schwoerer, 'No Standing Armies !' *passim*.

87. Weston, *English Constitutional Theory and the House of Lords*, 87–123.

88. 'Henry Powle', 'draft biographies for the History of Parliament Trust', ed. Henning. See note 89 below.

89. 'Richard Hampden', 'draft biographies for the History of Parliament Trust', ed. Henning. Hampden's leadership in the convention house of commons is said to have been almost unrivalled, Lacey, *Dissent and Parliamentary Politics in England, 1661–1689*, 228, 359, note 67. That Powle and Hampden influenced the proceedings of the convention house of commons at important junctures in the proceedings is undoubted. 'A Jornall of the Convention at Westminster', ed. Schwoerer, 245, 247, 248, 251, 259, 262. Thus Hampden helped moderate the tone of the debates, and when the time came for him to carry the resolution of January 28 to the house of lords, Powle urged members to accompany him, saying 'Pray gentlemen attend your chairman, for the lords take great notice how votes are attended.' *Ibid.*, 262.

90. 'Sir Thomas Lee', 'draft biographies for the History of Parliament Trust', ed. Henning. Weston, *English Constitutional Theory and the House of Lords*, 93, 118, 120.

91. *Ibid.*, 118, 120, 123. Usually John Somers is named as chairman of the committee of the convention house of commons that prepared the Bill of Rights, probably because of Macaulay; but, more recently, Michael Landon assigned the position to Treby. *The Triumph of the Lawyers*, 237, 238, 283, note 50. In fact, Treby served as chairman until February 7, and on the following day, for reasons that are obscure, Somers emerged as chairman in his place. *Journals of the House of Commons*, x, 15, 21–22, 23. Lois Schwoerer, who is preparing a study of the Bill of Rights, gave help on this point.

92. Petyt's library is described in note 28, Chapter 7 of this study.

93. *The Declaration of the Lords Spiritual and Temporal, and*

*Commons Assembled at Westminster* (London, 1689), 1–2. The Treby committee at first did not distinguish between the dispensing and suspending powers. Morrice MSS, Q, 457–58.

94. *Journals of the House of Commons*, x, 294. Williams, *The Eighteenth-Century Constitution, 1688–1815*, 33.

95. *Journals of the House of Lords*, xiv, 362, 418. H. M. C. *Twelfth Report, Appendix, Part VI. The Manuscripts of the House of Lords, 1689–1690*, 361.

96. Cobbett, *Parliamentary History of England*, v, 346. See also *ibid.*, v, 318.

97. Grey, *Debates of the House of Commons*, ix, 25. Morrice MSS. Q, 444. For the vote in the house of commons, see note 79 above.

98. Petyt, *Jus Parliamentarium*, 136, marginal note.

99. Grey, *Debates of the House of Commons*, ix, 12. See also 'A Jornall of the Convention at Westminster', ed. Schwoerer, 252 (Sir Henry Capell); 255 (Sir William Pulteney); and 258 (Sir John Maynard).

100. Grey, *Debates of the House of Commons*, ix, 19–20.

101. H.M.C. *Twelfth Report, Appendix, Part VI. The Manuscripts of the House of Lords, 1689–1690*, 15.

102. *Ibid.*, 15–16. Cobbett, *Parliamentary History of England*, v, 59.

103. Ogg, *England in the Reigns of James II and William III*, 226–27. Morrice MSS, Q, 445, 449, 453, 456.

104. H.M.C. *Portland Manuscripts*, iii, 439. The preface to Seller, *The History of Passive Obedience*, no pagination, has a passage reflecting the suddenness and completeness with which the contract idea preempted the center of the stage at the Revolution. See also Clarendon's comment in the house of lords. Cobbett, *Parliamentary History of England*, v, 76. Gough relates the idea of contract held earlier by Herle to that put forward at the Revolution. He thinks it almost a commonplace by the time of the Revolution. *The Social Contract: A Critical Study of its Development* (Oxford, second edition, 1957, reprinted 1967), 91.

105. Holmes, *British Politics in the Age of Anne*, 60.

106. Note 85 of this chapter of this study.

107. Quoted in Landon, *The Triumph of the Lawyers*, 219. The speech was printed as *The Speech of Sir George Treby, Kt. Recorder of the Honourable City of London to his Highness the Prince of Orange, December the 20th, 1688*. See also 'A

Jornall of the Convention at Westminster', ed. Schwoerer, 259–60.

108. Grey, *Debates of the House of Commons*, IX, 33. Sacheverell is mentioned in Weston, *English Constitutional Theory and the House of Lords*, 92–123, *passim*. He was appointed to the second Powle committee of 1673 and also to the committee at the Revolution that prepared the new coronation oath. See note 47 of Chapter 6 of this study and note 85 of Chapter 8.

109. Also requiring mention as representative of the ideological outlook at the Revolution is George Petyt, *Lex Parliamentaria, or, A Treatise of the Laws and Customs of the Parliaments of England* (London, 1690), licensed on December 6, 1689 and reprinted in 1707. Assigning sovereign power to parliament as a legislature, it borrows liberally from Atkyns and William Petyt. According to Atwood, also part of this group, 'the judgment of king, lords, and commons' was 'of uncontrollable authority'. Howell, *A Complete Collection of State Trials*, XI, 1312. Also to be consulted is Sir John Hawles' speech during the Sacheverell trial. *Ibid.*, XV, 118–19. Other pertinent materials include Henry Care's much reprinted *English Liberties*, 120–21, and the anonymous *University Loyalty*, 17–19. A tract of much more than ordinary interest, written when politics under Queen Anne were at a boil, is Benjamin Hoadly's *Original and Institution of Civil Government, Discussed,* published in 1709 although dated 1710 by the printers. A Lockean theorist, willing to justify revolution under the right circumstances, and the most vigorous clerical spokesman for the whig position in his generation, Hoadly had no qualms about making explicit use of the word 'co-ordination' in writing about lawmaking, despite its civil-war associations and the obloquy that it brought him from high tory writers like Charles Leslie. It is of the more interest that this work was published just before the house of commons voted that Hoadly merited the favor of that house for his strenuous espousal of revolution principles and as the impeachment trial of Sacheverell was getting under way. Hoadly summarized what he saw as the conflicting ideologies of his day – the theory of order as reflected in Filmer's patriarchalism and the community-centered view of government – and explained why the Filmerian scheme of government, in his view, had to be rejected. His explanation had the merit of relating the two ideologies to interpretations of the Glorious Revolution when he wrote : 'Neither can our whole

constitution, as consisting of king or queen, lords, and commons, be so much as agreeable to the will of God, according to
this scheme; or stand secure; if this [patriarchal scheme] be
once admitted. For, according to these principles, it is the will
of God that absolute uncontrollable authority, in making laws,
as well as executing them, should be lodged in the hands of
one single man : and all other forms are deviations from his
institution; the effect of popular madness; the voice of the
people, i.e. the voice of Belzebub, and the like. If this be true
therefore, it was so far from being blameable in a late king, to
endeavour to subvert this constitution; to destroy all appearances of any authority, co-ordinate with his own in legislation;
and to set up a dispensing power in himself over all laws; that
it was indeed his duty to do what he did : and the duty of a
Christian nation to thank him for bringing them into the right
way, and establishing them upon the only true foundation.
No wonder, therefore, that the writers who defend this scheme,
are perpetually railing at the pretended authority of lords and
commons, to make laws in conjunction with the king; and
crying up the glorious effects of absolute monarchy; and preparing men's minds to accept of it, or even to invite it in
amongst us, upon any terms : as it is, certainly, our indispensable duty to do, upon this scheme.' But this was not
Hoadly's view of the constitution. He continued : 'That
power [of the two houses] is co-ordinate with the king's in
legislation, without which the king can make no law,
according to the constitution : but without the authority
of the parliament, no law is of force. Therefore the houses of
parliament have a co-ordinate power in legislation. As they
without him, so he without them, cannot make a law : and as
it is he that enacts, so it is by their active authority likewise,
that every law is said to be enacted; and not only with their
passive consent. The members of one house are chosen voluntarily by the people; and in making laws, act entirely as their
representatives, in conjunction with the king : and therefore
are something more than a sluice to a mill, which is drawn up,
and let down entirely at the miller's pleasure; which is the
best compliment the author I have been speaking of can bestow
upon them. I wonder indeed, he could permit himself to go so
far : when even this low similitude will prove them to be so
necessary, that no law can be made without them. But we see
what such men are driving at, by fixing schemes upon Almighty

God; even to ruin the best contrived constitution, merely
because it is the result of human wisdom.' *The Works of Benjamin Hoadly* (London, three vols., 1773), II, 241–42. For the
ascendancy of Hoadly's position in the church of England after
the Jacobite rebellion of 1715, see Holmes, *The Trial of Doctor
Sacheverell*, 274–75. The eighteenth-century developments are
discussed in H. T. Dickinson, 'The Eighteenth-Century Debate
on the Sovereignty of Parliament', *Transactions of the Royal
Historical Society*, Fifth Series, XXVI (1976), 189–210. See
especially *ibid.*, 196, for an account of how the parliamentarian
formula regarding the human source of political power and
authority was now being utilized to reconcile the doctrine of
non-resistance with that of parliamentary sovereignty in king,
lords, and commons. Dickinson has expounded this position in
greater detail in his more recent *Liberty and Property: Political Ideology in Eighteenth-Century Britain*, 46–50.

<h2 style="text-align:center">APPENDIX</h2>

1. *An Examination of the Scruples of Those who Refuse to take
   the Oath of Allegiance*, 32. Allix's importance as a pamphleteer is assessed in Salmon, *The French Religious Wars in
   English Political Thought*, 154–55.
2. *A Letter to a Bishop concerning the Present Settlement, and
   the New Oaths* (London, 1689), 5–6. Four editions of this
   tract appeared in 1689. It was attributed at the time to the
   learned Thomas Comber, Dean of Durham, a great supporter
   of the earl of Danby at the Revolution but later a whig in his
   political credo. In his autobiography Comber denied that he
   had written the tract but expressed admiration for its argument. Curiously, however, a manuscript copy of the tract, in
   Comber's writing, is extant. Another author suggested is Dr
   Edward Gee, of the Manchester Gees, about whom little is
   known beyond the fact that he was made chaplain in ordinary
   to William and Mary, as was Comber. Introduction to *The
   Autobiographies and Letters of Thomas Comber*, ed. C. E.
   Whiting (Surtees Society, 1946). See also *ibid.*, I, 22; II, 170–71.
   There is also pertinent material in Ferguson, *A Brief Justifi-
   cation of the Prince of Orange's Descent*, 13–14, 15.
3. *A Representation of the Threatening Dangers, Impending over
   Protestants in Great Britain*, 30.

4. *A Friendly Debate between Dr. Kingsman, a Dissatisfied Clergy-man, and Gratianus Trimmer, a Neighbour Minister*, 44. This author wrote : 'All the gentlemen that I have discoursed with, who took up arms, profess they would never have taken arms against the king ruling by law, as he was bound to do; but look'd upon him [James II] as no king. *i.e.* no legal king of England in the exercise of his power'. *Ibid.*, 40.

5. Samuel Masters, *The Case of Allegiance in our Present Circum-stances Consider'd* (London, 1689), 12.

6. An anonymous pamphleteer inquired : 'Who shall take this forfeiture, supposing it be made, since the king hath no superior but God? I answer with Bracton, his court of barons, and great council, who share with him in the sovereignty, and represent the whole nation, with whom the compact is made'. And in another passage he wrote : 'In a mixt monarchy, if one of the estates will transgress all its limits, and swallow up the other two, they must then have a right to prevent this intoler-able mischief to the community; and where nothing else can secure the public, than taking the forfeiture, there they may do it, yea, must do it, or the legal government would certainly be dissolved.' *The New Oath of Allegiance Justified, from the Original Constitution of the English Monarchy*, 17, 18. For-feiture took place only when there had been 'a manifest attempt to change the nature of the government'. *Ibid.*, 16. The argu-ment for forfeiture may have come from Samuel Pufendorf. Salmon, *The French Religious Wars in English Political Thought*, 134, note 14. See, in particular, *A Full Answer to all the Popular Objections that have yet Appeared, for not Taking the Oath of Allegiance to their Present Majesties*, 33. This tract may have been written by Thomas Long. Seller, *History of Passive Obedience*, 115.

7. 'Some Short Considerations relating to the Settling of the Government; Humbly offer'd to the Lords and Commons . . . at Westminster', *A Collection of State Tracts, Publish'd on Occasion of the late Revolution*, 1, 176–77. The author may have been following George Lawson, whose *Politica Sacra et Civilis* was published under two different titles at the Revo-lution. That Lawson influenced Locke on this particular point is an important theme in Julian Franklin, *John Locke and the Theory of Sovereignty: Mixed Monarchy and the Right of Resistance in the Political Thought of the English Revolution* (Cambridge, 1978).

8. *An Examination of the Scruples of Those who Refuse to take the Oath of Allegiance*, 10, 11, 22, 26. The argument from Grotius was used earlier in the century to justify resistance to Charles I. See, for example, Marchamont Nedham, *The Case of the Commonwealth of England, Stated* [1650] ed. Philip Knachel (Washington, D.C., 1969), 35–36; Baxter, *A Holy Commonwealth*, 466–70, 479. For another argument from Grotius, used at the Revolution, see Goldie, 'Edmund Bohun and *Jus Gentium* in the Revolution Debate', 569–86.

9 Edward Stephens, *Important Questions of State, Law, Justice, and Prudence, Both Civil and Religious, upon the Late Revolutions and Present State of these Nations* (London, 1689), 4–5. See also 1–2 and 9. This was printed in the state tracts published at the Revolution. No mention is made of Grotius, but the debt is unmistakable in Tindal, 'An Essay concerning Obedience to the Supreme Power', *A Collection of State Tracts Published on Occasion of the late Revolution*, II, 434. This is, moreover, a succinct yet extraordinarily complete statement of the argument for resistance based on the co-ordination principle.

10. *Important Questions of State, Law, Justice, and Prudence*, 6.

11. *The Historian Unmask'd*, 34–36, 47–49. Long, 'A Resolution of Certain Queries concerning Submission to the Present Government', *A Collection of State Tracts, Publish'd on Occasion of the late Revolution*, I, 444, 450, 464. See also 'Some Short Considerations relating to the Settling of the Government; Humbly offer'd to the Lords and Commons . . . at Westminster', *ibid*, I, 176; 'The Proceedings of the Present Parliament Justified by the Opinion of the most Judicious and Learned Hugo Grotius; with Considerations thereupon', *ibid*., I, 178–84; and 'An Historical Account of Some Things Relating to the Nature of the English Government', *ibid*., I, 594.

12. Long, *The Historian Unmask'd*, 42. Other pertinent tracts are mentioned in note 89, Chapter 7 of this study. See also John J. Hughes, 'The Missing "Last Words" of Gilbert Burnet in July 1687', *Historical Journal*, xx (1977), 221–27, especially Hughes' description of Burnet's position, *ibid*., 222–23.

13. *Christianity, A Doctrine of the Cross: or, Passive Obedience, under any Pretended Invasion of Legal Rights and Liberties* (London, 1691), 68.

14. *Ibid*., 68–69.

15. *Second Treatise of Government*, ed. Laslett, 414, 455, 456. J. W. Gough, *John Locke's Political Philosophy* (Oxford, 1950),

N

102–15 According to Gough, Locke viewed the legislature as legally sovereign despite his reference to fundamental law in the *Second Treatise.*

16. *Second Treatise of Government*, ed. Laslett, Chap. xiv. John Dunn, *The Political Thought of John Locke* (Cambridge, 1969), Chap. 8, p. 127, etc. See also Charles D. Tarlton, 'A Rope of Sand : Interpreting Locke's *First Treatise of Government*', *Historical Journal*, xxi (1978), 71.

17. *Second Treatise of Government*, ed. Laslett, Chap. xix, p. 460. The statement above paraphrases Locke's comment, but it is not always easy to decipher his meaning since he first discussed what must happen if the legislature became arbitrary, only to switch to an account of the consequences of such behavior on the part of the supreme executive.

18. *Second Treatise of Government*, ed. Laslett, Chapter xix, especially pp. 460–61, 462.

19. *Ibid.*, 456.

20. *Ibid.*, 454, note.

# Bibliography

## MANUSCRIPT SOURCES

Bodleian Library. Tanner MS. 28, 34, 36, 103.

British Library. Additional MS. 34512, 34513, 34515.

British Library. Lansdowne MS. 737.

Dr Williams' Library. Roger Morrice Collection. MSS P, Q, and R. 'The Entring Book, Being an Historical Register of Occurrences from April An : 1677 to April, 1691.'

'Draft Biographies for the History of Parliament Trust.' 1660–90. Ed. Basil D. Henning.

Inner Temple MSS.

    Petyt MS. 512, Vols. L, M, N, and T.

    Petyt MS. 533, Vol. 15.

    Petyt MS. 535, Vols. 1–3.

    Petyt MS. 538, Vol. 17.

    Petyt MS. Miscellaneous MS. No. 61; No. 152.

Public Record Office.

    P.R.O. 30/24/6B.

    P.R.O. P.C. 2/53.

Savile, George, Marquess of Halifax. 'Prerogative.' Transcript of a manuscript in the possession of Dr Mark N. Brown. See below under 'Savile'.


## PRIMARY SOURCES

All law reports cited below, with the exception of those in the *Year Books*, are in the *English Reports*. 166 vols. 1865–1900; reprinted, 176 vols. 1900–30.

*An Account of Mr. Parkinson's Expulsion from the University of Oxford in the late Times*. London, 1689.

Acherley, Roger. *The Britannic Constitution: or, The Fundamental Form of Government in Britain*. 2nd ed. London, 1759.

Allix, Peter. *An Examination of the Scruples of Those who Refuse to take the Oath of Allegiance.* London, 1689.

Anderson, Edmund. *Les Reports du Treserudite Edmund Anderson.* London, 1664.

*An Answer to Dr. Stillingfleet's Sermon, by some Nonconformists.* London, 1680.

*The Arraignment of Co-ordinate Power.* London, 1683.

Assheton, William. *Evangelium Armatum: A Specimen; or Short Collection of several Doctrines and Positions destructive to our Government Both Civil and Ecclesiastical.* London, 1663.

  *The Royal Apology: or, An Answer to the Rebels Plea.* 2nd ed. London, 1685.

Atkyns, Sir Robert. *An Enquiry into the Power of Dispensing with Penal Statutes.* London, 1689.

  *The Lord Chief Baron Atkyns' Speech to Sir William Ashhurst, Lord Mayor Elect of the City of London.* London, 1693.

  *The Power, Jurisdiction and Priviledge of Parliament; and the Antiquity of the House of Commons Asserted.* London, 1689.

  *A Treatise of the True and Ancient Jurisdiction of the House of Peers.* London, 1699.

Atwood, William. *Fundamental Constitution of the English Government.* London, 1690.

  *Jani Anglorum Facies Nova.* London, 1680.

  *Jus Anglorum ab Antiquo: or, a Confutation of an Important Libel against the Government by King, Lords, and Commons.* London, 1681.

  *A Letter of Remarks on Jovian, by a Person of Quality.* London, 1683.

  'The Lord Chief Justice Herbert's Account Examined by William Atwood.' In T. B. Howell. *A Complete Collection of State Trials and Proceedings for High Treasons and Other Crimes and Misdemeanors from the Earliest Period to the Year 1783.* Vol. XI, cols. 1280–1316, London, 1811.

Aylmer, John. *An Harborowe for faithfull and Trewe Subjectes, agaynst the late Blowne Blaste, concerning the Government of Women.* Strassburg, 1559.

Bacon, Sir Francis. *The Letters and Life of Francis Bacon.* Ed. James K. Spedding. 7 vols. London, 1861–72.

  *Works.* Ed. James K. Spedding, Robert L. Ellis, and Douglas D. Heath. 10 vols. London, 1877–79.

Bacon, Nathaniel. *An Historical Discourse of the Uniformity of the Government of England.* 2 vols. in one. London, 1647.

Bagshaw, Edward (the Elder). *The Rights of the Crown of England as it is established by Law.* London, 1660.

    *Speech in Parliament, February the Ninth, 1640, concerning Episcopacy and the London Petition.* London, 1641.

Ball, William. *The Power of Kings Discussed: or, An Examen of the Fundamental Constitution of the Free-Born People of England.* London, 1649.

Barrington, John Shute. *The Revolution and Anti-Revolution Principles Stated and Compar'd.* London, 1714.

Bate, George. *The Regal Apology, or the Declaration of the Commons, Feb. 11, 1647. Canvassed.* London, 1648.

Baxter, Richard. *A Holy Commonwealth, or, Political Aphorisms opening the True Principles of Government.* London, 1659.

    *Reliquiae Baxterianae: or, Mr. Richard Baxter's Narrative of the most Memorable Passages of his Life and Times.* Ed. Matthew Sylvester. Vol. I. London, 1696.

Bellamy, John. *A Justification of the City Remonstrance and its Vindication.* London, 1646.

Benloe, William. *Les Reports de Gulielme Bendloes [and Dalison].* London, 1689.

Blackstone, William. *Commentaries on the Laws of England.* 4 vols. Oxford, 1765–69.

Bodin, Jean. *The Six Bookes of a Commonweale: A Facsimile reprint of the English translation of 1606.* Ed. Kenneth Douglas McRae. Cambridge, Mass., 1962.

*Book of Common Prayer.* Cambridge, 1663.

Bowyer, Robert. *Parliamentary Diary, 1606–1607.* Ed. David H. Willson. Minneapolis, 1931.

Brady, Robert. *A Complete History of England, from the First Entrance of the Romans under the Conduct of Julius Caesar, unto the End of the Reign of King Henry III.* Vol. I. London, 1685.

    *An Historical Treatise of Cities, and Burghs or Boroughs.* London, 1690.

    *An Introduction to the Old English History, Comprehended in Three several Tracts . . . Together with An Appendix . . . And a Glossary, expounding many Words used frequently in our Antient Records, Laws and Historians.* London, 1684.

Bramston, Sir John. *Autobiography.* Ed. Lord Braybrooke. Camden Society, 1845.

Bridge, William. *The Wounded Conscience Cured.* London, 1643.

Brooke, Sir Robert. *La Graunde Abridgement.* Ed. R. Tottell. London, 1586.

Browning, Andrew, ed. *English Historical Documents, 1660–1714.* Vol. VIII. London and New York, 1953.

Brydall, John. *The Absurdity of that New devised State-Principle, (Viz.) That in a Monarchy, the Legislative Power is Communicable to the Subject, and is not radically in Soveraignty in one, but in More.* London, 1681.

    *A New Years Gift for the Anti-Prerogative Men.* London, 1682.

Buchanan, George. *De Jure Regni Apud Scotos, or, a Dialogue, concerning the due Privilege of Government in the Kingdom of Scotland, Betwixt George Buchanan and Thomas Maitland.* N.p., 1687.

Burnet, Gilbert. *A Collection of Eighteen Papers, relating to the Affairs of Church and State, during the Reign of King James the Second.* London, 1689.

    *History of his own Time: with the Suppressed Passages of the first Volume, and Notes, by the Earls of Dartmouth and Hardwicke, and Speaker Onslow.* Vol. III. Oxford, 1823.

    *Some Sermons Preach'd on Several Occasions.* London, 1713.

Burnett, Thomas. *An Essay upon Government.* London, 1716.

Butler, Charles. *The Feminine Monarchie: or, a Treatise Concerning Bees, and the Due Ordering of them.* Oxford, 1609.

*Calendar of State Papers, Domestic Series.* 81 vols. 1603–1714.

*Calendar of State Papers and Manuscripts, Relating to English Affairs Existing in the Archives and Collections of Venice, and in other Libraries of Northern Italy.* Ed. Allen B. Hinds. Vol. XXXVIII (1673–75). London, 1947.

Care, Henry. *Animadversions on a Late Paper Entituled, A Letter to a Dissenter upon Occasion of His Majesties Late Gracious Declaration of Indulgence.* London, 1687.

    *English Liberties.* 4th. ed. London, 1719.

    *A Vindication of the Proceedings of His Majesties Ecclesiastical Commissioners against the Bishop of London and the Fellows of Magdalen College.* London, 1688.

Carte, Thomas. *An History of the Life of James Duke of Ormonde.* Vol. II. London, 1736.

Carthew, Thomas. *Reports of Cases Adjudged in the Court of King's Bench.* London, 1741.

*The Case of Allegiance in our Present Circumstances consider'd.* London, 1689.

*A Catalogue of the Names of the Knights, Citizens, and Burgesses, that have served in the last Four Parliaments . . . with the names of such Noblemen, Knights, and Gentlemen, as met in the Parliament at Oxford.* London, 1656.

*Certaine Sermons or Homilies Appointed to be Read in Churches in the time of Queen Elizabeth I.* Gainesville, Florida, 1968.

Charles I. *His Majesties Answer to the XIX. Propositions of Both Houses of Parliament.* London, 1642.

 *His Majesties Declaration to both Houses of Parliament . . . in Answer to that presented to him at New-Market the 9th of March 1641 [1642].* London, 1642.

 *The Works of King Charles the Martyr: with a Collection of Declarations, Treatises and other Papers.* 2nd. ed. London, 1687.

*Christianity. A Doctrine of the Cross: or, Passive Obedience, under any Pretended Invasion of Legal Rights and Liberties.* London, 1691.

Clarke, James S. *The Life of James the Second, King of England, etc. Collected out of Memoirs Writ of His Own Hand.* 2 vols. London, 1816.

Cobbett, William. *Parliamentary History of England: From the Norman Conquest in 1066 to . . . 1803.* 44 vols. London, 1806–38.

Coke, Sir Edward. *The Fourth Part of the Institutes of the Laws of England: Concerning the Jurisdiction of Courts.* Ed. Francis Hargrave. London, 1797.

 'Preface, to the Ninth Report.' *The Reports of Sir Edward Coke, Knt. in English, in Thirteen Parts Complete.* Ed. George Wilson. London, 1777.

 *The Reports of Sir Edward Coke.* London, 1826.

 *Systematic Arrangement of Lord Coke's First Institute of the Laws of England . . . With Annotations of Mr. Hargrave, Lord Chief Justice Hale, and Lord Chancellor Nottingham.* Ed. J. H. Thomas. Philadelphia, 1836.

 *The Third Part of the Institutes of the Laws of England. Concerning High Treason and other Pleas of the Crown and Criminal Causes.* Ed. Francis Hargrave. London, 1797.

*Collection of Papers Relating to Parliaments and the Penal Laws and Tests.* London, 1688–89.

*A Collection of Papers Relating to the Present Juncture of Affairs in England.* N.p., 1688–89.

*A Collection of State Tracts, Publish'd on Occasion of the late*

*Revolution in 1688, and during the Reign of William III*. 3 vols. London, 1705–07.

Comber, Thomas. *The Autobiographies and Letters of Thomas Comber*. Ed. C. E. Whiting. Surtees Society, 1946.

*Commons Debates, 1621*. Ed. Wallace Notestein, Hartley Simpson, and Frances Relf. 7 vols. New Haven, 1935.

Cowell, John. *The Interpreter or, 'Booke Containing the Signification of Words'*. Cambridge, 1607.

Craig, Sir Thomas. *De Unione Regnorum Britanniae Tractatus*. Ed. C. Sanford Terry. Edinburgh, 1909.

Cranford, James. *Plain English, or, The Sectaries Anatomized*. London, 1646.

Dallison, Charles. *The Royalist's Defence: Vindicating the King's Proceedings in the late Warre Made against Him*. N.p., 1648.

Dalrymple, Sir John. *Memoirs of Great Britain and Ireland [1681–92]*. 3 vols. London, 1790.

Davies, Sir John. *The question concerning Impositions, Tonnage, Poundage . . . fully stated and argued from Reason, Law, and Policy*. London, 1656.

*A Declaration of the Lords and Commons of Parliament Assembled at Oxford*. Oxford, 1644.

*The Declaration of the Lords Temporal and Spiritual, and Commons Assembled at Westminster. Presented to the King and Queen, by the Right Honourable the Marquess of Halifax*. London, 1689.

Denton, William. *Jus Regiminis: Being a Justification of Defensive Arms in General*. London, 1689.

Dering, Sir Edward. *Parliamentary Diary, 1670–1673*. Ed. Basil Duke Henning. New Haven, 1940.

D'Ewes, Sir Simonds. *Journal*. Ed. William Havelock Coates. New Haven, 1942.

*The Journals of all the Parliaments during the Reign of Queen Elizabeth*. London, 1682.

*A Dialogue at Oxford between a Tutor and a Gentleman, formerly his Pupil, concerning Government*. London, 1681.

Digby, Sir Kenelm. *The Royal Apology*. Paris, 1648.

Digges, Dudley. *An Answer to a Printed Book, Intituled, Observations upon some of His Majesties Late Answers and Expresses*. Oxford, 1642.

*A Review of the Observations upon some of His Majesties Late Answers and Expresses*. Oxford, 1643.

*The Unlawfulnesse of Subjects taking up Armes against their Soveraigne.* N.p., 1644.

Disney, William. *Nil dictum quod non dictum prius, or, the Case of the Government of England Established by Law.* London 1681.

Dodderidge. John. *The several Opinions of Sundry learned Antiquaries: . . . Touching the Antiquity, Power, Order, State, Manner, Persons and Proceedings of the High-Court of Parliament in England.* London, 1658.

Doughty, John. *The King's Cause Rationally, briefly, and plainly debated, as it Stands Defacto.* N.p., 1644.

Dugdale, Sir William. *The Baronage of England.* London, 1675.

*Life, Diary and Correspondence.* Ed. William Hamper. London, 1827.

*A Short View of the Late Troubles in England.* Oxford, 1681.

Dyer, Sir James. *Reports of Cases.* London, 1794.

Edwards, Thomas. *The Third Part of Gangraena.* London, 1646.

Egerton, Sir Thomas, Lord Ellesmere. *A Discourse upon the Exposicion and Understandinge of Statutes.* Ed. Samuel E. Thorne. San Marino, California, 1942.

'Speciall Observations Touching All the Sessions of the Last Parlement Anno 7 Regis and Etc.' In Louis A. Knafla. *Law and Politics in Jacobean England. The Tracts of Lord Chancellor Ellesmere.* Cambridge, 1977.

*The Speech of the Lord Chancellor of England, in the Exchequer Chamber, touching the Post-nati.* London, 1609.

Elyot, Sir Thomas. *The Boke named Governor.* Ed. S. E. Lehmberg. London, 1962.

Evelyn, John. *The Diary of John Evelyn.* Ed. E. S. de Beer. Vol. IV. Oxford, 1955.

*The Exercitation Answered.* London, 1650.

Ferguson, Robert. *A Brief Justification of the Prince of Orange's Descent into England, And of the Kingdoms Late Recourse to Arms.* London, 1689.

*A Brief Vindication of the Parliamentary Proceedings against the late King James II.* London, 1689.

*A Representation of the Threatening Dangers, Impending over Protestants in Great Britain, Before the Coming of His Highness the Prince of Orange.* N.p., 1689.

Ferne, Henry. *Conscience Satisfied, that there is no warrant for the Armes now taken up by Subjects.* Oxford, 1643.

*A Reply unto Severall Treatises Pleading for the Armes now taken up by Subjects in the pretended defence of Religion and Liberty.* Oxford. 1643.

*The Resolving of Conscience, upon this Question. Whether upon such a Supposition or Case, as is now usually made (the King will not discharge his trust but is bent or seduced to subvert Religion, Laws, and Liberties) Subjects may take Arms and resist: and whether that Case be now.* Cambridge, 1642.

Fiennes, Nathaniel. *A Second Speech . . . in the Commons House of Parliament. Touching the Subjects Liberty against the late canons and the new oath.* London, 1641.

Filmer, Sir Robert. *Patriarcha and Other Political Works.* Ed. Peter Laslett. Oxford, 1949.

Finch, Sir Heneage, First Earl of Nottingham. *A Treatise on the King's Power of Granting Pardons in Cases of Impeachment.* London, 1791.

Finch, Henry. *Law, or a Discourse Thereof.* London, 1627.

Fitzherbert, Anthony. *La Graunde Abridgement.* Ed. Tottell. London, 1565.

Forset, Edward. *A Comparative Discourse of the Bodies Natural and Politique.* London, 1606.

Foster, Elizabeth Read, ed. *Proceedings in Parliament, 1610.* 2 vols. New Haven, 1966.

*A Friendly Debate between Dr. Kingsman, a Dissatisfied Clergyman, and Gratianus Trimmer, a Neighbour Minister.* London, 1689.

*A Full Answer to all the Popular Objections that have yet Appeared, for not taking the Oath of Allegiance to their Present Majesties.* London, 1689.

Gardiner, Samuel Rawson, ed. *Parliamentary Debates in 1610.* Camden Society, 1962.

Gee, Edward. *The Divine Right and Original of the Civill Magistrate from God.* London, 1658.

*An Exercitation concerning Usurped Powers.* London, 1650.

*A Glance on the Ecclesiastical Commission.* London, 1690.

*Great Britain's Vote: or, God Save King Charles.* London, 1648.

*The Great Point of Succession Discussed.* London, 1681.

*Great and Weighty Considerations relating to the D. or Successor of the Crown.* London, 1682.

Grey, Anchitell. *Debates of the House of Commons from . . . 1667 . . . to 1694.* 10 vols. London, 1769.

Gutch, John, ed. *Collectanea Curiosa.* Vol. 1. Oxford, 1781.

Hale, Sir Matthew. *The Jurisdiction of the Lords House, or Parliament.* Ed. F. Hargrave. London, 1796.

　*The Prerogatives of the King.* Ed. D. E. C. Yale. Selden Society, 1976.

　'Reflections . . . on Mr. Hobbes : His Dialogue of the Lawe.' Sir William Holdsworth. *A History of English Law.* 3rd ed. Vol v. London, reprinted 1966, pp. 500–13.

Hall, Arthur. *An admonition to the Father of F. A. to him being a Burgesse of the Parliament, for his better behaviour therein.* London, 1579.

Hardwicke, Lord. *Miscellaneous State Papers. From 1501 to 1726.* Ed. Philip Yorke. Vol. II. London, 1778.

*The Harleian Miscellany: A Collection of Scarce, Curious, and Entertaining Pamphlets and Tracts . . . Selected from the Library of Edward Harley, Second Earl of Oxford,* Ed. Thomas Park. 10 vols. London, 1808–13.

Herbert, Sir Edward. *A Short Account of the Authorities in law, upon which Judgement was given in Sir Edward Hales His Case.* London, 1688.

Herle, Charles. *Ahab's Fall by his Prophets Flatteries: Being the Substance of Three Sermons. Upon 1. King. 22.22.* London, 1644.

　*An Answer to Dr. Ferne's Reply, Entitled Conscience Satisfied.* London, 1643.

　*A Fuller Answer to a Treatise Written by Doctor Ferne.* London, 1642. This is a revised and enlarged edition.

　*A Payre of Compasses for Church and State.* London, 1642.

Heylyn, Peter. *Aerius Redivivus: or, The History of the Presbyterians.* Oxford, 1670.

　*Certamen Epistolare, or, The Letter-Combate.* London, 1659.

　*The Rebells Catechisme.* N.p., 1643.

　*The Stumbling-block of Disobedience and Rebellion, Cunningly laid by Calvin in the Subjects Way, Discovered, Censured, and Removed.* London, 1658.

Hickes, George. *A Discourse of the Soveraign Power, in a Sermon Preached at St. Mary Le Bow, November 28, 1682. Before the Artillery Company of London.* London, 1682.

　*The Harmony of Divinity and Law, in a Discourse about not Resisting of Soveraign Princes.* London, 1684.

　*Jovian, or, An Answer to Julian the Apostate.* London, 1683.

　*A Sermon Preached before the Lord Mayor, Aldermen, and Citizens of London, at Bow Church on the 30th of January, 1681/2.* London, 1682.

Historical Manuscripts Commission. *Eleventh Report, Appendix, Part II. The Manuscripts of the House of Lords, 1678–1688.*
  *Twelfth Report, Appendix, Part VI. The Manuscripts of the House of Lords, 1689–1690.*
  *Thirteenth Report, Appendix, Part I. The Manuscripts of . . . the Duke of Portland, preserved at Welbeck Abbey.* Vol. I.
  *Fourteenth Report, Appendix, Part II. The Manuscripts of . . . the Duke of Portland . . . .* Vol. III.
  *Reports on the Manuscripts of the late Reginald Hastings, Esq. of the Manor House, Ashby-de-la-Zouche.* Vols. II and IV. Ed. Francis Bickley.

*The History and Proceedings of the House of Lords, From the Restoration in 1660 to the Present Time.* Vol. I. London, 1742.

Hoadly, Benjamin. *The Original and Institution of Civil Government, Discussed.* London, 1710. Reprinted in *The Works of Benjamin Hoadly.* Vol. II. London, 1773.

Hobart, Sir Henry. *Reports.* London, 1650.

Hobbes, Thomas. 'Behemoth : The History of the Causes of the Civil Wars in England.' *The English Works of Thomas Hobbes of Malmesbury.* Ed. Sir William Molesworth. Vol. VI. London, 1840.
  *Leviathan, or the Matter, Forme, and Power of a Commonwealth Ecclesiastical and Civil.* Ed. Michael Oakeshott. Oxford, 1946.

Holbourne, Sir Robert. *The Freeholders Grand Inquest.* N.p. 1648.

*The Honour of the Lords Spiritual Asserted: and their Priviledges to Vote in Capital Cases in Parliament Maintained by Reason and Precedents.* London, 1679.

Hooker, John (John Vowel alias Hooker). *The Order and Usage of the Keeping of a Parlement in England.* In Vernon F. Snow. *Parliament in Elizabethan England. John Hooker's 'Order and Usage'.* New Haven, 1977.

Hooker, Richard. *Ecclesiastical Polity: Book VIII.* Ed. Raymond Aaron Houk. New York, 1931.
  *Of the Laws of Ecclesiastical Politie; the Sixth and Eighth Books.* London, 1648.
  *Of the Laws of Ecclesiastical Polity.* Vol I. New York, 1965.

Howell, James. *Some Sober Inspections made into the Cariage and Consults of the late-long Parliament.* London, 1655.

Howell, T. B. *A Complete Collection of State Trials and Proceedings for High Treasons and Other Crimes and Misdemeanors from the Earliest Period to the Year 1783.* 34 vols. London, 1809–28.

Hudson, Michael. *The Royall and the Royalists Plea.* London, 1647.

Hughes, Paul L., and Larkin, James F., eds. *Tudor Royal Proclamations.* 3 vols. New Haven, 1964–69.

Hunt, Thomas. *A Defence of the Charter, and Municipal Rights of the City of London.* London, 1683.

*Mr. Hunt's Argument for the Bishops Right.* London, 1682.

*Mr. Hunt's Postscript for Rectifying some Mistakes in some of the Inferiour Clergy, Mischievous to our Government and Religion.* London, 1682.

Hunton, Philip. *A Treatise of Monarchie, Containing Two Parts: 1. Concerning Monarchy in generall; 2. Concerning this particular Monarchy.* London, 1643.

*A Vindication of the Treatise of Monarchy.* London, 1644.

Husband, Edward. *An Exact Collection of all Remonstrances, Declarations . . . and other Remarkable Passages between the Kings Most Excellent Majesty, and His High Court of Parliament.* London, 1642.

Hyde, Sir Edward, Earl of Clarendon. *A Brief View and Survey of the Dangerous and Pernicious Errors to Church and State in Mr. Hobbes Book, Entitled Leviathan.* Sheldonian Theatre, 1676.

*Calendar of the Clarendon State Papers.* Ed. O. Ogle and W. H. Bliss. Vol. I. Oxford, 1872.

*The Continuation of the Life of Edward, Earl of Clarendon.* Vol. III. Oxford, 1759.

*The History of the Rebellion and Civil Wars in England begun in the year 1641.* Ed. W. Dunn Macray. 6 vols. Oxford, 1888.

*The Life of Edward, Earl of Clarendon.* 3 vols. Oxford, 1827.

Hyde, Henry, Earl of Clarendon. *The Correspondence of Henry Hyde, Earl of Clarendon and of His Brother, Laurence Hyde, Earl of Rochester; with the Diary of Lord Clarendon from 1687 to 1690.* Ed. Samuel W. Singer. Vol. II. London, 1828.

Jacob, Giles. *A New Law-Dictionary.* London, 1729.

James I. *Political Works.* Ed. Charles H. McIlwain. Cambridge, Mass., 1918.

James II. *His Majesties Gracious Declaration to All His Loving Subjects for Liberty of Conscience.* London, 1688.

Jenkins, David. *Eight Centuries of Reports.* 3rd ed. London, 1771.

*Lex Terrae.* London, 1647.

*Vindication of Judge Jenkins, Prisoner in the Tower, the 29th Aprill, 1647*. London, 1647.

Johnson, Samuel. *An Argument Proving that the Abrogation of King James by the People of England from the Regal Throne, and the Promotion of the Prince of Orange, one of the Royal Family, to the Throne of the Kingdom in his stead, was according to the Constitution of the English Government and Prescribed by it*. London, 1692.

*Collected Works*. London, 1713.

*An Essay concerning Parliaments at a Certainty*. 3rd ed. London, 1694.

'Several Reasons for the Establishment of a Standing Army and Dissolving the Militia.' In T. B. Howell. *A Complete Collection of State Trials*. Vol. XI, cols. 1341–48. London, 1811.

Johnston, Nathaniel. *The Excellency of Monarchical Government, Especially of the English Monarchy*. London, 1686.

'A Jornall of the Convention at Westminster begun the 22 of January 1688/9.' Ed. Lois Schwoerer. With an introduction. *Bulletin of the Institute of Historical Research*, XLIX (1976), 242–63.

*Journals of the House of Commons, 1547–1714*. 17 vols.

*Journals of the House of Lords, 1578–1714*. 18 vols.

*The Judgment and Decree of the University of Oxford Past in their Convocation July 21, 1683, Against Certain Pernicious Books and Damnable Doctrines Destructive to the Sacred Persons of Princes, their State and Government, and of All Human Society*. Oxford, 1683.

Keble, Joseph. *Reports in the Court of Kings-Bench*. London, 1685.

Lambarde, William. *Archeion, or, A Discourse upon the High Courts of Justice in England*. Ed. Charles H. McIlwain and Paul L. Ward. Cambridge, Mass., 1957.

Langhorne, Richard. *Considerations Touching the Great Question of the King's Right in Dispensing with the Penal Laws*. London, 1687.

Laud, William. *The Works of the Most Reverend Father in God, William Laud D.D.* Ed. W. Scott and J. Bliss. 7 vols. in 9. Oxford, 1847–60.

Lawson, George. *An Examination of the Political Part of Mr. Hobbes his Leviathan*. London, 1657.

*Politica Sacra et Civilis: or, A Modell of Civil and Ecclesiasticall Government*. London, 1660.

Leicester, Sir Peter. *Charges to the Grand Jury at Quarter Sessions, 1660–1677*. Ed. Elizabeth M. Halcrow. Chetham Society, 1953.

Leslie, Charles. *Cassandra. (But I hope not). Telling what will come of it. Num.* 1. London, 1704.

The Constitution, Laws, and Government of England, Vindicated. London, 1709.

'The Rehearsals.' *A View of the Times, Their Principles and Practices.* Vol. v. 2nd ed. London, 1750.

L'Éstrange, Sir Roger. *An Account of the Growth of Knavery, under the Pretended Fears of Arbitrary Government, and Popery, with a Parallel betwixt the Reformers of 1677, and those of 1641, in their Methods and Designs.* London, 1678.

Considerations and Proposals in order to the Regulation of the Press. London, 1663.

The Dissenters Sayings, in Requital for L'Éstrange's Sayings. 3rd. ed. London, 1681.

The Free-Born Subject: or, The Englishman's Birthright. London, 1679.

A Short Answer to a Whole Litter of Libels. London, 1680.

A Letter to the Author of the Vindication of the Proceedings of the Ecclesiastical Commissioners concerning the Legality of that Court. Oxford, 1688.

A Letter to a Bishop concerning the Present Settlement, and the New Oaths. London, 1689.

A Letter to a Friend in the Country, Touching the present Fears and Jealousies of the Nation, and from whence they arise. London, 1680.

A Letter to a Friend, Shewing from Scripture, Fathers and Reason, how false that State Maxim is, Royal Authority is Originally and Radically in the People. London, 1679.

A Letter to a Gentleman at Brussels, Containing an Account of the Causes of the People's Revolt from the Crown. London, 1689.

A Letter to a Member of the High Court of Parliament, concerning the British Monarchy. London, 1689.

Littleton, Edward. *Les Reports.* London, 1683.

Locke, John. 'A Letter from a Person of Quality to his Friends in the Country.' *Works.* Vol. x. London, 1812.

Two Tracts on Government. Ed. Philip Abrams. Cambridge, 1967.

Two Treatises of Government. Ed. Peter Laslett. Cambridge, 1960. Rev. 1963. Published as a Mentor Book, 1965.

Long, Thomas. *The Historian Unmask'd: or, Some Reflections on the late History of Passive Obedience.* London, 1689.

Ludlow, Edmund. *A Voyce from the Watch Tower: Part Five:*

*1660–1662*. Ed. A. B. Worden. Camden Society, 1978.

Luttrell, Narcissus. *A Brief Historical Relation of State Affairs from September 1678 to April 1714*. Vol. I. Oxford, 1857.

Mackenzie, Sir George. *Jus Regium: or, the Just and Solid Foundations of Monarchy in General: and more especially of the Monarchy of Scotland: Maintained against Buchanan, Naphtali, Dolman, Milton, etc.* Edinburgh and London, 1684.

*The Manager's Pro and Con: or, An Account of what is said at Child's and Tom's Coffee Houses For and Against Dr. Sacheverell*. London, 1710.

Mantell, Walter. *A Shorte Treatise of the Lawes of England: with the Jurisdiction of the High Court of Parliament, with the Liberties and Freedoms of the Subjects*. London, 1644.

Marvell, Andrew. *Complete Works in Verse and Prose*. Ed. Alexander B. Grosart. Vols. II and IX. N.p., 1875.

Masters, Samuel. *The Case of Allegiance in our Present Circumstances Consider'd*. London, 1689.

*The Maximes of Mixt Monarchy*. London, 1643.

*Maximes Unfolded*. London, 1643.

Maxwell, John. *Sacro-Sancta Regnum Majestas: or; The Sacred and Royall Prerogative of Christian Kings*. Oxford, 1644.

Merbury, Charles. *A Briefe Discourse of Royall Monarchie, as of the Best Common Weale*. London, 1581.

Milbourne, Luke. *The People not the Original of Civil Power, prov'd from God's word, the Doctrine and Liturgy of the Established Church, and from the Laws of England. In a Sermon preach'd at the parish Church of St. Ethelburga, on Thursday, Jan. 30, 1706/07, being a day of solemn fasting and humiliation, appointed by law, for the execrable murder of King Charles I, of blessed Memory*. London, 1707.

*The Royal Martyr Lamented, Preach'd on the thirtieth of January*. London, 1708–20.

*The Traytors Reward, or, A King's Death Revenged*. London, 1714.

Milward, John. *The Diary of John Milward, Esq., Member of Parliament for Derbyshire, September, 1666 to May, 1668*. Ed. Caroline Robbins. Cambridge, 1938.

Mocket, Richard. *God and the King, or, A Dialogue, Shewing that our Soveraigne Lord King James being immediate under God within his Dominions, Doth Rightly claim whatsoever is Required by the Oath of Allegiance*. London. 1616.

Moore, Sir Francis. *Cases Collect and Report: Per Sir Fra. Moore.* 2nd ed. London, 1688.

Morrice, James. 'A Reading of the Midle Temple full of excellent good discourse and learninge circa 21 Eliz. R. [1578].' Edward T. Lampson. 'The Royal Prerogative, 1485–1603.' Ph.D. Dissertation, Harvard University, 1938. Appendix.

Muddiman, J. G. *The Trial of King Charles the First.* Edinburgh and London, 1928.

Nalson, John. *An Impartial Collection of the Great Affairs of State.* 2 vols. London, 1682–83.

Nedham, Marchamont. *The Case of the Commonwealth of England, Stated.* Ed. Philip Knachel. Washington, D.C., 1969.

Neville, Henry. *Plato Redivivus: or, A Dialogue concerning Government.* 2nd ed. London, 1681. Reprinted in *Two English Republican Tracts.* Ed. Caroline Robbins. Cambridge, 1969.

*The New Oath of Allegiance Justified, from the Original Constitution of the English Monarchy.* London, 1689.

Nicolson, William. *The English Historical Library.* Part III. London, 1699.

*No King but the Old King's Son, or, A Vindication of Limited Monarchy, as it was Established in this Nation, before the late War between the King and Parliament.* London, 1660.

Northleigh, John. *Remarks upon the Most Eminent of our Antimonarchical Authors and their Writings.* London, 1699. First published in 1685 as *The Triumph of Our Monarchy.*

Nye, Philip. *The King's Authority in Dispensing with Ecclesiastical Laws, Asserted and Vindicated.* London, 1687.

*Obedience due to the Present King, Notwithstanding our Oaths to the Former.* London, 1689.

*The Opinion of Divers Learned and Leading Dissenters, Concerning the Original of Government. Referring to the Doctrine of the Political Catechism.* London, 1680.

*The Oxonian Antippodes, or, The Oxford Anty-Parliament.* London, 1644.

Parker, Henry. 'Observations upon some of His Majesties late Answers and Expresses.' *Tracts on Liberty in the Puritan Revolution, 1638–1647.* Ed. William Haller. Vol. II. New York, 1934.

*The Parliamentary or Constitutional History of England.* Vol. XVII. London, 1755.

Penn, William, *The Great and Popular Objection against the Repeal of the Penal Laws and Tests Briefly Considered.* London, 1688. *Three Letters tending to demonstrate how the Security of this*

*Nation against all Future Persecution for Religion lys in the Abolishment of the Present Penal Laws and Tests.* London, 1688.

Pepys, Samuel. *The Diary of Samuel Pepys.* Ed. Henry B. Wheatley. 10 vols. London, 1903, 1904.

Petyt, George. *Lex Parliamentaria: A Treatise on the Laws and Customs of Parliament.* London, 1690.

Petyt, William. *The Antient Right of the Commons of England Asserted, or, A Discourse proving by Records and the best Historians, that the Commons of England were ever an Essential Part of Parliament.* London, 1680.

*Jus Parliamentarium: or, the Ancient Power, Jurisdiction, Rights and Liberties, of the Most High Court of Parliament, Revived and Asserted.* London, 1739.

*Miscellanea Parliamentaria.* London, 1680.

*The Pillars of Parliament struck at by the Hands of a Cambridge Doctor.* London, 1681.

Philipps, Fabian. *The Established Government of England Vindicated, from all Popular and Republican Principles.* London 1687.

Plowden, Edmund. *Commentaries or Reports.* London, 1816.

*A Political Catechism, or Certain Questions concerning the Government of this Land, Answered in His Majesties own words, taken out of His Answer to the 19 Propositions.* London, 1643.

Ponet, John. *A Shorte Treatise of politike power, and of the true Obedience which subjectes owe to kynges and other civile Governours, with an Exhortacion to all true naturall Englishe men.* N.p., 1556.

Poyntz, Sir Robert. *A Vindication of Monarchy.* London, 1661.

*Prayers and Thanksgiving to be used by all the Kings Majesties loving Subjects, for the happy deliverance of his Majestie, the Queene, Prince, and States of the Parliament . . . the 5 November 1605.* London, 1620.

*A Prelude to the Tryal of Skill between Sacheverellism and the Constitution of the Monarchy of Great Britain.* London, 1710.

*The Primitive Cavalerism Revived: or, A Recognition of the Principles of the Old Cavaleers.* London, 1684.

*Proceedings of the Short Parliament of 1640.* Ed. Esther S. Cope and Willson H. Coates. Camden Society, 1977.

*Protestant Loyalty Fairly Drawn, in an Answer to a Pair of Scandalous and Popish Pamphlets. The First Intituled 'A Dialogue at Oxford between Tutor and Pupil'.* London, 1681.

Prynne, William. *Brevia Parliamentaria Rediviva.* London, 1662.

This is volume III of *A Brief Register, Kalendar and Survey . . . of Parliamentary Writs.*

*Brief Animadversions on, Amendments of, and Additional Explanatory Records to, the Fourth Part of the Institutes of the Lawes of England; Concerning the Jurisdiction of Courts. Compiled by the Late Famous Lawyer Sir Edward Cooke Knight.* London, 1669.

*A Brief Register, Kalendar and Survey of the Several Kinds, and Forms of all Parliamentary Writs.* 4 vols. London, 1659–64.

*An Exact Abridgement of the Records in the Tower of London . . . Collected by Sir Robert Cotton.* London, 1657.

*The First Part of a Brief Register, Kalendar and Survey of the Several Kinds and Forms of all Parliamentary Writs.* London, 1659.

*The First Part of an Historical Collection of the Ancient Parliaments of England.* London, 1649.

*The Fourth Part of the Soveraigne Power of Parliaments and Kingdomes.* 2nd ed. London, 1643.

*A Plea for the House of Lords, and House of Peers.* London, 1658. First published in 1648, this tract was reprinted in a much expanded form in 1658 and 1659.

*The Second Part of a Brief Register and Survey of the Several Kinds and Forms of Parliamentary Writs.* London, 1660.

*The Soveraigne Power of Parliaments and Kingdomes: Divided into Four Parts together with an Appendix.* London, 1643.

*The Soveraigne Power of Parliaments and Kingdomes, or, Second Part of the Treachery and Disloyalty of Papists to their Soveraignes.* 2nd ed. London, 1643.

*The Treachery and Disloyalty of Papists to their Soveraignes, in Doctrine and Practise.* 2nd ed. London, 1643.

*The Treachery and Disloyalty of Papists to their Soveraignes, in Doctrine and Practise. Together with The First Part of the Soveraigne Power of Parliaments and Kingdomes.* 2nd ed. London, 1643.

Rapin-Thoyras, Paul de. *A Dissertation on the Government, Laws, Customs, Manners, and Language, of the Anglo-Saxons.* Trans. N. Tindal. London, 1730.

Rastell, John. *Les Termes de la Ley.* London, 1685, 1721.

Relf, Frances, ed. *Notes of the Debates in the House of Lords, Officially Taken by Robert Bowyer and Henry Elsing, Clerks of Parliament.* Camden Society, 1929.

Reresby, Sir John. *Memoirs.* Ed. Andrew Browning. Glasgow, 1936.

Ruffhead, Owen. 'Preface.' *The Statutes at Large, from Magna Charta to the End of the Last Parliament.* London, 1769.

Rushworth, John. *Historical Collections of Private Passages of State, Weighty Matters in Law, Remarkable Proceedings in Five Parliaments. Beginning the Sixteenth Year of King James Anno 1618. And Ending the Fifth Year of King Charles Anno 1629. Digested in Order of Time.* 8 vols. London, 1721–22.

Rutherford, Samuel. *Lex, Rex, or The Law and the Prince: A Dispute for the Just Prerogative of King and People.* London, 1644.

St Amand, George. *An Historical Essay on the Legislative Power of England,* London, 1725.

Sanderson, Robert. *Ten Lectures on the Obligation of Humane Conscience. Read in the Divinity School at Oxford, in the year, 1647.* Trans. Robert Codrington. London, 1660.

Savile, George, marquess of Halifax. 'Prerogative.' To be printed in *The Works of George Savile, Marquis of Halifax.* ed. Mark N. Brown. Forthcoming.

*The Secret History of the Court and Reign of Charles the Second, by a Member of his Privy Council.* Vol. I. London, 1792.

Selden, John. *Jani Anglorum Facies Altera.* London, 1610. Trans. Redman Westcot and reprinted 1683.

*Table Talk.* Ed. Sir Frederick Pollock. Selden Society, 1927.

Seller, Abednigo. *The History of Passive Obedience since the Reformation.* Amsterdam, 1689.

Sheringham, Robert. *The Kings Supremacy Asserted.* London, 1660.

Sidney, Algernon. *The Arraignment, Tryal and Condemnation of Algernon Sidney, Esq., for High Treason.* London, 1684.

*Discourses Concerning Government.* 2nd ed. London, 1704.

*Sidney Redivivus.* London, 1689.

Smith, Sir Thomas. *De Republica Anglorum.* Ed. L. Alston. Cambridge, 1906.

*Some Modest Remarks on Dr. Sherlock's New Book about the Case of Allegiance due to Sovereign Power, etc.* London, 1691.

*Somers Tracts. A Collection of Scarce and Valuable Tracts, on the most Interesting and Entertaining Subjects: but chiefly such as relate to the History and Constitution of these Kingdoms, selected from . . . Libraries, particularly that of the Late Lord Somers.* Ed. Walter Scott. 13 vols. London, 1809–15.

*A Second Collection.* London, 1750.

*A Third Collection.* London, 1751.

Spelman, Sir John. *The Case of our Affaires, in Law, Religion, and other Circumstances briefly examined, and Presented to the Conscience.* Oxford, 1644.

*A View of a Printed Book, Intituled Observations upon His Majesties late Answers and Expresses.* Oxford, 1643.

Squire, Samuel. *An Enquiry into the Foundation of the English Constitution.* London, 1745.

Stafford, William. *The Reason of the War.* London, 1646.

Stanford, Sir William. *An Exposition of the Kinges Prerogative.* Ed. Tottell. London, 1577.

*Les Plees del Coron, Divisees in Plusors Titles & Common Lieux.* Ed. Tottell. London, 1560 and 1574.

*State Tracts: Being a Collection of Several Treatises relating to the Government.* London, 1689. Republished, two volumes in one, 1693.

*Statutes of the Realm.* 11 vols. London, 1963.

Steele, Robert, ed. *A Bibliography of Royal Proclamations of the Tudor and Stuart Sovereigns.* Oxford, 1910.

Stephens, Edward. *Important Questions of State, Law, Justice, and Prudence, Both Civil and Religious, upon the Late Revolutions and Present State of these Nations.* London, 1689.

*The True English Government, and Mis-Government of the Four Last Kings, with the Consequences Thereof.* London, 1689.

Stillingfleet, Edward. *A Discourse Concerning the Illegality of the Late Ecclesiastical Commission . . . Wherein . . . an Account is given of the Nature, Original, and Mischief of the Dispensing Power.* London, 1689.

*The Grand Question concerning the Bishops Right to Vote in Parliament in Cases Capital.* London, 1680.

*The Subject of Supremacie: The Right of Caesar.* London, 1643.

*The Subjects Liberty Set forth in the Royall and Politique Power of England.* London, 1643.

Tomkins, Thomas. *The Rebels Plea, or, Mr. Baxter's Judgment, concerning the Late Wars.* London, 1660.

*Tracts on Liberty in the Puritan Revolution, 1638–1647.* Ed. William Haller. Vol. II. New York, 1934.

*A True Relation of the Manner of the Deposing of King Edward II.* London, 1689.

Twysden, Sir Roger. *Certaine Considerations upon the Government of England.* Ed. John Mitchell Kemble. Camden Society, 1849.

Tyrrell, James. *Bibliotheca Politica: or, An Enquiry into the Antient*

*Constitution of the English Government . . . Wherein all the Chief Arguments both for and against the Late Revolution, are Impartially Represented and Consider'd.* 2nd. ed. London, 1727.

*General History of England.* 3 vols. London, 1696–1704.

*Patriarcha non Monarcha.* London, 1681.

*University Loyalty: or, the Genuine Explanation of the Principles and Practices of the English Clergy, as Established and Directed by the Decree of the University of Oxford.* London, 1710.

Ussher, James. *The Power Communicated by God to the Prince, and the Obedience required of the Subject.* London, 1661.

Vane, Sir Henry. *The Tryal at the King's Bench, Westminster, June the 2d. and 6th, 1662.* N.p., 1662.

Vaughan, Sir John. *Reports and Arguments.* London, 1677.

*Vindiciae Veritatis.* London, 1654.

*Vox Populi, Vox Dei: Being True Maxims of Government.* London, 1709.

Walker, Clement. *Anarchia Anglicana: or, the History of Independency. The Second Part.* London, 1661.

    *The Compleat History of Independency. Upon the Parliament begun 1640. Continued till . . . 1660.* London, 1660–61.

Walton, Izaak. *The Life of Mr. Richard Hooker.* London, 1665.

Warwick, Sir Philip. *A Discourse of Government, as Examined by Reason, Scripture, and Law of the Land.* London, 1694.

    *Memoires of the Reigne of King Charles I.* London, 1701. Later ed. Sir W. Scott. Edinburgh, 1813.

Wellwood, James. *Reasons why the Parliament of Scotland cannot comply with the Late King James's Proclamation.* London, 1689.

Westcot, Redman. *The Reverse or Back-face of the English Janus.* London, 1682.

Whitelocke, Bulstrode. *Notes Uppon the Kings Writt for Choosing Members of Parliament . . . being Disquisitions on the Government of England by King, Lords, and Commons.* Ed. Charles Morton. 2 vols. London, 1766.

*William Lambarde and Local Government. His 'Ephemeris' and Twenty-nine Charges to Juries and Commissions.* Ed. Conyers Read. Ithaca, 1962.

Williams, Griffith. *Jura Majestatis. The Rights of Kings both in Church and State: 1. Granted by God. 2. Violated by the Rebels. 3. Vindicated by the Truth.* Oxford, 1644.

Wilson, John. *A Discourse of Monarchy, More particularly of the*

*Imperial Crowns of England, Scotland, and Ireland, According to the Ancient, Common, and Statute-Laws of the Same.* London, 1684.

*Jus Regium Coronae: or, the King's Supream Power in Dispensing with Penal Statutes.* London, 1688.

Womock, Laurence. *An Answer to the Gentleman's Letter to his Friend. Shewing that Bishops may be Judges in Causes Capital.* London, 1680.

Wood, Anthony. *Athenae Oxonienses: An Exact History of all the Writers and Bishops who have had their Education in the University of Oxford.* Ed. Philip Bliss. 4 vols. London, 1813–20.

    *Life and Times.* Ed. Andrew Clarke. Vols. II and III. 1891–95.

*A Word Without-Doors concerning the Bill for Succession.* London, 1679.

*Year Book.* 1 Henry VII. Ed. Tottell. London, 1555.

*Year Book.* 1 Henry VII. Ed. Maynard. London, 1679.

### SECONDARY WORKS

Abernathy, George R. Jr. *The English Presbyterians and the Stuart Restoration, 1648–1663.* Philadelphia, 1965.

Allen, J. W. *English Political Thought, 1603–1644.* London, 1938, reprinted 1967.

Ashley, Maurice. 'King James II and the Revolution of 1688 : Some Reflections on the Historiography.' *Historical Essays, 1600–1750, Presented to David Ogg.* Ed. H. E. Bell and R. L. Ollard. New York, 1963.

Aylmer, G. E., ed. *The Interregnum: The Quest for Settlement 1646–1660.* London, 1972.

    *The King's Servants: The Civil Service of Charles I, 1625–1642.* London, 1961.

Bacon, Matthew. *A New Abridgment of the Law.* Vol. III. London, 1786.

Bailey, J. E. *The Life of a Lancashire Rector during the Civil War.* Leigh, 1877.

Bate, Frank. *The Declaration of Indulgence, 1672.* London, 1908.

Baxter, Stephen. *The Development of the Treasury, 1660–1702.* London, 1957.

    *William III.* London, 1966.

Beddard, Robert. 'The Commission for Ecclesiastical Promotions,

1681–84 : An Instrument of Tory Reaction.' *Historical Journal,*
  x (1967), 11–40.

Behrens, B. 'The Whig Theory of the Constitution in the Reign of
  Charles II.' *Cambridge Historical Journal,* vii (1941–43), 42–
  71.

Birdsall, Paul. ' "*Non Obstante,*" A Study of the Dispensing Power
  of English Kings.' *Essays in History and Political Theory in
  Honor of Charles Howard McIlwain.* Ed. Carl Wittke. Cambridge, Mass., 1936.

Brown, Mark N. 'George Savile, Marquis of Halifax, 1633–1698.'
  Ph.D. Dissertation, Harvard University, 1964.

'Trimmers and Moderates in the Reign of Charles II.' *Huntington
  Library Quarterly,* xxxvii (1974), 311–36.

'The Works of George Savile Marquis of Halifax : Dates and
  Circumstances of Composition.' *Huntington Library Quarterly,*
  xxxv (1972), 143–57.

Browning, Andrew. *Thomas Osborne, Earl of Danby and Duke of
  Leeds, 1632–1712.* Vol. I. Glasgow, 1951.

Carte, Thomas. *An History of the Life of James Duke of Ormonde.*
  Vol. II. London, 1736.

Carter, Jennifer. 'The Revolution and the Constitution.' *Britain
  after the Glorious Revolution 1689–1714.* Ed. Geoffrey Holmes.
  London, 1969, 39–50.

*A Catalogue of the Petyt Library at Skipton, Yorkshire.* Gargrave,
  1964.

Chitty, Joseph. *A Treatise on the Law of the Prerogatives of the
  Crown.* London, 1820.

Chrimes, S. B. 'The Constitutional ideas of Dr. John Cowell.' *English
  Historical Review,* lxiv (1949), 461–93.

*English Constitutional Ideas in the Fifteenth Century.* Cambridge,
  1936.

Christie, W. D. *A Life of Anthony Ashley Cooper, First Earl of
  Shaftesbury, 1621–1683.* 2 vols. London, 1871.

Churchill, E. F. 'The Crown and the Alien from the Norman Conquest down to 1689.' *Law Quarterly Review,* xxxvi (1920), 402–
  28.

'Dispensations under the Tudors and Stuarts.' *English Historical
  Review,* xxxiv (1919), 409–15.

'The Dispensing Power of the Crown in Ecclesiastical Affairs.'
  *Law Quarterly Review,* xxxviii (1922), 297–316, 420–34.

'The Dispensing Power and the Defence of the Realm.' *Law
  Quarterly Review,* xxxvii (1921), 412–41.

Clark, G. N. *The Later Stuarts, 1660–1714.* Oxford, 2nd. ed. 1955, reprinted 1961.

Coate, Mary. *Cornwall in the Great Civil War and Interregnum, 1642–1660.* Oxford, 1933.

Cope, Esther. 'The Short Parliament of 1640 and Convocation.' *Journal of Ecclesiastical History*, xxv (1974), 167–84.

Cragg, Gerald R. *Puritanism in the Period of the Great Persecution, 1660–1688.* Cambridge, 1957.

Cuming, G. J. 'The Making of the Durham Book.' *Journal of Ecclesiastical History*, v (1955), 60–72.

'The Prayer Book in Convocation, November, 1661.' *Journal of Ecclesiastical History*, viii, 2 (1957), 182–92.

Daly, James. *Cosmic Harmony and Political Thinking in Early Stuart England.* Philadelphia, 1979.

*Sir Robert Filmer and English political thought.* Toronto, 1979.

Davies, Godfrey. *The Early Stuarts, 1603–1660.* 2nd ed. Oxford, 1959.

*The Restoration of Charles II, 1658–1660.* London, 1955.

Davies, J. Conway, ed. *Catalogue of Manuscripts in the Library of the Honourable Society of the Inner Temple.* 3 vols. London, 1972.

Dickinson, H. T. 'The Eighteenth Century Debate on the Sovereignty of Parliament.' *Transactions of the Royal Historical Society.* Fifth Series, xxvi (London, 1976), 189–210.

*Liberty and Property: Political Ideology in Eighteenth-Century Britain.* London, 1977.

Douglas, David C. *English Historical Scholars 1660–1730.* 2nd ed. London, 1951.

D'Oyly, George. *The Life of William Sancroft.* London, 1821.

Dunn, John. *The Political Thought of John Locke.* Cambridge, 1969.

Earl, D. W. L. 'Procrustean Feudalism. An Interpretative Dilemma in English Historical Narration, 1700–1725.' *Historical Journal*, xix (1976), 33–51.

Edie, Carolyn A. *The Irish Cattle Bills: A Study in Restoration Politics.* Philadelphia, 1970.

'The Parliamentary Challenge to the Royal Prerogative, 1660–1685.' Ph.D. Dissertation, University of Wisconsin, 1957.

'Revolution and the Rule of Law : The End of the Dispensing Power, 1689.' *Eighteenth Century Studies*, x (1977), 434–50.

'Succession and Monarchy : The Controversy of 1679–1681.' *American Historical Review*, lxx (1965), 350–70.

o

Elton, G. R. *England under the Tudors.* London, 1955, reprinted 1963.

*Studies in Tudor and Stuart Politics and Government.* Vol. II. Cambridge, 1974.

*The Tudor Constitution: Documents and Commentary.* Cambridge, 1962.

Evans, E. 'Of the Antiquity of Parliaments in England : Some Elizabethan and Early Stuart Opinions.' *History,* XXIII (1938), 206–21.

Feiling, Keith. *A History of the Tory Party, 1640–1714.* Oxford, 1924, reprinted 1965.

Foss, Edward. *The Judges of England.* Vol. VII. London, 1864.

Foster, Elizabeth Read. 'The Procedure of the House of Commons against Patents and Monopolies, 1621–1624.' *Conflict in Stuart England: Essays in Honour of Wallace Notestein.* Ed. William A. Aiken and Basil D. Henning. London, 1960.

'Proceedings in the House of Lords during the Early Stuart Period.' *Journal of British Studies,* V (1966), 56–73.

Frankle, Robert. 'The Formulation of the Declaration of Rights.' *Historical Journal,* XVII (1974), 265–79.

Franklin, Julian. *John Locke and the Theory of Sovereignty: Mixed Monarchy and the Right of Resistance in the Political Thought of the English Revolution.* Cambridge, 1978.

Furley, O. W. 'The Whig Exclusionists : Pamphlet Literature in the Exclusion Campaign, 1679–81.' *Cambridge Historical Journal,* XIII (1957), 19–36.

Gardiner, Samuel R. *History Of the Great Civil War, 1642–1649.* 4 vols. London, 1910–11.

Goldie, Mark. 'Edmund Bohun and *Jus Gentium* in the Revolution Debate, 1689–1693.' *Historical Journal,* XX (1977), 569–86.

Gough, J. W. 'Flowers of the Crown.' *English Historical Review,* LXXVII (1962), 86–93.

*Fundamental Law in English Constitutional History.* Oxford, 1955, reprinted 1961.

'James Tyrrell, Whig Historian and Friend of John Locke.' *Historical Journal,* XIX (1976), 581–610.

*John Locke's Political Philosophy.* Oxford, 1950.

*The Social Contract: A Critical Study of its Development.* Oxford, 2nd ed., 1957, reprinted 1967.

Greenberg, Janelle Renfrow. 'Tudor and Stuart Theories of Kingship : The Dispensing Power and the Royal Discretionary Authority in Sixteenth and Seventeenth Century England.' Ph.D. Dissertation, University of Michigan, 1970.

Greenleaf, W. H. *Order, Empiricism and Politics: Two Traditions of English Political Thought, 1500–1700.* London, 1964.

Gwyn, W. B. *The Meaning of the Separation of Powers.* New Orleans, 1965.

Haley, K. H. D. *The First Earl of Shaftesbury.* Oxford, 1968.

Hallam, Henry. *Constitutional History of England.* New York, 1859.

Hanson, Donald W. *From Kingdom to Commonwealth: The Development of Civic Consciousness in English Political Thought.* Cambridge, Mass., 1970.

Hardacre, Paul H. *The Royalists during the Puritan Revolution.* The Hague, 1956.

Harper, Lawrence A. *The English Navigation Laws.* New York, 1964.

Harrison, John and Laslett, Peter, eds. *The Library of John Locke.* Oxford, 1965.

Hart, A. Tindal. *William Lloyd, 1627–1717, Bishop, Politician, Author and Prophet.* London, 1952.

Havighurst, Alfred F. 'James II and the Twelve Men in Scarlet.' *Law Quarterly Review,* LXIX (1953), 522–46.

 'The Judiciary and Politics in the Reign of Charles II.' *Law Quarterly Review,* LXVI (1950), 62–78, 229–52.

Heuston, R. F. V. *Essays in Constitutional Law.* 2nd ed. London, 1964.

 'Sovereignty.' *Oxford Essays in Jurisprudence.* Ed. A. G. Guest. London, 1961.

Hexter, J. H. *The Reign of King Pym.* Cambridge, Mass., 1941, reprinted 1961.

Hill, W. Speed. 'Hooker's *Polity* : The Problem of the "Three Last Books." ' *Huntington Library Quarterly,* XXXIV (1971), 317–36.

Hinton, R. W. K. 'The Decline of Parliamentary Government under Elizabeth I and the Early Stuarts.' *Cambridge Historical Journal,* XIII (1957), 116–32.

 'English Constitutional Theories from Sir John Fortescue to Sir John Eliot.' *English Historical Review,* LXXV (1960), 410–25.

 'Was Charles I a Tyrant?' *Review of Politics,* XVIII (1956), 69–87.

Hirst, Derek. 'The Defection of Sir Edward Dering, 1640–41.' *Historical Journal,* XV (1972), 193–208.

Holdsworth, Sir William S. *A History of English Law.* 3rd ed. Vols. I–VI. London, 1908–24, reprinted 1966.

 'The Prerogative in the Sixteenth and Seventeenth Century.' *Columbia Law Review,* XXI (1921), 554–71.

Holmes, Geoffrey, ed. *Britain after the Glorious Revolution 1689–1714*. London, 1969.

*British Politics in the Age of Anne*. London, 1967.

*The Trial of Doctor Sacheverell*. London, 1973.

Horwitz, Henry. 'Parliament and the Glorious Revolution.' *Bulletin of the Institute of Historical Research*, XLVII (1974), 36–52.

*Revolution Politicks: The Career of Daniel Finch, Second Earl of Nottingham 1647–1730*. Cambridge, 1968.

Hughes, John Jay. 'The Missing "Last Words" of Gilbert Burnet in July 1687.' *Historical Journal*, XX (1977), 221–27.

James, F. G. 'The Bishops in Politics, 1688–1714.' *Conflict in Stuart England: Essays in Honour of Wallace Notestein*. Ed. William A. Aiken and Basil D. Henning. London, 1960.

Jones, J. R. 'The Clegate Case.' *English Historical Review*, XC (1975), 262–86.

Jones, J. R. *The First Whigs: The Politics of the Exclusion Crisis, 1678–1683*. London, 1961, reprinted 1966.

*The Revolution of 1688 in England*. London, 1972.

Jones, W. J. *Politics and the Bench*. London, 1971.

de Jouvenel, Bertrand. *Sovereignty; An Inquiry into the Political Good*. Chicago, 1963.

Judson, Margaret A. *The Crisis of the Constitution*. New Brunswick, New Jersey, 1949, reprinted 1964.

'Henry Parker and the Theory of Parliamentary Sovereignty.' *Essays in History and Political Theory in Honor of Charles Howard McIlwain*. Ed. Carl Wittke. Cambridge, Mass., 1936.

Kantorowicz, Ernst H. *The King's Two Bodies: A Study in Medieval Political Theology*. Princeton, 1957.

Keeler, M. F. *The Long Parliament, 1640–1641*. Philadelphia, 1954.

Keir, David L. 'The Case of Ship Money.' *Law Quarterly Review*, LII (1936), 546–74.

Kemp, Betty. *King and Commons, 1660–1832*. London, 1957, reprinted 1965.

Kenyon, J. P. 'The Revolution of 1688 : Resistance and Contract.' *Historical Perspectives: Studies in English Thought and Society in Honour of J. H. Plumb*. Ed. Neil McKendrick. London, 1974.

*Revolution Principles: The Politics of Party, 1689–1720*. Cambridge, 1977.

*Robert Spencer, Earl of Sunderland, 1641–1702*. London, 1958.

*The Stuart Constitution, 1603–1688: Documents and Commentary*. Cambridge, 1966.

*The Stuarts: A Study in Kingship.* London, 1958, reprinted 1966.

Kitchin, George. *Sir Roger L'Éstrange, a Contribution to the History of the Press in the Seventeenth Century.* London, 1913.

Kliger, Samuel. *The Goths in England.* Cambridge, Mass. 1952.

Knafla, Louis A. *Law and Politics in Jacobean England. The Tracts of Lord Chancellor Ellesmere.* Cambridge, 1977.

'New Model Lawyer : The Career of Sir Thomas Egerton, 1541–1616.' Ph.D. Dissertation, University of California, Los Angeles, 1965.

Lacey, Douglas R. *Dissent and Parliamentary Politics in England, 1661–1689.* New Brunswick, New Jersey, 1969.

Lamont, William. *Marginal Prynne, 1600–1669.* London, 1963.

Lampson, Edward T. 'The Royal Prerogative, 1485–1603.' Ph.D. Dissertation, Harvard University, 1938.

Landon, Michael. *The Triumph of the Lawyers.* Alabama, 1970.

Lee, Maurice D., Jr. *The Cabal.* Urbana, Illinois, 1965.

Lewis, Ewart. 'King above Law? "*Quod Principi Placuit*" in Bracton.' *Speculum,* xxxix (1964), 240–69.

*Medieval Political Ideas.* 2 vols. New York and London, 1954.

Lubasz, Heinz M. 'The Body Politic of the Kingdom. A Study of the Conceptual Origins of the Sovereignty of King in Parliament.' Ph.D. Dissertation, Yale University, 1959.

Macaulay, T. B. *The History of England from the Accession of James II.* 5 vols. New York, n.d.

McIlwain, C. H. *Constitutionalism Ancient and Modern.* Ithaca, 1947.

*Constitutionalism and the Changing World.* Cambridge, Mass., 1939.

*Growth of Political Thought in the West.* New York, 1932.

*The High Court of Parliament and its Supremacy.* New Haven, 1910.

McKenna, J. W. 'The myth of parliamentary sovereignty in late-medieval England.' *English Historical Review,* xciv (1979), 481–506.

Madan, Francis F. *A New Bibliography of the Eikon Basilike of King Charles the First.* Oxford, 1950.

*Oxford Books.* 3 vols. Oxford, 1895–1931.

Maddock, Henry. *An Account of the Life and Writings of Lord Chancellor Somers.* London, 1812.

Mendle, M. J. 'Politics and Political Thought, 1640–1642.' *The Origins of the English Civil War.* Ed. Conrad Russell. London, 1973.

Miller, John. 'Catholic Officers in the Later Stuart Army.' *English Historical Review*, LXXXVIII (1973), 35–53.

Neale, J. E. *Elizabeth I and her Parliaments, 1584–1601.* New York, Norton Library, 1966.

Nenner, Howard. *By colour of law: Legal Culture and Constitutional Politics in England, 1660–1689.* Chicago, 1977.

Nuttall, Geoffrey F. 'A Transcript of Richard Baxter's Library Catalogue.' *Journal of Ecclesiastical History*, III (1952), 74–100.

Nutting, Helen A. 'The Most Wholesome Law – the Habeas Corpus Act of 1679.' *American Historical Review*, LXV (1960), 527–43.

Oakley, Francis. 'The "Hidden" and "Revealed" Wills of James I : More Political Theology.' *Studia Gratiana*, XV (1972), 365–75.

'Jacobean Political Theology : The Absolute and Ordinary Powers of the King.' *Journal of the History of Ideas*, XXIX (1968), 323–46.

Ogg, David. *England in the Reign of Charles II.* 2nd. ed. 2 vols. Oxford, 1963.

*England in the Reigns of James II and William III.* Oxford, 1955, reprinted 1966.

Pallister, Anne. *Magna Carta: The Heritage of Liberty.* Oxford, 1971.

Pearl, Valerie. *London and the Outbreak of the Puritan Revolution.* Oxford, 1961.

'London's Counter-Revolution.' *The Interregnum: The Quest for Settlement 1646–1660.* Ed. G. E. Aylmer. London, 1972.

'Oliver St. John and the "middle group" in the Long Parliament, August 1643–May 1644.' *English Historical Review*, LXXXI (1966), 490–519.

'The "Royal Independents" in the English Civil War.' *Transactions of the Royal Historical Society.* Fifth Series, XVIII (London, 1968), 69–96.

Pinkham, Lucile. *William III and the Respectable Revolution.* Cambridge, Mass., 1954.

Pocock, J. G. A. *The Ancient Constitution and the Feudal Law.* Cambridge, 1957, reprinted 1967.

'James Harrington and the Good Old Cause : a study of the ideological context of his writings.' *Journal of British Studies*, X (1970), 30–48.

*The Machiavellian Moment: Florentine Political Thought and the Atlantic Republican Tradition.* Princeton, 1975.

'Robert Brady, 1627–1700. A Cambridge Historian of the Restoration.' *Cambridge Historical Journal*, X (1951), 186–204.

Pollard, A. F. *The Evolution of Parliament*. London, 1920.

Prest, Wilfred R. *The Inns of Court under Elizabeth I and the early Stuarts*. Totowa, New Jersey, 1972.

Proctor, Francis. *History of the Book of Common Prayer*. London, 1889.

Raphael, D. D. *Problems of Political Philosophy*. London, 1970.

Rex, Millicent B. *University Representation in England, 1604–1690*. London, 1954.

Robbins, Caroline. *The Eighteenth-Century Commonwealthman*. Cambridge, Mass., 1961.

Roberts, Clayton. 'The Constitutional Significance of the Financial Settlement of 1690.' *Historical Journal*, XX (1977), 59–76.

Roots, Ivan A. 'Cromwell's Ordinances. The Early Legislation of the Protectorate.' *The Interregnum: The Quest for Settlement 1646–1660*. Ed. G. E. Aylmer. London, 1972.

*The Great Rebellion, 1642–1660*. London, 1966.

Roskell, J. H. 'Perspectives in English Parliamentary History.' *Bulletin of the John Rylands Library*, XLVI (1963–64), 448–75.

Ruigh, Robert E. *The Parliament of 1624: Politics and Foreign Policy*. Cambridge, Mass., 1971.

Russell, Conrad. *The Crisis of Parliament: English History 1509–1660*. London, 1971.

ed. *The Origins of the English Civil War*. London, 1973.

'Parliamentary History in Perspective, 1604–1629.' *History*, LXI (1976), 1–27.

*Parliaments and English Politics 1621–1629*. Oxford, 1979.

'The Theory of Treason in the Trial of Strafford.' *English Historical Review*, LXXX (1965), 30–50.

Salmon, J. H. M. *The French Religious Wars in English Political Thought*. Oxford, 1959.

Schlatter, Richard B. *Richard Baxter and Puritan Politics*. New Brunswick, New Jersey, 1957.

Schochet, Gordon J. *Patriarchalism in Political Thought*. Oxford, 1975.

'Patriarchalism, Politics, and Mass Attitudes in Stuart England.' *Historical Journal*, XII (1969), 413–41.

'Sir Robert Filmer: Some New Bibliographical Discoveries.' *Transactions of the Bibliographical Society* (London, 1971), 135–60.

Schwoerer, Lois. *'No Standing Armies!': The Antiarmy Ideology in Seventeenth-Century England*. Baltimore and London, 1974.

Sirluck, Ernest. Introduction: Chapter I. *The Complete Prose Works of John Milton*. Vol. II. New Haven, 1959.

Sisson, C. J. *The Judicious Marriage of Mr. Hooker and the Birth of the 'Laws of Ecclesiastical Polity.'* Cambridge, 1940.

Skinner, Quentin. *The Foundations of Modern Political Thought*. 2 vols. Cambridge, 1978.

'History and Ideology in the English Revolution.' *Historical Journal*, VIII (1965), 151–78.

'The Ideological Context of Hobbes's Political Thought.' *Historical Journal*, IX (1966), 286–317.

Smith, A. G. R., ed. *The Reign of James VI and I*. London, 1973.

Snow, Vernon F. *Parliament in Elizabethan England. John Hooker's 'Order and Usage'*. New Haven, 1977.

Straka, Gerald. *Anglican Reaction to the Revolution of 1688*. Madison, 1962.

'The Final Phase of Divine Right Theory in England, 1688–1702.' *English Historical Review*, LXXVII (1962), 638–58.

Tanner, J. R. *English Constitutional Conflicts of the Seventeenth Century*. Cambridge, 1928, reprinted 1961.

Tarlton, Charles D. 'A Rope of Sand: Interpreting Locke's *First Treatise of Government*.' *Historical Journal*, XXI (1978), 43–73.

Thomas, Roger. 'The Seven Bishops and their Petition, 18 May, 1688.' *Journal of Ecclesiastical History*, XII (1961), 56–70.

Thompson, M. P. 'The Idea of Conquest in Controversies over the 1688 Revolution.' *Journal of the History of Ideas*, XXXVIII (1977), 33–46.

Tierney, Brian. 'Bracton on Government.' *Speculum*, XXXVIII (1963), 295–317.

Trevallyn-Jones, G. F. 'The Composition and Leadership of the Presbyterian Party in the Convention.' *English Historical Review*, LXXIX (1964), 307–30.

Trevor-Roper, H. R. *Historical Essays*. New York, 1966.

*Religion, the Reformation and Social Change*. London, 1967.

*Archbishop Laud, 1573–1645*. New York, 1965.

Tuck, Richard. '*Power* and *Authority* in Seventeenth-Century England.' *Historical Journal*, XVII (1974), 43–61.

Turberville, A. S. 'The House of Lords under Charles II.' *English Historical Review*, XLIV (1929), 400–17.

Turner, F. C. *James II*. London, 1948.

Underdown, David. *Pride's Purge: Politics in the Puritan Revolution*. Oxford, 1971.

Vile, M. J. C. *Constitutionalism and the Separation of Powers*. Oxford, 1967.

Wallace, John M. *Destiny His Choice: the Loyalism of Andrew Marvell.* Cambridge, 1968.

Wedgwood, C. V. *The King's Peace, 1637–1641.* New York, 1969.

*The King's War, 1641–1647.* London, 1966.

*The Trial of Charles I.* London, 1965.

Western, J. R. *Monarchy and Revolution: The English State in the 1680s.* London, 1972.

Weston, Corinne Comstock. 'The Authorship of the Freeholders Grand Inquest.' *English Historical Review*, xcv (1980), 74–98.

'Concepts of Estates in Stuart Political Thought'. *Representative Institutions in Theory and Practice.* 87–130. In *Studies Presented to the International Commission for the History of Representative and Parliamentary Institutions*, Vol. xxxix. Brussels, 1970.

*English Constitutional Theory and the House of Lords, 1556–1832.* London, 1965.

'Legal Sovereignty in the Brady Controversy.' *Historical Journal*, xv (1972), 409–31.

'The Theory of Mixed Monarchy under Charles I and After.' *English Historical Review*, lxxv (1960), 426–43.

Wharam, Alan. 'The 1189 Rule : Fact, Fiction or Fraud?' *Anglo-American Law Review*, i (1972), 262–78.

Wilkinson, B. *The Coronation in History.* London, 1953.

Williams, E. N. *The Eighteenth-Century Constitution, 1688–1815: Documents and Commentary.* Cambridge, 1960.

Willson, David H. *King James VI and I.* London, 1956, reprinted 1966.

Witcombe, D. T. *Charles II and the Cavalier House of Commons, 1663–1674.* Manchester, 1966.

Worden, Blair. 'Edmund Ludlow : The Puritan and the Whig.' *The Times Literary Supplement.* (January 7, 1977), 15–16.

Wormuth, Francis D. *The Origins of Modern Constitutionalism.* New York, 1949.

*The Royal Prerogative, 1603–1649.* Ithaca, 1939.

Wright, H. G. *The Life and Work of Arthur Hall of Grantham.* London, 1919.

Yale, D. E. C. *Hale as a Legal Historian.* Selden Society, 1976.

Sir Matthew Hale's *The Prerogatives of the King.* Selden Society, 1976.

'Hobbes and Hale on Law, Legislation and the Sovereign.' *Cambridge Law Journal*, 31 (1) (1972), 121–56.

Zagorin, Perez. *A History of Political Thought in the English Revolution*. London, 1954.

*The Court and the Country*. London, 1969.

Zaller, Robert. *The Parliament of 1621*. Berkeley, 1971.

# Index

comments on, 19–20, 81, 192,
286 n27, 373–5 n109
before 1642, 20–1, 29–32, 38, 47–
51, 87–8, 279–80 n79, 286 n24,
292 n58
and fundamental law, 20–1, 46–9,
286 n27, 326 n6, 378 n15
legislative activity of, 20–1, 85–6
88
Charles I stresses its law-making
function, 38, 49
treated primarily as a legislature
after 1642, 49–52
defined as the two houses, 63–4,
84
*See also* legal sovereignty,
controversy over; long
parliament; 'three estates'
parliamentarian formula
its tenets, 2, 57–8, 60–1
subverts the order theory of
kingship, 2–3, 83
among anti-court writers, 57–8,
60–1, 65–6, 267–8 n2, 289–90
n41
and the co-ordination principle,
58
not new in 1642, 58, 267 n2
noticed by Locke, 83, 176
imparts a divine sanction to the
community-centered view of
government, 83–4
in Charles II's reign, 176,
180–1, 350 n58
in Revolution tracts, 261, 365–8
n77
found at first in royalist writings,
267–8 n2, 289–90 n41
reconciles non-resistance with a
shared legal sovereignty, 375
n109
parliamentarian idology, *see*
community-centered view of
government
parliamentary sovereignty, *see* legal
sovereignty, controversy over

Pemberton, Sir Francis, 243
*People's Cause, Stated,* 328–9 n20
Peter, Hugh, 77–8, 300 n96
Peterborough, Henry Mordaunt,
second earl of, 225
Petyt, George, 373 n109
Petyt, Silvester, 344 n28
Petyt, William
his *Antient Right of the Commons of
England Asserted,* 135, 183–4,
187–91, 198
on the prescriptive right to
representation, 135, 186,
187–8, 189
on co-ordination, coevality and
legal sovereignty, 181, 183–4,
187–92, 252, 257, 343–4 n27
and the Brady controversy, 183–5,
185–7, 340 n8, 342 n16, 348
n49
and Prynne, 186–7, 187, 189, 217
and Dugdale, 187, 189
and a 'shared' law-making
power, 187, 191, 343 n27
and the *Freeholders Grand Inquest,*
187, 217, 341 n14
and the rule of 1189, 187–91,
342 n16
on the Norman conquest, 188–9,
191
on customary usage, 188–9, 191
his common-law argument for
early parliaments juridical, not
historical, 189, 342 n16
on the origin of the laws, 191
and the Answer to the Nineteen
Propositions, 191, 252, 344–5
n28
and the act for the preservation
of the king, 191–2, 252
and the address of the second
Powle committee, 192, 252
his modern view of parliament,
192, 256
and the 'three estates', 192, 345
n31